Strategy and human resource management

Peter Boxall and John Purcell

palgrave
macmillan

First published 2003 by
PALGRAVE MACMILLAN
Houndmills, Basingstoke, Hampshire RG21 6XS and
175 Fifth Avenue, New York, N.Y. 10010
Companies and representatives throughout the world

PALGRAVE MACMILLAN is the global academic imprint of the Palgrave Macmillan division of St. Martin's Press, LLC and of Palgrave Macmillan Ltd. Macmillan® is a registered trademark in the United States, United Kingdom and other countries. Palgrave is a registered trademark in the European Union and other countries.

ISBN-10: 0-333-77820-0
ISBN-13: 978-0-333-77820-3

This book is printed on paper suitable for recycling and made from fully managed and sustained forest sources.

A catalogue record for this book is available from the British Library.

Library of Congress Cataloging-in-Publication Data

Boxall, Peter F.
  Strategy and human resource management / Peter Boxall and John Purcell.
  p. cm. — (Management, work and organisations)
  Includes bibliographical references and index.
  ISBN 0-333-77820-0 (pbk.)
  1. Personnel management. 2. Organizational effectiveness. 3. Human capital.
I. Purcell, John, 1945– II. Title. III. Series.

HF5549 .B776 2002
658.3—dc21   2002072309

13 12 11 10
12 11 10 09 08 07 06

Printed and bound in China

Contents

Introduction

The last two decades of the 20th century witnessed a major growth of interest in strategy and human resource management. Reacting to the dramatic growth of new technology, of competitive uncertainty, and of regulatory reform, business leaders (and their counterparts in the public sector) looked for ways to design and implement more successful strategies. Consultancy practices responded to this explosion of interest. So too did the academic field of strategic management. It moved on from its base in prescriptive texts on 'business policy'. Academically, strategic management is now characterised by a range of theoretical schools, by extensive research (published in such learned journals as *Strategic Management Journal*), and by large academic conferences. Business schools have invested enormous resources in the teaching of strategy, both in MBA programmes and in the 'capstone courses' of major undergraduate degrees.

The situation is much the same in HRM. The term first gained prominence in the United States, where the most influential textbooks were initially published and where leading journals such as *Human Resource Management, Human Resource Management Review* and *Human Resource Planning* are based. Outside the United States, the significance of HRM has been recognised in the launch and growth of the *Human Resource Management Journal,* the *International Journal of Human Resource Management* and *Asia Pacific Journal of Human Resources.* Within business schools, and across more traditional academic departments, there has been an explosion of courses and publications concerned with the management of employment relations. It may have been fashionable to treat personnel management as a 'Cinderella' subject in the 1970s but few universities today treat HRM with quite the same disdain.

The growth of interest in strategic management and HRM has not, however, been accompanied by sufficient concern for integrating these two important fields of theory and practice. This is our argument for writing this book and our primary purpose. Too much of the literature in strategic management continues to downplay or disregard the human issues which affect the formation and execution of strategy.

Similarly, too much of the literature in HRM carries on the preoccupation of the personnel management literature with the individual technique – such as the selection test or the appraisal interview – and ignores the task of tackling problems with a mix of practices and investments relevant to management's objectives in the particular context. Both bodies of literature have their characteristic weaknesses. On the strategy side, it is the failure to fully appreciate the ways in which the management of people is strategic to success. On the HRM side, it is the failure to look up from the nooks and crannies of currently fashionable techniques to study the overall picture, to perceive the ways in which HR strategy might need to be integrated with other management functions and with the overall sense of direction.

Strategy and Human Resource Management is not organised around the sub-functions or 'classical monuments' of HR practice – selection, appraisal, pay, training, and so on – with the word 'strategic' slipped in front. The connections among these aspects of HR practice are inevitably considered by the book but sub-functional domains do not dominate the design of chapters as if they were self-contained 'solutions'. Instead, the book is designed around the need for a critical overview of what is important in HRM, of what HRM can and should contribute to business performance.

The book contains a number of distinctive features. It responds to Karen Legge's challenging questions (in her 1978 text) about the objectives of (what was then) personnel management by offering a framework for goal-setting in HRM. We argue that three goal domains are important in the strategic management of people in firms: labour productivity, organisational flexibility and social legitimacy. While many business analysts would readily accept that HR strategies should be judged by their impact on productivity and should help firms to build a capacity for change, we contend that the pursuit of legitimacy is also fundamental because firms are embedded in societies. This goal-setting framework binds the first and last chapters of the book together and acts as a touchstone throughout. The book also takes a distinctive approach to the definition of strategic management, arguing for the centrality of key HR issues in any credible notion of business strategy. The way we think about the strategic problems of firms makes an enormous difference to the ways we try to manage people. Our view is that a reasonably effective HR strategy is a necessary, but not a sufficient condition of business viability. An outstanding HR strategy may help to lay a basis for sustained competitive advantage.

As the field of strategic HRM has developed over the last ten years, a debate has raged over the role of context ('best fit') and universalism ('best practice'). We explore this debate, taking the view – shared by some in the field – that both unique context and general principles have a role to play in HR strategy. The book is designed with this tension in mind. As might be expected, we also work studiously with the contemporary emphasis on the resource-based view of the firm, with the notion that intangible assets can build positions of competitive strength. This is a very important body of work which quite obviously links the strategy and HRM fields. It thus gets due attention. We try in this area, however, to make some of the abstruse ideas more tangible and accessible. Areas much less often visited by writers on strategic HRM include the evolution of HR strategy across cycles of industry change, and the shape of HR strategy within multidivisional and multinational firms. These have been concerns of ours – we see them as important in the dynamic picture – and they play a key role in the final part of the book.

Lastly, we should note that our approach in each chapter follows a style based on three elements: theory, research and illustration. Like any academics, we aim to explain the important theory and to examine rigorous research on it. However, wherever possible, we try to bring the story to life with the more interesting illustrations – cases and vignettes – with which we are familiar. Overall, we think that *Strategy and Human Resource Management* is a novel synthesis of the HRM-strategy nexus: you be the judge.

PETER BOXALL AND JOHN PURCELL

Acknowledgements

My journey into strategic HRM started in the late 1980s/early 1990s at Monash University, where Peter Dowling was supervising my PhD and where the management school provided a stimulating and supportive environment. I am very grateful to Peter, to other colleagues there at the time, including Bernard Barry and Malcolm Rimmer, and to the Australian Government's sponsorship of the National Key Centre in Industrial Relations. The funding of the Centre enabled me to conduct serious fieldwork on HR strategy in Australian firms facing growing international competition. I am also very grateful to two other institutions and sets of colleagues: to the Business School at the University of Auckland, my home base and a world-class environment for research activity, and to the University of Bath, where I was a visiting Professor in the Work and Employment Research Centre in 1998. In respect of the University of Auckland, my thanks go to three Heads of the Management and Employment Relations Department who have, over the years, fostered a strong research culture: Marie Wilson, Kerr Inkson (now at Massey University), and John Deeks. In respect of the University of Bath, my sincere thanks go to Brian Bayliss, Head of the School of Management, and to my partner in this work, John Purcell, who was a terrific host during sabbatical leave. John and I began an edited book that year which did not materialise but which created a dialogue around key issues linking HR strategy and business performance. Those discussions, first in Bath and then in a visit by John and Kate Purcell to New Zealand, led to a major journal article and, eventually, to this book. Working with John has been a very engaging experience and I am very grateful for the full and frank exchanges we have had, always with good humour. We both thank Palgrave Macmillan and our series editor, Mick Marchington, for their faith in, and great patience with, this particular project. At Palgrave Macmillan, we especially thank Sarah Brown, Ursula Gavin and Brian Morrison.

As ever, my heartfelt thanks go to Marijanne and to our three sons, Chris, Andy and David, who do not mind being dragged around the world on these projects and who continue to teach me a lot about the management of people. Finally, a special word for my mother, Doreen Boxall, who always takes a great interest in my writing and to whom, like every one of her five children, I owe my grounding in the arts of communication.

PETER BOXALL

I first taught strategy and human resource management in 1995 to a group of Executive MBA students in the University of Bath. There was no text book, at least none that I liked, and much of what we explored together was experimental – built, in part, on their own experiences as practising managers from the private, public and voluntary sectors. Only rarely were any of them HR managers. Most were sceptical, at the start, about claims for the strategic importance of HRM but soon became enthusiastic as we tackled difficult questions linking HRM to performance and firm strategy. I owe these students a lot. Marking their assignments, based on the experience of their companies, has taught me a great deal. In a quite different way, final year undergraduates are terrific at theory and have a thirst for anything that tries to relate this to 'real' life. They, too, have suffered as I tried to find what strategy and HRM was really about. Others helped hugely. My research colleagues in the Work and Employment Research Centre in the School of Management at Bath have lived through research projects on 'leanness', telephone call centres, fostering and forcing change, contingent working, and especially two projects funded by the Chartered Institute for Personnel and Development on what we call 'People and Performance' and 'Growing Knowledge Intensive Firms'. In particular, I wish to record my debt to Nick Kinnie and Sue Hutchinson who have worked on most of these projects. I am very grateful to the Business School at the University of Auckland for helping to fund our visit there over Easter 2001, which allowed Peter and me to really get to grips with writing. Peter has been, as ever, a fund of knowledge and with a deep understanding of the critical issues. I cannot imagine a better collaborator and colleague. Cathy Aubin, the WERC secretary and many other things besides, has wonderfully turned scribbles and tapes into text, once I discovered that I could not write good English on screen. I am very grateful to her. Kate Purcell has often been supportive but also expressed cynicism 'as a sociologist' about the language and ideas of strategic human resource management. I value both more than perhaps she realises.

JOHN PURCELL

The authors and publishers wish to thank the following for permission to reproduce copyright material. They also wish to thank anyone not specifically mentioned here from whom material has been quoted but whose name(s) may inadvertently have been omitted, and on request will be happy to include appropriate acknowledgements to them in any future reprints of this book.

Atkinson, J. (1984) 'Manpower strategies for flexible organisations'. Originally published in People Management August: 28–31. (page 134)

Belbin Associates:

Belbin, M. (1981) *Management Teams: Why They Succeed or Fail*. Oxford: Butterworth-Heinemann. (page 44)

Blackwell Publishing Ltd:

Marchington, M. and Wilkinson, A. (2000) 'Direct participation'. In *Personnel Management: A Comprehensive Guide to Theory and Practice*. Edited by Stephen Bach and Keith Sisson. (page 167)

Mueller, F. (1996) 'Human resources as strategic assets: an evolutionary resource-based theory'. *Journal of Management Studies* 33(6): 757–85. (page 77)

Osterman, P. (1987) 'Choice of employment systems in internal labour markets'. *Industrial Relations* 26(1): 46–67. (page 9)

Schoenberger, E. (1997) *The Cultural Crisis of the Firm*. (page 103)

California Management Review:

Grant, R. (1991) 'The resource-based theory of competitive advantage: implications for strategy formulation'. *California Management Review* 33(2): 114–35. (page 99)

Chartered Institute of Personnel and Development:

For the quote taken from *Getting Fit Staying Fit* by Hutchinson, Kinnie, Purcell, Collinson, Terry and Scarborough (1998). (page 104)

Cornell University:

To print an extract from *Manufacturing Advantage*. Eileen Appelbaum, Thomas Bailey, Peter Berg and Arne L. Kalleberg, eds. © 2000 by Cornell University. (page 22)

Gittleman, M., Horrigan, M. and Joyce, M. (1998) ' "Flexible" workplace practices: evidence from a nationally representative survey'. *Industrial and Labor Relations Review* 52(1): 99–115. (page 67)

Godard, J. and Delaney, J. (2000) 'Reflections on "high performance" paradigms: implications for industrial relations as a field'. *Industrial and Labor Relations Review* 53(3): 482–502. (page 9)

Harvard Business School Press:

Eisenhardt, K.M., Kahwajy, J.L. and Bourgeois, L.J. (1997) 'How management teams can have a good fight'. *Harvard Business Review* July-August: 77–85. (page 45)

Hamel, G. and Prahalad, C. (1994) *Competing for the Future*. (pages 79/82)

Leonard, D. (1998) *Wellsprings of Knowledge: Building and Sustaining the Sources of Innovation*. (pages 80, 81, 82)

O'Reilly III, C.A. and Pfeffer, J. (2000) *Hidden Values*. (page 223)

Pfeffer, J. (1994) *Competitive Advantage Through People*. (page 62)

Pfeffer, J. (1998) *The Human Equation: Building Profits by Putting People First*. (page 63)

Walton, R.E., Cutcher-Gershenfeld, J.E. and McKersie, R.B. (1994) *Strategic Negotiations: A Theory of Change in Labor-Management Relations*. Boston, MA. (page 179)

John Wiley & Sons Ltd:

Goold, M., Campbell, A. and Alexander, M. (1994) *Corporate Level Strategy: Creating Value in the Multibusiness Company*. (page 216)

Hart, S.L. and Banbury, C. (1994) 'How strategy making processes can make a difference'. *Strategic Management Journal* 15: 251–69. (page 42)

Hedlund, G. (1994) 'A model of knowledge management and the N-form corporation'. *Strategic Management Journal* 15: 73–90. (Figure 4.6, page 83)

Koch, M. and McGrath, R. (1996) 'Improving labor productivity: human resource management policies do matter'. *Strategic Management Journal* 17: 335–54. (page 229)

Miles, G., Snow, C.C. and Sharfman, M.P. (1993) 'Industry variety and performance'. *Strategic Management Journal* 14: 163–77. (page 52)

Schmitt, N. and Borman, W. (eds) (1993) 'A theory of performance'. In *Personnel Selection in Organizations*. (Figure 7.2, page 138)

MIT Press:

Weinstein, M. and Kochan, T. (1995) 'The limits of diffusion: recent developments in industrial relations and human resource practices in the United States'. In Locke, R., Kochan, T. and Piore, M. (eds) *Employment Relations in a Changing World Economy*. (page 67)

Mrs M J Odiorne:

Odiorne, G. (1985) *Strategic Management of Human Resources*. (page 139)

Oxford University Press:

Gallie, D., White, M., Cheng, Y. and Tomlinson, M. (1998) *Restructuring the Employment Relationship*. (page 171)

Pan Macmillan Publishers:

Tuchman, B. (1996) *The March of Folly: From Troy to Vietnam*. (page 40)

Perseus Books Group*:

Freeman, R.B. and Medoff, J.L. (1984) *What Do Unions Do?* (page 176)

Personnel Publications:

McGovern, P., Gratton, L., Hope-Hailey, V., Stiles, P. and Truss, C. (1997) 'Human resource management on the line?'. *Human Resource Management Journal* 7(4) 12–29. (page 197)

Ward, K., Grimshaw, D., Rubery, J. and Beynon, H. (2001) 'Temporary workers and the management of agency staff'. *Human Resource Management Journal* 11(4) 3–21. (pages 131–2)

Sage Publications:

Rousseau, D. (1995) *Psychological Contracts in Organizations*. (page 152)

Taylor and Francis Ltd:

Passage from 'Are top human resource specialists "strategic partners"? Self perceptions of a corporate elite'. By Hunt, J. and Boxall, P. (1998) *International Journal of Human Resource Management* 9(5): 767–81. http://www.tandf.co.uk (page 41)

Thomson Learning:

Wallace, T. 'Fordism'. In *The IEBM Handbook of Human Resource Management* (1998). Edited by M. Poole and M. Warner. (pages 97–8)

Thomson Publishing Services:

Storey, J. (1995) *Human Resource Management: A Critical Text*. (page 3)

Watson, T. (1986) *Management, Organisation and Employment Strategy*. (page 155)

*Originally published by Basic Books

1

Human resource management and business performance

This book is concerned with the relationship between strategy and human resource management (HRM). Firms have always had some kind of strategy – though not necessarily a successful one – and have always engaged human labour. In order to form a useful purpose, and to pursue desired outcomes, organisations inevitably rely on the talents of people.

Our mission in this book is to explore the ways in which HRM is strategic to business success. We have three key objectives for this first chapter. First, we set up a definition of HRM. Because of our interest in linking HRM to performance outcomes, we then examine the question of goal-setting in HRM. This naturally entails a discussion of the tensions and trade-offs that these goals imply. Finally, as a way of introducing some of the key questions explored in this book, we outline the contemporary debate on 'high-performance work systems'. The chapter concludes with a short summary and with an explanation of what lies ahead.

Defining human resource management

The notion of human resource management (HRM) is used in this book to refer to all those activities associated with the management of employment relationships in the firm. The term 'employee relations' will be used as an equivalent term, as will the term 'labour management'. While there have been debates over the meaning of HRM since the term came into vogue in the 1980s, it has become the most popular term in the English-speaking world referring to the activities of management in the employment relationship.[1]

---

1 It is also important in the Francophone world, where courses and jobs in 'gestion des ressources humaines' are now commonplace.

1

We do not wish to use the term loosely, however. Definitions are important. They should not be rushed or glossed over, because they indicate the intellectual terrain that is being addressed. They suggest the relevant 'problematics' of the field – that is, they suggest what needs to be discussed and explained. Before proceeding, our definition will be clarified and elaborated.

HRM: covering all workforce groups

HRM is concerned with the management of all groups in the workplace. Thus, it includes questions about how managers themselves are managed. The evidence indicates that managers are generally managed differently from the rest of the workforce. Managers are typically managed in what Alan Fox (1974) describes as a 'high trust' manner: they enjoy large areas of discretion in their work and are assumed to support the best interests of the organisation. In his classic work, *The Practice of Management*, Peter Drucker refers to managers as 'the basic resource of the business enterprise and its scarcest' (1968: 139).

That managers are generally treated as a critical employee group is hardly surprising. But the point that HRM is concerned with the management of *all* employee groups needs to be made strongly because some academic approaches in the field of employment relations tend to look only at 'management-worker' relations (and, in some extreme cases, only at 'management-union' relations). These aspects are extremely important but, on their own, they do not define the 'universe' of employment relations in the firm.

HRM: involving line and specialist managers

It is also crucial to make the point that HRM is not the property of particular specialists. HRM is as an aspect of all management jobs. Line managers are intimately involved, usually hiring their own team and almost always held directly accountable for the performance of that team. In larger organisations, there may be permanent in-house HR specialists contributing specialist skills in such technical aspects of HRM as the design of selection processes, the formation of EEO (equal employment opportunity) policies, the conduct of collective employment negotiations, and training needs analysis. There may also be specialist HR consultants contracted to provide such important services as executive search, and assistance with major reformulations of salary structure and performance incentives. All specialists, however, are engaged in 'selling' their services to line managers, in working together with other members of the management team to achieve the desired results. In this book, the acronym 'HRM' is used to refer to the totality of the firm's management of work and people and not simply to those aspects where HR specialists are involved.

HRM: incorporating a variety of management styles

As our discussion so far should indicate, management may adopt a variety of approaches to managing employees. It is quite common for one approach to be taken to managers, another to permanent employees, and yet another to temporary and part-time staff. Not only are there differences *within* firms but there are also differences *between* firms. Osterman (1987), for example, refers to a range of 'employment subsystems' in firms. Purcell (1987) talks of a variety of 'management styles' in employee relations. These analyses recognise the fact that managers have at least some options in all contexts and make choices over time which add up to important differences in the way they manage people.

Our definition of HRM, then, allows for a wide variety of management styles. The notion of HRM is largely used in this sense in the United States where the term covers all management approaches to managing people in the workplace. Some approaches involve unions while others do not (see, for example, Milkovich and Boudreau 1997, and Noe, Hollenbeck, Gerhart and Wright 2000). It must be admitted, however, that most styles of labour management in the US *private* sector do not involve dealing with unions. This fact can mean that students of HRM there have much less exposure to theory on union-management relations than is typical in Europe and in the old Commonwealth countries of Canada, Australia and New Zealand.

In Britain, the rise of practitioner and academic interest in HRM sparked a debate about the term's meaning, its ideological presuppositions, and its consequences for the teaching and practice of industrial relations. Storey (1995: 5) defined HRM as a 'distinctive approach to employment management', one which 'seeks to achieve competitive advantage through the strategic deployment of a highly committed and capable workforce, using an integrated array of cultural, structural and personnel techniques.'

Similarly, Guest (1987, 1990) developed a model of HRM as a strongly integrated management approach in which high levels of commitment and flexibility are sought from a high quality staff. Some commentators went further than was implied by these sorts of definitions and saw HRM as a workplace manifestation of Thatcherite 'enterprise culture', as an ideology that would make management prerogative the natural order of things (see, for example, Keenoy and Anthony 1992). This view assumed rather a lot about the ability of management to orchestrate ideological changes in the workplace.

For research purposes, defining HRM as a particular style, as Guest (1987) and Storey (1995) do, is obviously a legitimate way to proceed. It opens up useful questions such as: what practices constitute a high commitment model of labour management?; what is the diffusion of such a model?; is the model more likely to occur in unionised or non-union settings?; and are the outcomes of such a model actually superior?

We are interested in all styles of labour management, and the ideologies associated with them, and pursue the sorts of questions about diffusion of particular models just noted (see, for example, Chapter 3). However, for the purposes of exploring the links between strategic management and HRM, we find that a broad, inclusive definition of HRM is more appropriate. The terrain of HRM includes a variety of styles. We are interested in which ones managers take in a particular context and why. The strategy literature requires this kind of openness because it recognises variety in business strategy across varying contexts (see, for example, Miles and Snow 1984, Porter 1985). It implies that there is no 'one best way' to compete in markets and organise the internal operations of the firm. If we are to truly explore the HRM-strategy nexus, we need relatively open definitions on both sides of the equation.

HRM: managing work and people, collectively and individually

Our conception of HRM is very close to the definition used by Gospel (1992) in his major study of the management of labour in Britain. Gospel defined 'labour or human resource management as a generic term' covering three main areas:

Work relations – the way work is organised and the deployment of workers around technologies and production processes;

Employment relations – the arrangements governing such aspects of employment as recruitment, training, job tenure and promotion, and the reward of workers;

Industrial relations – the representational systems which exist within an enterprise: in the British context this has often meant management-union relations and the process of collective bargaining.

One of the advantages of this broad view is that HRM is clearly seen as concerned with overall work organisation or work systems – with the way work is designed and allocated in the firm's approach to production or operations. We obviously need an understanding of the links among HRM, production, and technology in a business if we are to locate HRM in a strategic context. The firm creates value by the way it combines human and non-human resources (Penrose 1959). We do not wish to take the design of work as a given, something for which Peter Drucker once roundly criticised US personnel departments:

That the personnel department as a rule stays away from the management of the enterprise's most important human resource, managers, has already been mentioned. It also generally avoids the two most important areas in the management of workers: the organization of work, and the organization of people to do the work. It accepts both as it finds them (Drucker 1968: 332).

Work systems are, of course, associated with a whole array of employment or HR practices in the firm (for hiring, deploying, motivating, negotiating with, training, developing, reviewing and shedding the people needed to carry out the work). To cover all that this means, we find it convenient to talk of a firm's 'models of employment'. In other words, HRM is concerned with both the structure of work in a firm and with all the related employment practices that are needed to carry out the work. HRM is not simply about HR or 'people practices', it is about the management of *work and people* in the firm.

It then helps to recognise that the management of work and people includes both individual and collective dimensions (Purcell 1987, Storey and Sisson 1993). Gospel embraces the collective dimensions under the heading of 'industrial relations'. We incorporate industrial relations within the collective focus and add a fourth aspect to Gospel's model – individual dimensions. Doing this allows us to explore theories on the ways in which individuals are attached to, and managed by, firms. Our conception of the terrain of HRM, then, can be depicted as a two-by-two matrix (Figure 1.1). Figure 1.1 illustrates some of the research questions about HRM that can be posed by this kind of broad definition.

HRM: embedded in industries and societies

HRM, then, is concerned with managing people, individually and collectively. It is a management process carried out in firms – some small, some large, some very large, including multidivisional and multinational firms. While recognition of this fact is essential, the academic study of HRM has been criticised by industrial relations scholars for focusing too much on the firm and ignoring the wider context of the markets and societies in which the firm operates (see, for example, Strauss 2001). This is a fair criticism. The different HR strategies of firms are better understood if

Dimensions	Work systems	Models of employment
Individual dimensions	To what extent do individuals find the work they do intrinsically satisfying? What skill levels do jobs require of individuals and how do skill demands change over time?	To what extent can the firm attract, develop and retain individuals with relevant skills? To what extent do individuals regard their pay and benefits as fair and motivating?
Collective dimensions	To what extent is work organised on a team basis and how productive is teamwork? What kinds of status distinctions are created by work systems? Do work systems enhance trust levels and the quality of cooperation within the firm?	What mix of employment models is used in the firm and with what impacts? Where employment conditions are collectively bargained, what is the quality of union-management relations? What processes exist for introducing organisational change and how successful are they?

Figure 1.1 Individual and collective dimensions of HRM: some key questions

they are examined in the wider context that helps to shape them, something we shall certainly be arguing in this book. Work and HR practices are not developed entirely within a firm or controlled by that firm's management.

Firms are profoundly affected by the industries in which they choose to compete (Dunlop 1958). They often adopt similar employment practices to other firms operating with the same technology. Despite all the talk of globalisation by powerful corporate forces, nation states also exercise a major impact on the HR strategies of firms. Nations provide resources of physical infrastructure, politico-economic systems, educated workforces and social order. These resources are of variable quality across nations but are always significant. In exchange for the use of these resources, national governments impose certain regulations on how employees should be treated, with varying degrees of enforcement of these regulations. Firms, therefore, are always 'embedded in structures of social relations' (Granovetter 1985: 481).

The role of sectoral (or industry) and societal factors in influencing the HR strategies of firms is something we include within the terrain of HRM and, thus, within the focus of this book (particularly in Chapters 3, 9 and 10). The implicit model of HR practice as something entirely within the control of management in the individual firm is something we work hard to avoid.

Linking HRM to business performance

Having defined HRM in a broad, inclusive way, we can now examine the problem of goal-setting in HRM and introduce the contemporary debate on the role of HRM in business performance. A book that aims to connect strategy and HRM should pay close attention to the ways in which HRM influences organisational effectiveness. Strategic management is concerned with explaining significant variations in business performance. Thus, one of the key things that characterises academics working in *strategic* HRM is their interest in models and studies which link HRM to performance. It is not enough just to be concerned with one's favourite HR practice (this is better understood as 'micro-HRM'). One must be concerned, at the very least, with the impacts of practice – or better still, clusters or bundles of HR practices – on desired outcomes. This implies, of course, that we have some idea of what the desirable goals are.

The problem of goal-setting in HRM

It has never been easy to define the goals of labour management in the firm. In a classic analysis in 1978, Karen Legge noted that most textbooks on (what was then) personnel management sidestepped the difficult issue of desirable objectives by briefly referring to some statement such as, 'the optimum utilization of human resources in order to achieve the goals and objectives of the organization' (Legge

1978: 3). She pointed out that this kind of vague, ill-defined statement begged a number of important questions, including the question of *whose* interests were being served and what was meant by optimisation. Ignoring these (and other) troublesome questions, the textbooks moved quickly into the traditional exposition of personnel practices, depicted as ends in themselves (rather than as means or methods which might be relevant in some contexts and counter-productive in others). Despite the change of nomenclature, only a few HRM theorists have taken up the challenge of specifying a framework of goals by which the quality of HRM in the firm might be judged (notable examples include Beer, Spector, Lawrence, Quinn Mills and Walton 1984, Dyer 1984, Dyer and Holder 1988, Evans 1986, and Guest 1987).

In building a framework for goal-setting and evaluation in HRM, we should start from the obvious point that firms do not generally exist for the purpose of creating employment. It helps if we start by positing two broad goals for business firms (Boxall 1998, Drucker 1968, Gospel 1973). The first is the goal of securing viability with adequate profitability – with sufficient returns to shareholders so that their commitment is retained. This definition does not rely on a concept of 'maximisation' but does recognise that critical stakeholders seek a return that retains their involvement. Beyond this survival goal, firms *may* pursue some form of sustained competitive advantage or consistent and superior profitability. From this basic starting point (explored more fully in Chapter 2), it follows that the firm will need a combination of human and non-human resources (Penrose 1959, Mueller 1996) and it helps if managers identify goals for each of these essential elements. Our framework, then, is built on the basic model shown in Figure 1.2.

The framework argues that HRM ought to be concerned with three aspects of performance (or 'goal domains') that contribute to the firm's viability – its productivity,

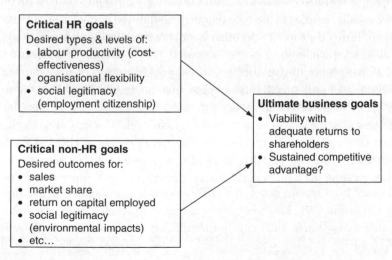

Figure 1.2 Critical goals in HRM: a basic framework

its flexibility, and its legitimacy. A superior performance in HRM – one which might earn the epithet of 'sustained competitive advantage' – implies an outstanding mix of outcomes across these three areas. This is not a simple matter and all sorts of blends of these goals are likely in firms. In practice, the extent to which goals are made explicit varies and it is inevitable that a firm's HR goals will be accompanied by various kinds of strategic tension or paradox (Boxall 1999, Cameron 1986, Evans and Genadry 1999), something we shall explore. Allowing for this kind of complexity, what does each goal domain entail?

Labour productivity (cost-effectiveness)

Profitability is inevitably critical in shareholder-owned firms. However, it can be affected by financial factors not connected to workforce management (such as movements in exchange rates), so it is better to focus on labour productivity as a measure of human resource management in the firm. We use the notion of labour productivity to mean the value of labour outputs in relation to the cost of labour inputs.[2] Several authors have argued that labour productivity ought to be seen as the primary goal of a firm's labour management (see, for example, Geare 1977, Heneman 1969, Osterman 1987). It is the touchstone against which every new HR policy ought to be evaluated: will it make labour more productive and will its costs, or the investment it implies, be justified? In other words, is it cost-effective?

The criterion of cost-effectiveness is the obvious one to apply to all proposed HR policies. HR policies, like any investment in the firm, should provide an adequate pay-back. Let's consider, for example, the idea of developing a formal performance appraisal process with written performance criteria and appraisal interviews. Such formal processes are almost immediately discounted in small firms. While they can be helpful, if well designed and relatively objectively implemented (see Chapter 7), they are usually regarded as too bureaucratic and thus too costly. The potential benefits do not justify the cost. On the other hand, the small firm's managers are likely to use timely, informal feedback on performance. This is certainly cost-effective and it would be foolish not to give direct feedback quickly in cases of poor performance. The objective of cost-effectiveness implies that the test of likely benefits to costs should be applied to every HR policy proposal.

Let's now raise the level of analysis to the system level. In 'macro' or strategic HRM, cost-effectiveness becomes a criterion for the overall system of HRM in the firm. Is the overall *combination* of HR philosophy, processes, policies, programmes and practices creating the human performance desired and is it doing so at reasonable

---

2   Physical measures of productivity which do not consider the value of production or the cost of labour are not quite the same thing and can be misleading (see, for example, Keltner, Finegold, Mason and Wagner (1999)).

cost (Godard 2001a)? Very expensive, high skill models of labour management, incorporating rigorous selection, high pay, and extensive internal development, are unlikely among small firms in the retail sector, for example. While firms in this sector should try to find ways of making competitive pay offers and of keeping their most effective staff, this does not imply that they should adopt the kind of HR system needed to compete with international consultancy firms or automobile manufacturers. Another example of the principle of cost-effectiveness is given by Godard and Delaney (2000: 488):

> ... in a nuclear power plant employing many workers, the costs of poor morale, (labour) turnover, and strikes can be high, so the benefits of HRM innovations will tend to be high. Firm size may also introduce important economies of scale, reducing the costs of HRM innovations per worker. Thus, in this plant, the benefits of new practices can be expected to exceed the costs. In a small, low-technology garment factory employing unskilled labour, the opposite may be true.

As Godard and Delaney (2000) imply, expensive HR practices are often justified where the production system is capital intensive or where high technology is involved. The actual level of labour cost could be quite low (say, ten per cent or less of total cost) but workers have a major effect on how well the technology is utilised or exploited. It thus pays to remunerate and train them very well, making better use of their skills and ensuring their motivation is kept high. As they find ways of making the equipment meet or even exceed its specifications, the unit cost of labour falls and productivity rises. Thus, in this kind of context, the firm can easily sustain high wage levels. It is more important *not* to alienate this kind of labour, because of the productivity impacts of disrupted production, than it is to worry about wage levels. As Osterman (1987: 55) explains:

> The concept of cost must be broadened to include potential as well as actual costs. Employees can impose costs on the firm through errors of various kinds. For example, a particular kind of capital equipment may be simple to operate and require little skill but yet be very expensive and subject to damage through employee error. Many firms will choose to employ higher-skill labour and create stable employment systems ... because of potential downside costs.

These examples help to illustrate the point that it is wrong to confuse wage levels with unit labour costs or, similarly, to confuse cost minimisation with cost-effectiveness. In certain cases, where markets are very competitive and where technology is limited and the work is labour intensive, wage levels are decisive in the assessment of cost-effectiveness. In these situations, cost-effectiveness does broadly equate with labour cost minimisation because labour cost levels have such a huge impact on the survival of firms. This is why so much basic apparel manufacture (such as undergarments), footwear manufacture, and toy manufacture, has moved to low wage countries (see Chapter 5). On the other hand, more complex and capital intensive design functions can usually be kept in high wage countries where a small team of well-paid designers uses computer-aided equipment and keeps in close contact with marketing colleagues and with retail buyers external to the firm.

Clearly, then, the problem of securing cost-effective labour, of making labour productive at reasonable cost, invites some careful thinking about likely costs and benefits. There are indeed situations where wage levels are in competition. When this occurs in manufacturing, firms worry about where to site production facilities to take advantage of lower wages. When it occurs in services, firms typically use employment practices that keep their service costs competitive: wages paid are relative to 'the going rate' in the local labour market (but rarely superior to it), the training investment is sufficient to ensure basic quality, and labour turnover levels are often high. Quality may be no better than average but this may be quite acceptable with customers if the price is right. On the other hand, there are situations where wages are not in competition but the interaction between labour and technology needs to be carefully managed to achieve high productivity. Here, high levels of HR investment pay high dividends and help to protect against disruption. Similarly, there are areas in the service sector, such as professional services, which are knowledge-intensive. Here, managers see the value of investing in higher salaries, extensive career development, and time-consuming performance appraisal because these practices foster the kind of expert interactions with customers that make it possible for the firm to secure and retain high value-added business.

The key point is that all firms should make an assessment of what kind of HR practices they need to make their use of labour cost-effective in the particular context they operate in. The driving question becomes: what HR practices are 'profit-rational' in which contexts? The criterion of cost-effectiveness runs across the management of labour in all business organisations. It does not, however, imply the same 'solutions' across all contexts.

Organisational flexibility

Labour productivity is something that is aimed for in a *given* context. In other words, given a particular market and a certain type of technology (among other things), it is about making the firm's labour resources productive at competitive cost. Unfortunately, change is inevitable and this suggests we need another goal domain in HRM: capacity to change or 'organisational flexibility' (Osterman 1987). The word 'organisational' is used here because employers typically seek forms of flexibility which extend beyond, but encompass, their employee relations (Streeck 1987).

In thinking about goals for organisational flexibility, it is useful to distinguish between *short-run* responsiveness and *long-run* agility. Short-run responsiveness includes financial flexibility (attempts to adjust the price of labour services) and numerical (or 'headcount') flexibility (which also has financial objectives). Thus, firms engaged in very cyclical activities often relate their permanent staff numbers to their calculation of the troughs in business demand rather than the relatively unpredictable peaks, seeking to offer overtime and ring in temporary staff if, and when, the workload surges. In other cases, firms seek to pay workers a mix of wages and profit-related bonuses, with the latter fluctuating in line with company fortunes. In both these cases, the emphasis is on adjusting labour costs to fit with changes in business revenues. Short-run flexibility also includes attempts to hire workers who are cross-trained or 'multi-skilled', combining roles that have historically been kept in separate job descriptions. Such 'functional flexibility' helps the firm to maintain a lower headcount but cope better with marginal improvements in product design or production processes.

Long-run agility, however, is a much more powerful, but rather ambiguous, concept (Dyer and Shafer 1999). It is concerned with the firm's ability to learn in an environment that can change radically. Does the firm have the capacity to create, or at least cope with, long-run changes in products, markets and technologies? Can it learn as fast or faster than its major rivals? Firms which employ too much labour on peripheral conditions, or which undermine core conditions too severely, may find this hard to achieve if their best workers move to better jobs as the labour market improves (Boxall 1996). Where this happens, it makes it more difficult for the firm to deepen its learning because of the instability of its work processes.

The problem we are noting here is the tension between actions taken to support short-run flexibility which actually undermine long-run agility. Like the productivity arena, the problem of creating desirable types and levels of organisational flexibility involves the management of some key tensions, as we shall argue further (below and also in Chapters 3, 6 and 9).

Social legitimacy

Without saying they are ever easy, productivity and flexibility goals very much reflect 'the business agenda'. They are needed to underpin profitability and economic survival over time. As goal domains in HRM, they are not, however, enough. Firms operate in societies, making use of human capacities that citizens and the State have nurtured and generated (for example, through public education). In this light, governments often exercise their right to regulate employment practices. Workers may also exercise sanctions against firms that offend social norms (either as individuals who decide not to work for certain kinds of firms or to work for them only with very limited commitment, or as unions which campaign against certain kinds of employment practice).

All of this means that the typical firm is concerned with its standing as an employer in society, or with its 'employment citizenship' (Boxall 1999). As Lees (1997) argues, legitimacy should be seen as an employer goal alongside the more market-oriented ones. More broadly, of course, the quality of the firm's reputation as an employer is only one aspect of its 'social legitimacy', which also includes such things as its impacts on the natural environment. There is a range of contemporary movements designed to encourage greater social responsibility in business and broader corporate reporting, including the notion of the 'triple bottom line' (financial, environmental and social) (Elkington 1997). In Chapter 11, we look more closely at the concept of the 'balanced scorecard' (Kaplan and Norton 1996, 2001) which recognises three key stakeholders in the firm: shareholders, customers and employees.

In practice, we see significant variety in the legitimacy goals of employers. Some employers seek only to comply minimally with their legal responsibilities in such areas as occupational safety and health. Others seek to go beyond compliance to forge a reputation as an 'employer of choice', as an exemplary employer from both the perspective of the State and that of potential workers. Multinational clothing and footwear companies, for example, are increasingly concerned that they do not acquire a reputation for employing Third World labour on exploitative terms, even where the direct employer is one of their sub-contractors. Levi Strauss, for example, while no longer able to retain huge production facilities in the United States, is still concerned to ensure that its foreign contractors comply with its code of employment ethics, as noted on its website.[3] Some firms are now actively competing for EEO (equal employment opportunity) awards or for favourable mentions in lists of the 'Best Companies to Work For'.[4]

To assist international firms to demonstrate ethical employment practice, a New York-based organisation called Social Accountability International has developed an international standard called SA (Social Accountability) 8000.[5] Companies seeking this standard, which incorporates key ILO (International Labor Organisation) conventions regarding child and forced labour, union rights, and health and safety, must be audited and certified by an accredited audit agency. Besides the initial audit of the company's employment practices, the process includes periodic 'surveillance audits'. While modelled on the well-known ISO quality system, SA 8000 requires auditors to consult with workers and their unions, and includes a mechanism for workers to bring complaints about non-compliance. Certified auditors currently include SGS (Société Générale de Surveillance) and BVQI (Bureau Veritas Quality International). Companies which are signatory members of SA 8000 (meaning their own factories and their suppliers must comply) include the world's largest mail-order business, Otto Versand, and the world's largest toy retailer, 'Toys R Us'.

This particular accountability standard identifies the important role that trade unions and, in European countries, works councils have played in improving the legitimacy of employment practices. When management reaches employment agreements with worker organisations, the legitimacy of the employment regime in the firm is usually enhanced, something we explore further in Chapter 8. The extent

---

3 See www.levistrauss.com/responsibility/conduct/guidelines.htm
4 For example, see www.fortune.com and www.workingwoman.com.
5 For the English version, see www.cepaa.org/Standard%20English.doc

to which firms can achieve high levels of legitimacy without mechanisms for employee participation in policy-making and enforcement is an interesting contemporary question.

Goals in HRM: building cause-effect chains

Setting up three overarching goal domains for HRM is, unfortunately, only a beginning. In practice, goal specification in HRM suffers from what might be called the 'Russian doll phenomenon': inside one goal, another is embedded (Boxall 1999, Legge 1978). This is illustrated in Figure 1.3. Setting goals for productivity could entail goals for work design, for employee competence or capability, for motivation, for labour cost and so on. And then the trail continues. Within a problem area like workforce capability and motivation, we would expect to see a range of goals relating to recruitment and selection (the 'buy' dimension of competence), training and development (the 'make' dimension of competence), and in pay and promotion (which are always key motivators).

Figure 1.3 illustrates the way in which goals expand to a third tier for one of the five problem areas identified in the second tier of the diagram: workforce capability and motivation. With a big enough page to work on, we could explode the model in Figure 1.3 out to a third tier for all of these five problem domains. We could also try to map some of the critical interactions. For example, it is well known that work organisation impacts in very important ways on employee motivation. We should have an arrow linking these two boxes. The same is true with trust and fairness: over

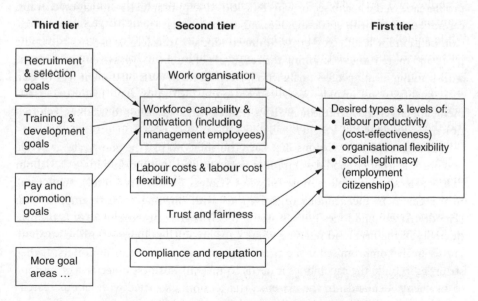

Figure 1.3 Expanding the goal-setting process in HRM

time, perceptions of trust affect motivation, so an arrow should link them as well. Companies that subscribe to Kaplan and Norton's (1996) 'balanced scorecard' develop these sorts of cause-effect chains, creating a 'theory of the business'. The value of taking this kind of approach in strategic HR planning is explored in Chapter 11. The key point we are making at this stage is that goals in HRM are complex and the process of improving goal-setting in HRM will be time-consuming but rewarding.

The reality of strategic tensions in HRM

Embarking on a process of goal-setting in HRM usefully confronts managers with the reality of 'strategic tensions' among HR goals, including trade-offs between employer and employee interests (Osterman 1987). As in business goal-setting generally, elements of paradox will be surfaced which call for some clever management (Cameron 1986).

Labour scarcity

One of the main tensions stems from the fact that firms need to compete in labour markets (Coff 1997, Windolf 1986). In all countries where forced labour has been eliminated, workers are free to resign and seek alternative employment. Firms must compete with others to secure talented staff, a problem that became severe in the global market for IT workers in the 1990s, particularly as the year 2000 approached, creating a major need to update computer systems. Labour shortages continue to be problematic in the health sector where various disciplines, such as radiation therapy, cannot keep pace with escalating demand as the average age of the population rises. Competition for health workers with internationally transferable skills is becoming more and more ruthless, straining the resources of public health systems all over the world. Young health professionals who have paid high levels of student fees to gain their qualifications, or older workers wanting to cash in on their historical investment, are targeted by recruitment firms that can arrange access to lucrative international assignments.

Well-resourced organisations that have the ability to pay the going rate or better, and are able to offer good development opportunities, tend to dominate the labour market, an issue we explore more fully in Chapters 7 and 9. As a result, many small firms remain fragile, tenuous organisations with ongoing recruitment problems (Hendry, Arthur and Jones 1995, Storey 1985). The goals of securing reasonable productivity in the firm, and building some capacity for development of the business, are seriously compromised if the firm cannot make competitive job offers. It then struggles to build the capabilities it needs to meet its business objectives or respond to its clients' demands. In the extreme, the tension associated with labour scarcity can become a full-blown 'capability crisis', compromising productivity and profitability and threatening the firm's reputation and viability. In tight labour markets, particularly, firms must evolve better recruitment and retention strategies if they are to compete effectively with well-resourced and artful rivals.

Labour motivation

A second major tension – associated with the motivation of worker behaviour once they are actually hired – has received major attention in the industrial relations literature over the last hundred years. The employment contract is an exchange relationship but, unlike the sale and purchase of commodities, it involves an ongoing and unpredictable interaction between the parties. Future behaviour matters to the parties but neither party can accurately predict it when they sign up. Both are relying on some element of trust and are therefore taking risks. As the pioneering industrial relations writers, Sidney and Beatrice Webb (1902: 658) put it, the labour contract is 'indeterminate'. Will the worker offer a conscientious, consistent level of effort over time? More seriously, the Webbs argued, on the other side of the coin, will the employer impose work pressures that are intense or make the worker suffer working conditions that are unsafe? Will the level of work pressure be subtly (or, perhaps, crudely) increased over time without any renegotiation of rewards? Such a process of 'work intensification' can undermine the initial trust extended to the employer by the worker and invite some form of retaliation (for example, reduction of work quality, absenteeism, disinclination to 'go the extra mile', and resignation). Overall, will the 'wage-effort bargain' become more or less satisfying for the parties?

It is impossible to anticipate all this in advance and silly to think that any written contract of employment could cover all the possibilities (Williamson, Wachter and Harris 1975). As Cartier (1994: 182) puts it, 'the contract of employment is inherently incomplete'. As a result, the law gives employers the right to issue what are commonly known as 'lawful and reasonable orders', something that sets up an ongoing problem of motivation for the firm because control of the behaviour of other human beings is always limited. When individuals are instructed to carry out work tasks, their discretion is never fully taken away from them (Bendix 1956). The employer, like the employee, must exercise some trust. As Keenoy (1992: 95) argues, 'no matter how extensive the controls, in the final analysis, management is reliant on employee cooperation'.

There is a huge body of literature examining the relationships between employer and employee interests in the workplace and their implications for motivation and cooperation. This literature varies depending on the ideological predispositions of the writers concerned. In terms of identifying different ideological approaches, the work of Alan Fox (1974) is widely cited. Fox makes an important distinction between 'unitarists' and 'pluralists'. Unitarists do not accept that there is any legitimate conflict of interest and have virtually nothing to offer on motivational problems apart from the simplistic advice to 'improve communications'. A unitarist position is sometimes found among the owner-managers of small businesses and among managers working in sectors where unions are unusual. On the other hand, managers in the 'pluralist' tradition accept that there are important conflicts of interest in the workplace. These include the trade-off between employee income and the profit of the firm, and the tension between employee control of work decisions and conditions and control by the employer (Keenoy 1992). However, pluralists also see an underpinning basis for cooperation in the intrinsic and extrinsic rewards that employment typically offers. They believe that tensions can be handled through good conflict management processes. Academics adopting a pluralist position typically argue that systems of union recognition and collective bargaining have an important role to play in expressing and alleviating workplace conflict.

Fox (1974) also discusses more extreme ideological positions. Radical writers, mostly Marxists, see much deeper problems in capitalist management that connect to the whole 'political economy' of the system (see, for example, Braverman 1974, and Hyman 1975, 1987). From this perspective, the sorts of solutions offered by pluralists are never seen as sufficient. Exploitation is seen as deeply embedded in the overall system of capitalism. Radical analysis is much more useful in identifying capital-labour tensions than it is in offering any kind of practical way forward within the current structure of our society (Sisson 1989: 7–8).

The position we adopt in this debate is of a pluralist nature. This needs to be elaborated somewhat further because of the diversity in the pluralist tradition (Hyman 1978, Blyton and Turnbull 1998). We recognise that serious conflicts over income and over employee discretion and work stress can affect the quality of workplace cooperation. Among other things, the motivation of workers is affected by the extent to which they find their work interesting, by how fairly they feel they are paid, by how fair they feel their workload is, by the extent to which they feel recognised and listened to, and by how much they feel they can trust management. These tensions are serious for the firm irrespective of the fact that workers do not typically have 'equal power' with management (Clegg 1975). In the most severe cases of conflict over these tensions, firms experience 'motivational crises' which depress productivity and profitability, and which threaten their viability. Any book on strategy and HRM ought to be very interested in the management of motivation and trust, both individually and collectively. We therefore explore these tensions much more fully in Chapters 5, 6, 7 and 8.

Change tensions in labour management

As implied by the motivational problem, change creates difficulties. The need to pursue productivity (and with it stability), while also pursuing flexibility, triggers a strategic tension around change management in the firm (Adler, Goldoftas and Levine 1999, Brown and Reich 1997, Osterman 1987). In Hyman's (1987: 43) memorable phrase, 'employers require workers to be *both* dependable *and* disposable'.

Change tensions pose major dilemmas within management strategy and include trade-offs with the security interests of workers.

To illustrate the difficult choices involved, suppose a firm's management decides (and manages) to place most of its operating staff on temporary employment contracts to provide for short-term flexibility of payroll costs. This reduces the level of fixed cost but is likely to create problems with employee turnover as skilled workers, who are generally capable of attracting a range of employment offers, move to more secure jobs elsewhere. Over time, the firm is likely to find that it fails to build the kind of learning process that underpins long-term growth and makes it more adaptable to radical change in technology. Too much emphasis on short-term flexibility may mean the firm is eliminated by competitors who learn faster and capture its market share. A firm, on the other hand, which employs all labour on secure permanent contracts to build a stable long-term labour supply (traditionally called 'labour hoarding') may find that it faces a cash crisis in a short-term recession that actually threatens its viability. The firm may have excellent long-term prospects but greater flexibility is needed in its staffing structure to ensure it can weather short-term variations in demand for its products or services. A firm with excellent long-term prospects may fail in the short-run for want of financial prudence.

The most resilient firms, then, are those which evolve a clever balance between short and long-run requirements for flexibility. This is much easier said than done. It has led in recent years to a strong level of interest in core/periphery models of employment. The debate over the theory and application of these systems is something we explore more fully in Chapter 6.

Contemporary explorations of the HRM-performance link: research on 'high-performance work systems'

The previous section should make it clear that the task of judging a firm's performance in HRM is complex and controversial. There is no single criterion of effectiveness for a firm's labour management. We have argued here for three – productivity (cost-effectiveness), flexibility, and legitimacy – which form *aspects* of what a firm needs to secure its viability. Pursuing productivity and flexibility goals inevitably involves the management of strategic tensions, including the problem of how to balance short-run needs for stable performance with long-run needs for agility. Acknowledging the role of legitimacy as a goal domain might seem enlightened but should not mask the fact that capital-labour trade-offs are inevitable. Even if good labour standards are respected, the contemporary firm almost certainly needs to make some difficult choices about work structures, pay levels, employment security, and career opportunities that conflict with the preferences of at least some, if not most, of its workers.

Beyond viability lies the notion of 'sustained advantage' or superior performance relative to intelligent rivals. The question of what constitutes a brilliant performance in HRM is something we ought to consider in the context of the broad literature on employment relations (including literatures on industrial relations, industrial sociology and institutional economics). Throughout the 20th century, there were a number of waves of interest in how to improve workplace performance. Ignoring the minor fads, this includes such famous attempts as Scientific Management or 'Taylorism', the Human Relations movement, and Total Quality Management (concepts we explore more fully in Chapter 5).

One of the most important of these initiatives in recent times is associated with the notion of 'high-performance work systems' (HPWSs). An influential book on *The New American Workplace* by Appelbaum and Batt (1994) helped to popularise this term. A subsequent book on HPWSs in US manufacturing, *Manufacturing Advantage* (Appelbaum, Bailey and Berg 2000), has built on this foundation. Research in other countries has picked up the theme, including Thompson's (1998, 2000) study of the British aerospace industry, and Lowe, Delbridge and Oliver's (1997) study of the global automotive components industry. The terminology used by researchers is somewhat diverse. Some refer to 'high-involvement management' (for example, Lawler 1987) while others, particularly in the UK, refer to 'high-commitment management' (HCM) (for example, Wood 1996). Both of these terms pick up a key theme within high-performance work systems, one highlighting the way they are supposed to increase employee involvement in decision-making and the other highlighting the way they are supposed to improve employee motivation and commitment. Neither term indicates the way such systems are expected to improve skills. Our preference is to use the more embracing terminology of HPWSs.

Business trends in the 1980s and 1990s: threats and opportunities

As might be expected, a concern with the competitiveness of firms underpins the contemporary interest in HPWSs. Figure 1.4 summarises the contextual factors commonly seen to have affected the management of labour in the 1980s and 1990s and created a need for higher performance. In this period, governments in the Anglo-American world significantly reformed the policies associated with the Keynesian post-war consensus. Domestic markets – for products, capital and labour – were substantially re-regulated in ways that exposed firms and workers to increasing levels of competition (known popularly as 'deregulation'). Not only were existing private sector firms affected by this process but privatisation of public sector entities extended the realm of the market and diminished union power (in respect of the UK, see Towers 1997). In virtually every study of management behaviour in the period, managers spoke of increasing pressures on the cost structures or competitiveness of their firms (see, for example, Frenkel 1994).

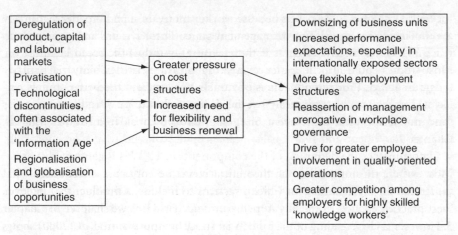

Deregulation of product, capital and labour markets		Downsizing of business units
Privatisation		Increased performance expectations, especially in internationally exposed sectors
Technological discontinuities, often associated with the 'Information Age'	Greater pressure on cost structures	More flexible employment structures
	Increased need for flexibility and business renewal	Reassertion of management prerogative in workplace governance
Regionalisation and globalisation of business opportunities		Drive for greater employee involvement in quality-oriented operations
		Greater competition among employers for highly skilled 'knowledge workers'

Figure 1.4 The 1980s and 1990s: commonly perceived contextual trends affecting the management of labour

Market liberalisation, however, has not simply posed threats. It has also enhanced opportunities to market products and services internationally and to increase market share at the expense of less agile firms. Furthermore, major advances in information technology over the period have created what Castells (1996: 66) calls the 'informational and global' economy. The increasing integration of electronic and computing technologies offers ways of significantly improving production and distribution processes across a range of industries, simultaneously challenging old ways of working and opening up new possibilities. In this *blend* of threat and opportunity, management and academic interest in the development of high-performance work systems is growing.

The notion of 'high-performance work systems'

Objectives and components of HPWSs

Like much of the literature on the links between employee relations and business performance, studies of HPWSs include a variety of outcome variables. Thompson (1998) uses one outcome variable – value added per employee. Lowe *et al.* (1997) employ a broader array of benchmarks including productivity, quality, defect rates and factory space utilisation. Appelbaum *et al.* (2000) report hard data on the company side as well as data on outcomes for workers. This is the most desirable kind of approach because it tells us about the extent to which *both* parties benefit from these 'innovative' work systems. A study by Ramsay, Scholarios and Harley (2000) also investigates the impact of HPWSs on employee outcomes, helping to examine whether these systems create higher performance at the expense of more stressed workers. In our view, all studies of HPWSs should include data on costs and benefits for *both* companies *and* workers because worker motivation and broader legitimacy are unlikely to improve if only management gains. These systems are more likely to reach high levels of effectiveness if they favourably influence employee attitudes. Most studies could also do better at creating measures of flexibility, particularly long-run agility. Productivity data is obviously needed (and the better studies collect it) but change pressures mean that the ability to shift to new productivity curves (and not just exploit the current one) ought to be considered (as we argue in Chapter 9).

Unfortunately, the definition of the components of HPWSs is confusingly varied. Most writers do not outline the theoretical structure (or cause-effect chain) that underpins their perceptions of which practices to include, a problem that bedevils 'best practice' models in the literature on strategic HRM, as we shall see in Chapter 3. However, a close reading of the influential study by Appelbaum *et al.* (2000) shows that they base their prescription on an old rubric called the AMO theory of performance. This states that performance is a function of employee ability, motivation, and 'opportunity'. Using mathematical notation:

$$P = f(A,M,O)$$

In other words, people perform well when:

- they are able to do so (they *can do* the job because they possess the necessary knowledge and skills);
- they have the motivation to do so (they *will do* the job because they want to and are adequately incentivised);
- their work environment provides the necessary support and avenues for expression (for example, functioning technology and the opportunity to be heard when problems occur).

This is just a very basic theory of performance (which is employed in Chapters 5 and 7 and elsewhere throughout this book) but it does offer a structure for identifying the desirable components of HPWSs.

A map of the generally anticipated linkages in HPWSs is shown in Figure 1.5. The work systems and employment models seen as supportive of high performance typically imply more rigorous selection and better training systems to increase ability levels, more comprehensive incentives (such as employee bonuses and internal career ladders) to enhance motivation, and participative structures (such as self-managing teams and quality circles) that improve opportunity to contribute (Appelbaum *et al.* 2000: 26–7, 39–46, 103–4). One of the key arguments running through the literature on HPWSs is that these practices work much better when 'bundled' together (Ichniowski, Kochan, Levine, Olson and Strauss 1996, MacDuffie 1995). The idea is that productivity is best served by the systemic interactions among these practices. Adding only one of the practices is likely to 'have no effect on performance' (Ichniowski *et al.* 1996: 319).

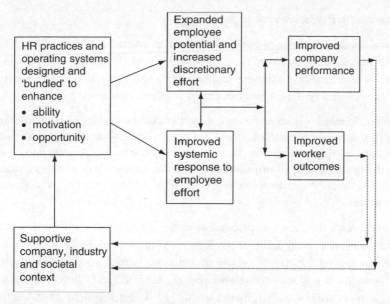

Figure 1.5 High-performance work systems: commonly hypothesised linkages

The contexts of HPWSs

While the general principle that HPWSs need to act on the elements of A, M and O to get results might be relevant across all companies, industries and societies, these contexts can, of course, be expected to influence the mix of policies and practices that make up a firm's attempts to create an HPWS (Whitfield and Poole 1997). The typical US policy prescription, for example, involves much less of a role for unions and other worker-representative bodies (notably works councils) than is generally the case in Europe (as discussion of 'best practice' models shows in Chapter 3). A fuller model of the conditions for high performance would inevitably need to recognise key contextual factors such as those associated with systems of employee 'voice' (discussed in Chapter 8) and the need for effective planning and investment by the firm's management (a key part of the company context), something we examine in Chapters 9, 10 and 11. One can also add into the context the important role of industry training institutions, something that has helped to foster higher company performance in a range of industries in Germany, as noted by various authors (for example, Steedman and Wagner 1989, Wever 1995). High performance is also a feature of clusters of firms in certain outstanding industries in Italy, as Appelbaum and Batt (1994) note. Networking and cooperation in generating 'social capital' serves them all well. As we will repeatedly emphasise in this book, it is wrong to analyse HRM and performance in the firm in an isolated way.

Outcomes of HPWSs: research so far

Research on the outcomes of current attempts to create HPWSs is still in its infancy. The major study by Appelbaum *et al.* (2000: 115), which examines three US industries (steel making, clothing manufacture, and medical electronics manufacture), provides fairly consistent evidence of win/win outcomes:

> Plant performance in each of the three industries examined is higher on the measures that matter to managers in those industries.[6] The opportunity-to-participate scale derived from the worker survey has a positive effect on worker outcomes as well. ... We find no support for the view that more participatory workplaces increase workers' stress. Importantly, we find a significant improvement in wages associated with the extent of the opportunity to participate.

This study, easily the most comprehensive so far, does suggest some cautions. It notes that conflicts are present and that tensions need to be managed. For example, those workers in apparel factories who have traditionally earned good bonuses from individual systems of performance-related pay, do not necessarily welcome team-based production systems (Appelbaum *et al.* 2000: 113–4). Such systems threaten the self-control and earning premium enjoyed by highly efficient workers under traditional forms of work organisation. Managers will often be sensitive to such feelings but still press ahead because, on balance, the new work systems are needed to enable some forms of apparel manufacturing to survive in a high wage country like the USA.

We would, however, be wise to question those lists of HPWS practices that always include teamworking. The principle of 'opportunity to participate' does not mean that teamwork should be treated as a kind of universal panacea. As Sewell (1998: 425) cautions, 'teamwork is not necessarily more liberating or morally edifying'. Like so many work and employment practices, teamwork should be seen as a variable – as something that varies in its value across different work contexts. In their study of automotive component manufacture, Lowe *et al.* (1997: 795) found 'mixed evidence on the use of teams, with a number of high-performance plants operating successfully without a recognizable team structure and a large number of plants with teams failing to perform to the highest standard'. The argument for greater teamwork in certain new types of work is examined more closely in Chapter 5.

On balance, the studies presented by Appelbaum *et al.* (2000) are quite supportive of the thrust of HPWSs. The other main piece of US data is much less sanguine. In a representative survey of US workplaces with more than 50 employees, Osterman (2000: 190) finds that the diffusion of work practices that foster flexibility, teamwork, and quality management is associated with 'a higher probability of layoffs in subsequent years and with no gains in wages'. As he explains, the development of new

---

6   For example, 'machine uptime' in the steel industry and 'sewing throughput time' in the apparel manufacturing industry.

forms of work organisation is likely to be accompanied by some negative forms of company restructuring in which at least some workers lose.

Clearly, there is much more work to be done on the conditions for, and the components and consequences of, high-performance work systems across a range of contexts. Indeed, on cost-effectiveness grounds, the value itself of such systems ought to be questioned (Godard 2001a, Guthrie 2001, Ramsay *et al.* 2000, Whitfield and Poole 1997). In what contexts are such systems profit-rational and is it possible, as Godard (2001b) implies, that such systems may be less desirable for both companies and workers in certain situations? Are there situations where the costs are not justified by the benefits for the firm and where the extra work pressure placed on workers makes it unhealthy for them? In theory, there are lose/lose possibilities as well as win/win ones and various shades in between. This kind of questioning is helpful if we want to explore the links between HRM and business performance with an open mind – and indeed we do.

Summary and structure of the book

In summary, this book adopts a broad, inclusive definition of HRM because we aim to explore the various ways in which HRM is critical for the performance of the firm. Human resource management (alternatively, 'employee relations' or 'labour management') includes the firm's work systems and its models of employment. It embraces both individual and collective aspects of people management. It is not restricted to any one style or ideology. It engages the energies of both line and specialist managers (where the latter exist) and typically entails a blend of messages for a variety of workforce groups.

The task of defining a set of goals in HRM has always proved difficult. In practice, managers and researchers need to spell out some cause-effect chains, starting from the ultimate goals of the firm and working back to key HR and non-HR objectives and so on within each stream. The model discussed in this chapter employs three goal domains for assessing the performance of HRM in a firm: labour productivity, organisational flexibility, and social legitimacy. These goal domains inevitably involve strategic tensions, including those associated with labour scarcity, labour motivation, and with change management.

The subject of strategic management is concerned with explaining significant differences in business performance. Hence, the field of strategic HRM must be concerned with the ways in which HRM influences the firm's performance. There is, in fact, a long tradition of research and practical experimentation with ways to lift business performance through smarter management of work and people. There are various models of what counts as 'smarter'. The current interest in 'high-performance work systems' is simply a recent expression of this interest. The literature in this area helps to introduce some of the questions which will be explored throughout the rest of this book.

In Part 1, three chapters look at the links between strategy and HRM. We have merely scratched the surface in this first chapter on the nature of strategy and the models of strategic management which have relevance for the management of labour. Chapter 2 explores the meaning of strategy and the process of strategic management, including its (very human) cognitive and political dimensions. In Chapter 3, we set up definitions of strategic HRM and HR strategy and examine the debate between universalist ('best practice') and contingency ('best fit') models of strategic HRM. Chapter 4 explores the implications for strategic HRM of the resource-based view of the firm. This is a key body of thought in contemporary strategic management which is richly laced with human issues. It is a perspective which informs much of the rest of the book.

Part 2 contains four chapters which aim to lay the basis of a strategic theory of labour management after Part 1 has undermined simplistic concepts of 'best practice'. It explores general principles that can be used to guide the strategic choices of firms across the four aspects of HRM that make up our definition. In Chapter 5, we examine work systems in the light of changing production priorities and in Chapter 6 we link ideas about work systems to models of employment that firms might potentially adopt. In Chapters 7 and 8, we review key theory and research on the individual and collective dimensions of labour management.

In Part 3, we apply strategy concepts and general principles of labour management to the analysis of HR strategy in complex and dynamic contexts. These include the contexts of industry-based competition (Chapter 9) and the contexts of multidivisional and multinational firms (Chapter 10). The final chapter (11) asks the 'where to from here?' question, examining ways in which the understandings of strategy and HRM developed in this book might be used to improve the quality of strategic planning in contemporary firms.

part 1

Connecting strategy and human resource management

2

Strategy and the process of strategic management

What do we mean by 'strategy' and 'strategic management' – and what role does HRM typically play in them? How might HRM play a more powerful, more effective role in strategic management? This section of the book is dedicated to these important questions. Because of diverse conceptions of strategy, the role of this first chapter in Part 1 is to establish a definition of this troublesome and over-worked word. In so doing, we consider the ways in which strategy is formed and re-formed in organisations – the *process* of strategic management. As the chapter will make clear, strategic management is a human process beset with all the pitfalls that characterise human attempts to make decisions in conditions of uncertainty, rivalry and limited resources. The major frameworks that have been used to interpret the role of strategic HRM are covered in the two chapters that follow this one. In those chapters, we review the main theories that have been put forward on the strategy-HRM linkage.

Defining strategy

As many writers have pointed out, the notion of strategy is subject to a confusing variety of interpretations. Much of the early literature in the field of strategic HRM leapt into the fray with little recognition that the notion of strategy needs careful handling. In order to describe what we mean by the word, it helps if we start with the negative. What definitions or conceptions of strategy are *not* helpful?

Strategy: misunderstandings and mis-firings

First, as Henry Mintzberg (for example 1978, 1990, 1994) has long argued, it is unhelpful to equate strategy with 'strategic plan'. A strategic plan is a formal document setting out an organisation's goals and initiatives over a defined time period. Strategic plans are characterised by a variety of formats: the time horizons vary, as

27

do the range of goals targeted, as do the activities that are planned for and the ways in which they are integrated with one another. Strategic plans are more likely to be found in large, complex companies which have major problems with coordinating efforts towards common goals (Grant 1998: 15–17). It is hard to see how any multi-divisional firm – facing the task of allocating its capital across business units – could cope without them. It is easy to see why such 'vast, diverse' firms as General Electric developed corporate planning in the 1960s (Whittington 1993: 71). Strategic plans are also more likely to be found in public sector organisations, which generally have strict requirements to disclose their goals and principal activities to politicians and the public. There are also certain industries where formal planning is *de rigeur*. It is impossible, for example, to undertake major construction projects without formal planning for the financial, architectural, material, labour and environmental implications. Official permission is not forthcoming without it.

However, the formality of strategic planning is unusual in small businesses – which often account for as much as half the private sector economy. Does this mean these firms have no strategy? Certainly not. It is possible to find *strategy* in every business because it is embedded in the important choices the managers and staff of the firm make about what to do and how to do it. In other words, when careful observers (such as would-be owners) make the effort, it is possible to discern the firm's strategy in its behaviour, in the characteristic ways in which the organisation tries to cope with its environment (Freeman 1995). As will be explained further below, we intend to base our understanding of strategy on the 'strategic choice' perspective. This conception of strategy means we should also treat 'with a grain of salt' the strategic plans we do find in the kind of organisations that use them. Formal planning documents rarely describe all of the organisation's strategic behaviour or keep track of all of its 'strategic learning' over time (Mintzberg 1990). We are not wanting to imply, however, that planning is unhelpful. Far from it. As we will explain further in Part 3 of the book and in the final chapter, the research suggests that good planning is very valuable in HRM. We are not anti-planners. The point we are making here is that strategy is best discerned in behaviour.

Secondly, it is unhelpful to make a hard distinction between 'strategy' and 'tactics' or between 'strategy' and 'operations'. This is a problem that has crept into business (and the new public sector management) from the military origins of strategy. In classical Greek, '*strategos*' is associated with the role of the general (Bracker 1980). In popular usage, we still tend to associate strategy with the lofty, orchestrating overview of the military commander. There are lots of problems with this imagery – including its restricted model of leadership and communication – but one major problem is the way it tends to imply that tactics or operations are things that can be mopped up afterwards, things that we have to do but which are not really important. Nothing could be further from the truth – in business and, for that matter, in war.

Sound operational planning and reliable delivery of service are essential to the success of any business. Take a 'High Street' or 'Main Street' bank, for example. If it cannot reliably organise its information processing – its receiving, storing and analysis of transactions – its chances of staying in business are slim. If it cannot run branch offices according to official opening hours or fails to maintain its ATMs[7] or its internet sites, it will lose customer support. In other words, certain key operational practices are strategic to success in all organisations. Going back to the military sphere, much of the German success in the First World War is attributed to German 'tactical excellence': the adaptable behaviour of well-trained soldiers in the field who coped better than most with the chaos that the fighting inevitably created (Ferguson 1998: 308–10). Much of the ultimate German failure, however, can be attributed to serious difficulty in forming and re-forming appropriate 'war aims' (Ferguson 1998: 282–6).

Astute leaders realise the importance of operational disciplines. In the management jargon of the 1980s – the era of *In Search Of Excellence* (Peters and Waterman 1982) – they understand the importance of productive workplace 'culture'. This is a reason why, in some enduring organisations, only those who have worked their way up from fundamental roles in the firm's production or sales processes can ever hold the top management posts (Pascale 1985). On the way up the organisation they should have learnt that there are strategic dimensions of all the key disciplines that constitute the business. Making a business successful is about giving due attention to the critical aspects of all the essential parts of the system, ensuring they are genuinely supporting the firm's mission and one another.

In adopting this perspective, some may think we are debasing the currency of strategy. If there are strategic aspects of all business disciplines, then there is no simple split between what the 'clever folk at headquarters' do and what the rest of us do. Where do we draw the line between the strategic and the non-strategic? It must be admitted that this is often a difficult thing to discern, not least because the environment changes in ways that surface new issues of strategic concern. Take the internet, for example. Ten years ago it seemed that retailers, particularly the small ones, could ignore the kind of *avant-garde* information technology on which it is based and its implications for sales and distribution processes. Now hardly anyone in retail can afford to be complacent about it, large or small.

It seems we need some way of discerning where the strategic issues lie. One thing we must definitely avoid is the profligate application of strategy language simply to impress. This has become something of a disease in the HRM literature. Very often writers in HRM have slapped the word 'strategic' in front of the old sub-functional categories of selection, appraisal, pay, and training to produce, as if by magic, a book on 'strategic HRM'. David Guest makes exactly the same point about much of the

---

7   Automatic teller machines

transition from personnel management to HRM – the covers of some textbooks have been changed but very little in between them (Guest 1987: 506). As he points out, and as many managers know, the titles of personnel departments have often been changed with little attempt to review the nature of the work they do. This kind of self-serving use of language leaves students and practitioners with no basis for distinguishing between the critical or strategic issues involved in running firms successfully and those which are of lesser significance. In the definitions that follow, we will attempt to provide a more meaningful set of markers.

Strategic problems and the strategies of firms

We are now in a position to move from the negative to the positive. In our view, strategy is best defined by making a distinction between the 'strategic problems' firms face in their environment and the strategies they adopt to cope with them (Boxall 1998: 266). Naturally, this means we believe that there is a real business environment, a relatively objective reality 'out there' that firms must deal with. The environment – political, economic, social and technological[8] – is not a fiction or something that can be trivialised in highly subjective word-games. The stark fact is that sooner, rather than later, firms face 'intelligent opposition' from rivals (Quinn 1980). They can also face quite threatening regulation from the State, and major fluctuations in markets. Even the most powerful firms, seemingly in control of their environment, will eventually face some kind of turbulence that threatens their position. Those who fail to understand their environment will fall foul of it.

The problem of viability

The fundamental problem, the most critical challenge, that the firm faces is that of becoming and remaining viable in its chosen market. Unless the firm has the *savoir faire* to compete in its chosen market, it is not going to be taken seriously by potential customers and investors. Another way of putting this is to say that all firms require 'table stakes': a set of goals, resources and capable people that are appropriate to the sector concerned (Hamel and Prahalad 1994: 226, Boxall and Steeneveld 1999). Decisions about these 'table stakes' are strategic. They are make-or-break factors. Get the system of these choices right – or right enough – and the firm will be viable. Miss a key piece out and the firm will fail. In other words, when we use the word 'strategic' to describe something, we are saying it is critical to survival, it is seriously consequential. We take, in effect, the common sense view that the word 'strategic' should indicate something of genuine significance for the future of the firm (Johnson 1987, Purcell and Ahlstrand 1994: 51–2).

8　Readers will recognise the PEST framework here. See, for example, Johnson and Scholes (1997: 93–9).

Continuing with our banking illustration, take the case of a company launching a new 'High Street' or 'Main Street' bank (Freeman 1995: 221). To be credible at all, it must have the same kinds of technology as other banks, a similar profile of products or services, the necessary levels of funding, systems of internal control, skilled staff who can make it happen 'with the gear' on the day, and a management team who can assemble these resources and focus the firm's energies on objectives that will satisfy its investors. Without an effective cluster of goals, resources and human capabilities, it is over before it starts (Figure 2.1). As Freeman (1995: 221) emphasises, much of the firm's strategy is formed in a 'package' when the original choice of competitive sector is made. A bank has to act like a bank: it comes with the territory.

The problem of viability is *the* fundamental strategic problem. While Figure 2.1 summarises the critical elements involved in it, it naturally over-simplifies the ambiguities, tensions and complexities involved. It is not necessarily straightforward to decide on the right mix of goals for the firm. Just take one example. Will the firm be more viable if it grows organically or by acquisition? There are costs and benefits in both strategies (Whittington 1993) and different firms in different sectors will read them in different ways at different times. Nor does a simple diagram like Figure 2.1 highlight the difficult relationships *among* resources that have to be managed. In business, different departments usually control some part of the firm's resources (Quinn 1980) but coordination among them is frequently difficult. As is often noted, 'marketing only promises what operations cannot deliver'.

What Figure 2.1 does highlight, however, is that there is no solution to the problem of viability *without* capable people. Appropriate human capabilities are strategic to the success of every firm. It is only people that pose the questions, 'What goals are appropriate for the business?' and 'What resources are relevant to our goals?', and

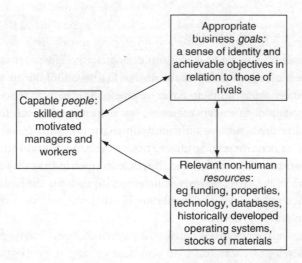

Figure 2.1   Three critical elements for the viability of the firm

take an interest in making the answers a reality. This is desperately obvious but it has to be said because there are dozens of books on strategic management which assume that good strategy appears out of nowhere: human beings do not seem to be involved or only as an afterthought.

Because the arrows go both ways, Figure 2.1 also highlights the fact that the three elements of goals, people, and other resources are *interactive* over time. While founding leaders are the first to develop goals (Boeker 1989), the sort of identity a firm acquires, and the sort of objectives it pursues, will attract some people to it and repel others from it. A firm like The Body Shop, with a reputation for environmentally friendly products, draws in workers who identify with such a goal (Grant 1998). Similarly, human capabilities and the firm's non-human resources interact with its goals over time. Take the example of a clothing manufacturing firm which hires workers who are not particularly flexible in their skills and invests very few funds in training. Such a firm may make lower cost garments, with adequate quality standards, but never be able to make complex or high quality branded clothing which commands a premium. The competitive goals of such a firm are limited by its historical investments in people and resources, a problem that will not be overcome quickly, if at all – a phenomenon noted in comparative studies of the British and German clothing industries (Lane 1990, Steedman and Wagner 1989). As is emphasised in the resource-based view of the firm (discussed in Chapter 4), the history of any firm is both a help and a hindrance: it enables management to contemplate some futures but makes other aspirations extremely difficult simply because the firm's 'routines' have been focused on other concerns (Nelson and Winter 1982).

The problem of viability, then, is the most critical problem facing the firm. It is a messy, interactive, dynamic set of concerns which we can simplify somewhat for theoretical purposes but never totally specify.

The problem of sustained advantage

While the problem of viability is the fundamental (though never static) strategic problem, there is a 'second-order' problem that lies beyond it. Firms which deal adequately with the viability problem have the chance to play in a higher level 'tournament': the contest among leaders of sound businesses to see which firm can secure the best rate of return. They are sufficiently in control of the survival issues to contemplate superior performance. In effect, this is not so much a problem as an opportunity, an opportunity to move beyond the pack and gain industry leadership (Boxall and Steeneveld 1999). It is, however, convenient to call it a problem because it is extremely difficult to achieve. As Chapter 4 will explain, it involves a complex mix of factors, human and non-human.

A firm which builds a relatively consistent pattern of superior returns for its shareholders has developed some form of 'competitive advantage' (Porter 1985) – or achieved what the economic theory of the firm has traditionally called 'rents': profits above what can normally be earned in conditions of 'perfect competition'. Chief executives are often incentivised for this higher level game: they may, for example, be promised certain bonus sums if the firm's profitability significantly exceeds the industry average or if its share price beats the average of its rivals over a certain timeframe. Their goal, if you will, is not to support perfect competition (which might be a goal of politicians) but to engineer *im*perfect competition favouring their firm.

How long such superior performance can be sustained is, of course, variable. We should not think that superior performance can be maintained indefinitely. It doesn't take what economists call 'perfect competition' for imitative forces to set in. There simply have to be serious rivals – as there are in any oligopolistic market – who detect that someone has achieved an unusual level of profitability and seek to compete it away. It is better to think of 'barriers to imitation' as having different heights and different rates of decay or erosion (Reed and DeFillippi 1990). And, as Barney (1991) reminds us, there is always the possibility of 'Schumpeterian shocks'. This refers to the great Austrian economist, Joseph Schumpeter's view that capitalism involves 'gales of creative destruction' (Schumpeter 1950: 84). These are major innovations in products or processes which can destroy whole firms and the sectors they inhabit. As he pointed out, this is a lot tougher than price-based competition.

The question of how to achieve competitive advantage is the dominant concern in the strategic management literature. Following theorists like Porter (1985, 1991), strategy textbooks in the last 20 years have typically assumed that competitive advantage is the dependent variable of interest in the whole subject. In our view, this emphasis is somewhat unbalanced. It focuses too much on how firms might make themselves different. Firms are inevitably different – in good, bad and ugly ways – but we think it is more balanced to use the notion of two strategic problems or dependent variables – viability and sustained advantage. In other words, firms must meet certain baseline conditions that make them similar to other firms (in their competitive sector and the societies in which they are based) while also having the opportunity to make gains from being positively different.

Our emphasis on the problem of viability is broadly consistent with the arguments of sociologists including 'organisational ecologists' (such as Carroll and Hannan 1995) and 'institutionalists' (such as DiMaggio and Powell 1983) who examine the processes that account for similarity among organisations. Recognition that firms face pressures to conform in order to gain social approval – or 'legitimacy' (one of the three key goals for HRM discussed in Chapter 1) – and have economic reasons to adopt successful strategies in their sector, is growing in the strategic management literature (see, for example, Deephouse 1999, Oliver 1997, Peteraf and Shanley 1997). In saying, then, that competitive advantage is a desirable end, we are not wanting to convey the impression that firms which pursue it will become completely different from their rivals. They will not. They will retain many similarities. If successful in securing competitive advantage, however, they will have some distinctive traits that give them superior profitability. Take the longstanding rivalry between Ford and

General Motors in the automobile sector, for example (Collins and Porras 1998, Pascale 1991). While Ford may have gained superior profitability over the last 15 years, they are both still car companies with huge similarities: while different in certain key respects, both are fundamentally viable firms characterised by many interchangeable products and processes.

The strategies of firms

In this context, the *strategies* of firms are their particular attempts to deal with the strategic problems they face. They are the characteristic ways in which the managers of firms understand their goals and develop resources – both human and non-human – to reach them. Some strategies are better than others in the context concerned: some address the problem of viability extremely well and others are simply disastrous – with every shade of effectiveness in between. The very best strategies are those which reach beyond the problem of viability to master the 'second order' problem of sustained advantage. When key requirements for viability are not addressed by a firm's strategy, its leaders either learn quickly where they are failing or the firm will fold up. In this sense, all firms have strategies but some have strategies that are much smarter than those of other firms. This is exactly what we observe in practice. The fact that someone has a strategy doesn't mean they are successful in their environment. It simply means they have a characteristic way of behaving.[9]

As noted earlier, we should not make the mistake of equating the strategies of firms with formal strategic plans. Following the 'strategic choice' perspective (Child 1972), it is better if we understand the strategies of firms as *sets of strategic choices*, some of which might stem from planning exercises and set-piece debates in senior management, and some of which emerge in a stream of action. The latter, called 'emergent strategy' by Mintzberg (1978) in a classic paper, is an inevitable feature of strategy. Once a firm commits to a particular strategy, such as a decision to enter internet banking, it is inevitable that the process of carrying out that commitment will involve learning which will shape the strategy over time. Commitments of this kind provide a structure or frame within which strategy evolves.

In defining a firm's strategy as a set of strategic choices we are saying that it includes critical choices about ends *and* means. A firm's strategy contains 'outward' and 'inward' elements. Firms face the problem of choosing suitable goals and the problem of choosing and organising appropriate resources to meet them. In effect, our 'strategic choice' definition draws on a 'configurational' or *gestalt* perspective (Meyer, Tsui and Hinings 1993, Miller 1981, Veliyath and Srinavasan 1995). To be

---

9 It is worthwhile pointing out that a firm or an individual's way of behaving could be quite opportunistic – but that may be the most effective strategy in a particular context. Individuals, for example, who stayed behind in London during the Blitz (in 1940–41) and bought up property when it was going cheap often became wealthy landlords later on. They were acting quite opportunistically but many people envy their astute behaviour now.

successful, firms need an effective configuration of choices involving all the key dimensions of the business. At a minimum, these include choices about competitive strategy (which markets to enter and how to compete in them), financial strategy (how to fund the business over time), operational strategy (what supplies, technology and methods to use in producing the goods or services), and human resource strategy (how to recruit, organise and motivate the people needed now and over time).

This definition means we do not use the terms 'business strategy' and 'competitive strategy' interchangeably (Boxall 1996). Competitive strategy is a sub-set of business strategy, an aspect that interacts with, and evolves with, other aspects of the firm's strategy over time. This is not an attempt to downplay competitive strategy. There is no doubt that decisions about sectoral choice and market positioning are very important, as we have already indicated. In the course of the next chapter, we will examine theory and research on the relationship between competitive strategy and human resource strategy and other factors – such as technology – which can affect this relationship.

Our discussion so far implies that business strategy is composed of a cluster of strategies covering the various 'functional silos' of the business: marketing, operations, finance and human resources. Another way of putting this, using stakeholder theory, is to say that business strategy includes key choices involving all the stakeholder groups: it covers critical aspects of the firm's relations with investors, customers, employees, suppliers and regulators (Donaldson and Preston 1995, Hill and Jones 1992). Business strategy is the 'system' of the firm's important choices, a system that could be well integrated around common concerns or which might have various weak links and 'foul-ups'. As noted before, there is nothing in this definition to say that a strategy is particularly clever.

A key issue associated with the strategic choice perspective is the question of what we are implying about the *extent of choice* available to firms. It is widely accepted in the strategy literature that firms in some sectors have greater 'degrees of freedom' than others enjoy (Nelson 1991, Porter 1985). Some environments are more benign – more 'munificent' – than others are (Pfeffer and Salancik 1978). Some firms are heavily constrained by competitive forces pushing them towards intense margin-based competition (something suppliers of supermarkets regularly complain about) while others enjoy a much more dominant position (companies like Microsoft come readily to mind). Consistent with John Child's (1997) reformulation of the strategic choice perspective, we believe it is important to steer a path between 'hyper-determinism', on the one hand, and 'hyper-voluntarism', on the other. That is, firms are neither fully constrained by their environment nor fully able to create it. Adopting a strategic choice perspective means that we see firms as experiencing a varying blend of constraint and choice somewhere in between these two extremes. The 'choice' in 'strategic choice' is real but its extent is variable.

Before moving on, we should note that this definition of strategy is based at the business unit level. This level is, in fact, the most logical one at which to define strategy because different business units are organised around markets or segments of markets which require different goals and clusters of resources (Ghemawat and Costa 1993). Theory and analysis in strategy stems, almost entirely, from the business unit level (Porter 1985, Kaplan & Norton 1996). However, we should note that more complex frameworks are needed to encompass corporate strategy in multidivisional firms. Questions about 'parenting' – about which businesses to buy and sell, which to grow organically and so on – are vital in multidivisional firms. We examine the different ways multidivisional firms take these choices and the role of *corporate* human resource strategy in Chapter 10.

The process of strategic management

If we take this view of strategy, strategic management is best defined as a *process*. It is a process of strategy-making: of forming and, if the firm survives, of re-forming its strategy over time. As we have already indicated, this may involve elements of formal planning, including the application of analytical techniques such as portfolio analysis (see, for example, Grant 1998, Porter 1985, Whittington 1993). It may involve set-piece debates among directors and executives, framed around policy papers and financial proposals. It may also involve *force majeure* if key power brokers – John Child's (1972, 1997) 'dominant coalition' – impose their will where they have the ability to do so. It will also, as Mintzberg emphasises (1978, 1990, 1994), *inevitably* involve a *learning* process as the managers of firms find out what works well in practice for them – or, we might add, what works better for their rivals. The transition in the strategy textbooks from titles such as 'Business Policy' and 'Strategic Planning' to 'Strategic Management' does indicate a realisation that strategy-making is a mixed, impure, interactive kind of process.

This description of the strategic management process implies that it is hard to do it well. Following Eisenhardt and Zbaracki (1992) and Child (1997), we see strategic decision-making as difficult in two key ways which need exploring in more depth: it is mentally or 'cognitively' tough and it is often politically fraught.

Strategic management and human cognition

Human cognition is a psychological term for thinking processes, for our ability to process information and make decisions. Research on cognition recognises the validity of Herbert Simon's observation, in his classic *Administrative Behavior*, that human beings are subject to 'bounded rationality' (Simon 1947). We cannot know everything about our environment, nor can we easily manipulate more than a handful of key ideas in a problem-solving situation: we are limited in the number of variables we can actively 'work on' as we wrestle with an environment which is much more complex than that. Our search for information is 'incomplete, often inadequate, based on uncertain information and partial ignorance, and usually terminated with the discovery of satisfactory, not optimal courses of action' (Simon 1985: 295).

While criticising the concept of optimisation or maximisation, we must be careful, however, to note that Simon was not saying that human behaviour is irrational: we can generally find goals or the element of *intent* in human action. When studying strategy in firms, we can find intent in both formal planning and in Mintzberg's (1978) 'emergent strategy' of action, a point that Mintzberg, unfortunately, fails to make clear. The nature of the intent may shift, and it may not be very clever in the eyes of rivals or through our own hindsight, but it is there.

Following Simon (1947), management theory does not typically employ the assumptions of '*homo economicus*': that tradition within economics which keeps alive a view of economic agents acting with all the information they need and with no debilitating debates or frustrating compromises over the firm's desirable direction or internal organisation. As many academics have quipped, this view of business behaviour is

---

1. We have reasons or goals for our actions but some of them are not very smart by other people's standards. Our powers of reasoning and our understanding of the world vary considerably.
2. We often have to act without knowing everything we'd like to: complexity and uncertainty are facts of life, especially in strategic management. Managers rely on 'mental models' which simplify and may distort the changing nature of their environment.
3. We often commit emotionally to a failing course of action and 'throw good money after bad'. People do not like to lose face.
4. We tend to search for confirming rather than disconfirming evidence to support our views (which is a common trap in employee selection, for example).
5. In problem solving, we often leap to a favourite or preferred solution without disciplining ourselves to diagnose the problem more deeply, mapping causes and consequences, generating real alternatives, and remaining truly open to the criticisms and refinements offered by others. Existing 'mental models' (about major cause-effect relationships in our world) tend to limit the range of our thinking about solutions to new problems.
6. No single executive in a large business is likely to have all the answers to complex, ambiguous problems: strategic management in large organisations needs teams of people with complementary strengths and styles.
7. Even if the need for management teamwork is recognised, knowledge of how things are done, and of how the firm might best respond to competitor threats or new technology, is dispersed throughout the firm, not held exclusively by farsighted or 'heroic' executives or high performing management teams.
8. The management process tends to repeat yesterday's success formula. It can take a long time to change the focus on 'what worked before' in a business. This opens up profitable opportunities for firms whose people can think differently. One firm's mindset or 'strong culture' is another firm's competitive opportunity.

Figure 2.2 Human cognitive issues affecting strategic management

largely unjustified but it makes the maths easier. Certainly, whoever thought of it first had no experience of University administration.

On a practical level, management can ill afford to assume it holds perfect knowledge or has outstanding problem-solving abilities. The work of strategic management, of finding a desirable path for the firm and managing its resources accordingly, is complex work that takes place in an environment of risk and uncertainty. As we have emphasised, it involves *systemic* factors – the problem of thinking not only within 'silos' but of identifying and coordinating a range of critical factors across the business. Figure 2.2, drawn from various sources (Barr, Stimpert and Huff 1992, Belbin 1981, Eisenhardt and Zbaracki 1992, Hambrick 1995, Isenberg 1984, Simon 1985), summarises some of the main findings of research on the cognitive problems of decision-making in firms. The overall effect of this research should be to induce some humility in the face of complex decisions. In respect of strategic decisions, it is much better to be 'often in doubt but seldom wrong' than 'seldom in doubt and often wrong'.

Barr *et al.* (1992) provide an interesting illustration of the cognitive problems of strategic management. They examine the quality of strategic decision-making in two US railway companies in the 1950s, a time when rail faced growing competition from other transport modes (particularly the growing trucking industry). Between 1949 and 1973, the number of major railway companies roughly halved (down from 135 to 69). Barr *et al.* examined the efforts of two companies, the Chicago & North Western (C&NW) and the Chicago, Rock Island and Pacific (Rock Island), to handle this threatening environment. C&NW is still in business but Rock Island went bankrupt in the mid-1970s. Barr *et al.*'s analysis of 50 letters to shareholders written by the directors of these companies is revealing. As the environment began to turn against the rail companies in the 1950s, both companies blamed *external* factors for their poor performance – such as the weather, Government programmes, and regulation. By about 1956, however, management at C&NW began to change its mental model, focusing efforts on *internal* factors (associated with costs and productivity) that management could control more effectively. This set in train (so to speak) a progressive learning process in which management strategies were improved by trial-and-error. This kind of shift in mental model did not occur at Rock Island until 1964, when an abrupt change of thinking occurred, by which time it was too late.

Barr *et al.* (1992) suggest that Rock Island's directors may have been caught in a 'success trap': having been prosperous for many years, they tended to dismiss the need for change even though the post-war environment was steadily moving against rail transport. This study is interesting because it demonstrates the way in which a dysfunctional mental model – one in which notions of cause-and-effect are well wide of the mark – can persist among the members of a senior management team. Not only was the environment clearly difficult but there were other firms – such as C&NW – that were handling it better.

Strategic management and organisational politics

Cases such as the demise of the Rock Island railway point to the role of cognitive strengths and weaknesses in strategic decision-making. There is no doubt that cognition – cleverness – counts for a lot in company success. Most of the research on human cognition, however, overlooks the fact that strategic decision-making is not simply about dealing with complex mental challenges in threatening environments. More than this is involved: politics matter, particularly in larger organisations. Strategic management is also about steering a course in a politically constituted organisation (Child 1972, 1997, Eisenhardt and Zbaracki 1992).

The point is well made in Child and Smith's (1987) study of Cadbury's attempts to transform itself in the 1960s and 70s. Facing the concentration and growth of retailer power and rising oligopolistic competition in a saturated home market, Cadbury needed strategic renewal. It needed to move away from some key elements of 'Cadburyism' – including a huge range of products and some key HR policies such as lifetime commitment – towards a more efficient model of manufacturing with better technology and fewer but more flexible (and well-paid) workers. The leaders who made this change happen were people who handled the cognitive problems well (they cleverly perceived which parts of 'Cadburyism' needed to change and which ought to be enduring). However, as Child and Smith (1987: 588) explain, they also had the power to influence events, the political position and credibility needed within the firm to effect change: 'The Cadbury transformation relied on the exercise of power as well as on the persuasive force of vision and its attendant symbols.'

Because firms are networks of stakeholder groups, we must expect that any major initiative involves *political* management, particularly where investors must be persuaded to support the initiative or where employee groups are being asked to make changes that threaten their interests (as was the case in the Cadbury transformation). This is one of the straightforward implications of the stakeholder theory of the firm (Donaldson and Preston 1995, Hill and Jones 1992) and of 'resource-dependence' theory (Pfeffer and Salancik 1978). In a nutshell, firms are beholden to stockholders (who supply financial capital) but they are also dependent on any stakeholder group (such as suppliers and key customers) that contributes resources that are valuable to the firm. Labour is powerful in this sense, as we noted in Chapter 1. Workers – employees and contractors – do not need 'equal power' to have influence with management, they simply have to have the power to affect performance in some significant way. This is almost invariably the case. It follows that dealing with the power of labour is something that should concern executives in all firms, irrespective of whether the workforce is unionised. Theories of strategic change in work and employment systems are something we examine closely in Part 2 of this book.

Dealing with the power of non-management labour is one of the most visible of the power dynamics in firms. It often hits the media. Less eye-catching but equally powerful is the loss of key employees who cannot be replaced, people with particularly scarce skills and good performance records who exercise their labour market power. The problem of retention of key workers began to stand out as a common problem in the 1990s and continues as a serious issue in the first decade of the 21st century. It has been a particularly severe problem in IT industries but also in the ever-expanding healthcare services, as noted in Chapter 1.

Much of the political difficulty of strategic management occurs within the management structure itself. Organisations offer managers opportunities for personal aggrandizement. The large enterprises of our time – the *Fortune 500* companies and the like – provide management 'careerists' (Rousseau 1995) with a huge domain for self-serving behaviour. Intra-management political problems are of two main types. On the more 'macro' level, departments acquire power when they are central to the fundamental strategy on which a business is founded (Boeker 1989). Managers who head the historically strong departments often fight change even when the larger picture indicates that strategic change is now needed. For example, a firm in which production has historically led the way may well suffer from serious managerial in-fighting if the marketing department grows in significance and starts to challenge production's power base.

On the more 'micro' level, individual managers have personal reasons to advance their own interests irrespective of whether they are located in a powerful department. Perhaps the most significant problem presented by this feast of opportunity is the way consideration for one's personal future often encourages managers to keep quiet about problems, to filter the bad news. Alternatively, individuals may try to fix blame onto their subordinates or peers as a way of displacing attention from their own performance. As we shall see in Chapter 7, performance appraisal systems are often compromised by management politicking.

When most managers in a team are afraid of introducing conflicting opinion, the organisation can suffer from 'groupthink' (Janis 1972, Morgan 1997: 219), a syndrome where executives close down debate prematurely and take decisions with negative consequences. The decision by the US Cabinet to invade Cuba at the Bay of Pigs is one of Janis's famous examples. In her classic study of flawed decision-making in a selection of great historical events ('from Troy to Vietnam'), *The March of Folly*, Barbara Tuchman (1996: 302–3), finds many cases of the tendency:

> Adjustment is painful. For the ruler it is easier, once he (*sic*) has entered a policy box, to stay inside. For the lesser official it is better, for the sake of his (*sic*) position, not to make waves, not to press evidence that the chief will find painful to accept. Psychologists call the process of screening out discordant information 'cognitive dissonance', an academic disguise for 'Do not confuse me with the facts.' Cognitive dissonance is the tendency 'to suppress, gloss over, water down or "waffle" issues that would produce conflict or "psychological pain" within an organization'. It causes alternatives to be 'deselected since even thinking about them entails conflicts'. In the relations of subordinate to superior ..., its object is the development of policies that upset no one.

The tendency to look after oneself is recognised by those branches of organisational economics (such as agency theory) which acknowledge that managerial interests can diverge from those of stockholders (see, for example, McMillan 1992, Rowlinson 1997). We cover these ideas (and their limitations) in Chapter 7. In the current chapter, it is simply important to note that the politics of executive ambition add complexity to the broader stakeholder-based politics we find in organisations.

Improving strategic management processes

Given cognitive limitations and political complications, what can be done to improve the quality of strategic decision-making in firms? And what role might human resource management play in this task?

The role of key HR decisions

In the light of what we know about cognitive problems, including the fact that human performance becomes increasingly variable in jobs of high complexity (Hunter, Schmidt and Judiesch 1990), it seems obvious that HRM should play a major role in improving the quality of strategic management. The greater the uncertainty and discretion involved in work, the more important it is to hire (or promote) people of high ability, with a well-rounded intellectual *and* emotional profile. There is evidence that senior HR specialists act on this view. In a study of human resource directors in the largest New Zealand corporates, Hunt and Boxall (1998) found a strong emphasis in their work priorities on developing executive capability and performance. In line with findings in the UK (Marginson, Edwards, Martin, Purcell and Sisson 1988), the primary concern of most of the senior HR specialists in the study was the management of managers, including recruitment, remuneration, development, succession planning and termination. One stated that they 'worked constantly' with the CEO of the company: 'looking at managers, identifying strengths and weaknesses, seeing who will go further and who needs to go' (Hunt and Boxall 1998: 772–3).

As the research of Hambrick (1987, 1995) emphasises, improving top team performance must be substantially about getting well-qualified people into the team in the first place. Constituting and renewing the top team, including the chief executive, and building the overall capability of management in the firm, is perhaps the most strategic concern of all in human resource management (Boxall 1994), as we shall argue further in Chapter 4.

The role of team building

While the core HR disciplines of recruiting and retaining top people must be involved if strategic management is to be improved, they are not, however, enough.

Skills in developing leadership and group processes – which are not often discussed in HRM textbooks – must also be involved. This is emphasised in the work of Stuart Hart (1992) who defines five styles of strategy-making (Figure 2.3). Hart's (1992) typology is useful because it specifies roles not only for executives but also for other members of the organisation under different modes of strategy-making. We can see a major shift in the way senior managers and other members of the organisation are expected to behave, from the command model at one end to the generative model at the other. Different modes might be appropriate to different contexts (a command style is needed in some crises) while firms might benefit from gaining the ability to combine different modes.

In a survey of the opinions of US chief executives, Hart and Banbury (1994: 266) find some evidence that 'firms which combine high levels of competence in multiple modes of strategy-making appear to be the highest performers'. Consistent with a resource-based view of the firm (which we explore in Chapter 4), they suggest that:

> ... a firm dominated by the command mode of strategy-making relies on the idiosyncratic capabilities of a single (or a few) individual(s). Should this person(s) leave the organization or be attracted away by competitors, the firm's strategy-making capability would be severely impaired. In contrast, a firm using symbolic, transactive[10], and generative processes of strategy-making demonstrates a more complex, deeply embedded capability

Descriptors	Command	Symbolic	Rational	Participative	Generative
Style	*Imperial* Strategy driven by leader or small top team	*Cultural* Strategy driven by mission and a vision of the future	*Analytical* Strategy driven by formal structure and planning systems	*Procedural* Strategy driven by internal process and mutual adjustment	*Organic* Strategy driven by organisational actors' initiative
Role of top management	Commander: provide direction	Coach: motivate and inspire	Boss: evaluate and control	Facilitator: empower and enable	Sponsor: Endorse and support
Role of organisational members	Soldier: obey orders	Player: respond to challenge	Subordinate: follow the system	Participant: learn and improve through self-evaluation against agreed criteria	Entrepreneur: experiment and take risks

Source: Adapted from Hart (1992)

Figure 2.3 Styles of strategy-making

---

10   We have changed the 'transactive' label to 'participative' in Figure 2.3.

requiring the concerted effort of hundreds (or even thousands) of people. Such an organization possesses a difficult-to-copy asset that could yield competitive advantage. Thus, firms able to accumulate several process skills into a complex strategy-making capability should outperform less process-capable organizations (Hart and Banbury 1994: 255).

Hart and Banbury (1994) note the need for further research on this idea – preferably involving multiple respondents and less subjective data. Their research, of course, does not tell us *how* firms could develop a greater range of strategy-making styles.

A small group of researchers and consultants has tried to identify ways in which management teamwork can be made more productive. One of the most celebrated frameworks is associated with the work of Meredith Belbin (1981). Belbin's model of eight team roles (Figure 2.4) has been used to analyse the strengths and weaknesses of many senior management teams. According to this theory, it is a mistake to construct management teams simply based on the functional expertise of individuals. Belbin argues that the most effective management teams enjoy a healthy mix of complementary *teamwork* styles. Such teams have at least one clever and highly creative individual (a 'plant'), are led by a chairman who knows how to use the talents of others, and contain a spread of other useful styles, for example, a 'monitor-evaluator' to provide some dispassionate intellectual appraisal of the plant's ideas, and a 'completer-finisher' and 'company worker' who will ensure sound organisation and follow-through (Belbin 1981: 93–9).

Belbin's ideas resonate with the research of Hart and Banbury (1994). They suggest that 'a winning company has a wider range of team-role strengths on which to draw than less successful companies' (Belbin 1981: 96). Teams uniformly low in IQ almost certainly fail but, conversely, those packed too full of pointy-headed geniuses often under-perform for want of complementary strengths in the other dimensions of effective teamwork.

The work of Kathleen Eisenhardt and her colleagues can also be used to help management teams perform more effectively – or learn to 'have good fights' (Eisenhardt, Kahwajy and Bourgeois 1997). Consistent with the view that strategic management involves both cognitive and political problems, she looks at ways to stimulate better conflicts, to avoid premature closure when key decisions must be taken (Figure 2.5). These suggestions, if followed, would help to diminish the deadening effect of hierarchy on the level of debate about strategy in a firm. To achieve this, of course, we must note the obvious point that the power to stimulate greater participation in strategic management lies in the hands of the current chief executive. Even when a company has built a more a participative culture, every time a new chief executive is appointed there is potential for decision-making to revert to an autocratic or closely-held style. Business organisations are not constituted as democracies. Disproportionate power keeps reverting into the hands of senior management. This should remind us how central key executive appointments are to the long-term success of the firm.

Type	Typical features	Positive qualities	Allowable weaknesses
Company worker	Conservative, dutiful, predictable	Organizing ability, practical common sense, hard-working, self-discipline	Lack of flexibility, unresponsiveness to unproven ideas
Chairman	Calm, self-confident, controlled	A capacity for treating and welcoming all potential contributors on their merits and without prejudice. A strong sense of objectives	No more than ordinary in terms of intellect or creative ability
Shaper	Highly strung, outgoing, dynamic	Drive and a readiness to challenge inertia, ineffectiveness, complacency or self-deception	Proneness to provocation, irritation and impatience
Plant	Individualistic, serious minded, unorthodox	Genius, imagination, intellect, knowledge	Up in the clouds, inclined to disregard practical details or protocol
Resource investigator	Extroverted, enthusiastic, curious, communicative	A capacity for contacting people and exploring anything new. An ability to respond to challenge	Liable to lose interest once the initial fascination has passed
Monitor-evaluator	Sober, unemotional, prudent	Judgement, discretion, hard-headedness	Lacks inspiration or the ability to motivate others
Team worker	Socially orientated, rather mild, sensitive	An ability to respond to people and to situations, and to promote team spirit	Indecisiveness at moments of crisis
Completer-finisher	Painstaking, orderly, conscientious, anxious	A capacity for follow-through. Perfectionism	A tendency to worry about small things. A reluctance to 'let go'

Source: Belbin (1981)

Figure 2.4 A typology of team roles

Conclusions and implications

This chapter provides a basis for exploring the role of HRM in strategic management. It is important to pause and reflect on the nature of strategy and strategic management before leaping into the theory and research on strategic HRM.

1 **Assemble a heterogeneous team, including diverse ages, genders, functional backgrounds, and industry experience.** If everyone in the executive meetings looks alike, then the chances are excellent they will probably think alike, too.
2 **Meet together as a team regularly and often.** Team members that do not know one another well do not know one another's positions on issues, impairing their ability to argue effectively. Frequent interaction builds the mutual confidence and familiarity team members require to express dissent.
3 **Encourage team members to assume roles beyond their obvious product, geographic, or functional responsibilities.** Devil's advocates, sky-gazing visionaries, and action-oriented executives can work together to ensure that all sides of an issue are considered.
4 **Apply multiple mind-sets to any issue.** Try role-playing, putting yourselves in your competitor's shoes, or conducting war games. Such techniques create fresh perspectives and engage team members, spurring interest in problem solving.
5 **Actively manage conflict.** Do not let the team acquiesce too soon or too easily. Identify and treat apathy early, and do not confuse a lack of conflict with agreement. Often, what passes for consensus is really disengagement.

Source: Eisenhardt *et al.* (1997)

Figure 2.5 'Building a fighting team'

Doing so will help to restrain us from superficial conclusions and misleading advice.

We have defined strategy by distinguishing between 'strategic problems' the firm faces in its environment, and the characteristic ways it tries to cope with them (its 'strategy'). As common sense tells us, the word 'strategic' implies something that is seriously consequential for the future of the firm. The fundamental strategic problem is the problem of viability. To be viable, a firm needs an appropriate set of goals and a relevant set of human and non-human resources, a configuration or system of ends and means consistent with survival in its competitive sector and the society (or societies) in which it operates. This obviously means that without certain kinds of human capability, firms are simply not viable. We take issue, then, with anyone who wants to downplay the significance of HRM in the firm. We find fault with those strategy texts which imply that key human resource concerns are not strategic. There is really no need for HR specialists to hang their heads in shame around the executive table, as if the critical dimensions of HRM were not important to the firm's success. As we shall argue further in the next two chapters, effective human resource strategy is a necessary, though not sufficient, condition of firm viability. We shall also examine the debate over the ways in which 'human assets' might lay the basis of sustained competitive advantage (which can be thought of as a 'second-order' or higher-level strategic problem). As we have argued in this chapter, however, firms which achieve some form of competitive advantage will not be completely different from those that do not – due to the need of all firms in the sector to have 'table stakes', features that make them strongly similar.

Strategy, then, is a set of strategic choices, some of which may be formally planned. It is inevitable that much, if not most, of a firm's strategy emerges in a stream of action over time. Strategy has both 'outward' and 'inward' elements – it includes both the firm's goals and the important means it uses to pursue them. How well these elements are conceived and coordinated is very variable. Saying that firms have strategy doesn't mean they are successful in their environment. Some firms fail, some secure viability with adequate returns, and some find ways of out-performing others for periods of time.

Strategic management, therefore, is the process used in the firm to develop critical goals and resources. It is a mixed, impure, interactive process, fraught with difficulty, both intellectually and politically. Improving the process of strategic management has a lot to do with HRM. It involves making some key HR decisions (about the appointment, development and promotion of key individuals) but it also involves astute team building activities, within the senior management team and throughout the organisation. There is some research suggesting that firms that develop multiple modes of strategy-making are likely to be superior performers. Developing and sustaining highly participative styles of strategic management is not easy, however. Business organisations are not democracies. Power keeps reverting to those at the top, a phenomenon that reinforces the critical importance of people decisions at the apex of firms.

3

Strategic HRM: 'best fit' or 'best practice'?

Perhaps one message – more than any other – has been communicated in job advertisements for HR directors over the last few years: whatever you do, help the firm to make its HRM consistent with its strategic direction, *integrate* HR strategy with business strategy. To many people this piece of advice seems obvious and straightforward. But is it? Could it be interpreted in quite different ways? Building on the concepts clarified in the previous chapter, our task in this one is to analyse the main ways in which theorists have argued that HRM should be integrated into strategic management.

The theory of strategic HRM does not, in fact, advocate a single way of linking HRM to strategy. Most theoretical debate around this nexus has been consumed with a contest between two normative models of how firms should link labour management to strategy. One model – the 'best fit' school – argues that HR strategy will be more effective when it is appropriately integrated with its specific organisational and broader environmental context. This school invites a string of questions about which are the most critical contingencies in this complex context and how they are best connected. The other model advocates universalism. It argues that all firms will be better off if they identify and adopt 'best practice' in the way they manage people. This is not straightforward either: it begs questions about how best practice is defined and about why we see such limited diffusion of most of the best practice models that are currently advocated, both within complex firms and across sectors of the economy. This chapter will explain each model more fully, reviewing the theoretical critique, and then examining what the research has to say. Readers will find that we take a very broad view of the research in reaching our conclusions and laying a basis for subsequent analysis in this book. To begin with, we need to flesh out our definition of strategic HRM and its companion term, human resource strategy.

Defining 'strategic HRM' and HR strategy

As Chapter 1 made clear, we do not associate HRM with any particular ideology or style of management. Low, moderate, and high commitment strategies exist, as do various shades of ideology. The practice of HRM incorporates all of these and we are interested in identifying and tracking trends in all significant patterns of employer behaviour over time.

What difference does it make, then, when we apply the adjective *strategic* to HRM? As explained in Chapter 2, our understanding of strategy is based on a 'strategic choice' perspective – something which can be applied to the whole of strategy and to its constituent parts, including human resource strategy. In this interpretation, the application of the adjective *strategic* implies a concern with the ways in which HRM is critical to the firm's survival and its relative success. There are always strategic choices associated with labour processes in the firm – whether highly planned or largely emergent in management behaviour – and these choices are inevitably connected to the firm's performance (Dyer 1984, Purcell and Ahlstrand 1994: 37–42). These choices are made over time by the whole management structure, including line managers and HR specialists (where they exist).

As also explained in Chapter 2, it is helpful to think of strategic choices on two levels: they either play a role in underpinning the firm's viability (make-or-break choices) or they provide a form of sustained advantage, accounting for major, ongoing differences in business performance. In adopting this understanding, it is convenient to refer to a firm's *pattern* of strategic choices in labour management (including critical ends and means) as its 'human resource (HR) strategy' (Dyer 1984).

To illustrate what we mean about strategic choices in HRM, take the case of a management consulting firm that aims to join the elite cluster of firms which are 'global' in their reach (Boxall and Purcell 2000). Firms such as PriceWaterhouseCoopers, McKinsey and KPMG are among the leaders in this sector. What might it take to join them? There is no doubt that firms in this 'strategic group'[11] must have highly selective recruitment and strong development of staff to ensure they can consistently offer clients high quality service on complex business problems. In this elite group of professional firms, a synergistic blend of certain human resource policies – such as proactive recruitment channels, high entry standards, high pay, employee ownership, and extensive professional education – is critical to credibility in the sectoral labour market. Firms of this type need these policies to attract and retain the talented people they want. On the other hand, we can draw something of a line between these critical elements of HRM and other aspects which are not really important. It is

---

11   A strategic group is a cluster of firms in the same industry that compete for clients in the same kind of way and develop strong 'mutual understandings' (Peteraf and Shanley 1997).

unlikely, for example, that there is much hanging on the firm's choice of job evaluation systems. Job evaluation systems allocate jobs to pay grades based on the skill, effort and responsibility they involve. If any one of a range of such systems supports its remuneration goals in recruiting and retaining highly qualified consultants, or doesn't perversely undermine them, then the choice among different systems is not critical. Similarly, the contracting out of payroll or benefits administration in such a firm is not a strategic dimension of its HRM. It is not difficult to meet the requirements of employment contracts in these areas and elite firms are not differentiated from lesser firms on this basis. What is vital, however, is that the firm's leaders put together the *system* of truly critical human and non-human resources that will help the firm to join the elite group of professional firms in this sector. However, it would be unwise to think that the firm's labour market reputation will be made quickly or that viability in the sector will be achieved solely through HR strategy (as our discussion of the resource-based view of the firm in the next chapter will make clear).

As a field of study, then, strategic HRM is concerned with the strategic choices associated with the use of labour in firms and with explaining why some firms manage them more effectively than others. It is helpful to spell out this definition in a very practical manner. Suppose an HR director is asked by a chief executive to conduct a review of the quality of HR strategy in a firm. What should such a review entail? We suggest the questions shown in Figure 3.1.

As the three questions in Figure 3.1 make clear, this kind of analysis is far from straightforward. In many firms, a major effort in data gathering would be needed to answer the first two questions. A study of these two questions nearly always reveals the need for better systems for measuring HR performance in the firm, as advocates of the 'balanced scorecard' have noted (Kaplan and Norton 1996: 144–5). There is still a marked tendency in firms to treat HR practices as ends in themselves and a lot of work is needed to map their links to one another, to other management activities and to important performance variables (for some key examples, see Chapter 11). The third question involves not only data analysis but some kind of theory about how to make HRM more effective in the firm, about how to improve the strategic management of human resources in it. This is the nub of the debate between advocates of 'best fit' and 'best practice' (Boxall and Purcell 2000).

---

1 What strategic choices in HRM (including key HR policies, practices, and investments and the overall system of these choices) are critical to the firm's performance?
2 How are managers in the firm making these choices – what processes are involved, including analytical and political processes, and how are strategic HR choices connected to other strategic choices in the firm?
3 How could the firm's HRM become more effective – what could be done in HRM to improve the firm's relative performance in its industry, perhaps even to the extent of generating some form of sustained competitive advantage?

Figure 3.1 Three questions for a review of HR strategy in a firm

Before exploring this interesting debate, we should note some complications to our conception of human resource strategy. Firstly, we should not assume that HR strategies are uniform within firms. It is wrong to conjure up the image of a single set of critical practices for managing people in the firm. The vast bulk of evidence suggests otherwise: firms rarely adopt a single style of management for all their employee groups. The HR strategies of firms typically include somewhat different styles for different occupational groups: 'internal labour markets' are segmented (Osterman 1987, Pinfield and Berner 1994, Purcell 1987), not least between management and non-managerial labour (Boxall 1992). In a nutshell, the pattern of strategic choices in a firm's employment relations is variegated (Purcell 1996, 1999a). This is something we explore very carefully in Chapter 6. Secondly, we have been talking as if the firm is a single business unit. As explained in our definition of strategy in Chapter 2, this is the easiest way to develop theory in strategic management. Reality, however, is much more complicated. Difficulties arise with multi-product and multidivisional firms, some of which are based on related diversification and others on unrelated diversification. Is there a role for corporate HR strategy in such firms and, if so, what should it be (Purcell and Ahlstrand 1994)? Can corporate HR strategy provide some form of 'parenting advantage' which adds value to what business units could achieve without corporate influence? This question is explored in Chapter 10. A third complication arises with international firms (as many multidivisional firms are). Where firms compete across national boundaries, in what ways should they adapt their employment strategies to local conditions? This is the concern of the fields of international and comparative HRM (see, for example, Boxall 1995, Brewster 1999, De Cieri and Dowling 1999). We touch on this problem in the course of this chapter but tackle it more fully in Chapter 10. Overall, our understanding of HR strategy is summarised in Figure 3.2.

On the basis of these definitions and clarifications, we are now in a position to examine the debate between 'best fit' and 'best practice' in strategic HRM.

Human resource (HR) strategy:
- consists of critical goals and means for managing labour
- inevitably affects the firm's performance
- is made by the whole management structure and not simply by HR specialists (where they exist)
- is likely to be partly planned and partly 'emergent' in behaviour
- is typically 'variegated' – different goals and means for different workforce segments (most notably for managers versus non-management labour)
- like strategy generally, is easiest to define at business unit level
- is more complex in multidivisional firms because of interactions among corporate/divisional and business unit levels
- is more complex in firms that compete across national boundaries

---

Figure 3.2 Characteristics of human resource strategy

Strategic HRM: the 'best fit' school

The 'best fit' or contingency school of strategic HRM covers a range of models which advocate fitting HR strategy to its surrounding context. Which elements of the context are 'privileged' or deemed important is variable. In one of the earliest sources, Baird and Meshoulam (1988) argue that HR activities, like structure and systems, should fit the organisation's stage of development – something they call 'external fit' (otherwise called 'vertical fit'). This implies informal, more flexible styles of HRM among start-up firms and more formal, professionalised styles as firms become more mature and increase the number and range of employees. It implies the need to cope with complex tensions between decentralisation and coordination when large firms diversify. Baird and Meshoulam also argue for 'internal fit', for the need to ensure that individual HR policies are designed to 'fit with and support each other' (1988: 122) (otherwise called 'horizontal fit'). Most models of 'best fit' are concerned with what is meant by 'external fit' and with how to achieve it. There are then flow-on implications for internal fit, a point to which we shall return.

'External fit': integration with competitive strategy

We think Baird and Meshoulam (1988) are making an important point, and we devote Chapter 9 to an exposition of how HR strategy is affected by industry and organisational life cycles. However, at this point we need to examine the most influential conception of 'external fit' to date: this is one in which fit is defined by the firm's competitive strategy rather than its stage of development. In this conception, the basic recipe for strategic HRM involves bringing HR strategy into line with the firm's chosen path in its product market (more accurately, this entails matching HR practices to the competitive strategy of a business unit). As those who follow the circuit will know, 'meeting the business needs' in this kind of way was the catch-cry of practitioner conferences on HRM right throughout the 1980s and 1990s.

One method for linking HR strategy to competitive strategy was developed by Miles and Snow (1984). In a well-known framework, they define three basic types of strategic behaviour. Firms they call 'defenders' have 'narrow and relatively stable product-market domains' (Miles and Snow 1984: 37). Defenders have a limited product line and aim to succeed through strong efficiencies. On the other hand, 'prospectors' continually search for product and market opportunities and aim to compete through innovation and prime mover advantages (Miles and Snow 1984: 37–8). Efficiency is a much lower priority. The third type, 'analysers', have some stable operations but also keep a lookout for opportunities to emulate creative rivals through fast follower strategies. Drawing on work done in the Canadian Pacific company, Miles and Snow posit a range of implications for HRM stemming from these three strategic types (see Figure 3.3).

Organisational/managerial characteristics	Defenders	Prospectors	Analysers
Competitive strategies	Limited, stable product line. Growth through penetration. Emphasis on efficiency	Changing product lines. Growth through innovation and market development	Stable and changing product lines. Some focus on efficiency but also 'fast followership'
Staffing and development strategies	Emphasis on internal training & development ('make')	Emphasis on recruitment ('buy')	Mixed approaches (both 'make' and 'buy' as needed)
Performance appraisal	Process-oriented and linked to training needs analysis	Results-oriented and linked to rewards	Mostly process oriented
Pay policies	Focused on internal equity	Focused on external competitiveness	Concerned with both internal equity and external competitiveness

Source: Adapted from Miles and Snow (1984)

Figure 3.3   Selected HRM implications of Miles and Snow's competitive types

While Miles and Snow's typology remains very influential in strategic management, it has been less so in the strategic HRM literature. The most heavily cited model of external fit in strategic HRM is associated with a framework developed by Schuler and Jackson (1987). This paper, and a subsequent stream of work (see, for example, Schuler 1989, 1996), has proven popular because it develops more fully the connections between competitive strategies, desired employee behaviours and particular HR practices. Schuler and Jackson (1987) argue that HR practices should be designed to reinforce the behavioural implications of the various 'generic strategies' defined by Porter (1985). A giant in the strategy field, Porter (1985) advises firms to specialise carefully in competitive strategy (Figure 3.4). In his view, firms should choose between cost leadership (achieving lowest unit costs in the sector), differentiation (based, for example, on superior quality or service), or focus (a 'niche play' in cost or differentiation). They should avoid getting 'stuck in the middle' or caught in a strategic posture which is mixed – neither fish nor fowl, one might say.

Schuler and Jackson (1987) took up Porter's framework to create what quickly became the best known model of its kind in strategic HRM (summarised in Figure 3.5). Returning to the third question we posed above, their model argues that business performance will improve when HR practices mutually reinforce the firm's (predetermined) choice of competitive strategy. To arrive at a desirable set of HR practices, Schuler and Jackson (1987) argue that different competitive strategies

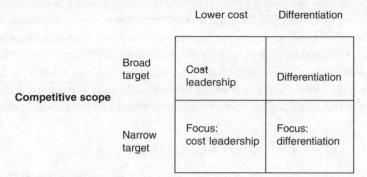

Competitive advantage

Lower cost   Differentiation

Broad target	Cost leadership	Differentiation
Narrow target	Focus: cost leadership	Focus: differentiation

Competitive scope

Source: Porter (1985)

Figure 3.4   Porter's typology of competitive strategies

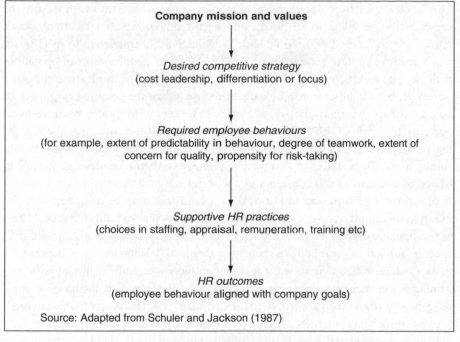

Company mission and values

↓

Desired competitive strategy
(cost leadership, differentiation or focus)

↓

Required employee behaviours
(for example, extent of predictability in behaviour, degree of teamwork, extent of
concern for quality, propensity for risk-taking)

↓

Supportive HR practices
(choices in staffing, appraisal, remuneration, training etc)

↓

HR outcomes
(employee behaviour aligned with company goals)

Source: Adapted from Schuler and Jackson (1987)

Figure 3.5   Linking HR practices to competitive strategy

imply different kinds or blends of employee behaviour. These inferences are drawn
from a major review of existing literature. If, for example, management chooses a
competitive strategy of differentiation through product innovation, this would call
for high levels of creative, risk-oriented and cooperative behaviour. The company's
HR practices would therefore need to emphasise '... selecting highly skilled individuals, giving employees more discretion, using minimal controls, making greater

investment in human resources, providing more resources for experimentation, allowing and even rewarding occasional failure, and appraising performance for its long-run implications' (Schuler and Jackson 1987: 210).

On the other hand, according to Schuler and Jackson, if management wants to pursue cost leadership (that is, to attain lowest unit costs in the sector), the model implies something a lot less attractive to the average employee. It suggests designing jobs which are fairly repetitive, training workers as little as is practical, cutting staff numbers to the minimum and rewarding high output and predictable behaviour.

The notion of external fit: theoretical critique

The model shown in Figure 3.5 provides a convenient basis for analysing the strengths and weaknesses of this body of theory.

Perhaps the most important criticism that can be made of models emphasising alignment of HRM with competitive strategy is that they overlook employee interests. They generally fail to recognise the need to align employee interests with the firm or comply with prevailing social norms and legal requirements (for example, Boxall 1996, Coff 1997, Lees 1997). While logic suggests that it is important to fit HRM to its competitive context because firms need the skills of people who can operate in their chosen markets, management inevitably faces the need to think about the other side of the coin. In other words, how does the firm 'fit' for the potential employee? As noted in Chapter 1, motivational issues are always central to human resource management. In Schein's (1977) classic model of 'psychological contracting', the 'matching processes' of HRM are needed to integrate business *and* employee needs, not simply to fit HR practices to competitive strategy (a theme we develop further in Chapter 7). As part of this consideration, Chapter 1 argued that legitimacy is usefully considered a strategic goal in HRM. What labour laws must be complied with (for example, minimum pay rates, safety regulations and maximum hours of work)? These are compliance and employee voice issues in HRM that should be recognised irrespective of the firm's competitive strategy (a theme we take forward in Chapter 8).

As a general rule, and despite the fact that employers typically enjoy superior bargaining power, managers must give thought to how they can meet the baseline needs of employees whose skills are crucial to the firm's survival. This is especially so in highly competitive labour markets where it is very hard to attract and retain talented individuals, as occurred in the markets for information technology (IT) skills throughout the 1990s. In effect, this criticism does not undermine the notion of a fit between competitive and HR strategy but says that the strategic goals of HRM are plural. While they do involve supporting the firm's competitive objectives, they also involve meeting employee needs and complying with social requirements for labour management. Multiple 'fits' are needed. The firm, after all, is a network of stakeholders.

A second criticism of models that aim to link HRM with competitive strategy concerns the lack of sophistication in their description of competitive strategy. Miller

(1992), for example, argues that competitive posture is multidimensional and subject to major variations across industries. There is evidence that the most resilient firms in some sectors are good at everything: they are superb 'all rounders', not just good at differentiation or cost leadership (see, for example, Cronshaw, Davis and Kay 1994, Murray 1988). Managing the workforce at one of these companies is unlikely to be based on relating practices to a *single* strategy in Porter's terms. It would be counter-productive if HR strategists devised HR policies for the workforce from a typology of competitive strategy that may be misleading in their specific context. Certainly, it would be extremely unwise if the management of managers in a firm needing variety in its competitive strategy was linked too much to a single competitive posture (Boxall 1992). As emphasised in Chapter 2, in a climate of strategic ambiguity and rivalry, it is desirable to build a management team which can think beyond its current competitive position and contemplate action outside its historical routines.

Again, however, this criticism does not invalidate the idea of a fit between HR strategy and competitive strategy. There are now several studies which can be cited as offering some support for the argument that firms try to relate a variety of HR practices to their competitive strategy (Bird and Beechler 1995, Delery and Doty 1996, Guthrie, Spell and Nyamori 2002, Peck 1994, Sanz-Valle, Sabater-Sanchez and Aragon-Sanchez 1999, Youndt, Snell, Dean and Lepak 1996). In a study of 200 Spanish firms, for example, Sanz-Valle *et al.* (1999) find that those with an innovation or a quality strategy do indeed provide more training and greater opportunities for employee participation than those pursuing cost leadership, as Schuler and Jackson's model predicts (for very similar results in a sample of New Zealand firms, see Guthrie, Spell and Nyamori (2002)). They also find that innovators pay better wages than those focusing on cost, again as the model predicts. However, the fit between HR strategy and competitive strategy is not total:

> Although some of our findings are consistent with Schuler and Jackson's (1987) assumptions, our study provides only partial support for their model. On the one hand, our results reveal that some HRM practices do not vary with strategy. For example, most of the companies prefer internal recruitment and have similar selection or appraisal criteria. Therefore, sometimes the job (managerial or non-managerial) has more influence on some HRM practices than firm strategy. (And) some of our findings are opposite to Schuler and Jackson's assumptions. For example, firms with a quality strategy have a more, not less, hierarchical payment system than companies with an innovation strategy (Sanz-Valle *et al.* 1999: 666).

These mixed results are typical for this kind of study and can also be seen in the other studies just cited. Definitional and method difficulties aside, these sorts of results suggest that current competitive strategy is indeed playing some role in shaping important aspects of HR practice but the correlation is never overwhelming. Other factors are exerting influence as well.

A third criticism then, is that the point just made implies that models of external fit in strategic HRM should give better attention to dynamics. While it is obviously important for management to implement certain key human dimensions of the existing competitive strategy, ongoing environmental change implies they should do more than this (Boxall 1992). A more helpful model for practice is one in which fit with existing competitive strategy is developed *simultaneously* with flexibility in the range of skills and behaviours that may be needed to cope with different competitive scenarios in the future (Wright and Snell 1998). HR strategy *should* give effect to the firm's current competitive goals, by recruiting, developing and retaining people with the sort of skills and motivations needed in the firm's competitive sector. However, it is also highly desirable that HR strategy encourage staff to think 'outside the square', that it help to build the sort of skills needed for new business capabilities in the future. Change, we are often reminded, is one of the few certainties of capitalism.

In effect, the last criticism reinforces the point that the strategic goals of HRM are complex and subject to paradox, as we argued in the first chapter of this book. Management would be unwise to focus solely on fit with any single variable (such as competitive strategy) in HRM because the objectives of labour management in the firm are inevitably plural – they cannot be encapsulated in one goal or summarised in a single theme. Aiming to meet current competitive needs in a cost-effective way is important but so too are goals for supporting organisational flexibility over time. In a changing environment, there is always a 'strategic tension' between performing in the present context and preparing for the future. And throughout all of this, there is a need to motivate employees by meeting their goals as far as possible. Along with the need to think about employee goals, there is the fundamental problem of compliance with labour laws and social norms for employing labour. Any HR professional accepting a job in a company that has not previously employed one knows that compliance objectives are among the first that need to be tackled. New HR specialists often refer to this work as 'putting out the fires'.

The companion notion of 'internal fit': theoretical critique

The criticism just made helps us to refine the companion notion to 'external fit' – 'internal fit' or internal coherence of HR policies and practices. In recent years, HR strategists have increasingly been advised that they should aim for positive 'bundling' of HR policies (MacDuffie 1995) – like our earlier example of elite management consulting firms. They have been advised to avoid 'deadly combinations': policies which work in directly opposite directions, such as strong training for teamwork but appraisal which only rewards highly individualistic behaviour (Delery 1998: 294). HR strategists have also been warned to avoid costly duplication of practices, such as over-designed selection systems where extra 'hurdles' add no further predictive power to the process (Delery 1998: 293). Consider the example of the firm that would benefit from structured interviewing and reference checking of job applicants but decides instead to design an 'assessment centre' with five or six kinds of test involved. Chances are that much of the assessment centre is an expensive white elephant. Little of value has been added for the considerable extra expense involved.

One of the more useful summaries of 'internal fit' is provided by Baron and Kreps (1999) who define three types of desirable consistency in HRM. The first type is 'complementary' fit or what they call 'single employee consistency': for example, ensuring that where firms use expensive selection approaches they also invest in training and promotion policies that aim to reduce labour turnover (thus increasing the chances of reaping rewards from their investment, as we argue in Chapter 7). In effect, this is the same point as Delery (1998) makes when he advises against 'deadly combinations'. The second type of fit is consistency across employees doing the same kind of work ('among employee consistency'). This type of consistency is a major reason for standardised employment conditions in firms, at least for the same occupational group (for example, all clerical staff). One of the main ways employers argue they are treating people equitably is by treating them all the same when it comes to employment conditions (such as standard working times and leave policies). The third kind of fit is what Baron and Kreps call 'temporal consistency': consistency of employee treatment across a reasonable period of time. 'In general, how employee A was treated today should not differ radically from how she was treated yesterday' (Baron and Kreps 1999: 33). Again, this principle makes good sense: employees like to be able to predict an employer's behaviour and can be seriously demotivated by reversals of employer policy (as we shall see in Chapter 7).

As far as it goes, this kind of advice is very reasonable. Is there anything wrong with it? Unfortunately, there is. While rightly emphasising the value of various forms of consistency, the notion of 'internal fit' tends to be discussed in a way that over-simplifies the paradoxical elements involved in managing people. The problem stems from the fact that the HR policies and practices of the firm are implicated in a range of strategic tensions, such as those we have just discussed between short-run focus and long-run flexibility (Boxall 1999, Evans and Genadry 1999). Even in small firms, more than one desirable theme will need to be transmitted through the firm's HR practices: a *blend* of messages about desirable skills and behaviour is needed (Wright and Snell 1998).

As an illustration, consider work by Pil and MacDuffie (1996) which forms part of a stream of research on automobile manufacturing. Arguably, this set of studies forms the best longitudinal, industry-based investigation of changes in work and employment practices available anywhere in the world. Pil and MacDuffie (1996) find a general increase in the use of 'high involvement' practices in the industry around the world: practices that foster higher skill and solicit greater commitment to, and creativity in, problem-solving. However, at the same time, firms have had to pursue downsizing, often of major proportions. As anyone with experience of the process knows, this is the kind of action that reduces trust in management and undermines employee commitment to the firm. This climate of insecurity, however, has not prevented management in automobile firms from seeking higher involvement from the (remaining) workforce. Here, then, is a critical tension: between needing more skilful, more creative work while not being able to hold traditional staffing levels and offer traditional levels of employment security. As Walton, Cutcher-Gershenfeld and McKersie (1994) put it, management increasingly needs a blend of 'forcing' and 'fostering' behaviour as it wrestles with the problem of renewing the firm, something we explore in Chapter 8.

We must be careful, then, with the concept of 'internal fit'. We should understand it *not* as reinforcing a single, desirable theme in HRM but as a process which involves balancing tensions among competing objectives, including tensions among competing interests. Striving for consistency is important but, at the end of the day, there is still an element of paradox in the way people are managed.

The evolution of models of 'best fit'

These sorts of criticisms do not invalidate 'best fit' models of strategic HRM but *can* be used to strengthen them. Much of the problem with contingency theorising in strategic HRM stems from the tendency of researchers to look for correlations between two variables, such as competitive strategy and HR strategy. Such models are attractively simple but they are 'too thin'. They miss much of the interactive, multivariate complexity of strategic management in the real world. While we should also try to avoid contingency models which are 'too thick' – throwing in everything plus the kitchen sink – we do need to evolve models that explain *most* of the important connections. Can contingency theory produce models which are useful (because they cover most of what really matters) without making the whole thing horribly complex?

In this regard, a more sophisticated approach to contingency theory involves 'configurational' thinking, as discussed in Chapter 2. We explained there that it is helpful to see business strategy as a configuration or *gestalt* of critical, interdependent elements. These elements include competitive strategy (sectoral choice and desired position), operations strategy (suitable supplies, technology, and methods), and appropriate strategies for finance, and human resources. In this conception, a superior business strategy is one that links all of these pieces in a more effective configuration. Taking such a view, we are more likely to uncover some of the important interactions among strategic variables in a business.

For example, we are likely to find that the impact of competitive strategy on HR strategy, at least in manufacturing, is affected by the dominant technology used in the sector and the firm (Boxall 1999, Purcell 1999b, Snell and Dean 1992, Youndt, Snell, Dean and Lepak 1996). When a manufacturing firm adopts advanced manufacturing technology, it may pursue up-skilling and quality management rather than the kind of de-skilling and task specialisation more appropriate to earlier technological forms, *even if* its competitive goal is to achieve the lowest unit costs in the industry. Getting workers who enjoy working with the technology and can make it reach its productivity specifications is the priority in such cases; even better if workers can take the machinery beyond its productivity specifications, as we note in the case of Chaparral Steel discussed in the next chapter. In this situation, then, the hypothesis that these workers would be best managed in a cost-minimising kind of way – as suggested by Schuler and Jackson (1987) – would not be supported. Rather, to enable the technology to reach its productivity potential (and create low unit costs), we need highly trained, well paid, relatively secure workers. They are likely to be employed in small numbers but their conditions are likely to be very attractive. On the other hand, if the firm is using low levels of technology (as in much of the apparel manufacturing sector), the implications are different. Here, a competitive strategy of cost leadership would most likely lead the firm to locate manufacturing in low wage sites, something that we noted in Chapter 1 has typically happened in this sector. Some, more differentiated forms of manufacturing (such as high fashion items linked to retailers through 'quick response' systems) can survive in high-wage countries but most other forms end up in low-wage countries.

Figure 3.6 depicts the chain of reasoning and implications for HR strategy across these two types of manufacturing. In both cases, we start our thinking from the same

Firm's choice of competitive strategy	Nature of productive technology in the sector	Worker actions and impacts of State regulation	Implications for HR strategy
Cost leadership	High technology or highly capital-intensive; often low staff numbers but key specialist skills very important to operations	If organised into unions, workers may extract more of a wage premium but this is not likely to affect the economics of the firm unless work practices are inefficient or unduly inflexible. Regulation by the State is not likely to have much relevance because wages and conditions are high in the sector	HR strategy should be based on developing and motivating workers to maximise the benefits of the technology (which will help to achieve the cost leadership strategy). Prediction: high-wage/high-skill models of labour management are cost-effective. Investments in creating 'high-performance work systems' are likely to be justified
Cost leadership	Low-technology, often highly labour-intensive operations and large scale	Here, strongly unionised workforces will strengthen the drive to locate operations in low-wage countries. Employment regulation could have a significant impact in setting the lower bound of wages and conditions	HR strategy is dominated by the need to survive in an environment where wages are in competition. Prediction: firms seek out low-wage sites where productivity is high and quality is acceptable. Firms will pay the going rate in the local labour market but avoid paying premium conditions or over-investing in training

Figure 3.6 Configurational thinking in HR strategy: two different scenarios

competitive strategy (cost leadership in this example) but then consider the role of technology in the sector. This leads us to a different set of conclusions in each case. We also include a column looking at the reactions of workers and the role of the State, something we argued earlier should always be considered. In the high-tech case, workers may be able to extract more of a wage premium if they are well organised but this is unlikely to be problematic for the firm unless work practices are bad for productivity and flexibility. It doesn't essentially change our predictions of the implications for HR strategy. In the low-tech case, typical of basic garment manufacture, unions and State regulation have the effect of setting lower bounds on wage-based competition in particular countries.

In summary, then, 'best fit' models argue that HR strategy becomes more effective when it is designed to fit certain critical contingencies in the firm's specific context. Figure 3.6 illustrates the way configurational thinking can add greater explanatory power to contingency models of HR strategy without getting too complicated. It is still, of course, possible to argue that too much is left out. Figure 3.7 offers our view of the range of factors that ought to be included in a fuller assessment in a firm of the factors that can influence HR choices. For convenience, it organises them into two broad categories. Economic and technological factors, both inside and outside the firm, do drive many choices in HR strategy. Here we include the firm's choice of sector (which determines much about what it needs to be), its competitive strategy, its dominant technology, its size, structure and stage in the industry life cycle. Alongside these we include the quality of the firm's funding and the general state of the economy. The figure also recognises that HR strategy will be shaped by a range of social and political factors. Labour is rarely passive and people will not necessar-

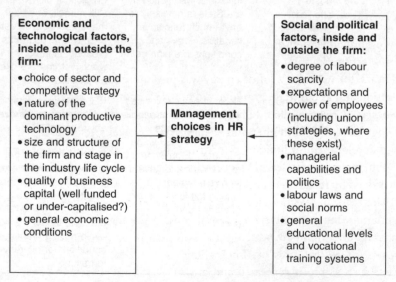

Figure 3.7   Major factors affecting management choices in HR strategy

ily buy into management policies if they have better options elsewhere or feel betrayed by past events. In any initiative in HRM, likely reactions from current and potential employees ought to be considered, and an assessment made of union strategies where unions exist. Management itself has issues to do with capability and politics which inevitably affect HR decision-making. As noted in Chapter 2, management doesn't necessarily make a good set of choices in HRM: limitations in cognitive abilities and debilitating politics will lower performance and may lead to outright failure. On the broader level, firms are 'embedded' in societies which regulate and influence them while also providing social capital of varying quality. The firm can never be the complete author of its own HRM.

Strategic HRM: the 'best practice' school

Those who advocate 'best practice' take issue with the sort of contingency theorising just described. In best practice thinking, a universal prescription is preferred. The staunchest advocates of best practice argue that all firms will see performance improvements if only they identify and implement best practice. This brings quite a different understanding of the problem of integrating HR strategy with the rest of business strategy. Integration with strategic management, in this conception, is about giving best HR practices the profile they deserve in the senior management process. It is about top management committing itself to key HR practices and 'going for it': researching the 'leading edge' of best practice, publicising commitments to specific best practices, measuring progress towards them and rewarding lower-level managers for implementing them consistently.

Models of best practice

Studies of individual best practices within the major categories of personnel work – such as selection, training and appraisal – have a very long tradition. During both World Wars, for example, a lot of energy was put into improving practices for officer selection and also into the training and motivation of (non-combatant) production workers (Crichton 1968, Eilbert 1959). The academic discipline of Industrial Psychology gained great momentum as industrial psychologists studied the prediction and development of human performance. Based on this tradition of work, and simply on management learning over time, aspects of best practice are widely acknowledged by researchers and practitioners (Delery and Doty 1996: 806, Youndt *et al.* 1996: 838). In selection, for example, hardly anyone would advocate unstructured interviewing over interviews carefully designed around job-relevant factors. Similarly, no one would advocate input-based performance appraisal for senior executives (such as measures of timekeeping) over processes that examine results achieved (such as profit generated and growth in market share). In effect, there is quite a lot of agreement on what constitutes 'bad' or 'stupid' practice.

It is when we go beyond these sorts of straightforward prescriptions about stand-ard HR practices and attempt to compile more comprehensive models that the problems multiply. There is also enormous variety in the number and type of prac-tices that are deemed to constitute a suitable *model* or *system* of best practices (Becker and Gerhart 1996: 785, Dyer and Reeves 1995: 658). Some models only mention four or five key practices while others have a dozen or more. Wood (1996) finds it useful to describe most of these models as 'high commitment management' (HCM) because strong identification with the firm tends to be a pervading theme. However, even this theme isn't always present because some best practice writers have moved so far towards the concept of 'employability' that employer-provided security has dis-appeared.

Arguably, the model that has highest profile with practitioners at the present time is associated with US writer Jeffrey Pfeffer's (1994) list of 16 practices for 'competi-tive advantage through people' (Figure 3.8). One interesting point about Pfeffer's list of practices is that both high pay and pay compression are deemed desirable. This means that people should be paid well but huge variations in their pay should be avoided so as to encourage teamwork and a sense of common destiny. Anyone with experience of remuneration consultancy in the USA knows that this goal is hardly ever achieved in corporate pay practice there: executive pay levels are very high by world standards and pay egalitarianism is rarely espoused as a virtue.

Unfortunately, it is difficult to see the underpinning logic in such a long list of practices. We need a more parsimonious way of summing up what is being argued. Youndt *et al.* (1996: 839) come close to a succinct summary of the thrust of current best practice models when they argue that:

> At their root, most (models) ... focus on enhancing the skill base of employees through HR activities such as selective staffing, comprehensive training, and broad developmental efforts like job rotation and cross-utilization. Further, (they) tend to promote empower-ment, participative problem-solving, and teamwork with job redesign, group-based incen-tives, and a transition from hourly to salaried compensation for production workers.

We may be able to make some progress in summarising the gist of best practice models by using the 'AMO' rubric referred to in Chapter 1 ('performance is a func-

1 Employment security	9 Training and skill development
2 Selectivity in recruiting	10 Cross-utilisation and cross-training
3 High wages	11 Symbolic egalitarianism
4 Incentive pay	12 Wage compression
5 Employee ownership	13 Promotion from within
6 Information sharing	14 Long-term perspective
7 Participation and empowerment	15 Measurement of the practices
8 Teams and job redesign	16 Overarching philosophy

Source: Pfeffer (1994)

Figure 3.8   Pfeffer's 16 practices for 'competitive advantage through people'

tion of ability, motivation and opportunity'). Firstly, best practice models typically include an emphasis on enhancing employee abilities or knowledge and skills through good recruitment and strong training. This is hardly surprising: firms concerned to make the best of human resources want better-than-average human potential to work on. Secondly, best practice models contain an emphasis on motivating desired behaviour through strong incentives (in Pfeffer's model, both incentive pay and employee ownership). Thirdly, best practice models include ways of opening up opportunities for better trained and more motivated workers to contribute their ideas through work redesign and indirect forms of employee participation. The AMO rubric is useful because it highlights the skeletal structure of the typical best practice prescription. It also helps to make the point that these models often parallel the notion of 'high-performance work systems' that we discuss in various parts of this book.

Models of best practice: theoretical critique

The first and most obvious criticism of best practice models has already been intimated – their sheer diversity. Lists of desirable practices vary significantly (Becker and Gerhart 1996, Dyer and Reeves 1995, Youndt *et al.* 1996). While we can all agree to avoid practices which are obviously dysfunctional or illegal, debate sets in after this point. Beyond a certain level of obviously sensible practices, managers start to think about their unique context. This naturally engenders diversity rather than uniformity in HRM.

Secondly, when definitions of 'best practice' are drawn from the four favourite sub-functions of Industrial Psychology – selection, training, appraisal, and pay – they tend to be weak or silent on the collective issues of work organisation and employee voice. This is one of the criticisms Marchington and Grugulis (2000) make of Pfeffer's (1998) most recent model (Figure 3.9) in which his 16 practices have been consolidated into seven. While Pfeffer (1994, 1998) is actually very positive about the way unions can enhance business performance, his lists of key practices seem to lack a strong commitment to independent worker representation and joint regulation. This makes his models much less relevant in a European context or in the manufacturing sectors of countries with active engineering unions, such as Australia, Canada and New Zealand.

1 Employment security
2 Selective hiring
3 Self-managed teams or teamworking
4 High pay contingent on company performance
5 Extensive training
6 Reduction of status differences
7 Sharing information

Source: Pfeffer (1998)

Figure 3.9 Pfeffer's 7 practices for 'building profits by putting people first'

As the previous point implies, advocates of 'best practice' tend to fudge the question of goals and interests, long identified by Legge (1978) as a problem with this genre of management literature. Part of the problem is the way in which practices seem to become ends in themselves, apparently disconnected from the company's goals in its specific context. And part of the problem concerns the divergent interests represented in the firm. *Whose* goals are being served? If 'best practice' serves both shareholder and worker interests, we can hardly object to it: similarly if we agree some practice is bad for both parties and should be avoided. But what if a practice is good for corporate returns but bad for workers? This is often the case with downsizing: share markets seem to rate companies more highly for doing it, cold comfort for the workers laid off. When this kind of trade-off emerges, do workers get a real voice in deciding the issue (Marchington and Grugulis 2000)? Best practice models are typically silent on these sorts of tensions. And what if a practice is good for executives but not good for either shareholders or waged workers? This is the problem, arguably, with many exit packages used for company directors dismissed or 'let go' because of disappointing performance: *they* benefit but the company and its other employees typically lose out. Pursuing these sorts of questions inevitably embarrasses models of 'best practice'. Have we gone far enough to say they should they simply be discarded? Let's pause to reflect on what the research has to say.

Best fit and best practice: assessing the research evidence

In assessing the evidence about the merits of 'best fit' and 'best practice', it is vital to remember the distinction between studies that examine what firms actually do (descriptive research) and models of how firms can do it better (normative or prescriptive theory). In this section, we review the body of descriptive research before the chapter concludes with our overall assessment of the debate.

The role of national context

When we stand back and think about the vast body of research on employment relations, it should be obvious, surely, that nations matter. It only takes a small amount of international travel to realise that nation states still have their own jurisdictions. Labour laws vary from country to country, including the degree of freedom given to unions to organise workers and engage in collective bargaining. On this one point alone, the universalist model of best practice cannot be supported.

There is overwhelming evidence against a universal set of HR practices based on national variations not only in law but also in cultural practices and management styles. Cultural norms and the unique history of different societies always make some difference to the methods of labour management, if not to the ultimate goal of employers for profit. As an example, consider Wever's (1995) study of the different approaches to labour relations in the US and Germany and their relative impacts on competitiveness. For her, the 'task facing German employers is to adapt some of the organizational lessons to be learned from the United States without sacrificing the strengths of the negotiated model' (Wever 1995: 17). She does not advise German firms to abandon their commitment to such institutions as industry-based collective bargaining and company-level works councils in pursuit of the kind of more individualistic, more flexible labour market implicit in much US 'best practice' thinking.

Appelbaum and Batt (1994), whose work on US models of high-performance work systems was introduced in Chapter 1, also underline the importance of national context. When looking beyond the USA for HPWS models, they identify four that are worth discussion: Swedish 'sociotechnical systems', Japanese 'lean production', Italian 'flexible specialisation' and German 'diversified quality production'. Each of these models (all of which have internal variations) are embedded in national laws, customs and management styles that vary from those of the USA. Just comparing three of these countries shows major differences (Figure 3.10). As Appelbaum and Batt argue, it is very difficult to transplant foreign models of high-performance work systems to the USA because of these societal contexts. While they support the idea of greater voice mechanisms for US workers, they realise this will have to be worked out in an American way. Most commentators on the USA recognise that the chances

Context	USA	Japan	Germany
Unionisation	Very low level (around 10% of private sector workers)	Well-established enterprise unions in the large corporations	Strong, industry-based unions with key involvement in vocational training (among other areas)
Power sharing: institutions	Collective bargaining only in workplaces where there is majority worker support	Collective bargaining at set annual time ('shunto' – the Spring Offensive) plus well established consultative processes	Industry-based collective bargaining plus very established tradition of codetermination (works councils and worker directors)
Management attitudes to joint governance	Apart from some cases of union-management 'partnerships', strong management resistance to any form of power sharing with unions	Japanese executives work with strong cultural norms that emphasise consultation, and have often been officials in the enterprise union	German managers have adjusted to codetermination and, while grappling with flexibility problems, see advantages in consensual decision-making

Sources: Appelbaum and Batt (1994), Taira (1993), Towers (1997), Wever (1995)

Figure 3.10 Key differences in industrial relations in three national contexts

of major reform there towards European-style works councils or worker directors are extremely small. In fact, the level of disagreement and inertia in the US political context is such that it seems almost impossible to achieve any kind of statutory change to US laws on collective bargaining (see, for example, Towers 1997).

Other illustrations of the role of national context are provided by studies which look at particular HR practices rather than whole employment systems. Wood's (1996) study of performance-related pay, for example, shows that notions of contingent pay (which US models of best practice often advocate) may be treated quite circumspectly in the UK, at least below the executive level. British manufacturing firms pursuing what Wood (1996) calls 'high-commitment management' are not likely to adopt this part of the typical American prescription, finding that salaried pay, rather than bonus and piece rate systems, better serves their objectives for high levels of employee involvement over time. In salaried systems of pay, it may well be easier to vary and refine goals over time, particularly where people are prepared to be somewhat flexible because they are relatively well paid (see Chapter 7).

Much more research could be cited but there is no need to be pedantic about what really ought to be an obvious point. While capitalist firms everywhere share the overriding goal of profitability, they do make a significant amount of adaptation to local laws, customs and institutions in their pursuit of shareholder wealth. Multinational firms opening branches around the globe are quite likely to orchestrate the management of senior executives from the centre (to ensure key objectives are pursued) and may well need to provide training in key work practices associated with the firm's proprietary technologies, but they will have to be careful with local labour laws in any country where these are actually enforced. Similarly, they will need to consider the impact of local cultural values (such as attitudes to discrimination) in any society where these influence workplace relations.

The role of sectoral and organisational context

The prevalence of diversity in HR practices based on national context or 'societal effects' severely undermines best practice models, but there are other objections as well. These models are further undermined by the impact of sectoral and organisational contexts. We discover increasing diversity when we examine research on the diffusion of 'best practice' *within* any major capitalist society. British research, based on the 1998 *Workplace Employee Relations Survey*, puts the spread of 'high-commitment' practices at no more than 14 per cent of workplaces (Cully, Woodland, O'Reilly and Dix 1999). The US research also shows limited diffusion. Through a cross-industry survey of private sector establishments with at least 50 employees,[12] Osterman (1994) estimates that some 35 per cent of US organisations of this size

---

12   A response rate of 65.5 per cent. The sample size is 694 firms.

have adopted at least two forms of 'innovative' work practice (defined as including teams, job rotation, TQM or quality circles) for at least 50 per cent of their core staff. These, he argues, can be thought of as 'transformed' organisations (although it seems quite a stretch of the imagination to imply that simply having job rotation and quality circles amounts to much that is radical!). When Osterman (1994) examines the characteristics of 'transformed' organisations, it becomes clear that sectoral and organisational variables are important in explaining why some firms have adopted more of these practices than others have. The survey indicates that the sort of employers most likely to adopt 'innovative' work organisation are engaged in sectors exposed to international competition, employ more advanced technology, and pursue competitive strategies which include a blend of quality and service dimensions as well as cost.

Another US survey, conducted by Gittleman, Horrigan and Joyce 1998), reaches similar conclusions. While both these surveys have very good response rates (unlike many US surveys of management practice), this survey is more comprehensive than Osterman's: it covers all US firms irrespective of size.[13] Gittleman *et al.* study the incidence of six work organisation practices: worker teams, TQM, quality circles, peer review of employee performance, worker involvement in purchase decisions, and job rotation. The survey finds that 58 per cent of the firms have *none* of these practices (this is the largest response). Size plays a major role: while 31 per cent of firms with over 50 employees have none of the practices, some 45 per cent have two or more, including 11 per cent who have four or more. Like Osterman (1994), the authors examine the factors that correlate with innovative work practices and conclude that 'Establishments that were introducing new technology, were in manufacturing, or were of large size were more likely to be making strides towards a flexible workplace' (Gittleman *et al.* 1998: 113).

Expert reviews, which stand back from a range of sectoral and organisational studies and assess the overall picture, reach the same sort of conclusion as Osterman (1994) and Gittleman *et al.* (1998). As Weinstein and Kochan (1995: 24) put it:

> ... the overriding conclusion based on available evidence is that innovations are partially diffused across ... industries and across the economy. Innovations are more widely diffused in (1) greenfield sites than in existing facilities, (2) in larger firms than in midsize and smaller firms, and (3) in high value-added industries such as autos, telecommunications, and computers than in clothing, finance, and health care.

Overall, research suggests that the sort of HR practices that foster high commitment from talented employees are most popular in those sectors where quality is a major competitive factor and where firms need to exploit advanced technology (as in complex manufacturing) or engage in a highly skilled interaction with clients (as in professional services). In these sorts of higher value-added sectors, firms need

13 An excellent response rate of 71.3 per cent using a nationally representative survey by the US Bureau of Labor Statistics. The sample size is 7895 firms.

more competence and loyalty from their employees and are more able to pay for them. In sectors where these conditions are not met – where output per employee is not high – employers adopt more modest employment policies. As research by Nord (1999) implies, they tend to adopt the kind of policies that will recruit and retain sufficient workers in the *relevant* labour markets. Where labour markets are still very loose (lots of labour in relation to the jobs available), working conditions have remained relatively static. This is why low-skill workers have not benefited much from productivity gains in 'high-tech' sectors: they do not benefit unless the economy becomes so short of labour that wage inflation reaches down into their sectors. According to Nord (1999), there is little 'trickle down' of productivity-driven wage inflation from a growing, knowledge-driven economy to the lowest-skilled workers.

This discussion should help to underline one of the points made in Chapter 1: cost-effectiveness is a key goal of employers. Employers will typically adopt more expensive models of HRM when they are competing in a sector which means they must do so (such models form part of 'table stakes') or when there is a clear pay-off from doing so. Considerations of cost-effectiveness are clearly an important part of the story of limited diffusion of models of 'best practice'.

Conclusions: the end of best practice?

Research on what firms actually do – descriptive research – makes life very difficult for the more extreme advocates of models of best practice. It demonstrates that methods of labour management are inevitably influenced by context, including societal, sectoral and organisational factors. Does this fact invalidate all 'best practice' thinking?

We think not. As noted earlier, there are some HR practices that only the very ignorant continue to use – because they are well known to be dysfunctional or perverse. There are sensible ways of going about such generic processes as job analysis and employee selection that everyone would be wise to follow. Things tend to get out of hand, however, when writers aggregate their favourite practices – and their implicit values – into more ambitious lists and offer them to the world at large. Such models generally overlook the way that context affects the shape of the HR practices that emerge in firms over time.

Many American models, for example, are unacceptable in environments where unions have a more central role in society – as in most of Europe and in Canada, Australia and New Zealand. Notions of legitimacy in employment practice vary across nations, and firms generally need to be sensitive to these variations. The economics of particular competitive sectors also makes a major impact on the way managers appraise the notions of 'best practice' that are offered to them. Models conceived by consultants for 'high-tech' firms tend to make little impact on managers in the warehousing, retail and hospitality sectors, for example. Similarly, managers of small firms are often indifferent to ideas dreamed up in much larger companies where HR specialists are available to help develop more formal HR policies and provide training to line managers. These reactions cannot all be put down to ignorance of better alternatives. It seems more likely that they stem from a concern with what is going to be cost-effective in the specific sector and organisation.

One way forward in this debate is to make an analytical distinction between the surface level of HR policy and practices in a firm and an underpinning level of processes and principles (Becker and Gerhart 1996, Purcell 1999b) (Figure 3.11). This is not a perfect distinction but it helps us to reconcile the tension between best fit and best practice in strategic HRM. We are most unlikely to find that any theorist's selection of best practices (the surface layer) will have universal relevance because context always matters, as the descriptive research demonstrates. It is, however, possible to argue that there are some more effective ways of carrying out the generic HR processes (such as selection) which all firms would be wise to follow. More powerfully, it is possible to argue that there are certain *desirable* principles which, if applied, will bring about more effective management of people. In effect, it is still possible to argue that, *ceteris paribus* (other things being equal), all firms are better off when they pursue certain principles (Youndt *et al.* 1996: 837).

Arguably, the most fundamental principle in labour management is the need to align management and worker interests, at least at the level of a contract that meets the baseline requirements of both parties. In any context where workers have some labour market choice or develop powerful organisation or enjoy strongly enforced labour market standards, this principle becomes more apparent – but it is always there. Research suggests that there are other principles too, albeit qualified in important ways by different contexts. In Part 2 of this book, we dedicate four chapters to 'searching for principles' in the management of people. This part of the book examines theories to do with work systems (Chapter 5) and associated models of employment (Chapter 6). It then looks at the individual (Chapter 7) and collective levels of analysis (Chapter 8). Having done this, Part 3 looks at special contexts that make a major impact on contemporary human resource strategies – the contexts of industry-based competition (Chapter 9), and of multidivisional firms and multinational operations (Chapter 10).

> *Surface layer*: HR policies and practices – heavily influenced by context (societal, sectoral, organisational)

> *Underpinning layer*: generic HR processes and general principles of labour management

Figure 3.11 The 'best fit' versus 'best practice' debate: two levels of analysis

In effect, the book is grounded on the assumption that *both* general principles *and* specific contexts play an important role in the theory and practice of strategic HRM. No one can seriously argue against the importance of 'best fit' or contextual thinking when managers come to consider their HR policies. However, there is still a valuable role for a concept of 'best practice' if it means a concern for underpinning principles of labour management and helps us to intelligently fashion particular practices to our specific context.

4

Strategic HRM and the resource-based view of the firm

In Part 1 of the book, we are concerned with fundamental concepts of strategic management and with their links to the management of people in firms. Chapter 2 established our preferred definitions of the major terms involved in studying strategy. It made the point that strategic management is a human process, dependent on human strengths, but also affected by our cognitive weaknesses and political agendas. This means that, at the very least, key choices about *whom* to place in leadership roles and *how* to build strategy-making processes are critical to the success of firms. Chapter 3 built on this basis to define what we mean by strategic HRM and HR strategy. It discussed the debate in the strategic HRM literature between contingency theory ('best fit') and universalism ('best practice'). The chapter concluded that *both* perspectives are important to organisational effectiveness. It argued that there are indeed some underpinning principles of people management which managers should follow if they aim to make the firm more successful. But it is also true that management inevitably faces the task of adapting the management of labour in the firm to its specific context – societal, sectoral and organisational. As should be obvious, fitting the firm to its environment is vital in any line of business.

The broad debate around the merits of contingency theory and universalism probably accounts for the largest body of literature in the field of strategic HRM. It dominated the field as it emerged into the limelight in the 1980s and remains very important in any kind of theory-building. Since the early 1990s, however, another body of thought has grown in significance. The strategic HRM literature has increasingly been influenced by a branch of strategic management known as the resource-based view of the firm (RBV). Relating the RBV to the best fit/best practice debate we have just been discussing, one might say that strategy theorists who work with the RBV aim to discover how a firm can build an *exclusive* form of 'fit'. How might a firm obtain and manipulate its resources – human and non-human – to become the best adapted, the most consistently profitable of all firms in its sector? This chapter aims to explain what is meant by the RBV, defining key concepts and exploring major models. In so doing, it examines the implications of the RBV for the strategic management of labour, helping to lay the basis for the rest of this book.

The resource-based view: origins and assumptions

The resource-based view is usually sourced to a remarkable book by a University of London Professor of Economics, Edith Penrose (1959). At the time, texts on the economics of the firm were dominated by discussion of 'equilibrium' conditions under different forms of competition. The main focus of these texts was on the relative merits of different types of market, including 'perfect competition', oligopoly and monopoly. While valuable in debates about market regulation, the traditional analysis ignored very important issues inside the 'black box' of the firm's operations, leaving the study of entrepreneurship and business management in a very rudimentary state within the discipline of Economics.

Arguing that her interest was different from that of the standard texts on the firm, Penrose set out to build a theory of the growth of firms. She made the basic, but critical, observation that the firm is 'an administrative organization and a collection of productive resources', distinguishing between 'physical' and 'human resources' (Penrose 1959: 31, 24).[14] Her understanding of the quality of the firm's human resources placed heavy emphasis on the knowledge and experience of the 'management team' and their subjective interpretation (or 'images') of the firm's environment (showing an early grasp of the kind of cognitive problems of strategic management discussed in Chapter 2). Her analysis proceeded from what has become a fundamental premiss in the theory of business strategy: firms are 'heterogeneous' (Penrose 1959: 74–8). As Nelson (1991: 61) puts it, competition ('perfect' or otherwise) never entirely eliminates 'differences among firms in the same line of business' and these differences account for major performance variations.

Penrose's ideas lay dormant for some time. Her work was not brought within the mainstream of strategic management theory until it was rediscovered by Wernerfelt (1984) and then by a string of other strategy writers from the late 1980s (for example, Amit and Shoemaker 1993, Barney 1991, Dierickx and Cool 1989, Conner 1991, Grant 1991b, Mahoney and Pandian 1992, Peteraf 1993). The result has been an explosion of interest in the resource-based perspective, focusing on the ways in which firms might build unique clusters or 'bundles' of human and technical resources that generate enviable levels of performance. Large scale reviews of the strategic management literature now routinely recognise the RBV as a major body

14 In passing, we might note that Penrose was one of the first theorists to adopt the 'human resources' terminology.

of thought concerned with explaining sources of competitive advantage (see, for example, Hoskisson, Hitt, Wan and Yiu 1999).

In effect, the growth of the RBV has provided a counterweight to the marketing-oriented models of strategic management which were dominant in the strategy textbooks of the 1980s. The best known of these models was associated with the works of Michael Porter (1980, 1985), discussed in the context of 'best fit' theory in Chapter 3. These models place greatest emphasis on critical choices associated with competitive strategy – primarily, choices about which industry to enter and which competitive position to seek in it. In so doing, these models make some fairly heroic assumptions (Boxall 1992, 1996). For example, they assume that the firm already has a clever leadership team which can make these sorts of choices effectively. They assume that the human resource issues that arise when particular paths are chosen, such as hiring and training a capable workforce, are very straightforward. They assume that culture change, when it might be needed to shift direction, is also unproblematic. In contrast, it is *exactly* these sorts of people issues that the resource-based view regards as strategic. In the RBV, the quality of the management process and of the firm's workplace culture are seen as major factors that explain enduring differences in business performance (see, for example, Barney 1991).

It can, however, be argued that the RBV is itself imbalanced, placing undue emphasis on the internal side of the old SWOT acronym (strengths, weaknesses, opportunities, threats). In a response to criticism from resource-based theorists, Michael Porter argues that 'resources are not valuable in and of themselves, but because they allow firms to perform activities that create advantages in particular markets' (Porter 1991: 108). Similarly, Miller and Shamsie (1996: 520) argue that the RBV needs 'to consider the contexts within which various kinds of resources will have the best influence on performance'. In a study of the Hollywood film studios from 1936 to 1965, they demonstrate how knowledge-based resources (such as the exceptionally creative skills of key writers and cinematographers, and big budget coordinating abilities) were more valuable to the studios in the relatively uncertain and turbulent environment of the 1950s when the advent of television seriously affected moviegoing habits. On the other hand, in the more stable conditions of the late 1930s and the 1940s (Wasn't everyone watching films in the War?), property-based resources (such as networks of theatres and long-term, exclusive contracts with particular actors) were more valuable for studio performance. In other words, the human talents that helped the studios to 'think and act outside the square' were indeed valuable when the context became less predictable.

Wernerfelt (1984: 173) did recognise the interplay of resources and markets when he said there is a 'duality between products and resources'. In other words, the strategic problem has both internal (strengths, weaknesses) and external (opportunities, threats) dimensions (Figure 4.1). These dimensions – what Baden-Fuller (1995) calls the 'inside-out' and the 'outside-in' perspectives on the strategic problem – are interactive over time. The point is well made. One should not get carried away with either

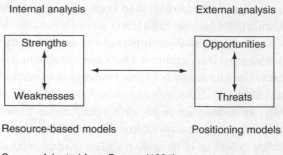

Internal analysis   External analysis

Strengths   Opportunities

Weaknesses   Threats

Resource-based models   Positioning models

Source: Adapted from Barney (1991)

Figure 4.1   Internal and external dimensions of the strategic problem

external or internal perspectives: both are necessary for a sufficient view of a firm's strategy. It seems safe, however, to suggest that what the resource-based perspective has achieved is a *re-balancing* of the literature on strategy, reminding people of the strategic significance of internal resources and their development over time.

Resources and barriers to imitation

What, then, are the basic definitions and concepts associated with the RBV? In the resource-based perspective, resources are not simply understood as assets in the formal accounting sense (which can be disclosed on a balance sheet) but include any feature of the firm with value-creating properties (Hunt 1995: 322). This means that aspects of the business that are not formally owned by it, such as the talents and interactions of the people who work in it, are not ignored but come within the realm of analytical interest. Wernerfelt (1984: 172) defined resources in the following way:

> By a resource is meant anything which could be thought of as a strength or weakness of a given firm. More formally, a firm's resources at a given time could be defined as those (tangible and intangible) assets which are tied semipermanently to the firm. Examples of resources are: brand names, in-house knowledge of technology, employment of skilled personnel, trade contacts, machinery, efficient procedures, capital etc.

In an interesting study of chief executive opinion about the value of different kinds of resource, Hall (1993) found that CEOs rated the quality of employee know-how and their firm's reputation with customers as their most strategic assets. It is easy to see why the RBV is so attractive to human resource specialists – here at last is a body of thought within strategic management in which people issues figure prominently.

Clusters of resources, understood in this broader way, can be sources of competitive advantage. Barney (1991), one of the most influential and accessible theorists in the RBV school, distinguishes between a competitive advantage which a firm presently enjoys, but which others will be able to copy, and 'sustained competitive advantage', a characteristic which rivals find themselves unable to compete away, despite their best efforts. In his conception, resources are valuable when they enable the firm to take advantage of market opportunities or deal particularly well with market threats in a way that competitors are not currently able to. The task is to manage these scarce resources in such a way that rivals are frustrated in their efforts to imitate or outflank them.

Using some fairly awkward terminology, RBV theorists are interested in the conditions that make desirable resources 'inimitable' and 'non-substitutable' (Barney 1991). As Coff (1997, 1999) and others point out (for example, Grant 1991, Kamoche 1996), it is important to add 'appropriability' to this list of traits. Not only must the firm be able to generate and defend sources of high performance[15], but the RBV assumes that the firm is able to capture the benefits for its shareholders. This is easier said than done because the firm is a network of *stake*holders. Some stakeholders, such as senior executives, have access to the kind of information and power which can enlarge their share of the firm's bounty. Qualities of desirable resources are shown in Figure 4.2.

Having defined these sorts of desirable traits, Barney (1991) notes that such resources are not immune to 'Schumpeterian shocks'. The great Austrian economist, Joseph Schumpeter, referred to the propensity for capitalism to generate 'gales of creative destruction' – radical breakthroughs which disturb technologies or basic concepts of business in the particular business sector (Schumpeter 1950). In the transportation sector, for example, inventions such as railroads, automobiles, and airplanes have had enormous impacts on the ways of providing transport that preceded them. We are currently living through a time when computerisation, telecommunications and the internet are making a major impact across various sectors of business. The vast majority of firms cannot protect themselves against such radical trends but there is scope for firms to differentiate themselves in ways which are relatively sustainable in a *given* competitive context. The issue is one of how management might build valuable, firm-specific characteristics and 'barriers to imitation'

Desirable resources are:
- **valuable and scarce:** worth something competitively and not easy to obtain
- **inimitable:** very hard to imitate or copy
- **non-substitutable:** very hard to neutralise with other resources which will meet the same ends
- **appropriable:** capable of providing a superior return to the firm's shareholders

Figure 4.2 Qualities of desirable resources

---

15 In the RBV literature, high financial performance is often described as 'rent', an old-fashioned term in Economics for profits above the normal level in competitive markets.

or erosion of them (Reed and DeFillippi 1990, Rumelt 1987). What, then, are the key barriers to imitation noted by resource-based theorists?

Unique timing and learning

Models proposed in the RBV typically place emphasis on the way that historical learning acts as a barrier to newcomers and slower rivals. Theorists cite the value to firms of 'unique historical conditions' (Barney 1991: 107), 'first mover advantages' (Wernerfelt 1984: 173) and 'path dependency' (Leonard 1998: 35). They argue that valuable, specialised resources (sometimes called 'asset specificity') are developed over time through opportunities that do not repeat themselves (or not in quite the same way). Competitive success does not come simply from making choices in the present (as positioning models of strategic management seem to imply) but stems from building up distinctive capabilities over significant periods of time.

In simple terms, RBV theorists argue that a sense of time and place matters: if you are not there at the time things are happening, you cannot expect to be successful. Others will take up the unique learning opportunity. As Woody Allen once quipped, 'fifty per cent of success is turning up'. Shakespeare expressed the same sentiment in a famous line from *Julius Caesar*: 'There is a tide in the affairs of men, which taken at the flood, leads on to fortune.' Or as Wernerfelt (1984: 174) puts it, in the rather prosaic language of business theory, 'if the leader executes the experience curve strategy correctly, then later resource producers have to get their experience in an uphill battle with earlier producers who have lower costs'.

The special value of timing and learning is widely understood in the business community. The difficulty of securing a firm's presence in an area where it has no experience is often a reason for take-overs. Directors of firms often feel they cannot make a mark in a new sector (or a new region) without buying an established player who has built up the necessary client base, employee skills and operating systems. The international accounting firms very often expanded this way in the 1970s and 1980s, taking over much smaller, but well regarded, firms around the world. The small firms thus absorbed provided important political connections, a pool of appropriately qualified staff and a well-established client base. Naturally, the owners of these firms also benefited enormously from the learning of the international firm, gaining access, for example, to special audit techniques, management consulting methodologies, and training systems developed at considerable expense elsewhere.

Social complexity

The phenomenon of historical learning or 'path dependence' is intimately linked to a second barrier to imitation – 'social complexity' (Barney 1991, Wright, McMahan and McWilliams 1994). As firms grow, they inevitably become characterised by complex patterns of teamwork and coordination, both inside and outside the firm.

Successful firms become strong clusters of 'human and social capital' (Lovas and Ghoshal 2000: 883). The network of these internal and external connections is a kind of natural barrier to imitation by rivals, a prime reason why firms in some sectors sometimes try to recruit an entire team of employees. Loss of all or most of an outstanding team of staff can decimate an organisation's reputation. Something like this happened in 1957 when eight key scientists and engineers working on the development of the silicon chip resigned from the Shockley Semiconductor Laboratory, a research and development company led by the Nobel laureate physicist, Bill Shockley: 'Their mass departure cut the productive heart out of the laboratory, leaving behind a carcass of men working ..., on the four-layer diode project plus a bunch of aimless technicians and secretaries ... (Riordan and Hoddeson 1997: 252). The group left to form Fairchild Semiconductor. The rest, as they say, is history.

Mueller's (1996) discussion of 'resource mobility barriers' is one that places strong emphasis on socially complex attributes of firms. Mueller argues that sustained advantage stems from hard-to-imitate routines deeply embedded in a firm's 'social architecture' (Mueller 1996: 774). By contrast, he sees little enduring value accruing to the firm from top management's codified policy positions (which are easily imitated because of their public visibility). Indeed, he implies that little value is created by those senior managers who are highly mobile:

> Corporate prosperity not seldom rests in the social architecture that has emerged incrementally over time, and might often predate the tenure of current senior management. ... The social architecture is created and re-created not only or even primarily at senior management levels in the organization, but at other levels too, including at workgroup level on the shopfloor (Mueller 1996: 771, 777).

According to Mueller, outstanding *corporate* value is more likely to come from persistent, patient management processes that, over time, encourage skill formation and powerful forms of cooperation deep within the firm. These processes generate valuable new combinations or 'bundles' of human and non-human resources for the firm.

Causal ambiguity

A third type of resource barrier noted in the RBV literature – causal ambiguity – is more controversial. As with social complexity, ambiguity about the cause/effect relationships involved in the firm's performance is an inevitable outcome of firm growth (Barney 1991, Reed and DeFillippi 1990). It can take some time to figure why an established firm has become successful and to discern how successful it really is. There is no doubt that firms wanting to acquire other firms should be very careful in the 'due diligence' process that precedes (or ought to precede) the purchase of another business. There are inevitably elements of ambiguity about a firm's performance, as there are about the performance of individuals and teams.

Having said this, it is likely that causal ambiguity is over-rated as a barrier to imitation (McWilliams and Smart 1995). Human rationality is always bounded, as was noted in Chapter 2, but if one pushes the notion of causal ambiguity too far, management is virtually meaningless, as is theory (Priem and Butler 2001). The 'paradox of causal ambiguity' has recently been explored by a study in two US industries: textiles and hospitals (King and Zeithaml 2001). This study examined the way senior and middle managers perceive the competencies of their organisations and their links to competitive advantage. Interestingly, the study was one in which chief executives were very keen to participate (which is quite unusual given 'survey fatigue' among managers in the USA). It involved finding out how other members of their senior team and a cross-section of middle managers understood the firm's resources and their impacts. CEOs were interviewed and the other managers selected in the 17 firms were surveyed (with very high response rates). The study contains evidence that high-performing firms benefit from building consensus across management levels about the resources that enable them to out-perform rivals. Understanding of the links between competencies and firm performance *ought* to be high. This doesn't mean, however, that all aspects of particular competencies will be transparent because there is always some degree of ambiguity embedded in organisational culture and employee know-how. As we explore further below, 'tacit knowledge' is always present in organisations.

The findings of this study are consistent with the arguments of advocates of the 'balanced scorecard' (Kaplan and Norton 1996, 2001) who claim that, given enough effort, it must be possible within business units to evolve a broad theory of how the business works or might work better (see Chapter 11). Not only this, but the benefits of having agreement about where we are going and how we are getting there must be more valuable than confusion and working at cross-purposes! It seems, then, that while causal ambiguity will always be present to some degree, it is likely to be a less important barrier to imitation than the processes of historical learning and social interaction that characterise established firms.

Applying the resource-based view: managing capabilities

The discussion so far might convince us that the RBV contains some important insights but leave us wondering what we can do about it. How can all this talk of valuable resources and barriers to imitation be made less technical?

Most practical application of the RBV hinges around defining and managing a company's competencies or capabilities. One of the more popular frameworks is associated with the work of Hamel and Prahalad (1993, 1994). They argue that competitive advantage, over the long run, stems from building 'core competencies' in a firm which are superior to those of rivals. Their notion of a core competency is very close to the concept of a 'distinctive competency' discussed in the older strategy texts as something the firm did particularly well. Their definitions of the term (shown in Figure 4.3) place strong emphasis on analysing a firm's collective skills: skills found in the complex teamwork embedded in the firm.

The writings of Hamel and Prahalad are important for leaders of multidivisional firms (discussed in Chapter 10). CEOs and directors of these firms are encouraged to identify the underlying clusters of know-how in their companies which transcend the artificial divisions of 'strategic business units' – or which might do so, if they were appropriately managed. Sony's 'unrelenting pursuit of leadership in miniaturization' – manifesting itself in various products over time – is one of Hamel and Prahalad's standard examples (Hamel and Prahalad 1994: 119). They argue that companies which make the effort to understand their core competencies (and envision the core competencies they ought to build) are much less likely to get left with outdated products or miss important new applications of a knowledge base. In effect, their work is an argument for developing a 'knowledge-based', rather than a product-based, understanding of the firm. This might be a simple distinction to make but it suggests quite a profound change in the way corporate directors review company strengths and analyse their strategic opportunities.

A similar analysis is advanced by Leonard (1998) who uses the word 'capability' instead of 'competency' (but is concerned with the same idea). Her framework helps executives to identify the distinctive or 'core capabilities' underpinning their products or services. Core capabilities are 'knowledge sets' composed of four dimensions: the 'content' dimensions which include the relevant employee skills and knowledge and technical systems, and the 'process' dimensions which include managerial systems, and values and norms (Figure 4.4). Her framework is perhaps the most helpful in terms of spelling out the HR implications. This is because managerial systems include the critical HR policies needed to recruit, develop and motivate employees with the relevant skills and aptitudes (Leonard 1998: 19). Employee development and incentive systems are a key part of her notion of core capability. She also emphasises the interlocking, systemic nature of the four dimensions and the resulting tendency of

---

A 'core competency':
- is a bundle of skills and technologies that enables a company to provide particular benefits to customers
- is not product specific
- represents ... the sum of learning across individual skill sets and individual organisational units
- must ... be competitively unique
- is not an 'asset' in the accounting sense of the word
- represents a 'broad opportunity arena' or 'gateway to the future'

Source: Excerpted from Hamel and Prahalad (1994: 217–28)

Figure 4.3 Hamel and Prahalad's notion of 'core competency'

1 **Employee knowledge and skill**: This dimension is the most obvious one.
2 **Physical technical systems**: But technological competence accumulates not only in the heads of people; it also accumulates in the physical systems that they build over time – databases, machinery, and software programs.
3 **Managerial systems**: The accumulation of employee knowledge is guided and monitored by the company's systems of education, rewards, and incentives. These managerial systems – particularly incentive structures – create the channels through which knowledge is accessed and flows; they also set up barriers to undesired knowledge-creation activities.
4 **Values and norms**: These determine what kinds of knowledge are sought and nurtured, what kinds of knowledge-building activities are tolerated and encouraged. These are systems of caste and status, rituals of behaviour, and passionate beliefs associated with various kinds of technological knowledge that are as rigid and complex as those associated with religion. Therefore, values serve as knowledge-screening and -control mechanisms.

Source: Leonard (1998: 19)

Figure 4.4   The four dimensions of a 'core capability'

core capabilities to become 'core rigidities' over time, unless firms learn to practise continuous renewal. According to Leonard (1998: 30), every strength is also simultaneously a weakness. The recognition that firms can also have weaknesses or 'distinctive inadequacies' is an aspect of the RBV that ought to be given greater attention, as West and DeCastro (2001) have recently argued. Some weaknesses can result from having 'too much of a good thing', as Leonard implies, while others can simply be 'bad things' (such as not developing sufficient skills in environmental analysis and change management).

In outlining her model of how firms might develop outstanding capabilities, Leonard (1998: 5–16) discusses the interesting case of Chaparral Steel, a very successful US 'minimill', employing around 1000 people. While only the tenth largest steel producer in the USA, Chaparral is regularly a world leader in productivity:

> ... in 1990, its 1.5 person-hours per rolled ton of steel compared to a US average of 5.3, a Japanese average of 5.6, and a German average of 5.7. Chaparral was the first American steel company (and only the second company outside of Japan at the time) to be awarded the right to use the Japanese Industrial Standard certification on its general structural steel products (Leonard 1998: 6).

With strong values and incentives supporting the creation of new knowledge, Chaparral employees have pushed the company's equipment well beyond its original specifications:

> The rolling mill equipment its vendor believed (was) limited to 8-inch slabs is turning out 14-inch slabs, and the vendor has tried to buy back the redesign. The two electric arc furnaces, designed originally to melt annual rates of 250,000 and 500,000 tons of scrap metal, now produce over 600,000 and 1 million tons, respectively (Leonard 1998: 11).

Leonard explains how Chaparral has achieved these results through building an 'interdependent system' of employee skills and technical systems supported by HR policies, practices and cultural values:

> Chaparral's skills, physical systems, learning activities, values and managerial philosophies and practices are obviously highly interdependent. Competitively advantageous equipment can be designed and constantly improved *only* if the workforce is highly skilled. Continuous education is attractive *only* if employees are carefully selected for their willingness to learn. Sending workers throughout the world to garner ideas is cost-effective *only* if they are empowered to apply what they have learned to production problems (Leonard 1998: 15–16, italics in the original).

Leonard's model, then, places emphasis on the fact that cleverly developed systems of this kind – where the parts reinforce each other in powerful ways – are very hard to imitate. This is certainly the view within Chaparral. Leonard (1998: 7) notes that the CEO is happy to give visitors a full plant tour, showing them almost 'everything and ... giving away nothing because they cannot take it home with them'. This kind of story lends some support to the argument made earlier that unique learning and social complexity are more significant barriers to imitation than causal ambiguity.

'Table stakes' and distinctive capabilities

While sources of valuable differentiation are very important in the RBV, it is worth injecting a note of caution here. A problem with some writing in the RBV is the tendency of authors to focus only on sources of idiosyncrasy, thus exaggerating differences between firms in the same sector. As we argued in Chapter 2, all viable firms in a sector need some similar resources in order to establish their identity in the minds of customers and secure legitimacy in broader society (Carroll and Hannan 1995, Deephouse 1999, Peteraf and Shanley 1997). For example, banks must act like banks (having the requisite information technology and the typical range of services, for instance). They must satisfy investors and regulators that they can behave as responsible repositories and lenders of funds. Without these baseline features, banks lack legitimacy and recognition in wider society.

Writers in the RBV do not generally understand the important role of social legitimacy as a corporate goal. However, it is a strength of the frameworks outlined here that the authors do see the importance of 'table stakes' (Hamel and Prahalad 1994) or 'enabling capabilities' (Leonard 1998). These are features of the business which enable participation in the industry but which do not make the firm distinctive or account for superior performance.

Leonard (1998) makes useful distinctions among three kinds of capabilities: core (which are superior and cannot be easily imitated), supplemental (which add value to core capabilities but can be easily copied), and enabling (which are necessary conditions of being in the sector). These distinctions are shown in Figure 4.5. Both Leonard (1998) and Hamel and Prahalad (1994) note the dynamic nature of capabilities: over time, one company's distinctive or core capability (such as outstanding quality) tends to be emulated by other firms. It then becomes part of the 'table stakes' in the industry and firms that seek superior performance must search for other ways to differentiate themselves. Hamel and Prahalad (1994: 232) note this dynamic in a case most of us can attest to – that of automobile manufacturing:

> ... in the 1970s and 1980s quality, as measured by defects per vehicle, was undoubtedly a core competence for Japanese car companies. Superior reliability was an important value element for customers and a genuine differentiator for Japanese car producers. It took more than a decade for Western car companies to close the quality gap with their Japanese competitors, but by the mid-1990s quality, in terms of initial defects per vehicle, has become a prerequisite for every car maker. There is a dynamic at work here that is common to other industries. Over long periods of time, what was once a core competence may become a base-line capability.

From an HR perspective, 'table stakes' or 'enabling capabilities' include the minimum HR policies and practices required by each firm to play the competitive game (including similar types of work organisation and employment conditions) (Boxall and Steeneveld 1999, Boxall and Purcell 2000). The type of minimum 'HR system' inevitably varies by sector. There are, for example, strong similarities in the way car plants employ labour and strong similarities among retail chain stores. The differences between these two sectors in skills required, working conditions, team processes and so on are very significant. The key point is that viable firms in a particular business sector are *partially* rather than totally idiosyncratic. Valuable resources, then, include some elements in common with other firms in the sector and some differences.

Towards the knowledge-based view

Standing back from the commentary so far, it should be clear that the management of knowledge plays a key role in resource-based models of the firm. For Hamel and

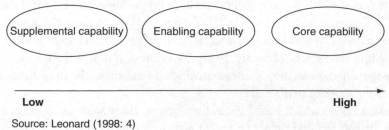

Source: Leonard (1998: 4)

Figure 4.5   Strategic importance of capabilities to the firm

Prahalad (1994), building a focus on knowledge management is much more important than the historical focus of Western firms on product management. For Leonard (1998), understanding the 'wellsprings of knowledge' is the key issue in the long-run renewal of the firm. The RBV, then, encourages researchers to focus on knowledge and its creation and exploitation within firms (Grant 1991, Hoskisson *et al.* 1999).

There is really no point in making a distinction between the resource-based view (RBV) and the knowledge-based view (KBV) of the firm. Whichever of these labels we apply, we end up with same argument – that it is a firm's ability to learn faster than its rivals, and adapt its behaviour more productively, that gives it competitive advantage (see, for example, Kamoche and Mueller 1998). On a practical level, executive interest in the area is increasingly dominated by models of knowledge management, of how to identify, protect and enlarge a firm's 'intellectual capital' (Edvinsson and Malone 1997, Stewart 1998).

In terms of the implications for HR strategy, some of the more important ideas so far are contained in the work of Hedlund (1994) and Nonaka and Takeuchi (1995). They start, like most writers in the area, from Polanyi's (1962) classic distinction between 'tacit' and 'explicit' (or 'articulated') knowledge. Tacit knowledge is 'nonverbalized or even nonverbalizable, intuitive' while explicit or articulated knowledge is 'specified either verbally or in writing, computer programs, patents, drawings or the like' (Hedlund 1994: 75). Figure 4.6 illustrates this distinction across four levels of analysis, starting with the individual and moving up to the 'inter-organisational' domain. The distinction helps to explain why firms are vulnerable to labour turnover. They can never entirely capture what individuals know. Some of what we know – including many of our best skills – cannot be reduced to writing or to formulas. When we leave the firm, we take this knowledge with us. When whole teams leave, as was noted earlier in a case from the semiconductor industry, the effect can be devastating.

	Individual	Group	Organisation	Inter-organisational domain
Explicit knowledge	Knowing calculus	Quality circle's documented analysis of its performance	Organisation chart	Supplier's patents and documented practices
Tacit knowledge	Cross-cultural negotiation skills	Team coordination in complex work	Corporate culture	Customer attitudes to products and expectations

Source: Adapted from Hedlund (1994: 75)

Figure 4.6 Types of knowledge

On the basis of this simple but important distinction, Nonaka and Takeuchi (1995: 70) argue that firms trying to become more innovative need to improve the interaction between tacit and explicit knowledge: 'Unless shared knowledge becomes explicit, it cannot be easily leveraged by the organization as a whole. ... Organizational knowledge creation is a continuous and dynamic interaction between tacit and explicit knowledge.'

They cite the example of how Matsushita developed an automatic home bread-making machine in the late 1980s. The key problem for the firm was how to mechanise the kneading of dough. Kneading is a skill which lies embedded in the tacit knowledge of master bakers:

> Dough kneaded by a master baker and a machine were x-rayed and compared, but no meaningful insights were obtained. Ikuko Tanaka, head of software development, knew that the (Osaka) area's best bread came from Osaka International Hotel. To capture the tacit knowledge of kneading skill, she and several engineers volunteered to apprentice themselves to the hotel's head baker. Making the same delicious bread as the head baker's was not easy. No one could explain why. One day, however, she noticed that the baker was not only stretching but also 'twisting' the dough, which turned out to be the secret for making tasty bread. Thus she socialized the head baker's tacit knowledge through observation, imitation, and practice (Nonaka and Takeuchi 1995: 64).

In this case, explicit knowledge which could be applied to new product development was won from a process of participation in learning tacit skills well outside the individual's personal background.

This is just one illustration. The process of knowledge creation is examined in much greater depth in Nonaka and Takeuchi's (1995) important book. Our main interest lies in their theory of the kind of corporate culture and HR strategy that support greater knowledge creation. Key aspects of their argument have been selected and summarised in Figure 4.7. Their ideas are obviously based on their perception of how leading Japanese companies, such as Kao Corporation and Matsushita, have become successful innovators. However, much of what they argue resonates with the major RBV models we have discussed: those of Hamel and Prahalad (1994) and Leonard (1998). There is the same emphasis on building a concept of business strategy heavily based around knowledge rather than simply product concepts. There is also strong emphasis on the idea that certain cultural practices (such as 'information democracy') and HR policies (such as 'multifunctional careers') underpin the development of the 'learning organisation' (Senge 1992). If firms are to create better learning systems, it is obvious that management will need a process for reviewing company culture and HR policy.

The RBV and human resource strategy

It should be obvious that resource- and knowledge-based models of strategic management are replete with references to the human dimensions of resources. A large

Knowledge strategy	The leadership of 'knowledge-creating companies' should develop a vision for what sort of knowledge should be developed in the firm.
Multi-functional careers and cross-functional teams	Individual employees can contribute more to knowledge creation when they have been trained in more than one function and when they regularly participate in cross-functional teams.
Triple career ladders	There should be career ladders for (1) managers, (2) technical specialists and (3) project leaders. A project leader is an 'intra-firm entrepreneur' who should be well rewarded for this 'frontier' role.
Competing internal development teams	There is value in positive 'redundancy': having different internal teams working on the same project who then argue over the advantages and disadvantages of their approaches.
Information democracy	All employees should have equal access to corporate information so that they can interact on equal terms. Job rotation, open meetings and collegial decision-making should be practised to democratise information flows.

Source: Adapted from Nonaka and Takeuchi (1995)

Figure 4.7 HR dimensions of the 'knowledge-creating company'

part of any firm's strengths – and weaknesses – stems from the calibre of the people employed and the quality of their working relationships. Before we conclude this chapter, we should take stock of the implications of the RBV for the theory of strategic HRM.

At the most elementary level, the resource-based view of the firm provides a conceptual basis, if we were ever in any doubt about the matter, for asserting that key human resources can be sources of competitive advantage. Taxonomies of valuable resources always incorporate an important category of 'human capital' (Barney 1991) or 'employee know-how' (Hall 1993) and resource-based theorists stress the value of the complex interrelationships between the firm's human resources and its other resources: physical, financial, legal, informational and so on (see, for example, Penrose 1959, Grant, 1991, Mueller 1996). This much is self-evident.

Moving beyond this basic point, we need to understand *what* it is that can be exceptionally valuable about human resources and *how* the management of a firm might develop and defend these sources of value. Identifying what is really valuable and protecting it with 'barriers to imitation' is at the heart of resource-based thinking. In terms of the 'what' question, it helps to make a distinction between 'human capital advantage' and 'organisational process advantage' (Boxall 1996, 1998). Because employment relationships are generally 'relational' rather than 'spot contracts' (Kay 1993: 278–9), firms have the possibility of generating human capital advantage through recruiting and retaining outstanding people: through 'capturing' a stock of exceptional human talent, latent with powerful forms of 'tacit' knowledge.

Organisational process advantage, on the other hand, may be understood as a function of historically evolved, socially complex, causally ambiguous *processes* such as
team-based learning and cross-functional cooperation – processes which are very
difficult to imitate. Both human capital and organisational process can generate
exceptional value but are likely to do so much more powerfully when they reinforce
each other (Boxall 1996). In a nutshell, 'human resource advantage', or exceptional
value in human resources, can be traced to better people employed in organisations
with better process.

To understand the positive potential, it helps to think about the negative. We are
all aware of ways in which firms fail to realise the full benefit of human talent. Some
firms may have highly capable managers but fail to maximise the interplay of their
talents as a result of excessive in-fighting between their departments (Hambrick
1995). Highly talented non-managerial staff may also be recruited but find that the
firm fails to offer opportunities which extend their talents. The firm's 'stars' may thus
become disillusioned and leave, or stay and fail to reach their potential (sometimes
referred to as 'internal resignation') (Boxall 1996). Or talented executives and specialists may make major contributions to the firm but capture most of the benefits
for themselves through excessively generous share options and bonus systems (Coff
1997). In these and other ways, human capital may be squandered or perform below
its potential.

Obviously, then, there is widespread agreement that the quality of a firm's human
resources *can* provide it with sources of exceptional value. The major source of
debate concerns the 'how' question (Boxall and Steeneveld 1999). It focuses on the
role of human resource management in assisting firms to build competitive advantage (Wright *et al.* 1994). The question most often posed is: are HR policies and practices competitively valuable? Or are they far too common and well-understood to lay
the basis for advantage, lacking that imperfect mobility essential to competitive
superiority? Certainly, this is true of policy positions – which can simply be run off
on a photocopier or downloaded from the internet. As Mueller (1996) argues, it is
hard to see any distinctive value in policy *per se*.

The value of an HR *system* or HR strategy – understood as a system of critical ends
and means – is another matter. Leonard (1998) argues that HR systems and cultural
norms are an important part of valuable capabilities. Arguably, the scarce and hard-
to-imitate value stems from the historically developed, socially complex elements,
including the way in which they have formed important systemic connections over
time. Thus, while knowledge of individual HR policies is not rare, the knowledge of
how to create a positively reinforcing blend of HR philosophy, process, practice and
investment *within* a particular context is likely to be very rare. The *systemic* quality
of highly effective HR strategy is likely to be very important. 'Human resource advantage' cannot simply reside in a single individual but must be more broadly based in
the management structure and process (Boxall 1998). It doesn't help a firm to have
a superb HR thinker in the management team if there is a lack of the related elements

that can turn this insight into advantage: chief executive commitment, consistent line manager support for critical HR practices over significant time periods, (at least) adequate financial resourcing, sympathetic management accounting systems, and so on. We take this argument further in Chapter 9 in our discussion of the role of HR strategy across cycles of change in industries.

In summary, then, human resource strategy, supported by other sympathetic elements, can enable a firm to build sources of sustained competitive advantage. In any industry, there are likely to be particular firms which have built 'human resource advantage' in this sense. The evidence discussed by Leonard (1998) certainly implies that Chaparral Steel has built human resource advantage in the US steel sector. On the other hand, the majority of surviving firms in an industry are likely to have HR strategies which support their survival but which do not confer advantage. Arguably, most (surviving) firms are 'mainstream' or 'median' employers whose HRM is sufficient to underpin their viability but not otherwise impressive. Firms that fail altogether have often fallen short in the critical human capital they need to be viable, as studies of young, vulnerable firms attest (Bates 1990, Storey 1985).

Before moving on, we should note that there is a problem with thinking about resources only at the level of the firm or even at the level of the industry. This is because nation states affect the resources available to firms and the HR strategies they can pursue (an issue we take further in Chapter 10). Countries provide variable resources of physical infrastructure, politico-economic systems, educated workforces and social order. Some firms and industries have a 'head start' in international competition because they are located in societies which have much better educational and technical infrastructure than others (Boxall 1995, Porter 1990). American, British, German and French firms, for example, are all assisted by the existence of long-established traditions of excellence in higher education which enhance the knowledge-creating capacities of business organisations. German firms tend to enjoy major advantages in manufacturing arising from technical training systems superior to those typically found in English-speaking countries (Steedman and Wagner 1989, Wever 1995). The point here is that the potential to develop human resource advantage does not lie solely in the hands of managers within firms.

Conclusions and implications

There is no doubting the fact that the resource-based perspective is an important set of spectacles for viewing the strategic problems facing the firm. It focuses on the analysis of internal strengths and weaknesses, paying particular attention to the ways in which firms can develop valuable resources and erect barriers to imitation of them. It is not, however, without conceptual weaknesses. Strategy analysts should remember that firms always exist in environments: resources are not ends in themselves but are useful when they create value in markets. More broadly, resources are valuable when they win some form of stakeholder support for the firm. The stake-holders that matter include not only shareholders but also employees, the State and the public at large who have expectations that the firm will use society's resources in legitimate ways. We must also avoid getting carried away with the resource-based notion of idiosyncrasy or differentiation. To be sure, superior firms have distinctive features but all firms in a sector need some similar resources in order to identify their line of business and meet standard customer expectations. From the perspective of HRM, we should also note that the RBV, like most of the strategy literature, can become too absorbed with the firm as the unit of analysis. Human resources vary in quality across nations and this variability affects the strengths that firms are capable of building.

As the name itself implies, resource-based frameworks present an account of strategic management which is richly laced with *human* resource issues. These HR issues include strong concerns with the management of human knowledge or with the development of 'learning organisations'. Managing knowledge inevitably means managing both the company's proprietary technologies and systems (which *do not* walk out the door at the end of the day) and the people (who *do*). It implies man-agement of the ongoing interaction between these two aspects of a firm's knowledge system. Clearly, then, when we take a resource-based perspective on the strategic problem, questions of human resource strategy are going to loom large. How to attract, deploy, motivate and develop people is going to be central. So is the question of how to manage workplace culture. The reader won't be surprised that we regard this as entirely appropriate. We aim, however, to build on the RBV while staying alert to its conceptual weaknesses.

In the rest of this book, resource-based issues remain important. In Chapter 6, we take up the implications of resource-based thinking about 'core competencies' by looking at the way firms often use core/periphery employment structures as they try to develop critical human resources. We link the RBV to the debate within employ-ment relations about the 'flexible firm'. The theory of how firms can build good human capital – how they might build alignment with talented individuals – is examined in Chapter 7. Here we link this resource-based question to agency theory and the theory of psychological contracting. We also look at what studies of job sat-isfaction can tell us. Our exploration of the resource-based view continues in vari-ous parts of the rest of the book. In Chapter 9 we look at how HR strategy is affected by cycles of industry change, exploring the question of how firms might develop what Dyer and Shafer (1999) call 'organisational agility'. In Chapter 10, we examine the HR problems of multidivisional and multinational firms, the sort of firms that most interest theorists like Hamel and Prahalad (1994). Chapter 11, the final in the volume, returns to the RBV in a very practical way, examining its implications for the practice of strategic planning.

part 2

Managing people: searching for general principles

5

Work systems and the changing priorities of production

One of the most distinctive features of the millennium age has been the growth of competition in virtually all countries and in nearly all sectors of the economy, whether publicly owned or privately financed. More precisely, massive companies or whole sectors in previously secure national markets, have been forced to change the way they operate to meet threats to their market or financial position. Companies in many areas have found that it is no longer possible to rely on market strategies or 'positioning' to maintain dominance in terms of market share or profitability. Instead, the requirement has been to look internally at all aspects of the way the organisation functions in order to improve efficiency and, crucially, to reduce costs. Often this means getting more out of existing operations without further major capital investment. In particular, this search has focused on labour effort, costs and productivity. In so doing, attention is increasingly turned to the design of work systems or ways in which work is organised and workers managed and controlled.

In general terms, there has been a move away from the type of work systems which dominated the organisation of production in large factories in the early and mid years of the 20th century. This has been called mass production, or 'Fordism', or more generally embodied in the Scientific Management principles of F. W. Taylor, with a strict distinction between management and labour in the planning and execution of work. In this form of work organisation, jobs were designed to minimise discretionary behaviour among workers, with precise routines enforced on how and when work was to be performed and little or no opportunities provided (or expected) for employees to make suggestions for process improvements or technical innovations. The organisational logic for the design of work is typified as low discretion, with routine tasks undertaken in a low trust work environment (Fox 1974).

91

In the 1980s, new forms of work organisation began to emerge with emphasis placed on multi-skilling, team based work organisation, and generally higher levels of employee discretion in the execution of work tasks. A necessary feature of successful work organisation in these work systems is a higher level of trust in workers to be 'right first time' and for them to undertake their own quality inspection. These new work systems have been variously described as 'Japanisation' (Oliver and Wilkinson 1992), 'world class manufacturing' (Schoenburger 1982), 'flexible specialisation' (Piore and Sabel 1984), 'total quality management' (Wilkinson and Willmott 1995) or, simply, 'lean manufacturing' (Womack, Jones and Roos 1990). As noted in Chapter 1, the particular human resource consequences of these new forms of work organisation have been described as 'high-performance work systems' (HPWSs) in North America (for example, Appelbaum and Batt 1994, Becker and Gerhart 1995) and 'high-commitment management' (HCM) in the UK (for example, Wood and Albanese 1995).

While by no means universal in their coverage, these new work systems have been fundamental in focusing attention on the way work is organised and its link with performance. One key influencing factor is the degree to which employees are competent and motivated to exercise discretion in carrying out their job or tasks, seen for example in multi-skilling and forms of involvement. The importance of discretionary behaviour and the opportunity to exercise discretion is central to most of these new models of work organisation (as explained in Chapter 1). As such, the experience of everyday work under these new forms of work organisation has changed for many people, especially the way management control is exercised over the work process, becoming more participatory and less overtly authoritarian. That is, the form of management control changes with greater emphasis placed on involvement, quasi-self management through teams and, in some work settings, emphasis placed on strong or explicit organisation culture whose purpose is to elicit commitment and motivation. Changes have also had profound implications for union-management relationships and more generally 'employee voice' systems, as discussed in Chapter 8.

This chapter explores these changes to work organisation by first outlining the features of the dominant model of the mid 20th century, that of Fordism in particular and low discretion work models in general, sometimes loosely described as 'command and control' models of employment. It then traces the growth of competitive pressures which led many to first question the efficacy of these low discretion forms of work organisation and then experiment and apply other work systems characterised by higher worker discretion at the point of production, whether in the shop, factory floor or office. While much of the early experience of these forms of higher discretion work systems was initiated in manufacturing greenfield sites, or new start-up companies, they spread in some sectors, like automobile assembly to many, but by no means all plants (MacDuffie and Pil 1996). More recently, HPWSs have been linked to customer service management in retail and banking, and to knowledge

management in professional service companies. Attempts have been made to introduce some of the features of HPWSs into the public sector with the growth of the
'new public management' and the adoption of marketisation strategies by public
authorities around the world.

The implications for people management in terms of the requirements to reduce
costs, improve quality, be quicker in meeting market demands, and in innovation,
are discussed using lean production or 'lean work processes' as a particular example.
This allows us to explore the tensions that exist between the 'hard' and 'soft' features
of these new work systems. The effects on HRM are traced through to the growth of
forms of HRM associated with high levels of performance. An important distinction
is made between the design of appropriate policies and their application. This draws
attention to the crucial role of front-line managers, and to the way these managers
are themselves managed.

Trends in work organisation: from Fordism to flexible specialisation

The origins of low discretion, low trust work systems

At the time when Adam Smith was writing his famous text in 1776, *The Wealth of
Nations*, with its analysis of the massive efficiency gains to be achieved by the detailed
division of labour, factory owners in the emerging industry of cotton manufacture
were taking advantage of new mechanised processes, like power looms, to create radically new forms of work organisation. Initially employing large numbers of children,
usually taken from the parish workhouses, owners like Samuel Gregg in Styal, just
outside Manchester, and Robert Owen in New Lanark near Glasgow brought to an
end the centuries old system of 'putting-out' whereby merchants would contract
home workers using the hand-powered, hand-built, looms they owned, to produce
bundles of fabric or clothing. Putting-out was slow and inefficient, and at harvest
time family workers would work in the fields. The great advantage of the factory system, then as now, was that it allowed capitalist, or managerial, control to be exerted
over the whole work process, especially the workers. Continuous labour availability
on one site enabled the efficient use of new forms of power (water and steam) to be
applied to new machinery like power looms and the spinning jenny (Deane 1969:
87, Jones 1994).

Under the factory system, operatives became machine minders working at the
pace set by the machine, not themselves. They were paid a wage, often linked to output and, working very long hours, undertook a single task or a small number of
linked tasks requiring some dexterity but little skill. Each task might take no more
than a few minutes and then had to be repeated again, and again. Thus, short cycle
tasks were boring and simple and repetitive, and workers had to be disciplined to
stay at their work stations, unable to move to another task or another job. Benevolent

owners, like the two just mentioned, would provide housing, schooling and (compulsory) Sunday worship but little else in terms of training or careers. Discipline was strict and power was vested in overseers or foremen. The language at the time, and common through the 19th century, and much of the 20th, of 'the master and his hands' is especially instructive. The implication, as Watson (1986) observes, was that workers were machines using motor not mental skills.

Factories were designed by engineers to function as large engines of cogs and wheels rationally linked together. This metaphor of organisations as rationally co-ordinated interlocking parts is still prevalent today and it denies humanity and human emotion (see Morgan (1997) for a wonderful analysis of the ways of thinking about or imagining organisation). As work was de-skilled through task fragmentation and the detailed division of labour, and as workers no longer owned their own means of production, being reliant, as wage slaves, on the owner and his management agents, individuals were dehumanised.

In a wider sense, this was no more than a reflection of social structures and beliefs in society at the time on the brutish nature of the emerging working class. However, questions were increasingly being asked by novelists like Dickens and Mrs Gaskill, and social reformers like Seebohm Rowntree, about the social consequences of the 'dark satanic mills', as William Blake called them. Early factory legislation, bitterly opposed by the owners, outlawed the employment of the youngest children and limited some of the worst excesses of dangerous working practices and conditions. The factory system had to adapt to survive, despite the warnings of dire consequences of economic collapse from capitalists (who then, and now, saw meddling social reformers and interventionist politicians as anti-business). It did so remarkably well as yet new efficiencies were found, often by replacing people with advances in technology: capital-labour substitution as it is called. That is, far from increases in labour costs forced by legislation leading to loss of markets, it tended to spur a search for innovation and efficiency, as observed in the introduction of a minimum wage in the UK in 1999 (for the first time).

Taylorism and Fordism as improvements to the factory system

A vitally important conclusion can be drawn from this brief historical analysis. The mental models of the early factory owners about the way work should be organised, strongly supported by economic theorists from Adam Smith onwards and by statisticians like Babbage, became the standard or default model for the design of work organisation. This fundamental assumption of the best way to organise work in factories, and subsequently in factory-like offices, spread around the world and remains the dominant pattern today in many workplaces, and many countries. Subsequent developments, whether that pioneered by Henry Ford (Glover 1998), or turned into a new science of management by F. W. Taylor (Warner 1998), were premised on the assumption that the work organisation of the factory, of de-skilled, low discretion work, performed by machine-like humans, could be made yet better and more efficient. The fundamental principles of the factory system remained unchallenged and were seen as both normal and inevitable.

What Taylor advocated and Ford put into practice was the application of strict scientific principles based on measurement (time and motion study, for example) and the absolute division of responsibility between management and labour. The former did the thinking, planning and directing and the latter were required to obey instructions, mind the machines and remove the product. If worker resistance to the factory regime became problematic then the answer was to pay higher wages in return for compliance and discipline, as Ford did, nicely stimulating demand for his own cars. If absenteeism and labour turnover problems were experienced, then perhaps a welfare department (the forerunners of personnel management) could be used to visit sick workers, more for reasons of control than compassion, or some type of compensatory benefits provided. If workers organised themselves into trade unions, then these were to be resisted – that is, until national governments in many countries, disturbed by the potential breakdown in social order in the first half of the 20th century, intervened and, one way or the other, persuaded or forced many, but not all, companies to recognise these unions, thereby giving workers some workplace influence, as discussed in Chapter 8.

The factory systems had to adapt at the margins, and had to take account of changing social mores and the emerging democratic imperative in the wider society, but the fundamental principles of work organisation first developed by the early factory owners of the late 18th century remained unquestioned and largely unchallenged.

Technology became more sophisticated, factory size grew hugely, divisions of labour developed among the managerial and professional classes and a new breed of office worker emerged. Here, more bureaucratic and paternalistic forms of management control were used, often because of the close proximity of these staff, the white collar workers as they were called, to their bosses. Factory workers were kept at a distance on the shop floor and labour control was more technical, deriving from the work process itself (Edwards 1979). For as long as there were workers prepared to labour in such workplaces and provided the product produced had a ready, sustainable and profitable market, the economic system of mass production work organisation would remain intact. Fundamentally, the assumed subservient role of labour in the industrial, commercial and the growing public services sectors remained unchallenged until the 1970s.

Challenges to Fordism and Scientific Management

Efforts were made in the middle decades of the 20th century to boost productivity and efficiency through improving management and leadership and by adopting new ideas about motivation and satisfaction. This became known as the Human Relations School (see Watson (1986) for an excellent analysis). While increasing concern was expressed about working conditions and worker motivation, the fundamental principles of work organisation or job design were questioned by few. There appeared to be little interest, for example, in utilising the mental and cognitive abilities of individual workers or of allowing or 'empowering' workers to exercise greater discretion over work routines, or to engage in non-routine activities like problem-solving. Human relations was essentially a form of benevolent paternalism: strong on welfare but less interested in power-sharing or 'empowerment'.

It was not until the 1970s that new ideas about the organisation of work and the division of labour began to influence enough senior managers and strategists to make a difference in suggesting new routes to competitiveness. In part, this came from a growing rejection of the principles of Scientific Management and its alienating effect on workers following the upsurge in industrial conflict in the late 1960s (Crouch and Pizzarno 1978). This was itself a reflection of the deep social changes that took place in the 1960s. After two decades of full employment in most advanced industrial nations, labour supply for blue collar or manual work in factories, and in the public services, was increasingly drawn from immigrants, whether so called 'guest workers' in Germany or Black Commonwealth citizens in the UK. Great interest was shown in alternative forms of organisation design, in ownership, and in work organisation. This ranged from the Volvo experiments in humanising the assembly line (Berggren 1992), to the Mondragon worker cooperatives in the Basque region of Spain (Whyte and Whyte 1989), and more broadly to alternative social and political approaches seen in the Yugoslavian workers' self-management movement. However, it was the oil crisis of the mid 1970s, triggering a period of declining productivity which, taken with the beginnings of global competition especially from the Japanese, led to the emergence of 'post-Fordism' (Wallace 1998: 367–8). This rather unsatisfactory term is used to describe a variety of new approaches to markets, consumers and workers, and in the new global marketplace, to the relative inability of governments to control the economy.

One vitally important part of post-Fordism was, and is, the adoption of new forms of work organisation, described by Piore and Sabel (1984) as *flexible specialisation*. This involved the move to a new production or work system which 'recognises the possibility for strategic choice over production techniques, working practices and organisational forms' (Wallace 1998: 368). Flexible specialisation is built around the ideas of organisational decentralisation and innovative production techniques managed on a daily basis by multi-skilled and flexible workers themselves. Employees are usually organised in teams or cells (as in 'cellular manufacturing'), often producing goods and services for smaller niche, or customised, markets. Here the economies of scale reaped in mass production are replaced by 'economies of scope'. This is the flexible use of both technologies and people to produce product variety more customised for the end user. If Henry Ford is famous for his marketing dictum that 'you can have any colour you like provided it is black', under mass customisation and the concomitant production system of flexible specialisation the adage is, 'you can have whatever colour, and any model, you want, when you want it'. This has huge implications for work organisation, the place of employees in the production or work process and, crucially, for human resource management. Figure 5.1 shows the difference between Fordism and post-Fordism for labour and management, as helpfully summarised by Wallace (1998).

Fordism	Post-Fordism
Economy competition, technology and production process	
Protected national markets	Global competition
Mass production of standardized products, economies through fixed capital and labour productivity within the production process. Stock control on a just-in-case basis	Flexible production systems/small batch/multiple products in niche markets, economies through capital productivity between production and distribution. Stock control on a just-in-time basis
Bureaucratic, hierarchical and vertically integrated organizations, split into dispersed and remote site plants or branches	Flatter and flexible organizational structures alongside organizational decentralization, organizations moved to greenfield sites
Technology focused upon single purpose machinery	CNC, multi-purpose and adaptable machine tools
Compete by full capacity utilization and cost cutting	Compete by innovation, diversification, sub- contracting
Domination of manufacturers over retailers, producers over users	Domination of retailing
Labour and management	
Fragmented and standardized work tasks, strict division between mental and manual labour	Flexible specialization/multi-skilled workers, open ended tasks with closer integration of mental and manual labour
Semi-skilled workforce represented by large general trade unions	Multi-skilled workers with no-strike agreements or by derecognition. Management strategies aimed at achieving high individual performance and people identified as a key organizational resource
	Management theories lean towards human relations management supported by numerically flexible peripheral workers
Wages collectively bargained at national level	Individualized payment – PRP
Low trust/low discretion, majority employed in manufacturing sector and blue collar jobs	High trust/high discretion, majority employed in service sector/white collar jobs
Little 'on the job training', little formal education required for most jobs	Regular 'on the job' training, greater demand for knowledgeable workers

Small managerial and professional elite utilizing scientific management	Growing managerial and professional class/service class
Industrial/economic change seen as natural process of facilitating mass production and consumption	Need for change viewed as a natural result of facing up to economic crises and depressions
Fairly predictable labour market histories	Unpredictable labour market histories due to technological change and increased economic uncertainty
Politics, culture and Ideology	
Trade union solidarity and class based political affiliation	Decline in trade union membership and class based political affiliation
Importance of locality/class/gender based lifestyles	Fragmentation and pluralism, 'global' village
Cultural icons are the television set, the cinema, the theatre, other forms of collective entertainment, and the package holiday	Culture becomes individualized and fragmented through the Walkman, the computer game and travel becomes individualized through the packaging of the independent holiday
Mass consumption of consumer durable 'You can have any colour as long as it is black' (Ford)	Individualized consumption/consumer choice 'You can have any colour or size or shape you want' (Benetton)

Source: Reproduced with permission from Wallace (1998)

Figure 5.1   From Fordism to Post-Fordism in the management of labour

Pressures to improve competitiveness and their implications for HRM

The profound implications of flexible specialisation or post-Fordism more generally were not restricted to the manufacturing sector but spread much more broadly and deeply throughout all sectors of advanced economies. The global crisis of the late 1970s and 80s involved substantial changes to the competitive environment in all sectors of the economy. The way companies and governments responded brought new tensions and uncertainties to the world of work, and the position of employees in the enterprise. In particular, it helped change the way a growing number of executives thought about the links between 'people management' and the search for competitive advantage, that is the place of human resource management in strategy analysis.

Human resource management, or personnel management as it was then called, did not feature at all when strategy analysis first emerged as a business, and especially business school, discipline in the 1960s and 70s. One could search the index of the plethora of strategy books for any reference to people, employees, workers or staff without success. The reason for this was that business strategy, as we explored in Chapter 2, was primarily about the relationship between the firm and its competitive environment. What happened inside the company was, as one leading analyst asserted, all to do with implementation, just as tactics are the implementation of battle strategies. Implementation 'comprised of a series of sub-activities which are primarily administrative', wrote Andrews in 1968 (quoted in Hoskisson *et al.* 1999: 422). This remains much the view of some leading strategy thinkers today, like Porter, who talks of 'operational effectiveness as given' (1996: 74).

The assumed role of human resource management for operational effectiveness was to ensure continuous production at the lowest cost possible. The primary purpose for HRM was the achievement of order, stability and cost control. This required a concentration on the mechanisms for the institutionalisation of industrial conflict through the regulation of terms and conditions of employment, the adoption of job evaluation, for example, to bring order into pay systems, and work study and industrial engineering to define jobs and tasks as precisely as possible. In the many big workplaces of the 1960s and 70s (many with over 5000 workers on a site), the job of the personnel department was fundamentally one of securing an adequate labour supply while the industrial relations managers were required to keep the peace.

Whether it was the recession triggered by the oil crisis in the mid 70s or the opening of markets to Japanese competition in the same decade, seen in the eradication of the British motorcycle industry for example, is not important. The economic certainties of the long post-war boom came unstuck and with it attempts by governments to control the economy through devices like incomes policies and indicative planning. These were typical features of 'neo-corporatism' and, in some countries, tripartite regulation between the State and associations of labour and employers (Crouch 1979). Market turbulence began to undermine the sense of certainty. Business planning timescales were reduced from five years to three and then even shorter. Strategic thinking about the importance of human resources changed significantly, as indicated in the previous chapter on the resource-based view of the firm:

> When the external environment is in a state of flux, the firm's own resources and capabilities may be a much more stable basis on which to define its identity. Hence, a definition of a business in terms of what it is capable of doing may offer a much more durable basis for strategy than a definition based on needs (e.g. markets) which the business seeks to satisfy (Grant 1991: 116).

What was painfully realised in the light of Japanese manufacturing success, seen for example in the Toyota production system (now copied directly by Ford), with its focus on waste reduction and flexibility, was that operational and human resource management was no longer simply a matter of 'implementation' or 'administration'. Unchanged, the old forms of work organisation and associated systems of HRM could become a source of competitive *dis*advantage. Transformed to flexible specialisation with what were then innovative HR practices, the new forms of work organisation had the potential to contribute to competitive advantage in a way unimaginable in the 1960s. The implications were well put by the founder of one of the major Japanese manufacturing companies to a group of visiting Western business leaders in 1985:

> Your firms are built on the Taylor model: even worse, so are your heads. With your bosses doing the thinking, while the workers wield the screwdrivers, you are convinced deep down that this is the right way to run a business. For you the essence of management is getting the ideas out of the heads of the bosses and into the hands of labour. We are beyond the Taylor model: business, we know, is now so complex and difficult, the survival of the firms so hazardous in an environment increasingly unpredictable, competitive and fraught with danger, that their continued existence depends on the day-to-day mobilisation of every ounce of intelligence. For us the core of management is the art of pulling together the intellectual resources of all employees in the service of the firm. Only by drawing on the combined brain power of all its employees can a firm face up to the turbulence and constraints of today's environment. (Konosuke Matsushita)

Globalisation

It is important to be clear about the nature and sources of the dramatic change to the business environment since they impact in different ways on HRM. Take 'globalisation'. This is not just another term for the growth in competition but refers to a number of interrelated developments. First is the significant, planned reduction in tariff barriers between countries and regions. The days have far gone when the Australian Government would increase tariff barriers to protect Australian jobs when wage awards were approved by the Federal Arbitration Commission, as they did in the 1950s. World trade has increased significantly and low labour cost areas become preferred operational areas for multinational companies.

This is especially important in those sectors where the ratio of labour costs to total costs is fairly high, as in clothing, footwear, component assembly and data processing, and skill requirements are relatively low. This is not surprising given that hourly compensation costs in Korea, for example, were 63 per cent lower than in the USA, and 69 per cent lower than the European average in 1999 (but were, even so, significantly higher than in Sri Lanka (97 per cent lower than the USA) and Mexico (89 per cent lower than the USA) (Figure 5.2).

The implications of these marked differences in wage costs were that intense pressure was placed on unit labour costs (the combination of wage cost and productivity) of firms in the advanced industrial nations. In many cases, plants were opened in developing countries and closed in the home country, and significant job losses occurred in those establishments that remained. In some cases, established firms redefined themselves as retailers, moving out of manufacturing in their home base completely, for example the shoe company, Clarks, which closed its last factory in the UK (in Weston-super-Mare) in 2001, moving production to Taiwan.

In order to reduce costs, work was intensified for the remaining employees in the 'home' economies in an effort to boost output per employee. As multinational com-

Country	US $ per hour
Germany	26.18
Sweden	21.58
Netherlands	20.94
Japan	20.89
United States	19.20
United Kingdom	16.56
Australia	15.89
Canada	15.60
New Zealand	9.14
Korea	6.71
Taiwan	5.62
Mexico	2.12
Sri Lanka*	0.47

*1998 data

Source: US Department of Labor (2000): Table 2

Figure 5.2 Hourly compensation in US dollars for production workers in manufacturing, 1999

Note: includes pay for time worked, holiday pay, bonuses and insurance and benefit plans

panies increasingly had factories and offices in many countries, they were able to play one location off against another, to reward the efficient with new investment and new model work (as in the motor industry) and to bargain with governments for development grants as an inducement to keep existing plants open (Mueller and Purcell 1992). This globalisation trend was accelerated as multinational firms spread development costs and efficiencies by designing and marketing products on a global scale, seen in the so called 'world car' or the standardisation of household and pharmaceutical products and seen too in financial markets. Globalisation was also associated with the growth in the number of mergers and strategic alliances stretching across national borders, for example in pharmaceuticals, motor cars and management consultancy companies (discussed in Chapter 10). Faced with these global competitive pressures, the capacity of national unions to protect the jobs of their members and working conditions was significantly eroded. New forms of relationships with company management had to be developed, as we discuss in Chapter 8.

These pressures were by no means restricted to manufacturing. Governments and regional economic areas such as the European Union dismantled regulations that had protected industries in the past, whether by the abolition of retail price maintenance, or the deregulation of particular sectors as in banking or airlines, for example. In airline deregulation, which took place in the USA in the 1980s and in Europe was begun in the 1990s, the effect was that the protected routes 'owned' by an airline were opened up to competition. Now labour cost increases could no longer be passed on automatically to the captive customer. New, low cost airlines entered the market like People's Express in the 1980s in the USA and Easyjet and Ryan Air in Britain ten years later. As labour costs are the largest component of variable costs in the industry, huge pressure was placed on finding means of achieving cost reduction. This could be done by efficiency improvements such as shorter turnaround time, as achieved in South West Airlines, for example (O'Reilly and Pfeffer 2000) and by job loss and work intensification, or by outsourcing or franchising to operators with lower wage rates (Cappelli 1995).

The pattern of low cost, new entrant firms rapidly taking market share from long established companies repeated itself in many industries like telecommunications, information systems, banking, insurance and finance. In each, established players found the rules of the competitive game had changed. Now they, too, had to find ways of rapidly introducing new technologies or systems in order to reduce costs drastically while improving quality and the speed of customer service. This had to be done by finding better ways of managing operations and people. It is no wonder that two of the managerial preoccupations of the 1990s became 'benchmarking' and the 'management of change'.

Privatisation and the impact of market forces in the public sector

Pressures to reduce government expenditure as a proportion of gross domestic product, for example, in order to meet the criteria for joining the Euro, and to reduce government debt, were associated with large scale privatisation of government owned industries. Pioneered by Mrs Thatcher's Government in the UK in the 1980s, this approach to minimise the role of the State quickly spread around the globe and was enthusiastically supported by the International Monetary Fund and the World Bank. New forms of government action came in the form of State-sponsored regulators and auditors whose jobs were to ensure that privatised firms were not exploiting 'captive' customers. Regulators had the power to order significant reductions in prices, as they did, for example, in UK water companies in 2000. This had dramatic consequences for jobs in the sector. Governments, whether national or supra-national like the EC (now EU), ordered that markets be opened up to competition, as for example in telecommunications. Utilising the latest technologies and building on the changing nature of customer markets with the growth of telephone and internet access, many new companies were able to enter the market. They had significantly lower cost structures compared to the existing, long established firms which were burdened with sunk costs and high exit costs. Pressure to reduce these costs while improving quality and adopting new technologies was, and remains, intense. This is especially the case in the finance sector, in telecommunications, and in information technology companies.

The force of change was experienced, too, in those parts of the public or government sector that could not be privatised. This is the public service sector of hospitals, central and local government which has no significant independent source of revenue beyond taxes. Here the import of 'new public management' (Ferlie, Ashburn,

Fitzgerald and Pettigrew 1996) sought to replicate private sector competitive strategies. This could involve compulsory competitive tendering of service provision, such as school meals, refuse disposal or hospital facilities management, or the creation of proxy markets to force competition. This was achieved in health care through the artificial splitting of the purchasers from the providers of services. The outcome for workers in the UK public sector has been a significant intensification of work effort in the 1990s (Green 2001) with teachers and health workers exhibiting higher than average levels of stress (Smith 2001). Similar intensification of effort was observed in manufacturing, especially in the 1980s (Green 2001).

The impact of competitive forces on human resource management

The outcome of all of these various pressures, which accumulated in the 1980s and 90s, always in different forms and at different speeds in various sectors, was to undermine old certainties and question the fundamental assumptions of people management. Perceptions of job security for many collapsed (Doogan 2001). There was, and remains, plenty of evidence that for some workers their experience of work in this period got worse as institutional and statutory protection of jobs and unions were removed, and firms struggled to survive in competitive markets by downsizing, by cost cutting and work intensification (Edwards and Whitson 1991, Wood 1989). In low-wage-cost developing countries, new factories precisely adopted the Taylorist principles of Scientific Management (Wilkinson, Gamble, Humphrey and Morris 2001). In effect, post-Fordism is an exaggerated Western phenomenon.

However, in some workplaces, often those using more advanced technology and operating in highly competitive export markets (Osterman 1994), alternative strategies of fundamental significance to the world of work and the way management thought about HRM became evident. These were based around achieving cost advantage, productivity improvements and the ability to meet customer demands by tapping into the sources of employee commitment, motivation and innovation. This was most usually achieved through an extensive adoption of teamworking as the fundamental building block of the organisation (Procter and Mueller 2000).

Changes in customer expectations on speed of delivery and quality and new product development, whether in manufacturing or services, place pressure on companies to be flexible and innovative:

> Now the central focus is on drastically compressing development times ... as well as speeding up the order to delivery cycle. Time in production has to be managed to accommodate these new imperatives: the manufacturing base has to be capable of rapidly and smoothly adjusting to continually changing product configurations and the specific demands of the moment ... Time has become the competitive strategy of the firm (Schoenberger 1997: 45).

The implications for jobs and work are immediate:

> Because of the premium placed on speed, reliability, and quality of output in the new environment, workers must be encouraged to co-operate and to discipline themselves to the work process. For example, if things go wrong on the line, operators must have the knowledge to intervene directly and immediately (*ibid*: 51).

Time compression requires just-in-time (in place of just-in-case) and right-first-time working, and more especially a speedy response to market changes, customer expectations and advances in technology. Time compression is particularly powerful in its effects on reducing the organisational 'space' available for thinking, planning and responding. Whereas before, with the functional division of responsibilities within the firm, managers had time to plan and coordinate, now the need is for agility and flexibility in quick response to customer and supplier needs. This tends to promote both a reduction in hierarchical levels and bureaucracy and a decentralisation to work areas directly responsible for meeting customer needs. For example, right-first-time, and the need for quick responses, put a premium on the direct contact between employees and the customer. This can be in talking directly to front-line staff in telephone call centres, or industrial customers having direct contact with team leaders or team members themselves in their suppliers' companies. Increasingly, senior management have to rely on their employees' discretion and judgement – to trust them in a way that was unimaginable in earlier generations.

Associated with time compression, as a feature of many markets, is the increasing uncertainty and unpredictability of the competitive environment. One HR manager in an insurance company put it this way:

> Time scales have been reduced to change every 12 or 15 months so you cannot say that change is a one off thing. You do not plan for it: it's evolutionary, so it happens all the time with us. I suppose the final message is that we try for change all the time; it is not something where we say we are going to change in 18 months' time – it's continuous. This puts pressure on the organisation. Now it is being much more able to focus on the customer, very much needing staff who are helpful individuals, able to find solutions rather than problems, being able to make decisions. Now front line staff have to take responsibility. They can actually now provide customers with money, compensation there and then, which in our company was unheard of (Hutchinson, Kinnie, Purcell, Collinson, Scarbrough and Terry 1998: 92).

Task integration in teamworking

The effect of these pressures, whether down the supply chain in the face of customer requirements for speed and flexibility, or in consumer markets where buyers want immediate access to goods or services (as in 24 hour telephone or internet operations), can be to change significantly the way work is performed and the whole design of work systems. It requires tight coupling of activities previously separated in time and space in the hierarchical, functionally designed firm. This is often linked to the development of teams and teamworking as the fundamental building block of the organisation. Teams can provide the means to coordinate work tasks between people, they can provide a means for learning and development, and become a social unit with a form of self, or more accurately, quasi-self-governance (Mueller 1994). The economic or efficiency outcome of teamworking is generally positive through the integration of tasks and alignment of the organisation structure (Batt 2000).

Teamworking, if properly designed, allows for four necessary types of task integration to occur. These are illustrated in Figure 5.3.

First, the requirement is to integrate mental and manual work within work teams or among employees directly, rather than leave the thinking to the managers and the doing to the workers. This type of integration is typically found in problem-solving activities such as *kaizen* teams or quality circles and project activities. These 'offline' activities, doing non-routine work (for example, working on the introduction of a new model or new system), can be combined with 'online' work. An example here would be where quality is controlled by employees directly. A very good example of this type of integration is in the Toyota NUMMI plant in California where there is far above average performance in efficiency and flexibility (Adler, Goldoftus and Levine 1999). Here, the team is the unit for work allocation between members, achieving the horizontal coordination of tasks (Dunlop and Weil 1996).

The second form of integration comes from the efficiency improvements associated with combining specialist work roles within operational teams. This means, for example, that responsibility for maintenance and quality inspection, previously carried out by specialists in different departments, is brought within the ambit of the team as far as the members have technical competence to do so. In some cases, individuals with special skills will work as team members. Within service companies, like telephone banking or in retailing, team members may be trained in dealing with

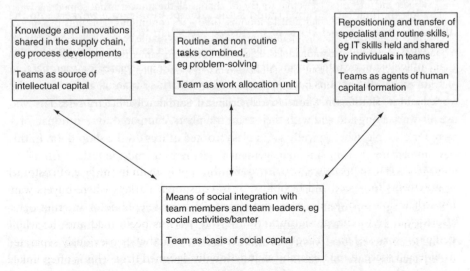

Figure 5.3 Task integration with team structures: activity, example and processes

customer complaints or handling difficult customers, or some team members may have special skill or experience in software or IT systems. Thus, multi-skilling does not just mean that individual workers have to learn and use a wider range of skills (which they do – see Gallie, White, Cheng and Tomlinson (1998)) but team members have a wider variety of skills available to them within their control, to use as and when required. In this type of integration, the team becomes a repository of knowledge, and the avenue or agent for learning, a crucial part of human capital formation that enables people to act in new ways.

The third form of integration crosses organisational boundaries by linking the supplier with the customer in an interactive way. This involves active information sharing and the development of supply partnership based on levels of trust as well as commercial contracts. In a quality car assembly plant, for example, track and assembly workers are members of teams that regularly meet with suppliers to discuss problems and improvements. In the clothing or apparel industry, the use of what is called 'modular' production is predicated on close contact between the big retailers and the manufacturers via the electronic point of sale (EPOS) bar code system, and through discussions on style changes. In software development houses, designers are located on the client's premises working closely with their staff, and in relational marketing, via the telephone or internet, employees are directly involved with customers. Information flows increase significantly between supplier, customer and client. The effect is to make organisations less opaque and less hierarchical since much information flows horizontally rather than vertically up and down the management levels. It means, too, that teams can become a source of innovation in process improvements in direct contact with clients. In this sense, teams form the prime building block of the intellectual capital of the firm by being or becoming 'a community of practice' (Batt 2001).

The fourth, final type of integration is the attempt to integrate workers into the cultural or organisational fabric of the firm, rather than treat them as outsiders or lesser citizens. At a trivial, yet symbolic level, this is seen in the adoption of the language of inclusion or integration. All employees become 'associates' or 'members', in place of earlier distinctions between 'workers' and 'staff' or manual and white collar workers. More significantly, some managerial tasks are devolved to team leaders who usually work alongside and with their team members, compared to traditional foremen, for example, who typically sat in glass fronted offices on the shop floor. In this way, immediate or front-line management is less remote and the task of front-line managers and team leaders changes to give more emphasis to training, coaching and encouraging better performance.

Social integration, or at least the attempts at it, can be seen in social and 'fun' activities organised on a team-by-team or office basis. The attempt is to blur the old rigid distinction between local managers and workers. The job of the supervisor, or team leader, focuses more on gaining worker involvement and commitment through information sharing, knowledge transfer, and discussion as well taking part in social activities and banter. It is questionable how far this extends to senior management, but information and communication flows from top management usually increase to raise awareness of customer needs, quality and overall firm performance. The aim is to gain higher levels of employee commitment to the work process, the end user and the organisation as a whole. This is sometimes called 'affective commitment' where employees wish to remain part of the firm and see membership as important to them and their sense of worth. This social integration of team members with each other and with team leaders, where it occurs, is strongly associated with the development of 'social capital', seen by Nahapiet and Ghoshal (1998) as fundamental to the achievement of organisational advantage.

The people management implications

The overall effect of these four types of integration in team-based forms of work organisation is that employees often gain greater discretion over their jobs, and how they perform them, and, in particular, how they interact with others, whether fellow workers or front-line management.

One study of 'high-involvement' organisations showed that the volume of communication interchange between team members and significant others in the production process about operational, customer-related or work routines was much higher than in 'control-orientated' work systems (Gant, Ichniowski, and Shaw 1999). This type of teamwork is also associated with work satisfaction. 'Jobs that allow workers to use their knowledge and skills, provide some autonomy and provide opportunities for learning, lead to higher levels of job satisfaction' (Berg 1999: 130). Teamwork and task integration have behavioural implications of fundamental importance to HRM. Trust levels have to improve, means have to be found to motivate employees to use this discretion, greater reliance is placed on employees to solve problems, and new skills obtained to take on a wider number of tasks and learn new ways of working, often discovered by the employees themselves.

The team becomes the focal point for learning, and for work pressure exerted by customers and employees on each other. In an extensive study using a variety of data sources, Green (2001) noted that in 1986 some 37 per cent of employees in the UK said they were subject to work pressure from clients or customers, but by 1997 this had risen to 54 per cent. In the same period, the proportion who reported that they were subject to work pressure from fellow workers or colleagues rose remarkably from 29 to 57 per cent. 'It seems that peer pressure has come into its own as a source of labour intensification' (Green 2001: 70). This is strongly confirmed by the Bath People and Performance study (Hutchinson et al. 1996, 1998). Many of those interviewed said that 'they could not let their mates down'. The team was a social entity, and, of course, a social construction. This type of 'concertive' control by team members over themselves is, suggests Barker (1993), more powerful than other, more traditional methods of control to gain worker compliance with management's requirements.

Eileen Appelbaum and her colleagues, following the work of Bailey (1993), in their extensive study of high-performance work systems (Appelbaum, Bailey, Berg and Kalleberg 2000), identified three linked crucial processes in managing people for high performance. These were based around the fundamental requirement for employees to use discretionary effort effectively. 'Workers need appropriate motivation to put forth discretionary effort, they need to have the necessary skills to make their effort meaningful, and employers had to give them the opportunity to participate in substantive shop-floor decisions through the way the work was organised' (*ibid*: 26).

The starting point is the design of jobs and tasks, a point observed by Patterson, West, Lawthorn and Nickell (1998) in their study of HRM and performance in medium-sized manufacturing companies in the UK. Job-cycle time, or the time to complete the whole task, is fundamental. If the job task takes a minute or so to perform, and is repeated endlessly through the shift, there is very little opportunity for discretionary behaviour or process improvement unless non-task, offline, time for problem solving, communication and involvement is designed into the working day or week. This is as true of call centres, where some simple transactions, such as rail timetable inquires, are restricted to 20–30 seconds, as it is in some jobs in manufacturing. Elger and Smith (1998) noted in a study of component assembly work in Japanese greenfield site companies that job times were typically of a very short duration and there was very little scope for employees to change the work methods or make suggestions. Thus work design, or more generally work organisation, plays a central role in 'providing non-managerial employees with the opportunity to contribute discretionary effort through participation in shop floor problem solving and decision making' (Appelbaum *et al.* 2000: 26). In terms of the AMO theory of performance introduced in Chapter 1 (ability, motivation, opportunity), work design provides the opportunities for performance. In an extensive study of the motor industry across the globe, MacDuffie (1995: 217–18) noted the 'organisational logic' of gaining a strong integration between flexible production (typically seen in product or service variety combined spatially and temporally), work systems (the way routine and non-routine tasks are combined usually in teams), and HPWS practices concerned with motivation, involvement and learning. This is shown in Figure 5.4.

Tensions between operational and social processes: the example of lean production

It is important to recognise that flexible specialisation and high-performance work systems were introduced to improve efficiency and profitability, not for social or ethical reasons. Work often becomes more challenging and stressful and some argue that the new work processes are but a new form of Taylorism (Warner 1994). In effect, there is a tension between the production need for quality output and the social organisation of work necessary to ensure that workers are motivated and competent. This tension is seen particularly clearly in lean production or lean processes. Figure

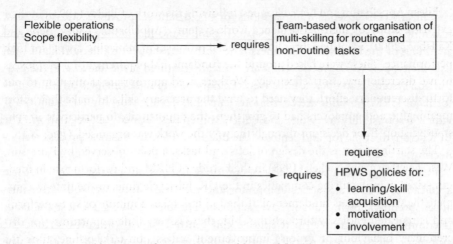

Figure 5.4   The organisational logic of flexible operations

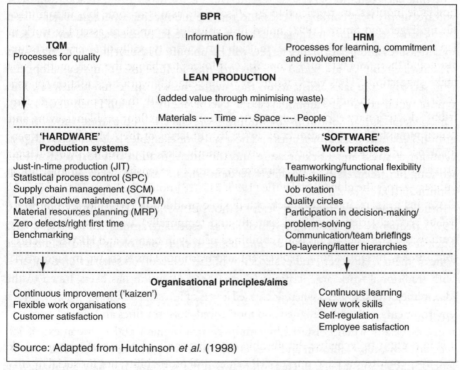

Figure 5.5   The HR implications of lean business processes: hardware and software

5.5 summarises the implications by drawing a distinction between what is termed the 'hardware' and the 'software' of the new ways of organising work under lean processes. 'Hardware' is shown on the left hand side starting with Total Quality Management (TQM) and lists the requisites of the production or the operational system, and the consequent implications for organisational processes. Measurement, planning and process interactions between people and technology are fundamental attributes of the hardware of leanness. The 'software', shown on the right hand side, lists the type of work practices that are typically required if the 'hardware', the production system, is to operate effectively. The organisational principles on which new forms of HRM are built are continuous learning, flexible work practices and individual responsibility for work and effort, sometimes termed 'self-regulation'. The BPR acronym at the top and centre of the diagram refers to 'business process reengineering'.

In most lean processes the new operational systems are bolstered by extensive application of control systems to monitor and measure compliance and detect variances speedily, allowing for corrective action and problem-solving. Work surveillance is common. For example, in telephone call centres, typical measures include the automatic measurement of call length against prescribed time, calls waiting to be answered, the abandoned call rate, the time taken to 'wrap up', and call availability (the time the customer service representative is actively on duty). In addition, there will frequently be recording of calls and remote monitoring where managers listen in to ensure that scripts and greetings are used properly. Where the task involves selling, measures and performance targets will be ubiquitous. Surveillance in retailing is via closed circuit TV and video cameras and may include use of 'mystery shoppers', who secretly score sales assistants on their willingness to smile and be helpful. This type of requirement for 'emotional labour' can be highly stressful (Hochschild 1986). The general spread of forms of auditing of quality and output (now deeply entrenched in schools, universities and hospitals, for example) is associated with perceptions of stress and work pressure and the intensification of effort seen in long working hours. Stress is increasingly recognised as a modern occupational illness (Smith 2001).

Studies of worker responses to lean methods of working (Hutchinson *et al.* 1996, 1998) frequently cite growing levels of stress, especially among team leaders, who often feel caught in the middle as both team worker (one of 'us') and as manager (one of 'them'). However, studies also show higher levels of job satisfaction compared with traditional work organisations (Berg 1999). Attention has been drawn to the 'disciplined worker' thesis where increased levels of job satisfaction are found in work environments with well designed and monitored work routines and surveillance systems, especially when bolstered by employee involvement and in a context of job security. Edwards, Collinson and Rees (1998) note the paradox of work and surveillance, or as we put it here, the tension between the 'soft' and the 'hard', in managing work systems. Involvement is constrained 'by a continued reliance on discipline and monitoring ... (However) there (are) genuine benefits to workers in problem-solving since most workers (are) satisfied with their level of work effort, and since acceptance of quality and trust in management (go) along with more and not less strict controls' (*ibid*: 470).

Managing the tensions: the crucial role of front-line managers

In effect, there is a trade-off between the 'hardware' and 'software' requirements in lean processes and in high-performing work systems generally. Too much emphasis on the hardware and a form of neo-Taylorism occurs, marked especially by bullying and pressure tactics by managers. Too much emphasis on the software, the behavioural aspects of lean working, and production levels may fall. How much time should be given to problem-solving, or training and skill acquisition, or to team briefing and communication? The two subsystems, soft and hard, are in tension and getting the balance right is difficult, especially when there are pressures from shareholders, customers, suppliers, or competitors.

Cost-cutting and downsizing can put intense pressure on new work systems, as noted in research on TQM (Edwards *et al.* 1998). It is not so much a question of having the skill, motivational and involvement-focused HR policies in place, as making them work. What brings these policies alive is the behaviour of managers, especially the immediate managers or team leaders. The way these managers are able to achieve this balance and bring policies alive is itself a reflection of the organisational control systems, for example, the type of hard, financial performance measures used, compared with the more qualitative data more typically found in HRM. It is often to these team leaders that responsibility is devolved rather than directly to team members themselves, thus making their role pivotal (Delbridge, Lowe and Oliver 2000: 127). The ability of front-line managers to bring these HRM policies alive is an outcome of the way these managers are themselves selected, managed, motivated and rewarded. Thus, the type of HPWSs required for flexible specialisation need to be considered in relation to both non-managerial employees and their managers.

In research in the branches of a Canadian bank, Bartel (2000) noted the relationship between high-performing branches and branch mangers who talked to their staff and involved them in decision-making, compared to lower-performing branches where management was more remote. This implies that many of the HR policies designed to suit high-performance work systems, or flexible specialisation, can only be applied by line managers, as has often been argued in the debate on 'returning HRM to the line' (McGovern, Gratton, Hope-Hailey, Stiles and Truss 1997). But it also means that managing the managers is crucial, especially in giving them space to undertake and learn people management skills. Thus, the HRM implications of new ways of working are profound not just in terms of worker skill, motivation and involvement, but in terms also of eliciting the appropriate management leadership skills to make these policies 'come alive'.

Conclusions and implications

One of the most important, if not the most important, influences on people's experience of employment is the way their work is organised. The social and technical organisation of work – what people do, what they do it with, and how they work with others – deeply affects the level of skill and prior training needed, and the extent to which individuals can use their mental abilities. It is the most important source of job satisfaction or motivation to perform. Work organisation also deeply influences the opportunities to participate in decision-making. As such, it is a fundamental building block in HRM. Strategically, too, work organisation is the fulcrum of the operation of the firm where people combine with technology, and interact with customers and suppliers. Responsibility for the design of work systems, then, can never be wholly the responsibility of the HR professional. Indeed, for much of the short life of the personnel and HR specialism, work organisation has been taken as given. For much of the period of mass production, and its equivalent in offices and service organisations, the role of personnel specialists was to ensure an adequate supply of appropriately trained workers, and to keep the peace with the trade unions when necessary. The origins of the factory system, based on the fragmented division of labour and management control over workers, later made 'scientific' by F. W. Taylor, were deeply embedded in the mental maps of managers around the world as to the way work ought to be organised, not for themselves of course, but for the industrial and office proletariat.

What is loosely called the 'transformation of work' involved the adoption in some workplaces of new forms of work organisation. This has more often been the case in advanced industrial countries which have relatively high labour costs, but pools of experienced and trained workers. The new forms of work organisation tend to be based around the adoption of teamworking, multi-skilling and the integration of routine with non-routine tasks, thus requiring higher levels of discretionary behaviour. Since employees now exercise greater choice in what is done, when and how, the problem for management becomes that of how to ensure people are motivated to perform, obtain the skills to do so, and are provided with opportunities to participate. In so doing, the advantages for the firm are often seen in lower unit labour costs (since fewer people, working better, improve efficiency); the ability to meet customer or end-user needs quickly (since employees are more likely to be in direct contact with customers); and to produce at higher quality or reduce defect levels (since quality is built into the work processes of 'right first time' and workers solve problems as they occur). Thus, the operational requirements of 'quicker, better and cheaper' can only be delivered by new forms of work organisation and HPWSs. Add to this the requirement for innovation in product and processes that has become much more prevalent in the millennium age, and the need for strategic thought and action in the way people are managed, and the way they 'deliver' business strategies, is evident. This is seen, for example, in the new lexicon of 'the learning organisation', 'knowledge management', and 'the agile corporation'.

It is important not to exaggerate these trends, or to underestimate the difficulties in designing and implementing high-performance work systems. There is an inevitable trade-off or tension between the 'hardware' and 'software' of such work systems: between the requirements of operations and those of the people who perform them. These work systems can be fragile and can be associated with higher levels of stress and work intensification. But they can also be a source of greater job satisfaction and a sense of achievement.

At their most successful, these types of work organisation can be a source of sustained competitive advantage since, try as they might, other firms find it hard to copy, at least for a long time, the unique, idiosyncratic way people and technology combine, learn and adapt. In some sectors, the adoption of HPWSs has become an industry norm, or a 'table stake', and those unable or unwilling to adopt these work practices find they are at a competitive disadvantage. Meanwhile, in workplaces with routine, repetitive work and few requirements for innovation (and there are plenty of these), the fundamentals of the factory system with the division of labour, surveillance and direct management control, remain the most effective and most cost-efficient way of organising work. This will remain the case for as long as there is a ready supply of labour, as in developing countries, and working conditions do not challenge tenets of social legitimacy sufficiently to trigger government intervention or international outrage against low pay and child labour, for example.

The implication is that strategic choice is necessary in designing work systems and integrating them with, and within, the way people are managed, motivated, skilled and provided with opportunities to participate. These choices are logically derived from wider competitive strategies of what sort of markets and what sort of competition the firm wishes to face now and in the future. The simple 'decision tree' model from competitive strategy to HR strategy is, however, deceptive, as we explained in Chapter 3. An organisation's choice of work system will be influenced as well by social and ethical values, and by the labour market and legislative context in which it is set. New forms of work organisation are driven in part by labour shortages and the inability to drive down costs by cutting wages. That is, the relationship between competitive strategies and HRM is more symbiotic than directive.

6

Linking work systems and models of employment

Work restructuring of the sort analysed in the previous chapter changes roles and responsibilities and has implications for the wide range of HR policies linked to human capital acquisition, motivation and involvement. A focus on HPWSs is often associated with downsizing (redundancy and job loss) and de-layering (the removal of a layer or layers of command in the management hierarchy). Osterman's (2000) research on 'high-performance work organisations' in the USA (HPWOs or, as used more commonly in this book, HPWSs) found that they generated a higher probability of layoffs in subsequent years while also experiencing a growth in jobs. This paradox 'implies that the layoffs associated with HPWOs are better thought of as reorganisation than as reductions in enterprise size' (*ibid*: 192). Unlike the industry studies of Appelbaum *et al.* (2001), Osterman's survey of US workplaces with 50 or more employees argues that the adoption of HPWSs has not improved wages for the workers involved (as noted in Chapter 1). Thus, while workers may find their jobs more meaningful, and even enjoyable (Freeman and Rogers 1995), it seems likely that the benefits of the adoption of HPWSs are mixed. HPWSs may meet criteria for productivity and flexibility improvements, but improvements in social legitimacy are less often achieved (the three goal domains of HRM established in Chapter 1). Osterman (2000) questions the long-term sustainability of these systems and wonders if they may trigger passive resistance from the workforce. Interestingly, he shows how the presence of a union in an establishment introducing HPWSs 'sharply reduced the probability of . . . associated layoffs. Evidently unions were able to deploy their power effectively' (Osterman 2000: 191). The union effect is discussed in Chapter 8. The purpose of this chapter is to look at restructuring by asking how the firm, in the context of its environment, establishes different models of employment and how these have been changing in recent decades.

Restructuring is associated with terms like 'outsourcing', 'core-periphery', 'contingent labour' and, more generally, 'externalisation'. All, in different ways, refer to the growing tendency for firms to differentiate their labour force strategies between the internal, where employees have relative job security and access to training in return for task flexibility and high-paced work, and the external. Here, the links between the individual worker and the firm are less certain but in return economic rewards may, for those with rare skills, be higher while others may gain little. In some cases, workers are employed by a temporary work agency and not by the firm which becomes, in effect, a client. Or they may be employed by the outsourced contractor, for example a haulage contractor which took over the contract to run the firm's transport fleet. Here, the drivers still work from the same locations, and may even drive the same vehicles, but they are now employed by a new organisation, often on revised terms, once the transfer period, protected in Europe by legislation, is over.

This trend to redraw the contractual map of employment raises a whole set of questions that each firm has to deal with if the aim is to develop strategic human resource management delivering productivity, flexibility and legitimacy. For example, in Chapter 4, looking at the implications of the resource-based view, we noted how a number of authors saw one of the critically important parts as being the ability to erect 'mobility barriers' so that the firm's crucial and rare human resource capability or strength stays and provides 'rent'. Retention is a crucial issue in managing employees with such rare attributes and this tends to drive aspects of HR policy in these firms. But can and do all employees of the firm exhibit such rare attributes linked to creating customer value? Some jobs are routine although essential like security, certain clerical functions, accountancy and aspects of the HR function. Here, one option may be to lower mobility barriers, or to put it in economist language, to reduce the exit costs such that if the firm wishes to reduce numbers employed it can do so easily. One way of doing so in some call centres, for example, is to rely on the growing student labour market while others use agency staff (Grimshaw, Ward, Rubery and Beynon 2001). Neither party has high expectations of the longevity of the employment relationship. Is it then possible – and desirable – for the firm to attempt to erect mobility barriers for some while simultaneously reducing them for others? And how does the firm know who is 'core' and who is 'periphery'? What impact do factors of social legitimacy inside and outside the firm, reflected, for example, in labour law, social beliefs and union responses, have on this? What influence do workers themselves have on whether to opt to be the loyal company worker or, as sometimes described, to be a 'mercenary' in the modern flexible labour market? Who in any case are the winners and losers in this 'new labour market'?

The rise and disintegration of the internal labour market

There is, of course, nothing much new in this bifurcation between insiders and outsiders in the labour market. Go to the Printers' Arms or the Bricklayers' Inn or other typical English city-centre pub and the chances are that this was the place where, in the mid 19th century, skilled artisans in a particular trade met each evening with the local secretary of the union to hear of job availability with those masters willing to pay the union rate. Some craftsmen 'tramped' from town to town in search of jobs and knew the named pub which gave the chance of lodgings and a place to meet fellow craft workers. This is not that much different from meetings in motorway service stations or 'satellite offices' of peripatetic professionals using face to face exchanges in addition to web, e-mail and fax communication methods to swap market information, to network and learn from each other. Some of these people will be self-employed while others will be contract workers, but very few of them will have normal or standard contracts of employment.

In the mid to late 19th century an employment contract, and indeed the whole idea of employment, as opposed to paid work, was unusual. Dockers queued each morning to be picked by the gang master for work and paid per hour, a practice which continued up until the post-Second World War period, both in the UK and in the USA, as shown in the 1960s film *On the Waterfront*. This type of spot contracting, or daily or hourly employment, was common in many industries but habit and familiarity tended to give an impression of permanency for many, until, that is, the trade cycle returned and unemployment rose. With no social security system, large families, and usually only one wage earner in the family (the father), economic downturns triggering wage cuts and unemployment were widely feared. This reliance on the external labour market, with its uncontrolled fluctuations, had deleterious consequences for workers, of course, but increasingly too for employers. This was especially the case in the emerging industries which used more sophisticated technologies and work processes, like gas companies, steel works, the railways and chemicals. This is where distinctive worker skills and safe working practices were necessary to operate the plant, implying the need for some form of training and some form of investment in people. Capital accumulation, economies of scale and the development of national or even international markets led to the creation of large firms, the requirement of a cadre of managers and the development of 'rules' of employment exclusive to, and inside, the firm. The result was the emergence of the 'internal labour market' in large firms (Doeringer and Piore 1971, Jacoby 1984, Osterman 1982). Marsden (1999: 3) sees this as 'one of the two great innovations lying behind the rise of the modern business enterprise. The first was the development of new supplies of capital. The second has revolutionised the organisation of labour services, providing firms and workers with a very flexible method of coordination and a platform for investing in skills.'

Rules in the internal labour market

The internal labour market (ILM) developed as a means of establishing some form of control over the labour market and the labour process. This was developed not just by employers for their own benefit, to keep valued workers by offering a form of career and job security and to ensure discipline, for example, but was favoured by governments and the emerging trade union movements as a means to help reduce conflict through a process of 'institutionalisation'. This focused on the emergence of rules to govern the employment relationship. The authorship of these rules is discussed in Chapter 8 but here it is the nature of these rules used to regularise employment and especially to build and manage expectations that is important. Osterman (1987) sees these rules coalescing into four groups. Each is a form of exchange relationship as expressed in 'a fair day's work for fair day's pay', otherwise known as the 'wage-effort', or more broadly the 'effort-reward bargain'. Arbitrary acts by immediate bosses and 'unreasonable' refusals to work by workers were increasingly brought within the ambit of employment law, but in large companies, especially those with trade unions, social regulation went much further. Jobs became defined and the implicit job description of who does what became codified. These *job definition rules*, the first of Osterman's categories, typically get redefined only periodically because of technical change or the introduction of new forms of work organisation. Thus 'multi-skilling', often a key part of HPWSs (high-performance work systems), is an attempt to reclassify and open up jobs through 'job enlargement', or sometimes, 'job enrichment'.

Career development rules refer to the extent to which more senior, or more rewarding, jobs are reserved for 'insiders' to provide some basis of career development or career expectation. In its most developed form, the ILM has a single, or very few, 'ports of entry' (such as graduate recruitment) and with subsequent progression up the career ladder based on understood criteria such as seniority, qualifications or promotion panels. Here 'cradle to grave' employment systems emerged over time for salaried or white-collar employees especially, closely linked to the emergence of forms of bureaucratic control (Edwards 1979). In bureaucratic control, jobs were not defined by the technology used to produce the product, and the concomitant operational or production process (the assembly line where 'technical control' is more likely to be used), but were based on social relationships: employees were expected to show loyalty, commitment and compliance. These attributes came with organisational experience, developing a form of what we now call 'social capital'. Of course, such public and private bureaucracies were better suited for stable circumstances and slow change. Come the rapid adoption of information technology, the opening of markets and the focus on cost regulation, and the fundamental requirements for internal career development rules cannot be sustained in their entirety. Choices have to be made about who stays and who goes and the terms of a new relationship are based less on career than on performance.

This merges into the third of Osterman's categories, that of *job security rules* and the extent to which explicit commitments are made to individuals about the expected time they can hope to stay within the firm. In this context, it is widely believed that the move in recent years has been to the loose idea of 'employability' rather than employment security. Here the onus is placed on the individual to ensure the accumulation of training and experience in order to remain attractive in the labour market, whether internal or external. The employer may provide opportunities for human capital development but it is up to the individual to take advantage of them.

The fourth of Osterman's rule types relates to *wage rules*. How is the person's salary or wage to be determined? In the simple or direct control of early industry (and still found in small owner-managed firms around the world), it is at the behest or whim of the owner or the owner's agent, the manager, for as long as the individual worker concurs. Labour law in most countries tries to limit arbitrariness by (often) requiring written contracts of employment, a limit on the hours to be worked in a week, or a minimum number of days of holiday required, both paid and unpaid and, in some cases, with minimum wage rates established. ILM wage rules crucially revolve around the effort-reward relationship and the need for job classification rules to be reflected in wage differences (or differentials) to establish a linkage with the career development process. Thus, the crucial choices are the design of salary scales, the way in which the individual moves up the scales and the extent to which payment is linked to performance. Job evaluation is the typical way in which the 'worth' of one job is rated against the worth of others to create a finely tuned internal set of job hierarchies clustered into grades. Traditionally, the logic of job evaluation was to create 'felt-fair' job grades linked to pay, with no account taken of individual worker attributes such as hard work, enthusiasm or laziness, since these were covered by the rules in the other subsystems (promotion under career rules, dismissal for incompetence under job security rules). This presupposed that rates of pay in the external market moved slowly and generally at the same pace for most people. However, when the demand for one occupation rapidly increases, for ICT professionals for example, this becomes untenable. Demand varies hugely in the external market for different types of skills, creating pressures that go well beyond the ILM rules. The move to a performance orientation through a focus on customers and their satisfaction has also driven the fashion for pay related to performance.

Limits to internal labour markets

In effect, in its most elaborated form, the ILM became the defining feature of sophisticated personnel management in the 1960s and 1970s (Foulkes 1980) but had within it structural flaws which rendered it increasingly inappropriate for the more turbulent circumstances of recent decades. One of the structural flaws that became apparent was the conservatism of ILMs as practised in many firms. This became noticeable in two ways. First, not surprisingly, employment systems tended to reflect the social divisions in the society in which they existed. This was seen in the divisions between manual and non-manual, works and staff, and a hierarchy of privilege seen in the allocation of cars and car park spaces, holiday entitlements, and canteens demarcated by status. Once enshrined in rules and justified with a veneer of rational decision-making, it becomes hard to bring about change, with each group concerned to protect their own vested interests in the system. That is, whilst the rules exist to reflect wider social structures, they simultaneously tend to reinforce these same divisions by their very existence and the fact they are embedded formally in rule books, and cognitively in beliefs and expectations. Change is difficult; the system is 'sticky'. The very stickiness of the system can lead to the adoption of alternative systems seen in outsourcing or even in plant relocation to new sites in another country or region where the external rules are less rigid and the internal market rules have yet to be created.

The second conservatism, which also derived from wider social beliefs and structures, is that ILMs tended to be profoundly gendered (Wajcman 2000) such that the dominant model was that of a male, full-time worker pursuing a career while women were trapped in secondary labour markets with less access to training both inside and outside the workplace, undertaking 'women's' work whether as unskilled or trapped in the lower levels of the professional occupations. W.H. Whyte's (1956) famous study of the American corporation in the mid 1950s was appropriately called *The Organization Man*. The growth in women's labour force participation, now near to reaching parity with men in many societies, and the wider social changes in gender relations have profoundly questioned the legitimacy of the sexual division of labour, both ethically and practically. In the 1950s and 60s, when production industry supported relatively full employment amongst male manual workers, married women formed the 'obvious' fresh source of labour to support the expansion of service sector industries in Britain (and elsewhere) (Bruegal and Perrons 1998). Legislation in the external labour market challenged, to a degree, the assumptions embedded in the internal system, seen in moves to establish rights to equal pay and protection against discrimination. This, combined with labour market demand pressures and changes to the number of women, especially graduate women, entering the labour market, provided the context in which firm strategies for employment systems were, and continue to be, shaped. That is, unlike the assumptions in most American models of employment systems (for example, see Bamberger and Meshoulam (2000)), choices are set within a social context. HR strategists, like any other, are not totally free agents.

In a detailed study of the erosion of ILMs in four British organisations (a bank, a major retailer, a telephone company and a local authority), Grimshaw *et al.* (2001) note how in different ways the fundamentals of ILMs – job permanence, career progression, wage systems, narrow ports of entry and access to training – were all challenged. They conclude that for low skilled workers:

> The transformation in career path and opportunities for skills development is drastic. Entry into the contemporary large organisation may require intermittent periods of employment as a temporary agency worker, rather than direct recruitment onto a permanent contract subject to a pre-determined period of probation. Internal job ladders may be horizontal rather than vertical, with greater emphasis on external opportunities for promotion ... Practices of delayering mean that entry and exit through the organisation is more likely to occur at the same point on the job ladder as there are limited opportunities for internal career progression. Finally, the volume of inflows and outflows through some

organisations has risen with the use of temporary employment contracts, and job security has been weakened by policies of outsourcing and downsizing (p 50).

In all of these ways, the process of erosion has involved a move from internalisation to externalisation but it is a question of degree rather than the wholesale dismantlement of ILMs. The process has two important attributes. First, externalisation is also associated with 'individualisation': that is, a focus on each individual worker (a wider term than 'employee'). In particular, the process of opening up the internal labour market to the external market, which is more volatile, is linked to risk sharing or a risk burden being placed on the worker. If ILMs gave job security and guaranteed incomes, among other benefits, then product market fluctuations and profit ups and downs were borne by the employer, who took the rough with the smooth. With the individualisation of pay linked to performance, reduced job security and the growth of contingent contracts with little protection, some of these risks are shifted to workers, especially those who are now working for agencies or have contingent or short term contracts.

Second, internalisation was, in part, a reflection of social beliefs about the good employer. As Grimshaw *et al.* (2001: 46) note in traditional ILMs, opportunistic behaviour by employers (such as redundancy, taking advantage of employees) is minimised by its potential negative impact on the reputation of the organisation amongst future labour market recruits. However, they note that now the emphasis on financial markets runs counter to this, with share prices improving when redundancies are announced. Share-based compensation schemes for senior executives no doubt add to this pressure. In tight labour markets, especially for skilled employees, company (and sector) reputation is important for recruitment and employees have expectations of training, participation and security. Where there are high levels of unemployment, or where the rate of change in the unemployment level is negative and growing, expectations of job insecurity rise and the value of ILMs becomes disconnected from perceived reality. Doogan (2001) notes a major paradox where, in the UK at least, perceptions of job insecurity rose dramatically in the 1990s while actual job tenure – the length of time people work for the same employer – also grew. This was particularly the case for part-time workers. His explanation is that insecurity is, or has been, 'manufactured' and is a conscious strategy of Government that arises from attempts to increase productivity and competitiveness, especially in the public sector (p 439). The same could apply to large firm restructuring or downsizing, although whether this is a conscious strategy to 'manufacture insecurity' is more questionable, even though the term 'positive insecurity' is sometimes used to explain why insecure workers tend to work longer hours, take less time off sick and give more effort, or at least try to be seen to give more effort. As Heery and Salmon (1999) note, (in)security has three dimensions – as a job property, as an environmental phenomenon in which jobs exist, and as a subjective experience affecting employee attitudes to security. In ILMs as classically defined and experienced, job security was high in both the job and the wider labour market. This influenced attitudes to it – a belief in jobs for life. Now, even though the actual experience of many is long term employment, the environment has changed as major job cuts are announced regularly. This, in turn, has changed some people's attitudes towards job insecurity, both in fearing it and accepting its inevitability, and indeed its legitimacy. This marks a weakening of the ILM as the dominant model of the employment system if we see it as a social construction guiding beliefs and behaviours. This is true whether or not ILMs exist as a statistical 'fact'.

Differentiated models of employment

The end of the dominance of the inclusive ILM has been associated with substantial rethinking and reconceptualisation of employment models within organisations. This is sometimes seen in terms of core and periphery, where privileged employees in the core are differentiated from, and to a degree buffered by, more 'peripheral' workers who may be employed by the firm or may be external to it yet provide labour for it. Of course, as we have already noted, ILMs were often demarcated internally on hierarchical and gender lines, but the logic of these new employment models is different, based on analysis of the value of employees' work to the organisation in helping to meet end user requirements, and in the uniqueness of skills and knowledge held by employees (Lepak and Snell 1999). The underlying question is simple to ask, but difficult in practice to answer: should the organisation seek to develop and nurture its human talent or hire externally as and when required? In the language of operational management, the choice is between 'make' or 'buy'. Since, however, the answer is going to vary between different occupational groups within the firm, the question is whom to 'buy' and whom to 'make' and how to distinguish between them.

A good starting point is shown in Figure 6.1. This divides the type of occupational groups in the firm into basic quadrants classified by the type of skill or knowledge

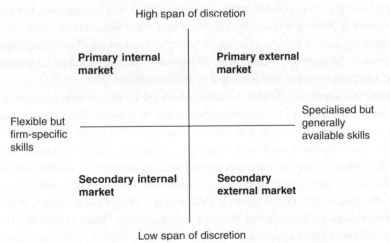

Figure 6.1 Organisational and firm-specific labour markets

required to do the job and the extent to which work has high or low levels of discretion – that is, the degree to which individuals have choice about how and when they use their skill and knowledge. We noted in the previous chapter how HPWSs crucially rely on higher levels of discretionary behaviour. High-discretion jobs used to be confined to the upper echelons of the organisation, the managers and professional workers, at the time of the dominance of Scientific Management. Now they can include operational employees working in teams in some parts of the 'lean organisation'. Of course, there remain plenty of organisations still divided between employees and managers in the traditional way.

The inclusion of the horizontal axis in Figure 6.1, relating to the type of skill and knowledge required, makes for a more subtle distinction between the types of employees. Some jobs require specialised skills which are generic or generally available in, and supplied by, the external labour market (for example, professional workers, whether in ICT, medicine, law or education). The prime requirement here is for the organisation to recruit from the external market people who are already qualified and reward them accordingly. To do their job, provided the tasks required of them are appropriate for their skill, they need very little specific understanding of the organisation and how it works beyond a familiarisation with office routines. Should the organisation employ them on open, long-term contracts or should it 'buy' them for their specific skills for as long as these are required? It may be that these skills are needed for only a short period or for less than full-time working. The option becomes available of using external contractors or specialist agencies on short, fixed-term contracts. It may also be that there is insufficient expertise in the organisation to manage a particular skill set and the use of external experts provides an opportunity to learn from them or leverage their skill (Matusik and Hill 1998). These professionals constitute the primary external market, the top right quadrant in Figure 6.1. What sort of human resource management is appropriate for these types of workers? We consider this in detail later in the chapter but for now it is appropriate to note that the type of linkage with the organisation is akin to a client relationship centred on transactions. Thus, the type of psychological contracting (explored in Chapter 7) is more likely to be transactional, specific and time-limited rather than open-ended and relational (Rousseau 1995).

The secondary external market is also inhabited by people requiring little, if any, particular knowledge of the organisation where they work. Here, though, jobs are designed to require little skill and discretionary effort. These are de-skilled jobs and the people doing them need little training, and are expected to perform effectively from the first day. Traditionally, this type of work is seen in low-skilled manual work like cleaning or packaging. In the service economy it is often undertaken by agency workers – in call centres, for example (Ward *et al.* 2001). One agency, in a presentation to prospective clients, listed the advantages of using their contract staff (Purcell 1999a) for these types of jobs as:

- enhances flexibility ('turn on and off like a tap')
- no legal or psychological contract with the individual
- you outsource the management problems associated with non-core staff
- greater cost efficiency (on average 15–20 per cent).

This agency was selling its services on the basis that the client organisation could focus its strategic human resource management on its core workforce and leave the management problems of non-core workers to the agency. This meant the agency would deal with the recruitment, selection, remuneration, control and turnover of the non-core workers. The implication is that firms will often find it hard to manage differentiated employment systems.

The more complex a job, and the more a variety of skills for routine and non-routine tasks are combined in the same job, the more likely it is that skill requirements are for flexibility related to the specific needs of the organisation. This is shown on the left hand side of Figure 6.1. In the resource-based view of strategy (Chapter 4), emphasis is placed on human capital and organisational processes being rare, hard-to-copy and idiosyncratic. These idiosyncratic contingencies linked to path dependency (the historical pattern of learning in the firm) can become a source of sustained competitive advantage since competitors find it hard to copy, at least for a while. Thus:

> Behind most definitions of core employees is the common theme of product, service or organisational knowledge that can never be bought but has to be created . . . core employees are those requiring some organisation specific skill, knowledge or attitude in order to be effective both in their own job and the degree of support provided to others, especially the areas of resource strength. It is these employees who are most likely to require or benefit from . . . high commitment management (Purcell 1996: 19).

The distinction between the primary and the secondary internal markets shown in Figure 6.1 makes a lot of sense. The primary internal employees are those with high levels of discretion requiring high levels of skills and competency, much of which is derived from the organisation. These workers, and the way they learn and interact with each other, managing knowledge and developing high levels of social capital seen in shared languages, codes of behaviour, rituals and so forth (Nahapiet and Ghoshal 1998) constitute the human resource strength of the organisation. As such, since it takes time (investment) to develop this distinctive human capital and organisational process, 'organisations may logically emphasise *commitment-based* HR systems that focus on long-term relationships and internal development of skills . . . (requiring) an open and trusting culture' (Snell, Lepak and Youndt 1999: 180–1). These are the employees where the question of resource immobility becomes important. Thus, managing retention is critical especially when the external labour market is buoyant. So too is performance management since employees need to be motivated to exercise discretionary behaviour. Boxall (1998: 268) sees these employees as the 'inner core', consisting of 'those managers, technical specialists and strategically located workers who are responsible for valuable innovations or for successful imitation . . . Loss of key members of the inner core undermines the firm's capacity to adapt to a changing environment and to lead adaptive change in the industry'.

The secondary internal market (called the 'outer core' by Boxall (1998)) consists of people with appropriate industry skills providing customer service, for example, who require good knowledge of the firm's products and services to be effective. They provide crucial support to the inner core and have to have a thorough understanding of 'how things are done'. Thus, 'the inner core . . . provides the "adaptive capacity" of the firm while the outer core provides it with "credible operational capacity"' (Boxall 1998: 268). While inner core workers in the primary internal labour market are needed for innovation and adaptive learning, especially in relation to the firm and its markets and competitors, the outer core (the secondary internal labour market) are required for excellence of routines and dependability. Here, too, labour turnover can be a real problem if it gets too high (over 20 per cent, for example, in call centres) and the need is to achieve high levels of organisational commitment and positive working relationships at the individual and collective level.

Does theory help differentiate between types of employment systems?

Transaction cost analysis

The model of internal and external, primary and secondary labour markets in the firm, or at least the large firm, is intuitively appealing. The problem is that it is too generalised and managers often have difficulty in choosing between types. Indeed, such models as shown in Figure 6.1 are always ideal-typical abstractions. We describe each quadrant at the extreme or the 'pure' edge. In reality, many companies will be clustered in the middle with no clear evidence on who is, let alone who should be, core or periphery, internal or external. How then to choose? The work of the American economist, Oliver Williamson (1975, 1985) is, at first sight, helpful here but, as we shall see, does have major limitations when applied in the 'real' world.

Williamson built on the work of Coase (1937) to focus on the cost of economic transactions, otherwise known as transaction cost analysis (TCA). This allows the fundamental question of 'why employ anyone?' to be answered, or more pertinently, 'who should be employed by the firm and when?' and, alternatively, 'should people be contracted to provide a service?' In the former, employment is restricted to, and in part controlled by, the 'hierarchy' of the firm while in the latter 'the market', meaning the external labour market, is the prime mechanism for providing and pricing labour in the short term. In labour law, the distinction is between a 'contract of employment' and 'a contract for services', the latter applying especially to the self-employed. TCA can be used to think about the most efficient, least cost way of organising employment in terms not only of how the negotiation of the contract price is best achieved but also the best way to control the labour process, the effort side of the effort-reward relationship. Thus TCA allows for the inclusion of the 'transactions' or activities required to monitor employee performance and ensure that skills are used appropriately and effectively.

There are four attributes of transactions that inform the analysis. These are:

- *asset specificity*: the extent to which the assets (knowledge, skill) required and held by people doing the task are generally available or specific to the firm;
- *uncertainty*: the extent to which the task performed can easily be defined, structured and made predictable or involves 'uncertainty', or has idiosyncratic elements that rely on individuals to use their discretion;
- *frequency*: the extent to which the tasks are performed with high frequency or are needed periodically or for short periods;
- *ease of measurement*: how simple and cost effective it is to measure the extent and effectiveness of task activity and completion.

Figure 6.2 uses the four elements to suggest how TCA can inform decision-making in different employment models.

TCA can be used to predict that the use of contingent labour (the American term for limited duration contracts whether agency staff, fixed-term contract workers, casuals or freelance workers) will be high when:

- the task performed is easily defined and has few elements (single-skilled as opposed to multi-skilled), that is, low uncertainty;
- workers performing the tasks do not need organisation-specific knowledge, for example about customers, products, services or procedures, to be effective, that is, asset specificity is low;
- the requirement or demand for these tasks is periodic or thought to be infrequent (for example, staff are needed to launch a new product or meet exceptional demand). In these cases, length of service would be low with no promises of contract renewal, that is, frequency is (relatively) low;

Attribute of transactions	Internal labour market ('hierarchy')	External labour market ('market')
Asset specificity	high	low
Uncertainty	high	low
Frequency	high	low
Ease of measurement	difficult	easy

Source: Williamson (1975, 1985)

Figure 6.2 Transaction cost analysis applied to different employment models

- task performance is easily measured, for example using automated surveillance systems commonly found in call centres and supermarkets and where the pertinent measure is of outputs (number of calls, sales and so on) rather than inputs (attitude, motivation, skill). Performance measurement is easier to do when tasks are 'stand alone' and unrelated to the work of other people.

Behind much of this type of analysis are the twin issues of work organisation design and the form of management control to ensure that what ought to be done is done. 'Internal' jobs, especially those associated with the adoption of HPWSs and lean processes, become more complex and multi-faceted. As we saw in the last chapter, this tends to increase the requirement for employee discretionary behaviour. Thus, one can hypothesise that the internal labour market – the hierarchy in Williamson's terms – will be used when there is a need for trust, open ended contracts, and the building of a relationship between the firm and the employees seen in high levels of organisational commitment. Trust between managers and employees is crucial in HPWSs and lean processes since managers have to trust workers without continuous checking and control.

HR architecture and configurations

Lepak and Snell (1999) combine TCA with theories derived from the resource-based view (as discussed in Chapter 4) and human capital theory (Becker 1964) to suggest a more comprehensive view of the elements of what they term 'HR architecture'. The root proposition of human capital theory is that the firm will invest in employee skills only when it is justifiable in terms of future productivity. The Lepak and Snell model is shown in Figure 6.3.

There are strong similarities with Figure 6.1 but Lepak and Snell move the debate on employment models significantly further by suggesting how different models are associated with different relationships and different types of what they call 'HR configurations'. The familiar pattern of the HR configuration for ILMs, the 'inner core', is found in quadrant 1. The high value external market (for such people as design engineers, ICT specialists, recruitment specialists) is shown in quadrant 2. Here advanced skills are required, the relationship is symbiotic and the HR configuration is predominantly market driven. Where tasks require neither unique (that is, organisation-specific) human capital, nor valuable skills, the key words are 'contracting', 'transactional' and 'compliance' (quadrant 3). Quadrant 4, however, is unusual. Lepak and Snell (1999: 40–1) give an example of an attorney (solicitor) who knows the firm well and understands its needs and ways of working. Either for reasons of size, or preference of either party, the relationship is a contract for services which continues beyond one transaction. The relationship is one of alliance, partnership and collaboration. Outsourcing or sub-contracting takes on these attributes where a longer-term relationship is required so that both parties have a deep understanding

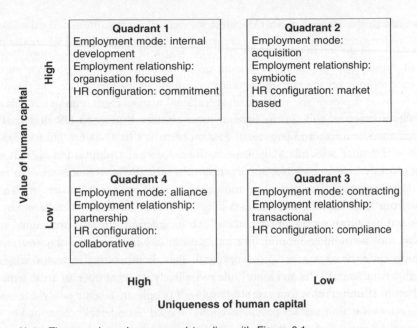

Quadrant 1	Quadrant 2
Employment mode: internal development	Employment mode: acquisition
Employment relationship: organisation focused	Employment relationship: symbiotic
HR configuration: commitment	HR configuration: market based

Quadrant 4	Quadrant 3
Employment mode: alliance	Employment mode: contracting
Employment relationship: partnership	Employment relationship: transactional
HR configuration: collaborative	HR configuration: compliance

Value of human capital — High / Low

High / Low

Uniqueness of human capital

Note: The axes have been moved to align with Figure 6.1

Source: Adapted from Lepak and Snell (1999)

Figure 6.3 Summary of Lepak and Snell's 'human resource architecture'

of the other (Marshall 2001). The importance of quadrant 4 is that it draws attention to the interrelationship between trends in outsourcing and supply chain relationships and similar developments in strategic human resource management. Thus in quadrants 2, 3 and 4 the contract relationship may be with the person or it may be with a labour market intermediary like a temporary work agency (which have grown rapidly in the last decade), or with a sub-contractor or outsource provider. Only quadrant 1 is unambiguously internal and commitment-based, requiring direct employment by the firm itself.

Choosing employment systems in practice

These theories of employment systems are elegant, and they provide a useful basis for thinking through the strategic issues, but they are only partial. Four types of limitations apply. There is no consideration of employer choice in the design of work systems; the firm is considered as an entirely free agent unencumbered with environmental constraints from the labour market, the financial system and wider institutional arrangements and beliefs; the costs and benefits of moving from one type of employment model to another are not considered; and the preferences of the workers themselves are ignored. Let us take each of these in turn.

Choices in the design of work systems

The nature of the job in terms of the type and degree of skill required is fundamental to all employment models. The assumption is that there is a single decision tree where decisions on the type of market to compete in lead to choices on the technology to be deployed and the type of operational management required. Job design configurations are made in the light of these choices, leading to HR decisions on recruitment, training and pay levels. The problem is that tasks are often confused with jobs. Under Scientific Management, the division of labour is fragmented into single tasks wherever possible, but organisations actually have choices on what tasks to cluster together. The typical presumption of HPWSs is that greater efficiencies flow from multi-tasking and multi-skilling of jobs, and the social construction of jobs and beliefs about the importance of job satisfaction can lead organisations to design jobs more in the round. The more multi-tasked a job, and the greater the interdependency of one person's work with that of others (as in teamworking – another fundamental design choice), the more likely it is that internal arrangements will apply. If universities, for example, employed people on 'teaching only' contracts, then external labour market providers could be used (wonderfully described by the columnist Laurie Taylor as 'Dons-U-Like') or people employed on single semester contracts. If the expectation is that the university lecturer will not only teach but be a tutor to students, engage in research, write papers, represent the university at conferences, engage in administration, undertake student admission and be responsible for the quality of his or her own work, then a long-term relational-type employment system is likely. The latter will be more attractive to potential quality recruits than the former, so that the quality and quantity of labour supply is affected by the choice of work systems. The choice of work systems is one of the fundamental building blocks of strategic HRM, a key argument in this book. It cannot be just taken for granted.

Environmental constraints

The second objection to or limitation of the theories is that, as in classic Anglo-American approaches to theories of the firm, the assumption is made that choices are unconstrained, or rather they can be used to suggest what ought to happen if there were no limitations on choice in a 'perfect' world. People in the real world often despair of this type of thinking. Two types of environmental constraints are particularly important in influencing choices on employment systems. First, continuing skill shortages in many economies, even where there is unemployment, create severe limits on the choices available to employers. Logic may dictate that jobs be externalised and job design simplified so that lower skilled people can be used. These types of low-paid, low-security jobs may well be filled if workers have few choices of alternative employment. In a period of high unemployment in the UK in the 1990s, for example, nearly all new jobs were part-time and/or temporary. As the economy recovered and unemployment fell between 1997 and 2001, most new jobs created were full-time and open-ended (mistakenly called 'permanent'). That is, the employer needed to make jobs more attractive when the labour market was tight. At times they may be unable to do so, and may have to rely on external agencies to supply workers at a higher price, even though their preference is to offer 'permanent' employment.

A good example here is nursing staff in the UK and the Netherlands where shortages, exacerbated by high levels of labour turnover and a failure to manage retention, have led to a rapid growth in the numbers of agency nurses (Audit Commission 2001). Nurses earn more for agency work than they do from the Health Service direct, on top of which the agency takes a fee. Why does this happen? It is a good example of a mismatch in employment systems. Traditionally the Health Service had an employment system built around strong internal labour markets for the various professional groups. However, professionals typically exhibit characteristics of the primary external market, or in Figure 6.3, quadrant 2, where contracting and market-based HRM are predicted. Strong internal labour markets, as we have explored, are 'sticky'. It is institutionally extremely difficult and expensive to adjust the wages of all to allow rates for one occupational group to be raised to the market level. And this presupposes that the solution is money, rather than such things as family-friendly policies, better teamworking within a hospital or a reduction in work-based stress.

Labour markets are strongly influenced by wider societal institutions, whether labour law, collective bargaining or wider social values. The change in the law following the election of New Labour in the UK in 1997, and the adoption of employment directives from the European Commission, led to agency workers, those on fixed contracts and others like freelancers who, in effect, worked only for one firm, getting improved rights such as four weeks of paid holiday per year. For many employers, the cost advantages of externalising employment disappeared. Agencies had to adapt to meet the new operating environment and began to offer holiday pay, sick pay and, in some cases, training and careers. That is, they had to show themselves as good employers, and both of the leading agencies in the UK decided to recognise trade unions. Koerne, Pot and Paauwe (2001) see the growing social legitimacy of temporary work agencies in the Netherlands as crucial in explaining the growth in penetration of agency work there. They note that this social factor is completely ignored by Williamson (1975, 1985), or rather, he 'takes it as given'. In other words, employer choice of employment systems is heavily influenced by the institutions and social values of the country in which they operate.

Figure 6.4 shows the reasons given by UK employers in 1998 for using agency and fixed-term contract workers. Some of the reasons fit neatly with the theories, such as 'obtain specialist skills', while other items listed reflect the labour market problems mentioned earlier, such as 'unable to fill vacancies'. The biggest categories (short-term cover, maternity or annual leave replacement) are attributes of an internal

Reason	Contingent agency workers	Fixed-term contract workers
Matching staff to peaks in demand	38	34
As a trial for a permanent job	–	22
Short-term cover for staff absence/vacancies	59	–
Cover for maternity leave or long/annual leave	16	10
Unable to fill vacancies	19	–
Obtain specialist skills	12	17
Freeze on permanent staff numbers	11	15
Other/unspecified	4	18

Notes: As percentage of the employers who use both or either form of contingent employment. An employer may give more than one reason.

Source: Cully *et al.* (1999)

Figure 6.4   Reasons of employers for use of contingent workers (percentages)

labour market where high levels of job security for insiders are reflected in the temporary use of outsiders to fill short-term vacancies. This helps to explain why the use of contingent workers is highest in those countries with the strongest institutional and legislative protection provided to people in employment. 'Matching staff to peaks in demand' also fits the theory in respect of 'frequency'. The firm does not know if there will be continuous (high-frequency) use of extra labour so relies, for a while at least, on the external labour market.

The final specified reason, 'freeze on permanent staff numbers' is illustrative of how financial, and especially share market pressures impinge on HRM. Here, head office dictates that no new employees can be taken on either because of a financial crisis or to influence the stock market (for an example, see Grimshaw *et al.* 2001). This can have dramatic consequences. One senior IBM manager said of his firm in 1996, following the dramatic loss of market and virtual collapse of the company in the 1980s:

> IBM halved its numbers of direct employees from 440,000 to 225,000 worldwide but we still had the same overall number of jobs as before, around 500,000. We have just shifted their status. The group will never go back to full employment in any way. It got its fingers too badly burned in the 1980s (quoted in Purcell 1999a: 246).

Costs in externalising employment systems

Choices of employment systems are strongly influenced, then, by a variety of external factors, financial, social and legislative, as well as the specific condition of the external labour market. But they are also strongly influenced by organisational history and the beliefs and values of the decision-makers. New entrants to a market, or firms opening greenfield sites, may choose quite different arrangements from well-established firms. This is illustrated in the different routes taken by two firms competing head-to-head in the industrial bottled gas market in the mid 1990s in the UK (Purcell 1996). British Oxygen was a long established player in the market with a dominant share. Air Products was a relatively new entrant but with lots of experience in the USA. In 1992, British Oxygen needed to improve delivery, cut costs and get customers to trade up where possible. They had a large existing distribution fleet. Painful negotiations with the drivers' union led to new hours of working, wider job responsibilities including customer relations, more training and cab-based information technology. Drivers became seen as key staff in direct contact with customers. At the same time, Air Products decided to outsource distribution to a specialist haulage contractor. There was no expectation here that drivers would know anything about gas beyond safety considerations. In the case of British Oxygen, drivers were considered a core part of the firm because they always had been, not because they possessed distinctive organisational knowledge or skills. Indeed this knowledge of the customer and the skill about gas systems had to be learned once the decision was made to give them customer relations responsibilities.

A similar case in New Zealand involved the privatisation of gas companies. Meters in domestic properties need to be read, but are meter readers just 'data harvesters' (single-task jobs suitable for outsourcing) or are they front-line customer service representatives (Peel and Boxall 2001)? There is no right answer. It depends on the uncertain and emergent process of strategy making as we explored in Chapter 2. All we can say with certainty is that the boundaries of employment systems have to be drawn somewhere and increasingly this involves a mixture of the internal and the external. Theory tells us which group should be in the core and why. In practice some firms choose the core for historical or institutional reasons and then design the jobs and the employment relationship to fit these core attributes, as in the case of British Oxygen. This is explicable. 'Many activities in firms ... are so taken for granted or so strongly endorsed by the firm's prevailing culture and power structure that decision-makers no longer even question the appropriateness or the rationality of these activities' (Oliver 1997: 700). To put it another way, the moral as well as the economic and financial exit costs are too high, or are unquantifiable. Thus, in practice, firms choose the boundaries of their employment systems for a whole variety of reasons, not just or only according to the tenets of economic rationality.

In a detailed study of why a bank and a telecommunications company came to use agency staff for customer service work, often at high levels (for example, up to 65 per cent of staff in one telecommunication centre), and the difficulties encountered, Ward et al. (2001) were able to discern six types of factors influencing the choice. These are:

- the desire for greater numerical flexibility due to increased uncertainty associated with technological change and new forms of competition;

- the need to respond to changes in external labour market conditions;
- the coupling of corporate performance targets to employment levels, leading to a need to mask true staffing statistics;
- corporate-level pressure to reduce labour costs;
- the generation of internal flexibility in order to meet job security and redeployment targets for core staff;
- the provision of a cheap screening process to assist recruitment and selection procedures.

Ward *et al.* (2001) note that these factors were often contradictory in the two cases. Internal needs for flexibility and performance were at odds with corporate requirements for a jobs freeze, as was the need for customer service in situations where there was a high labour turnover of agency staff. Local managers found difficulty in managing relationships with the agencies.

Changing employee expectations

There is one final consideration overlooked in theories of employment which is important. This relates to the expectations of employees themselves. Peel and Boxall (2001) note how the preference of the gas meter readers themselves, at times forcibly expressed, was an important factor influencing the contracting or employment routes. In another case, Kessler, Coyle-Shapiro and Purcell (1999) showed how 'outsourced' employees preferred being employed by a specialist computer facilities company where, in effect, they were core employees, to their previous jobs in the local authority where there appeared to be few career opportunities. In the UK, in the depth of a recession in 1993, 43 per cent of temporary workers said they really wanted a permanent job while by 1997 this had fallen to 37 per cent. Asked a separate question about whether they were looking for a permanent job, 38 per cent of women (who make up just over half of the contingent workforce) and 27 per cent of men said they were not (Cam, Purcell and Tailby 2001).

Why do some people not want a permanent job? Some (and it is a growing number) are students who need to fund their studies, others are retired or have taken early retirement and, in the case of many women (and some men), the 'domestic division of labour' is the dominant force explaining employment choice. In some cases, too, permanent jobs are restricted to full-time jobs so that women especially, who take 80 per cent of part-time jobs, may say they do not want a permanent job because they believe it will in effect be full-time. It is also the case that those workers with a highly marketable skill in demand by a variety of employers use the labour market to their advantage. Some are able to build an impressive career history working on the latest technology in well-known companies and get high levels of pay. This may suit the lifestyle especially of young people. Half of contingent workers in the UK are under 35 years old. For some people, the option to be a contingent worker may provide the opportunity to achieve a work-life balance and a career which permanent employment does not offer. This, in part, explains the growth in agency nurses in hospitals and the growth of fixed-term contracting amongst professional workers. Albert and Bradley (1998), in a study of men and women accountants, showed that professionally qualified women especially felt that they had little control over their work and their working lives when they were employed by one of the big four accountancy/consulting firms. In contrast, women accountants working for specialist agencies, which supplied accountants to firms when required, felt they were much more in control. Perceptions of lack of control, they argued, drive women from large firms to temporary agencies. Now all the large accountancy firms have policies on work-life balance and attempt to introduce family friendly policies. In part, this is to meet the new demand for social legitimacy, especially in regard to women professional staff and to satisfy the Government, but it is also because they are finding it hard to keep staff beyond the first few years. Thus, one important factor influencing employer choice of employment systems are the views and behaviour of employees and potential employees themselves. Another is the role of trade unions, discussed in the next chapter.

Conclusions and implications

A common way to display the different types of employment systems is to use a set of concentric rings showing the core and two different types of peripheral workforce, a diagram based on the influential work of Atkinson (1984) (Figure 6.5). The external ring shows people who provide work for the firm but are not employed by it. Some may work in outsourced areas such as IT, canteens, distribution or facilities, and increasingly HR professionals. Others are, in effect, in-sourced to work on the employer's premises but are supplied by, and contracted to, a third party provider like temporary work agencies. In some call centres, for example, up to 70 per cent of the customer service representatives are agency workers. Trainees in unemployment areas can be employed by Government agencies but gain work experience from the firm. Some freelance workers, home workers and other self-employed may also provide work for the firm. The middle ring are employees of the firm yet their status is tangentially engaged, often in routine or single-skill work. This ring is divided into two categories but linked by the common requirement for numerical flexibility. Here the employer wishes to, or is able to, flex the number of people working and the number of hours worked to suit the varying demands of the product market over the year. This may be through the use of limited duration contracts (peripheral group 2) or the use of both overtime hours and extra shifts and natural wastage (peripheral group 1). Natural wastage is based on the expectation that there will be reasonable levels of labour turnover and the employer will not seek to erect mobility barriers to reduce this unless it is very hard to get replacements. At the centre are

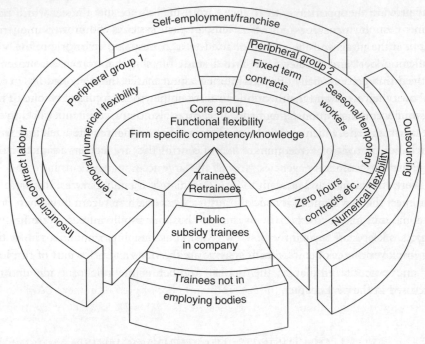

Source: Adapted from Atkinson (1984)

Figure 6.5 Core-periphery (flexible) employment model

core employees. Here we expect to see high levels of functional flexibility (as in multi-skilling) and a reliance on firm-specific competency and knowledge. Following Boxall (1998) we can further divide these into an inner and an outer core.

The implication of the model, and indeed of the various theories of differentiated employment systems, is that the firm should pursue strategies of both core and periphery simultaneously. However, there is little evidence of highly planned and coordinated core-periphery employment models. Both Osterman (2000) in the USA and the WERS 98 survey in the UK (Cully, Woodland, O'Reilly and Dix 1999) found it rare for firms to exhibit the attributes of *both* numerical and task flexibility *simultaneously*. Instead, some chose the task flexibility route, especially in workplace transformation to HPWSs, while others, often using traditional production and operational systems, looked to numerical flexibility to change labour supply in line with varying labour demand. In particular, there was very little evidence that firms used numerical, peripheral flexibility deliberately in order to buffer core employees from the vagaries of the market (in other words as a type of resource immobility measure), unless forced to do so by agreement with unions to provide job security, or because of legal protection against redundancy as in Germany and Spain, for example. Marsden (1999) explains this modest take-up of the complete core-periphery model by suggesting that employment systems are socially and institutionally embedded in the societies of which they part. It may also be that the social and ec nomic costs of managing a variety of employment systems within the same firm, except at the margin, are too complex and too high, despite the rhetoric of the 'virtual company'. Nevertheless, as we have discussed in this chapter, there is evidence of the disintegration of fully-fledged internal labour markets, and perceptions of job insecurity have grown even though long-term employment security remains. That is, socially and institutionally embedded practices also change over time. The growing use of agencies to supply labour to fill vacancies and the way the agencies themselves are changing as the market matures will lead to further adaptation in employment systems.

There is evidence, as Marsden (1999: 3) admits, of a rapid growth in the use of contingent labour in most advanced industrial societies, albeit from a relatively low base. In part, this may be because of changes in labour supply influencing employer choices, such as the huge increase in women in paid employment and a rise in the number of young people who combine study with employment for part of the year or day. Another trend that is easily predicted in countries with ageing populations and low population growth is the rise in the number of post-retirement people who seek to re-enter the labour market one way or the other as contract or contingent workers.

The importance of the analysis of employment systems is that the old certainties of the Monday to Friday, 9 to 5, typical job and work pattern (which may in hindsight seem to have occurred in only two decades after the Second World War in advanced industrial societies and even then only for some employees) are melting, as are the traditional divisions between manual, staff and managerial workers. In their place, new theories about the strategic value of work and workers in providing value to the firm (such as the RBV, a central framework in this book) are influencing management thinking. Even if mixed employment systems are relatively unusual, there is clear evidence of different types of systems in different sectors. Some firms choose to build their employment systems around internal development with commitment-based policies. This is typical of HPWSs. Others emphasise transactional relations where compliance is required, for example in traditional work organisations with clear divisions of labour. Knowledge-intensive firms, especially ones that are growing rapidly, like software houses for example, require a growing number of professionally qualified employees and often have little time for internal training and development. These types of new organisations will tend to have employment systems based on markets with rates of pay moving every few months. The prime need is to acquire people from the external market and then to keep them in the firm (Swart and Kinnie 2001). In due course, as the firm expands and as the rate of growth slows, the need will be to move from a market-based acquisition mode to one more affected by notions of internal development and commitment, with increasing rules to regulate employment relationships. The question of how HR strategy evolves as firms grow and industries mature is taken further in Chapter 9.

7

Managing individual performance and development

Chapters 5 and 6 have explored principles associated with the organisation of work and linked these to models of employment. Within this broad framework, we now turn to issues associated with managing individuals. Without compromising the importance of the specific context in which the firm is located, what guiding principles should inform the management of individuals in the firm?

Traditional personnel management (now sometimes called 'micro' HRM) and the discipline of industrial psychology have always been concerned with managing individual performance within the given structure of work and employment. The focus (or 'level of analysis') has usually been on individual HR practices (such as particular selection, appraisal or training techniques). Textbooks in this tradition typically cover a range of practices across the 'individual human resource cycle' (Figure 7.1). The cycle of employing and managing individuals includes a trail of techniques stretching from job analysis through selection, pay, appraisal, training and so on. In

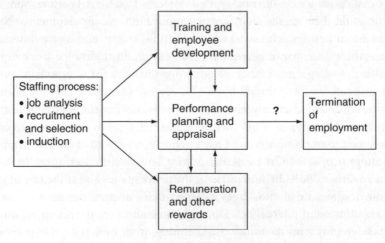

Figure 7.1 The individual human resource cycle

most cases, the performance of the individuals recruited is acceptable or better and the cycle is concerned with the links from performance appraisal to training, to remuneration, and to other forms of reward (such as promotion systems). However, in some cases, performance management will identify the sort of poor performance or misconduct that leads to contract termination.

Those readers wanting an in-depth commentary on each of the elements of the individual human resource cycle can consult one of dozens of books available in their home country. It is often helpful to build one's knowledge of these functions by studying a book written about a particular country because national law and institutions can then be considered in each area. (For example, different countries have somewhat different laws on privacy and discrimination which affect recruitment and selection practices.) We do not intend to summarise all this material in a book on strategy and HRM, nor should we. Our interest is in the critical, underlying issues or *connecting* theory as one passes through the HR sub-functions. This is important for general managers and any other managers, including HR specialists, wanting to participate in the strategic debate in the firm. We need underpinning theory on the management of individual performance and development to enable senior managers to take a more strategic approach to the management of people in the firm. What should senior managers assume about abilities and dispositions at work as they consider the way their firm typically manages individuals? What theory will help firms to manage the firm's individual 'human assets' more intelligently?

The performance equation

If we are concerned to manage individual human performance more effectively, we should actually start with a theory of human performance. In Chapter 1, we referred to the 'AMO theory' of performance. This states that individual performance is some function of the individual's abilities, motivation, and their opportunity to succeed in the specific context (which covers factors like the quality of resources available and channels for influencing management decisions):

$$P = f(A,M,O)$$

On the colloquial level, this model has been around for a long time. Academically, a more formal version of AMO theory can be found in the work of the industrial psychologists, Campbell, McCloy, Oppler and Sager (1993) (Figure 7.2) and in an HR strategy text written by Dreher and Dougherty (2002). In this model, ability is broken down into 'declarative' knowledge (what we know about things) and 'procedural knowledge and skill' (how we actually go about things). The elements of motivation are also usefully identified. However, the role of 'opportunity' is not clearly acknowledged. As a result, some writers use the Campbell *et al.* (1993) model but add an environmental factor ('E') into their equations (see, for example, Macky and

$P = f$ {Declarative knowledge} $\times$ {Procedural knowledge & skill} $\times$ {Motivation}		
Facts	Cognitive skill	Choice to perform
Principles	Psychomotor skill	Level of effort
Goals	Physical skill	Persistence of effort
Self-knowledge	Self-management skill	
	Interpersonal skill	

Source: Campbell *et al.* (1993)

Figure 7.2   Determinants of job performance

Johnson 2000). We think it is important to have an O or E factor in the equation because this helps to make the point that individual performance is embedded in a context. To be sure, individual attributes have a huge impact but even the most able and motivated people cannot perform well if they lack 'the tools to finish the job'.[16] The great quality management guru, Edwards Deming (1982), was fiercely critical of US systems of performance appraisal for blaming poor performance on individual workers rather than tackling the sources of variation in the production system. He included performance appraisal among the 'seven deadly diseases' of American management. While this criticism tends to under-rate the role of individual discretion in work, a factor which is always present (Bendix 1956), it does point to the key influence of technological choices and types of work organisation in many manufacturing environments.

What, then, are the implications of the performance equation? For one thing, it clearly reminds us that firms should aim to hire, develop and retain 'motivated capability': people who have the *can do* (ability or capability) and the *will do* (motivational) factors relevant to the job. From this basic premiss, some authors have developed typologies of human performance to assist employee development and succession management activities. One such model, akin to the BCG matrix of business types (see Chapter 9) and adapted from Odiorne's (1985) 'human resources portfolio', is shown in Figure 7.3. The implicit argument here is that performance management needs to be adjusted to handle different performance types effectively. All firms need some blend of 'stars' and 'solid citizens' while aiming to minimise the numbers who fall into the problematic categories – 'marginal performers' and 'chronic under-achievers'. Star employees have the sort of qualities that are important for pathfinding but solid citizens make things happen reliably once direction has been decided. The idea of an 'all star' company is impractical because firms need to manage *both* change *and* stability: they need to find a way forward while also reaping the profits to be made in a given context. A high-performing team is much more likely to have a blend of performance qualities, as Belbin (1981) has demonstrated (see Chapter 2).

16   One of wartime Prime Minister Winston Churchill's most famous pleas was: 'give us the tools and we will finish the job'.

Marginal performers	Stars
Ability: could be generally adequate but not able to handle high-pressure situations or weak in a couple of critical performance domains; or slightly below most performance standards but capable of improvement through greater personal efforts to improve know-how	*Ability*: advanced, highly respected technical experts, very capable general managers or highly creative business winners; over time, perceived as having star abilities by most people in the workplace and probably the industry
Motivation: may be inconsistent in motivation ('blowing hot and cold'); or generally motivated but occasionally depressed	*Motivation*: always operate with the necessary motivation; often capable of several periods of outstanding achievement in a single year; but may be vulnerable to 'burnout' if over-extended for too long

Chronic under-achievers	Solid citizens
Ability: may have misrepresented their abilities at recruitment; or may be carrying major intellectual or emotional weaknesses which have never been appropriately dealt with; or may be an example of the 'Peter Principle' (promoted to the level of their incompetence)	*Ability*: possess valued technical or managerial know-how related to established business operations; help to ensure the organisation can reliably deliver what it has promised its customers
Motivation: may be seriously depressed; or annoyingly inconsistent in motivation; or perversely motivated; or may be highly motivated but unable to bridge major gaps in their experience and abilities	*Motivation*: always operate with the necessary motivation; generally capable of sustaining performance through some periods of high pressure in a single year

Source: Adapted from Odiorne (1985)

Figure 7.3 A typology of performance types

The sort of model shown in Figure 7.3 is sometimes used by firms to map the talent they have in particular teams, and plan their recruitment, development and performance management strategies accordingly. It is not, however, a precise, well-researched framework. It is simply a loose approximation to reality. Reality is always more complex. While recognising the important role of ability and motivation, we ought to base our conceptions of how to manage individuals on a more secure footing. Our concern in the rest of the chapter is to outline theory and research that can assist.

Managing employee ability

Levels and types of ability vary enormously across the human population. Research consistently demonstrates the huge impact of intelligence or 'general cognitive ability' on performance (Hunter and Hunter 1984, Hunter, Schmidt, Rauschenberger and Jayne 2000, Judge, Higgins, Thoresen and Barrick 1999). Besides intelligence, education and life (including work) experience make key impacts on a person's abilities. Except in cases of very discouraging or traumatised backgrounds, more intelligent people secure a better education and gravitate towards more demanding work (Baumeister and Bacharach 2000). The process of tackling more challenging work develops their abilities further, increasing their value to potential employers and thus further enhancing their advantages over others. It is not surprising that more intelligent people earn more and get promoted more often (Baumeister and Bacharach 2000, Judge *et al.* 1999). They may not be happier with the intrinsic dimensions of their work, something we shall explore further below, but they do get employed in more complex and better paid work.

The crucial role of recruitment and selection

When one looks at the size of the recruitment industry around the world, it seems that practitioners act as if recruitment and selection is the most important human resource function. The research on the critical role of ability in explaining performance suggests they are *not* wrong to do so. Failure to recruit workers with appropriate competence will doom the firm to failure or, at the very least, to stunted growth. As stressed in Chapter 3, firms need to attract and nurture people with the kind of abilities that will make the firm productive in its chosen sector. This is the primary way in which HR strategy needs to be 'fitted' to business strategy.

While firms should aim to recruit effectively at all levels of ability, the need to recruit astutely is particularly important where higher levels of discretion or specialised blends of skills are required in the work. As job complexity increases, so does the range of human performance (Hunter, Schmidt and Judiesch 1990). Thus, as we move up from low complexity work (such as routine clerical work) to jobs where greater ambiguity is involved in decision-making, differences in skills and judgement become more pronounced. It is quite possible for one professional, such as a lawyer or an accountant, to be several times better than another at the same task. The phenomenon of large performance variation is also commonly recognised in sales work, such as insurance sales (Hunter *et al.* 1990). Some people simply lack the blend of cognitive abilities and personality traits needed (such as a friendly manner plus the ability to close the sales deal) and should not be recruited at all. Among those who do have the threshold abilities, the performance range will still be enormous. Firms commonly find they need 'sales compensation packages' which allow high achievers to earn a much higher pay packet through bonus systems that link personal productivity to rewards.

Recognising the crucial role of ability in performance, the literature on recruitment and selection is vast. Our concern is not to summarise it but to point to underlying principles. Highlighting the key messages in this literature, it is important to make a distinction between selection practices and recruitment strategies. Selection is about choosing among job candidates. It is about how to make fair and relevant assessments of the strengths and weaknesses of applicants. It is deeply concerned with the value of particular practices. Recruitment strategy is best understood as the way in which a firm tries to source or attract the people among whom it will ultimately make selections. Recruitment strategies include attempts to sell the organisation as an attractive place to work and attempts to reach better pools of candidates. Some firms that are having difficulties in the labour market succumb to the temptation to over-sell jobs, with the result that appointees become disillusioned and resign fairly quickly.

The literature on selection is an area where concepts of 'best practice' have a very logical place. The fundamental issue is how to make selection more valid: how to use techniques that improve the ability of firms to predict good performers (for a valuable review, see Rynes, Barber and Varma 2000). As has been noted before in this book (Chapter 3), hardly anyone would recommend unstructured interviews over interviews where questions have been based on a careful job analysis or over the use of work sample or cognitive ability tests. Regardless of what kind of job is involved, the selection literature offers valuable insights into how the process can be made more effective for employers and fairer for job candidates.

The focus of the recruitment literature is somewhat different. The literature here has many more gaps (for a recent review, see Taylor and Collins 2000) and the notion of 'recruitment strategy' needs further development. One of the few papers in the area which is useful for considering the strategic questions was written by Windolf (1986). Windolf identifies the task of profiling the ideal kind of candidate and the choice of recruitment channels (among search, advertisements, networking and so on) as key dimensions of recruitment strategy. We would add a third dimension to these: the quantity and quality of inducements offered to job candidates. Some firms are powerful recruiters because they are sufficiently well-resourced to be able to pay wage premia, which increases their ability to pick and choose in the labour market. The capacity to offer better pay and greater internal development makes it easier for firms to build 'high-performance work systems' and out-compete under-capitalised firms (see chapters 1, 5 and 9).

With this addition, we find the typology of recruitment strategies developed by Windolf (1986: 238–46) a useful framework. An adapted version is shown in Figure 7.4. Firms vary in their labour market power (the vertical axis). They also vary in the extent to which management is creative and proactive in forming and reviewing recruitment strategies (the horizontal axis). This framework usefully makes the point that some firms ('status quo' recruiters) have resource advantages but do not use them thoughtfully. Their recruitment practices tend to be conservative, often recruiting from the same social strata and age groups without challenging the way this can discriminate against certain kinds of job-seekers. On the other hand, 'innovative' firms attempt to recruit talented people who can help them develop a stream of new products and processes. They therefore use all possible channels to generate a 'heterogenous group of applicants'. Another proactive type, the 'autonomous' firm, plans

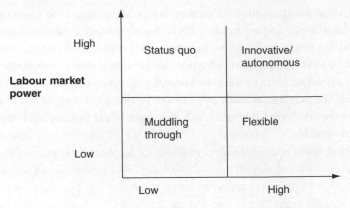

Management creativity and proactivity in
recruitment activities

Source: Windolf (1986: 239)

Figure 7.4   A typology of recruitment strategies

very carefully for all types of recruitment and aims to 'cream off' the best candidates
whatever the condition of the labour market. Most firms classified as 'muddling
through' or 'flexible' are small or medium-sized and cannot offer above-average conditions. They gain some power in slack labour markets but face serious difficulties
when labour markets are tight. The two types of firm are differentiated on the basis
of the HR expertise they bring to their problems. Flexible firms are more thoughtful: they make more astute use of what little power they have.

The key implication of Windolf's (1986) framework is that firms have something
to gain from more creative use of their resources. This is particularly so for small
firms competing against much better resourced rivals. As a general rule, more proactive employers do better in tight labour markets. At the present time, this may
include opening up channels for workers over the age of 40. A lot of companies,
including many which are well-resourced, still imagine recruitment to be about
attracting young workers, fresh from colleges or after only a few years in the labour
market. Such conservatism is increasingly out of step with the rise in the average age
of the workforce.

It is also outdated to think that firms can always recruit exactly the experience they
want in individuals. Sometimes they can but this shouldn't always be the primary
focus of the recruiter. Providing candidates have the baseline qualifications needed
in the role, a more creative approach is to focus on hiring the underlying potential
of individuals. If trying to build a strong core of workers around whom a 'high-
performance work system' will be based, or if trying to create 'organisational agility', it
is important to recruit for long-run trainability and adaptability (see Chapters 6 and
9). Specific know-how of company routines can be developed over time if the individual has the cognitive ability to learn and the motivation to keep learning.

Finally, we should note that recruitment and selection are nearly always joint management processes of some kind: both line and specialist managers are involved (Dany and Torchy 1994: 74–5). For example, line managers hire their own team in consultation with HR specialists who have helped them form a recruitment plan and selection criteria and who may have assisted with shortlisting. Where there are no in-house HR specialists, advice and services of this kind may be obtained from a recruitment agency (see Chapter 6). In some cases, where firms are building HPWSs, teams of workers may carry out hiring functions themselves but, again, this may involve some use of specialist HR expertise.

The complementary role of training and development

This discussion of the crucial role of recruitment and selection ('buy') helps to put training and development ('make') in its context. As our discussion indicates, 'make' cannot be a total alternative to 'buy'. This is obviously true on quantitative grounds: at some point, there has to be an inflow of talent. More importantly, it is true on qualitative grounds. Given the fact of major ability differences in the population, training in companies should be seen as a complement to, rather than a substitute for, careful recruitment.

Having said this, all companies have something to gain from encouraging informal and incidental learning on the job (Hendry, Arthur and Jones 1995, Marsick and Watkins 1990). This may simply involve exposing new workers to the skills of experienced performers. This approach is sometimes colloquially referred to as the 'SBN' system – 'sit by Nellie' (with the sub-text: 'and do what she does').[17] This may be complemented by some formal on- and/or off-the-job training in technical skills where the expense can be justified by the fact that such skills are needed for acceptable job performance. Much training in the use of new computer software is of this nature. Informal learning and short-run training are probably the most common approach among small firms in English-speaking countries. The expense is kept down and the costs of losing good workers through 'poaching' – an ever-present risk in tight labour markets – is minimised. The overall approach is often described as a 'deficit model' (simply based on bridging obvious performance gaps). It is wrong to criticise small firms for this kind of pragmatic attitude to training investment. They are acting in an economically rational manner and the problem of under-investing in employee development lies in wider national and industry institutions over which they have no control (see, for example, Lane (1990)).

The opportunity to use training more powerfully really arises where firms have invested more comprehensively in recruitment, and thus built a labour pool with greater long-run potential (and consequently greater aspirations). Such firms would

---

17   For an historical reference to the role of 'Nellie' in employee training, see Crichton (1968: 33–4).

be unwise not to maximise the investment. In this context, training and development offer the kind of complementary potential recognised in models of high-performance work systems (see Chapters 1 and 5). Such firms are well placed to consider more ambitious training strategies which involve moving beyond immediate demands in jobs to longer-run employee development. The key principle here is that, in the context of a superior investment in work and employment practices, employee development should not be restricted to a deficit model. Rather, it should aim to build the firm's agility over the long-run (Dyer and Shafer (1999), see Chapter 9).

Unlike short-run training, long-run development plans involve a more balanced mix of formal training and education (typically off-the-job) and informal coaching and teambuilding (typically on-the-job). Formal learning is important to enhance the individual's grasp of relevant theory (the template through which they understand their experience) and their ability to tackle abstract problem-solving. This kind of development becomes more powerful when individuals also, or subsequently, face a more challenging work environment in which their informal learning is extended (Marsick and Watkins 1990).

Performance appraisal systems: valuable, if astutely managed

The argument here implies that the most important thing a firm can do to improve individual performance is to learn to recruit and retain more effectively. We have stressed the crucial role of thoughtful recruitment strategies and valid selection practices and the complementary role of training and development, especially where significant investment has been made in the staffing process. Improving retention is something we shall explore further below. What about performance planning and appraisal systems? Performance appraisal (PA) systems are formal methods of planning and evaluating employee performance which involve employee interviewing (typically annually). Quite commonly they include some form of employee development planning (although some firms separate these activities).

Clearly, our argument implies that it is wrong to conflate performance appraisal systems with 'performance management'. Individual performance is managed through a variety of techniques – from recruitment to termination (Figure 7.1). Current reviews stress that PA systems can play a productive role in this mix of techniques, but only if they are managed astutely (Bradley and Ashkanasy 2001, Latham and Latham 2000, Marshall and Wood 2000). People have long been able to see a valid and important role for formal performance appraisal, particularly in major organisations with large numbers of salaried staff (Huber and Fuller 1998).

Research in Britain shows that PA systems are growing as a key way of managing individual performance, particularly in managerial and professional work (Gallie, White, Cheng and Tomlinson 1998). As noted above, the spread of performances in work with higher levels of discretion is vast and it seems only logical to manage each 'human asset' in an individualised manner. PA systems can form a basis for individual work planning, for discussing 'critical success factors' in the job, and can provide the key (if not the only) input to decisions on merit-based salary increases, training, promotions, and international transfers. It is hard to see how multinational firms, involved in time-consuming expatriate management, can operate without a formal PA system for assessing performance and potential (Dowling, Schuler and Welch 1994).

The problem we must wrestle with is that good intentions in the PA area have often been associated with disappointing outcomes. As well as huge variability in how (or even whether) managers conduct formal interviews, research has long confirmed the existence of 'rater bias', stemming from use of invalid performance criteria and lack of representative data on performance (amongst other things). As a result, some industrial psychologists now routinely distinguish between 'objective' and 'rated' performance in organisations (Hunter *et al.* 2000). The implication is that good performers are insufficiently recognised. They also tend to be frustrated with senior management because PA systems raise expectations of links to rewards and development which are often not forthcoming. Too many managers see appraisal interviews as a chore to be got out of the way (as another management system with which they are forced to comply). Their staff typically see them as an opportunity to have their good work rewarded and further developed. Staff are often concerned with the links to the other parts of the HR cycle (Figure 7.1). Not surprisingly, then, a key concern in the appraisal literature over many years has been similar to that in the selection field: how to make the whole process more valid or how to improve its 'cognitive properties' (Huber and Fuller 1998).

Cognitive problems must have something to do with the frustration with PA systems and better management training is bound to be part of the answer, providing it actually involves effective practice at better techniques (Latham and Latham 2000). However, in recent years, some key writers in the literature have started to realise that the problem is not simply cognitive. The idea that better training is the answer assumes that managers are not perversely motivated. The work of writers such as Murphy and Cleveland (1991), who point out that managers have goals of their own which may not include giving accurate appraisals and who act in a political context, is attracting greater attention (Huber and Fuller 1998, Latham and Latham 2000). This kind of approach resonates with the work of Kets De Vries and Miller (1984) who discuss a range of dysfunctional managerial behavioural and personality syndromes including 'powerholic' and 'workaholic' problems, and infantile jealousies of more productive people.

Admitting the possibility of motivational and political problems implies that senior managers must improve accountability mechanisms around PA systems – for example, requiring lower-level managers to summarise and justify all proposed evaluations in advance of interviewing any employees (Marshall and Wood 2000). Senior managers can also improve systems by spending time better clarifying their purposes and how key linkages to rewards and development will actually be achieved consistently in practice (Marshall and Wood 2000). All of this is a tall order. It seems, then, that PA systems can be used effectively when they are well-led and well-resourced. In this light, small firms might be well advised to stick with good informal performance management and some 'golden rules' (such as aiming to hire as well as they can and intervening early in any case of poor performance). In large organisations, however, such as large public companies and government ministries, this will not do. The problems of planning work and rewarding performance are simply too great to rely on informal methods. The challenge in these contexts remains one of making formal PA systems reach more of their potential.

Motivational theory

Vital and substantial though it is (Hunter *et al.* 2000), ability is not the only factor explaining performance. In order for performance to occur, workers must also choose to apply their capabilities with some level of effort and consistency. Motivated capability is the quality that firms most need from individuals. This means that firms must offer workers sufficient incentives to attend work and do an adequate job. Like the employer, the employee is motivated to enter an employment relationship when:

- the benefits of doing so (such as wages, intrinsic enjoyment, social standing) outweigh the costs (such as increased stress and travelling costs);
- these benefits do so in the light of alternatives to that employment (such as alternative job offers or staying at home).

In other words, there must be sufficient levels of mutuality in the relationship if employment is to be stable (Barnard 1938, Watson 1986). The extent to which employment relationships meet both parties' needs is, of course, variable. It is possible to imagine a range of implications depending on the extent to which business and employee interests are mutual or aligned (Boxall 1998) (Figure 7.5).

The key question, then, becomes one of finding ways in which firms can create the motivational environment they desire. Motivation is a variable. What explains high and low levels? In this section, we consider the two main perspectives that have come to dominate theory on motivation in the workplace – agency theory (drawn from organisational economics) and the theory of psychological contracting. We round the section out with a discussion of job satisfaction and long-run development, of the problem of retaining highly motivated workers over significant periods of time. This may sound old-fashioned but that is far from the case.

Agency theory and incentive alignment

While economists recognise the role that different levels of ability or 'human capital' play in the lifetime earnings of workers (see, for example, McConnell and Brue (1995)), by far their main focus in performance management is on the question of

Quality of alignment between business and employee interests	Short-term business context	Long-term business context
Weak	Likely to have chronic HR problems (eg high labour turnover, low productivity) which create, or contribute to, business failure	Likely to become victim of major market changes because of loss of key value generators and low motivation among remaining staff
Adequate	Likely to recruit and retain a competent workforce but motivational levels are unlikely to support any forms of 'human resource advantage'	Likely to survive as a credible member of the industry but not to develop any leadership position through human resources
Strong	Creates the motivational basis to move beyond basic viability issues and develop superior short-run productivity	Creates the motivational basis to secure the employees likely to play a decisive role in the long-run direction of industry change

Source: Boxall (1998)

Figure 7.5   Likely implications of different levels of mutuality

motivation. In organisational and personnel economics, the problem of individual performance is largely seen as one of aligning the incentives of employers and employees (Lazear 1999, Tomer 2001). Much of this thinking derives from a classic paper by Jensen and Meckling (1976: 308) which helped establish the field of 'agency theory':

> We define an agency relationship as a contract under which one or more persons (the principal(s)) engage another person (the agent) to perform some service on their behalf which involves delegating some decision making authority to the agent. If both parties to the relationship are utility maximizers, there is good reason to believe that the agent will not always act in the best interests of the principal. The principal may limit divergences from his/her interests by establishing appropriate incentives for the agent and by incurring monitoring costs designed to limit the aberrant activities of the agent.

Employer-employee relationships are seen as a class of principal-agent relationships, all of which are defined by the fact that the interests of the two parties may diverge. As we argue in Chapter 1, this is a realistic assumption: employers and employees should be seen as having mixed motives.

The standard prescription in agency theory is that principals should find ways of ensuring win/win outcomes with their employee agents. The typical employee in mind is a manager and the context is one in which the principal cannot know all that the manager knows about running the firm. The technique typically advanced is the individual bonus or share incentive scheme. The idea is to ensure that the agent benefits only when the principal benefits (for example, through a sustained rise in share price relative to rival firms in the same sector).

As far as it goes, this is very straightforward advice. It is hardly novel: bonus schemes have been used in capitalism for centuries and were heavily advocated in the Scientific Management movement of the first half of the 20th century (Kessler 1998). What agency thinking really amounts to is a theory of the value of monetary rewards in shaping employee behaviour at work. It is an argument that extrinsic rewards matter to employees and that making such rewards contingent on some form of measured performance will help the firm perform better. The first part of this proposition is certainly true. The main reason for working is the need to earn money to live – sometimes called the 'provisioning motive' (Rose 2000). It is not the only motive, however, and organisational economics is very weak at understanding the psychological and sociological motives that affect higher levels of work performance, as the economist John Tomer (2001) notes. We shall have more to say about this below.

However, the other part of the agency proposition, that contingent rewards – performance-related pay (PRP) – are good for firms is something that needs very careful qualification. There is no doubt that company directors and senior executives have benefited from the explosion of performance pay schemes because these have helped to inflate executive pay (Bartol and Durham 2000). This might have something to do with the fact that directors and senior executives are simultaneously principals and agents – they are supposed to represent shareholder interests but are mostly employees with interests of their own. It is much less obvious that shareholders have benefited and, as such, PRP schemes have created more, rather than less, shareholder concern with agency problems at the apex of public companies (see, for example, Bruce and Buck 1997, Conyon 1997).

An awareness of research outside the agency theory tradition would help. One very interesting piece of work is a study of practices used to manage executives in US public companies. In this study, Martell and Carroll (1995) obtained detailed responses on HR practices for managing top management members, as well as assessments of business performance, in a sample of 115 strategic business units based in 89 Fortune 500 companies. The study found that the practices associated with better management performance were:

- very selective recruitment (but whether executives were hired from within or outside the group did not have an impact);
- high external relativity in pay (implying that firms should try to pay executives well in terms of the labour market but should not worry excessively about internally driven notions of pay relativity in compensation management – rather a blow to advocates of expensive 'job evaluation' systems);
- rigorous use of performance planning and review (while there were no relationships between the bonus systems used in these firms and business performance).

Martell and Carroll's study reinforces the argument in this chapter about the crucial role of recruiting for good ability in the first instance. It also produces interesting evidence that having ongoing dialogue around desirable objectives for executives is more important in fostering good performance than having bonus systems. Of course, this does not invalidate the need to pay them well in terms of the external labour market, something which correlates with hiring the best candidates. What the study suggests is that the desired results of bonus systems (getting managers to focus on the right things) can be achieved more effectively (and, almost certainly, more cheaply) by strong attention to performance planning and feedback.

It is not hard to see why agency theorists are blind to this kind of study. They seem to have fixed on a solution (contingent pay) before really having studied the problem (what counts as good performance in different contexts and what mix of practices might best encourage it). In the practical field of HRM, this kind of solution-before-problem thinking is nearly always dangerous.

The better research in the agency theory tradition is based much less on 'stylised facts' and much more on studying what works in practice. One of the more useful contributions is contained in a study of worker bonuses conducted by Edward Lazear (1999). Lazear gained access to the records of the Safelite company, a firm which installs automobile window glass, and which changed in 1994 from time-based to piece-based pay (with a minimum hourly wage guarantee). Full data was available on worker output before and after the change in the pay system. The data revealed that overall productivity increased by 44 per cent after the change to performance-related pay. Lazear was able to show that the firm benefited in two ways: high-potential workers increased their output (an 'incentive effect', as predicted by the theory). But he was also able to show a 'sorting effect': the rate of labour turnover of higher performers dropped and more workers of high ability were attracted to the firm. At the same time, those of lower ability tended to leave in search of more secure payment regimes elsewhere. By the end of 1995, Safelite's workforce was on average much more productive than it had been when associated with time-based wages alone. The study is valuable because Lazear (1999) notes some of the critical contingencies which make it a case where individual bonuses will work well: the work is actually very individualised and quite observable. Cooperation in teams (which is better assisted by pay compression) is not important in this company's business.

Most pay researchers would validate the importance of these contingent factors and also argue that other factors will come into play over time (see, for example, Kessler 1998). Very often, performance pay systems become demoralised. There is an initial incentive effect but changes in the business context that employees cannot control – such as a downturn in the economy or the entry of a powerful, new rival firm – mean that the bonuses disappear or fall to a level that is no longer significant enough to motivate. This is a point that is predicted by expectancy theory which we explore below. There are also the issues that arise when performance pay is based on qualitative assessments of performance. This means that subjectivity plays a key role

(Kessler and Purcell 1992). The PRP scheme is dependent on the quality of the performance appraisal system that feeds into it. As we have seen, this can be quite variable. It is little wonder that even in firms that are very committed to some form of PRP, management finds it necessary to tread very carefully in the way it designs links from appraisal to pay adjustments (Kessler and Purcell 1992).

Generally speaking, agency theory could do better at spelling out the contingent factors that foster or limit the use of 'at-risk' models of performance-related pay. Again, work outside the agency frame can help to refine the contingent factors that affect pay system design. Wood's (1996) study of pay systems in a sample of British manufacturing firms pursuing 'high-commitment management' is instructive. Most US models would advise such firms to adopt a serious element of contingent remuneration but Wood finds that UK manufacturers pursuing higher employee commitment are circumspect about bonuses. If using any form of PRP, they are more likely to add merit pay permanently into the salary (so it is not 'at risk' from year to year). When one reflects on Wood's findings there is a strong, intuitive logic to them. Employers may well avoid individual bonus systems if they discourage the kind of involvement the firm seeks (Wood 1996: 65, 72). One of the risks in bonus systems is that they will create 'perverse incentives': behaviour which produces rewards but which channels the worker's actions too narrowly and which doesn't help to build a more flexible and comprehensive awareness of the firm's unfolding needs (Kessler and Purcell 1992).

These cautionary tales suggest that agency theory cannot function as a major theory of employee motivation. It can point to the basic principle of interest alignment between employers and employees but this is hardly 'rocket science'. The question of the best ways in which to align interests through pay needs careful handling (Kessler 1998). As a general rule, pay systems should be designed to recruit and retain the people the firm needs, as Martell and Carroll's (1995) study demonstrates. After that, they can be used to incentivise certain kinds of valued behaviour but only when certain key conditions are met. With individual bonuses, this means ensuring that team effects are not important and that workers are able to reach high performance through their own discretionary efforts, and without company resources or other factors limiting them. In field-based sales work, these conditions can quite often be achieved and sustained for serious amounts of time. If, however, such conditions cannot be carefully orchestrated or are not desirable (because high levels of team cooperation are wanted), firms should tread warily. The same argument applies at any level of PRP (individual, team, company, or mixed). The sort of difficulties that can arise mean that careful firms ensure that full consultation with the workers and managers concerned is undertaken in any new form of pay system design.

The theory of psychological contracting

As noted in our commentary on agency theory, social and psychological processes play a major role in the employment relationship alongside economic ones. While agency theory constitutes an attempt to understand individual performance management from an economic perspective, the emerging theory of psychological contracting represents an attempt to do so from a more psychological stance. Sociological concepts are still mainly concerned with larger groups (the workforce as a collective) and are discussed in the next chapter.

The concept of a 'psychological contract' may be a useful way of analysing the quality of individual employment relationships within the firm. We need some way of doing this because a majority of employment relationships in English-speaking countries are based on individual contracts and involve employees who are not unionised. It is absurd to continue to lump all non-union employment relationships into a single category. This is often a weakness in the industrial relations literature, as McLoughlin and Gourlay (1992) have argued. What patterns are there and what accounts for different levels of satisfaction with individual employment?

Early sources on the notion of psychological contract placed their emphasis on shared expectations between the employer and the employee (Coyle-Shapiro and Kessler 2000, Wolfe Morrison and Robinson 1997). Schein (1978: 48) defined the psychological contract as 'a set of unwritten *reciprocal expectations* between an individual employee and the organization'. He developed a simple model which argued that successful employment relationships involve *matching* organisational needs with individual needs (Schein 1977, 1978). Individual needs are seen to be changing across early-career, mid-career and late-career phases. There was really very little theory in the model except the basic point that employment requires an ongoing alignment of interests between employers and employees.

In recent years, Denise Rousseau (1995) has become the most prominent theorist of psychological contracting in employment relationships. She defines the psychological contract as an individual's beliefs about the terms of their relationship with the organisation that employs them. Spot or 'transactional' contracts have very little psychological content but the standard, open-ended employment relationship has lots of 'relational' content (McLean Parks and Kidder 1994, MacNeil 1985), as we argued in Chapter 1. A range of contrasts is usually made between transactional and relational contracting (Figure 7.6). These types are best understood as located at the ends of a continuum, rather than as absolute categories. Readers will note the parallels here with models of core (very relational) and peripheral (much more transactional) models of employment discussed in Chapter 6.

An example of how a psychological contract is formed is shown in figure 7.7. For Rousseau, the employment contract is 'fundamentally psychological – agreement exists in the eye of the beholder (1995: 6)'. The rectangular boxes indicate the individual's thinking and work orientations while the words in the ovals indicate processes from the organisational side. The formation of the individual's psychological contract is shaped by recruitment claims and company policies but also by social cues in the work environment. The diagram helps to illustrate how difficulties can arise. The individual in this case forms the view that they are being promised early

Transactional contracts	Relational contracts
Specific economic conditions (eg wage rate) as primary incentive	Emotional attachment as well as economic exchange
Limited personal involvement in the job (eg working relatively few hours, low emotional attachment)	Whole-person relations (eg growth, development)
Close-ended time frame (eg seasonal employment, two to three years on the job at most)	Open-ended time frame (ie indefinitely)
Commitments linked to well-specified conditions	Both written and unwritten terms (eg some terms emerge over time)
Little flexibility (change requires renegotiation of contract)	Dynamic and subject to change during the life of the contract
Use of existing skills	Pervasive conditions (eg affects personal and family life)
Unambiguous terms readily understood by outsiders	Subjective and implicitly understood (ie conditions difficult for third party to understand)

Source: Rousseau (1995: 91–2)

Figure 7.6 The continuum from transactional to relational contracting

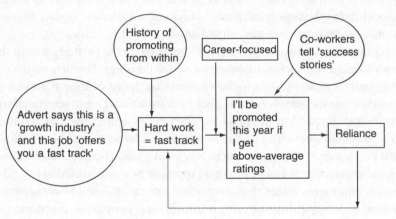

Source: Rousseau (1995: 34)

Figure 7.7 An illustration of the formation of a psychological contract

promotion in exchange for hard work (people often conflate 'hard work' with performance, concepts which may overlap but which do not perfectly coincide because of ability and resourcing differences). Their personal assumption that they can be promoted in a single year is just that: a personal assumption. It may have been encouraged by the recruitment rhetoric but it is not grounded in anything the employer has specifically promised. In actual fact, something like two per cent of individuals are promoted in this organisation in a single year (Rousseau 1995: 34), so the individual is more than likely heading for disappointment and disillusionment.

Given the prevalence of scenarios like that depicted in Figure 7.7, it is not surprising that research on psychological contracting finds that psychological contracts are frequently 'violated' (Wolfe Morrison and Robinson 1997). A widely-cited study by Robinson and Rousseau (1994) argues that violation of the psychological contract is the norm rather than the exception. The study tracked 128 MBA graduates two years after their graduation. Some 55 per cent said their psychological contract had been violated over this short time frame. Robinson and Rousseau (1994) inject a sense of proportion into this. There are obviously degrees of violation. Some aspects of an employee's psychological contract are more significant than others. There may also be violations which are recognised and explained by management. In certain situations, employees accept as credible the explanations they are given for violations (Rousseau 1995: 127).

The risk with more serious violations of psychological contracts is that employees leave prematurely (before the employer has had a good payback) or stay and adjust their 'organisational citizenship behaviours' (OCBs) (Organ 1988). OCBs include a range of cooperative and caring behaviours that can be very valuable to collegial relations, teamwork and client service in a firm. If an employee who has tried to work hard feels violated in some important aspect of their psychological contract, they are likely to work less sacrificially in future. Much as predicted by Adams' (1965) famous 'equity theory', they adjust their work inputs (effort) to take account of the lowered outputs (rewards) they are actually experiencing at work.

There are, however, serious problems with the approach that Rousseau (1995) takes to the notion of psychological contract. As Guest (1998) argues, Rousseau's model makes the psychological contract entirely subjective, something only in the head of the employee. This means that it cannot be seen in any meaningful way as 'contractual'. If one cares about the plain meaning of words, Rousseau's definition cannot be supported. To have a psychological contract must mean that employer and employee *share* some common understandings that go beyond what was written in their employment agreement, as earlier writers on psychological contracting argued (Coyle-Shapiro and Kessler 2000).

Guest (1998) also points to the huge difficulty that multiple agency presents in large organisations. Given the fact that so many managerial actors can be involved in the recruitment and then the ongoing performance management of an individual, it is hard to see how management can ever maintain a consistent set of psychological messages. Violation is almost inevitable and perhaps employees come to realise and accept this. Why do not we simply go back to the study of the very important construct of job satisfaction, recognising that satisfaction is affected by the dynamics of promises made, kept and broken?

While these are serious difficulties, Guest (1998) still sees some value in the notion of psychological contract as a way of analysing the variety of individual employment relationships that exist in today's labour market. Perhaps the greatest value, as demonstrated in the last chapter, is that it can be used in the analysis of core-periphery employment models in firms. In core-periphery models, management is often trying to send a different set of messages to different groups which vary in their centrality to the firm's mission.

The role of expectancy theory in psychological contracting

Another problem with much of the writing on the psychological contract is that it tends to degenerate into discussion of seemingly dichotomous states (relational versus transactional, insider versus outsider, long-term versus short-term and so on) with insufficient regard to the analysis of factors that explain positive and negative dynamics in psychological contracting. One key paper which presses the whole area forward has been written by David Grant (1999). Grant points out that concepts of psychological contracting really stem from expectancy theories of motivation. The key dimensions of expectancy (or expectations) theory are shown in Figure 7.8. The text boxes with borders are the elements of the pure theory of expectancy while the other parts of the diagram have been inserted to build a more comprehensive model of individual performance. We have done this by drawing on the work of Tony Watson (1986), whose concept of the implicit contract is synonymous with the psychological contract, and by drawing on the performance equation which is fundamental to this chapter.

Expectancy theories of motivation do not tell us about the content of human motivations (about pay, status and intrinsic job satisfaction, for example) but make the fundamental point that our ongoing motivation at work is affected by the expectations we form and our experience of whether these are met over time. On a practical level, it tells us three quite important things. First, impossible goals will frustrate rather than motivate. There is no point in putting forth effort if we are being set up for failure. We might try once or twice but, over time, we need to believe that our efforts can achieve the results desired. Secondly, unrewarded goals may be ignored. In other words, people are indeed motivated by obtaining rewards. This, of course, is something to be very careful about when designing PRP schemes, as noted earlier. Companies should avoid rewarding certain kinds of behaviour that are ultimately dysfunctional for the firm. Thirdly, expectancy theory implies that firms cannot motivate good performers at all unless they have rewards that these people value. It is impossible to employ some people, for example, unless the work interests them and the pay meets their threshold expectations. Over time, to keep people motivated, the firm needs a virtuous cycle in which the rewards that people value do come to them when they perform. In other words, expectancy theory implies that organisations without attractive rewards will fail and that faith in the reward system needs to be maintained.

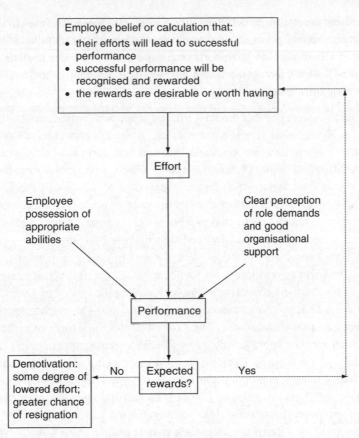

Source: Adapted from Watson (1986: 119)

Figure 7.8 The expectancy theory of motivation and performance (with added factors to recognise the full 'performance equation')

Grant (1999: 331) explores these principles through a framework in which he defines four types of psychological contract and in which he lays strong emphasis on the need for management to match reality with its rhetoric:

- the *congruent contract* (where management's 'rhetoric' in HRM appeals to employees and 'coincides with their perceptions of reality'). Previous experiences 'tally with the content of the rhetoric';
- the *mismatched contract* (where 'the rhetoric fails because it has no appeal to the employee and does not match the perceived reality'). This can happen, for example, when past experience tells employees management cannot deliver on its rhetoric;
- the *partial contract* (where 'parts of the rhetoric appeal to the employees and parts do not'). 'For example, the employee may feel that rhetoric promising

personal development reflects reality, while at the same time they may feel that rhetoric linking personal development to increased levels of pay does not';

- the *trial contract* (where 'rhetoric is given a chance to prove itself and become reality'). This can happen where employees are prepared 'to "buy in" to the rhetoric on a "wait-and-see basis" '.

The fourth category in this model – the trial contract – introduces the basis for a dynamic analysis. Grant (1999) reports a case in the UK consumer electronics sector ('Renco') where data was obtained through two periods of data gathering on employee attitudes, some 18 months apart. Renco, a Japanese-owned company, opened a greenfield site at which Japanese practices of shopfloor participation and a cooperative approach to industrial relations were promised. Workers were keen to give this approach a chance (a trial psychological contract). After 18 months, however, management practice had diverged significantly from the initial rhetoric. Key Japanese-style consultative practices were allowed to decay. Employees did not experience consistent opportunities for involvement. The trial contract passed away as employees revised their effort (for example, lowering the quality of work) in a 'quid pro quo' for a disappointing management performance. The psychological contract shifted back to a mismatched one. The case illustrates the danger of raising expectations which are then subsequently dashed because management doesn't care about follow-through on rhetoric. Cynicism is bred in this kind of environment and any future 'change management programmes' will have serious credibility issues.

Grant's (1999) analysis helps to pinpoint the central role of expectations in any theory of employee motivation. Like agency theory, expectancy theory says that employees must be offered the incentives that appeal to them (which typically, of course, extend beyond monetary rewards). However, expectancy theory adds the valuable point that faith in the reward system needs to be maintained over time. There is an unfolding psychological exchange in employment which needs some careful management if motivation is to be sustained or enhanced. It is, of course, unrealistic to expect that firms could ever meet the kind of subjective interpretations of desirable rewards that Rousseau's (1995) conception of psychological contracting suggests. However, firms are well advised to promise only what they are actually committed to delivering because of the dangers of a mismatch between the rhetoric of management style and the reality of daily management practice.

'Expressivism' and the drive for personal growth

The theory of psychological contracting helps to highlight the important question of how to sustain employee motivation over time. Perhaps the most useful work in this context is associated with studies of job satisfaction. Studies of job satisfaction and of labour turnover tell us some important things about 'what workers want'.

A key contribution is contained in the major study of social change and economic life (SCELI) in Britain conducted in the late 1980s. This study contains a survey of some 4000 employees (Penn, Rose and Rubery 1994).[18] Through the SCELI study, Michael Rose (1994) has developed a theory of intrinsic job satisfaction. This theory does not account for all job satisfaction because extrinsic factors (such as pay) and satisfaction with management style also matter, as Rose (1994) acknowledges. However, the crux of Rose's theory is that people are satisfied in their jobs (and more loyal to their companies) when the skills they use in their job ('job-skill') match the skills they actually have ('own-skill'). This is quite a refreshing argument because it implies that most people can be happy in their work, irrespective of how brainy they are. The key factor is finding a job which uses the talents one has.

In this respect, Rose (1994) defines three categories. The first are the under-utilized whose talents are not fully engaged (own-skill greater than job-skill). University students doing low-skilled jobs while studying often fall into this category but so too does anyone working in a job which does not make good use of their talents. The second group are matched (own-skill approximates job-skill) while the third category are under-qualified (own-skill less than job-skill). These categories are refined somewhat further in Rose's (1994) analysis of the satisfaction levels of the three groups (shown in Figure 7.9). The composite satisfaction levels indicate how people in these categories feel, on balance, about their work. The study indicates that people who feel their talents are under-employed at work are the most unhappy while those where talents needed and possessed are equivalent are generally satisfied with their work. The findings on the under-qualified represent an amusing but dangerous story.

Skill situation of subgroup	Satisfaction level
Under-utilized	
Low job-skill, moderate own-skill	−27
Moderate job-skill, high own-skill	−15
Low job skill, high own-skill	−13
Matched	
Low job-skill, low own-skill	+1
Moderate job-skill, moderate own-skill	+5
High job-skill, high own-skill	+4
Under-qualified	
Moderate job-skill, low own-skill	+12
High job-skill, moderate own-skill	+13
High job-skill, low own-skill	+33

Source: Rose (1994: 261)

Figure 7.9 Types of skill-matching and satisfaction levels

18 The SCELI sample was drawn from six localities – Aberdeen, Coventry, Kirkcaldy, Northampton, Rochdale and Swindon – but very closely matches the 'class composition' of Britain as a whole.

People who are obviously inadequate for their work feel quite happy. Not surprisingly, they are the group which is best pleased with management (Rose 1994: 258). After all, management's failure to deal with their incompetence has been very rewarding.

This study illustrates why half of Adams' (1965) equity theory is wrong. Studies confirm that people generally adjust their effort if they feel fair rewards are not forthcoming, as predicted by equity theory (Watson 1986). However, Adams argued that people who feel over-rewarded would try to lift their game. While it's more than likely that some do this, the evidence in Rose's (1994) study suggests that many are quite happy with this sort of inequity. As subsequent psychology has argued, people often find ways of rationalising unfair advantages that come their way and are capable of inflating their performance through 'self-serving bias' (see, for example, Kruger (1999)).

The key point to be taken from Rose's (1994) work, however, is the value of choosing employees who are interested in the work being offered because they find it a good deployment of their abilities. This is the old notion of 'person-job' or (more broadly) 'person-organisation' fit (for a recent review, see Kristof (1996)). It implies that economic motives alone cannot account for long-term employee behaviour. Intrinsic satisfaction, and opportunities to grow in the work, are very important alongside economic drivers, something that is regularly demonstrated in surveys of IT professionals.[19] While people work to meet material needs, the motive of 'expressivism' is also significant, particularly among contemporary growth occupations (Rose 2000). As a general rule, workers embrace job-related change which encourages their personal development but which doesn't threaten their other interests.

The adult life cycle and the drive for personal growth

The drive to express one's personality in work is supported by life-cycle theory, which suggests that there will be several times over a person's adult life when they will seek major developmental challenges. According to life cycle theorists, the adult life cycle consists of alternating periods of *stability* (structure-building) and *transition* (structure-changing) (Levinson 1978, Levinson and Levinson 1996, Sheehy 1977). In each stable period, the emphasis is on pursuing one's goals and values *within* a given structure of key choices. In the transitional periods, one 'questions and reappraises the existing structure, to explore various possibilities for change in self and world, and to move toward commitment to the crucial choices that form the basis for a new life structure in the ensuing stable period' (Levinson 1978: 49). At the transitional points, some people 'externalise' their inner turmoil

---

19 See the regular surveys of job satisfaction conducted in the IT industry by Lucent Technologies: www.lucent-networkcare.com/surveys.

more than others: changing their job, their address, their spouse, perhaps their country of domicile.

Research indicates that up to about the age of 30, most men and women are experimenting with the workplace, finding out what kind of work they do or do not like. Labour turnover rates are generally much higher among the under-30s than other age groups, something which has been true for a very long period of time in Britain (Burgess and Rees 1998). The pattern of stability alternating with change across the life cycle is likely to be similar for both sexes (Levinson and Levinson 1996, Sheehy 1977). There is greater variety, however, in women's patterns (see, for example, Gilligan 1982). Women who focus on being mothers, and have no paid (or very incidental) employment after their first child is born, have a life pattern which is obviously very different from the typical male one but which involves life challenges of its own. On the other hand, women who are not, or choose not to be parents, may have very similar career orientations to men. Paid employment is a very central life interest, if not the most important thing. A third pattern includes those women who try to balance family and employment (Buxton 1998), either on the basis of part or full-time employment.

Where paid employment makes up a significant element of their life, we can expect both men and women to seek some regular growth opportunity (such as acquiring new skills in the latest technology or extending interpersonal skills from one career context to another, or shifting from employee to self-employed or from part-time to full-time). Periods of reflection and change will naturally occur throughout the lifespan. As a rough rule of thumb, talented people seek some kind of significant stimulation every three to four years. The challenge of retaining high performers over the long run, then, becomes one of providing a setting in which developmental challenges can be navigated in-house.

This analysis puts an interesting spin on the issue of change in the workplace. We are frequently told that employees are resistant to change. However, research on job satisfaction and life-cycle theory suggests that people leave firms because their employer cannot offer them *enough* stimulating change. Generally speaking, firms can do better at designing growth opportunities for individuals. Three categories of growth are shown in Figure 7.10. Only one of these categories involves hierarchical techniques. A good use of performance appraisal systems (see above) lies in the way they can be used to open up a dialogue around personal growth opportunities, a use which would make them more sympathetic to the rise of 'expressivism'. From the viewpoint of improving the firm's retention of good performers, this is a better use of the appraisal interview than a tiresome review of past performance (see, for example, Latham and Latham 2000). Good performance should be informally and regularly acknowledged while the annual 'appraisal' interview becomes a vehicle for encouraging the employee to discuss development interests and a forum for planning ways to match these with opportunities in the firm.

Examples of intra-functional growth	Examples of cross-functional growth	Examples of hierarchical growth
On-the-job training	Job rotation (temporary) or reassignment (permanent)	Promotion within department
More challenging task assignment(s) in the same job	Temporary secondment across functions	Acting headship of department
Individual research projects	Participation in multidisciplinary project groups	Management development courses
Off-the-job educational/training courses	New career start in-house	Appointment to general management
Conference participation		
Study trips to other firms		

Figure 7.10   A menu of growth opportunities in the workplace

Conclusions and implications

What principles, then, have strategic significance when it comes to the management of individual performance and development? The key argument in this chapter is that the performance equation ($P = f(a,m,o)$) has a universal relevance in workplaces. Individual performance is a function of ability, motivation and opportunity. As a result, whatever the level of the firm's resources, recruitment activities are going to be critical. Wherever labour markets are tight, firms are well advised to make recruitment practices more proactive, selection practices more valid, and training practices as complementary as possible. The greater the investment in staffing (better selectivity and greater inducements), the greater the benefits to be gained from strong internal development. While small firms can make do with good informal methods of performance feedback, large firms should aim for greater validity in performance appraisal, particularly in work involving high levels of discretion. We realise now, of course, that this is as much a problem of managing organisational accountabilities and politics as it is a technical one of improving system design and managerial training.

The attraction and fostering of relevant human ability is clearly of vital importance in all firms that want to grow. This doesn't mean that motivation should be neglected. It might help to put it this way: within the limits of the firm's available resources, managers should act as if recruitment of good ability counts for everything in performance management. Once people are recruited, however, they should act as if motivation is everything.

Agency theory emphasises the important role of aligning the economic interests of employer and employee. The more win-win games that can be created through the firm's reward systems, the better the firm will do. However, this is much easier said than done. It takes some very careful design, with good employee involvement and due regard to critical contingencies, to minimise perverse incentives in pay systems. Pay strategies have a very important role to play in recruitment and retention but other practices (such as good performance goal setting) can be more effective in structuring employee focus on the job (Martell and Carroll 1995).

Maintaining faith in the rationality of the reward system is something that should be striven for, as the theories of psychological contracting and expectancy imply. In this context, rewards are much broader than the economic. Job satisfaction and life cycle research increasingly point to the rise of 'expressivism' in the workplace. Where firms are concerned about improving the long-term retention of high performers, attention should be given to ways of opening up greater opportunities for personal growth. As Rose (1994) demonstrates, much of this has to do with matching individual skills and potential to the skills required in the job. Fortunately for firms, this is a principle that is relevant to work of all skill levels. It suggests that even firms of limited resources have opportunities to foster higher levels of employee satisfaction and commitment.

8

Managing employee voice in unionised and non-unionised firms

'Employee voice' is the term increasingly used to cover a whole variety of processes and structures which enable, and at times empower, employees, directly and indirectly, to contribute to decision-making in the firm, and occasionally in the wider society. Over many decades, indeed since industrialisation, voice mechanisms have taken many forms and been labelled with a wide variety of terms. The way these have changed indicates the shifting priorities and values associated with different types of voice systems. 'Worker participation', favoured in the 1960s and 1970s, gave way to 'employee involvement' in the 1980s while for a short period in the 1970s the term 'industrial democracy' was used to imply the need for wider employee rights through the appointment of worker directors. Beyond, and stretching back over the last century, there has always been a strong interest, especially from the political left and among some but by no means a majority of trade unions, in forms of worker self-management and worker cooperatives where changes in ownership provided the best means of exerting influence (Bradley and Gelb 1983, Oakeshott 2000). Many of the ideas for employee participation and involvement come not from 'best practice' in human resource management linked to improved economic performance but from political philosophy and action in the political economy, and from the trade union movement. Thus, while many chapters in this book are concerned with the links between aspects of HRM and business outcomes, here our concern is more with the social and political forces which impinge on management decision-making. We need to ask how and how extensively should, and can, employees have a voice in decision-making, as well as how managers might respond to these pressures. Much of the current thinking and action, whether at the level of the State or the enterprise, has its origins in industrial relations systems that evolved in different ways in each country in the 20th century.

Origins: industrial relations and the representation of worker interests

In industrial relations, the focus for the best means of representing worker interests has been on collective bargaining and collective consultation. This focus emphasised the primacy of unions as the main, and at times, exclusive organisations representing the views of employees where they are recognised to do so. Here expressions such as 'joint regulation' drew attention to the union role in negotiating the basic rules of the contract of employment from pay levels to methods of dealing with redundancy and procedures for handling grievances and discipline in the workplace. Forms of collective bargaining and consultation, where management and employee representatives met to discuss matters of common, and sometimes conflicting interest, became established avenues for the interaction between management and labour. These meetings became 'institutionalised', seen in the regularity of the contact between the 'parties' in Joint Negotiating Committees or Joint Consultative Councils, and the outcomes in terms of 'rules' shaping the employment relationship. At the peak of union influence in the decades following the Second World War in most advanced industrial nations, analysis of joint regulation paid particular attention to:

- where the bargaining was undertaken (the location of bargaining at workplace, company, industry or national levels);
- the subjects bargained over (the scope of bargaining from periodical pay negotiations to broader issues of management decisions on capital investments, for example);
- who the negotiators were (whether local representatives or lay officials and managers in the workplace or full-time national union officers with their opposite numbers in employers' associations);
- the type or style of bargaining, whether fundamentally based on adversaries meeting to allocate or distribute resources, or to work together to seek to find solutions to workplace difficulties. In the terms developed by Walton and McKersie (1965), the former was termed 'distributive bargaining' while the latter was 'integrative bargaining'.

Two fundamental principles, or some would say beliefs, stood behind all analyses of industrial relations. The first was that conflicts of interest between owners (capital) and employees (labour) were inevitable in that, even while working together for mutual survival, shareholders would rationally wish to maximise profits while workers would want more pay and job security (recall Chapter 1). The second was that, while it was never possible to eradicate this conflict, it could be expressed, and accommodations reached, once each party recognised the legitimate interests of the other and was prepared to engage in dialogue and negotiation. Thus, as in politics, there could never be one single source of authority or legitimate power based on ownership, but instead it was necessary to recognise a plurality of interests and inter-est groups which would need to learn to live together and resolve their differences without resort to force. However, this would only happen if each party recognised the ability or power of the other to do it harm if relationships broke down. Thus the language of industrial relations, especially in Anglo-American countries, was infused with what might now seem the language of an industrial cold war: power, conflict, negotiation, accommodation. Given the levels of industrial conflict which engulfed countries at various points and in ways which are (currently) unimaginable to those born after 1970, it was not surprising that the State intervened sometimes to try to crack down on emergent or powerful union movements and at other times to seek mutual solutions and avenues where conflict could be expressed peacefully.

The link between politics and industrial relations is important since in this area, or sub-system, of human resource management, the State has often played a major role and what has been learned in political science and philosophy has echoes with-in the modern enterprise. It is not possible, even if it were desirable, to look at ques-tions of employee voice only through the lens of productivity and flexibility. Here the issue of legitimacy (as we discussed in Chapters 1 and 3) is fundamental and few nation states leave this to the owners of capital to resolve themselves, unfettered by legislation or social stigma ('the unacceptable face of capitalism', as one British Conservative Prime Minister once said of a major employer which suddenly closed a factory without any discussion or warning). If the British monarchy's royal pre-rogative came somewhat spectacularly to an end on the executioner's block on 30 January 1645, so the issue in the world of work is not whether, but how much, restriction should be placed on the managerial prerogative. If modern democracies are based upon political citizenship how far can there be any concept of industrial citizenship? If the exercise of arbitrary power by those in authority in government is constrained by laws giving rights to citizens, and enforced by the judiciary, how far can equivalent rights be applied in the world of paid employment and how can they be enforced?

There are not, and never can be, any right or conclusive answers to these ques-tions, just as there can be no finite code of ethics universally accepted by all. It may be convenient to justify the utility of various forms of employee voice mechanisms against the template of profitability, and we will do so later in this chapter, but it is never sufficient since, ultimately, questions of legitimacy and human rights have also to be faced. In seeking to evaluate the outcomes of particular forms of voice or par-ticipation, it would be more sensible to use the reverse test of degrees of damage caused. Do employee voice arrangements significantly endanger the enterprise by reducing performance and creating conditions of competitive *dis*advantage? Using this test, it is hard to think of any employee voice mechanism, as currently practised, which is economically seriously damaging. Even this test, however, is flawed since it still confuses ends and means. Ultimately the justification for employee voice is as an end value in its own right. As such, it is always contentious and subject to reinterpretation as different generations of power-holders in the enterprise and the wider political system have to deal with industrial and ethical problems.

These problems in the first half of the 20th century, when the foundations of industrial relations were laid, were mainly about strikes and cycles of intense industrial unrest which threatened social order. The solution then was the focus on the recognition of trade unions and an emphasis on the process of collective bargaining, described by one leading American professor in the 1950s as 'the great social invention that has institutionalised industrial conflict' (Dubin 1954: 44). The State, in many Anglo-American countries especially, but also in the Nordic countries, strongly endorsed this in the way they ran their own public sector organisations and persuaded employers to engage in some formal discussion with trade unions, often at industry or sectoral level through employers' associations.

The linkage between social democratic or labour parties in the political arena and trade unions in the industrial sphere meant also, especially in the post-Second World War period, that workers' interests were reflected in political agendas with unions recognised as 'social partners' at the national level in many European countries, and legislation passed to enhance worker rights to information and consultation. Within the Anglo-American tradition historically, the emphasis was on worker rights 'won' at the bargaining table by strong, well-organised trade unions. The principle was one of 'voluntarism'. The alternative route more often found in continental European, or more specifically Northern European countries, was the provision of rights enshrined in law and applied universally across the economy. Thus in the UK, for example (but also in Canada and the USA), voluntary agreements on information, consultation and joint regulation were found in many different forms in a patchwork of agreements in individual companies and sectors. In the Netherlands and Germany, however, rights were established in law. Collective bargaining agreements became legal minima applied to all firms in a sector whether they had union members or not, and all firms beyond the very smallest were required to have a works council and to provide information and discuss with workers a range of issues to do with the organisation and future direction of the firm. In some of the larger companies in Germany, a further requirement was for worker directors to work with other board members to 'co-determine' key aspects of strategy.

The foundation and subsequent enlargement of the European Union (EU) in the last three decades of the 20th century, taken with a serious decline in union membership and union power in many countries, but especially in Britain, has led to marked changes in the landscape of worker participation and to a degree a convergence in systems of representation. With it has come a new language of 'partnership' and an emphasis on more effective ways of incorporating employee opinion into decision-making. Across the whole of the EU, large 'European companies' with establishments of over 150 employees in two or more member states are now required to establish European Works Councils (EWC) to receive information on future plans and performance and discuss appropriate action. When firms merge or are taken over, there is a need for established rights to be preserved and discussions held. In cases of redundancy, explanations must be provided and meetings held with representatives of the employees to review how these should be implemented. And by the mid years of the first decade of this century, national systems of consultation or works councils will need to be established in all but the smallest workplaces. None of these procedures are restricted to unionised firms. They apply equally to all but the smallest places of work but the form they take may vary, especially whether representation is focused on union elected officials or, more generally, employee representatives. The combination of these new institutions providing substance to employee voice systems, and the very different environment in which unions operate, has had marked effects on the role and operation of trade unions. This is discussed in detail later in this chapter. It is necessary, first, to provide an overview of the many different types of voice systems that can be applied. While legislation can dictate the form that some involvement and participation systems take, it can never specify how organisations manage or deal with such structures. It is always the case that if management does not wish to engage in meaningful dialogue with its employees and their representatives, it can render legislatively imposed voice systems largely worthless. While the political and social environment impinges more obviously and more directly here than in any other area of human resource management, organisations still have choices, and if they wish to, these forms of involvement can be made strategic, or rendered trivial nuisances. Meetings of an EWC, for example, can be perfunctory once-a-year gatherings or they can be embedded into the fabric or culture of the firm, contributing to effectiveness and employee wellbeing.

Choices in employee voice systems

In any analysis of voice systems allowing for, or encouraging, employees to have a say, and thus an influence in decision-making, five linked questions need to be addressed:

1 How much say/involvement/participation is envisaged in the scheme?
2 Over what sort of decisions?
3 Taken at what level in the enterprise, or beyond in the wider political economy?
4 Who is involved and, if a representative, how elected or selected?
5 What are the enforcement mechanisms both to keep the system going and to ensure that action follows?

The first question is the most important since it will strongly influence the form the answers to subsequent questions take. In the German co-determination and consultation legal framework, there is a clear delineation of types of involvement or degrees of influence. Elsewhere, especially in Anglo-American societies, there is much more ambiguity but it is still possible to suggest a scale based on the extent of influence allowed or expected. This is shown in Figure 8.1. Marchington and Wilkinson (2000: 343) display this diagrammatically as an 'escalator' of participation (Figure 8.2).

The types of decision and their location in the managerial hierarchy can attract different degrees of involvement. For example, decisions on health and safety will often (and in many countries must by law) involve employee representatives in the evaluation of risks and their avoidance in current operations and in the purchase of new technology. In some extreme cases, safety representatives have the right to delay or veto a decision if there is a danger to life and limb. In the same firm, it would be most unusual for employees to have the same degree of voice over product marketing or distribution decisions, but in a thriving system of consultation it may be that management are held to account for these decisions, especially if there is a prospect of economic damage. Examples here may be evidence of declining quality in a car manufacturer, or pricing and shelf display in a biscuit-maker in its relationship with a dominant supermarket, or a major plant location and investment decision in a

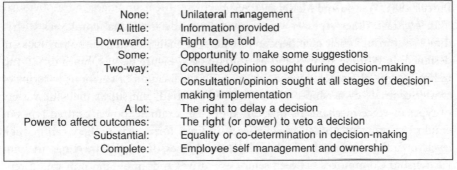

None:	Unilateral management
A little:	Information provided
Downward:	Right to be told
Some:	Opportunity to make some suggestions
Two-way:	Consulted/opinion sought during decision-making
:	Consultation/opinion sought at all stages of decision-making implementation
A lot:	The right to delay a decision
Power to affect outcomes:	The right (or power) to veto a decision
Substantial:	Equality or co-determination in decision-making
Complete:	Employee self management and ownership

Figure 8.1 Scale of participation or involvement allowed to employees and their representatives

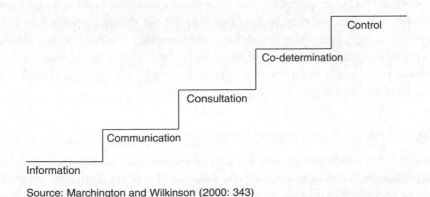

Source: Marchington and Wilkinson (2000: 343)

Figure 8.2 Marchington and Wilkinson's escalator of participation

multinational company. In most cases of consultation and lesser voice systems, the 'right of last say' rests with management but the extent to which employees believe their views are listened to, and so sometimes have influence, is important in the way employees evaluate voice systems and judge management effectiveness. This in turn has a tendency to increase job satisfaction and organisational commitment (Appelbaum *et al.* 2000, Guest and Conway 1997).

If the scale of involvement varies by type of decision and by its location (in the corporate board in the case of major plant location; at the plant, department or level of the team in the example of declining quality), then this in turn strongly influences the nature of the voice system. Some types of involvement in all but the smallest companies will require a system of representation with a few employees elected or selected to represent their co-workers. Here involvement is indirect and questions are posed on how the tenor and outcome of joint meetings is communicated amongst 'constituents', and how, and to what extent, representatives take soundings before meetings, especially when dealing with confidential information. The quality of the underlying relationship in terms of levels of trust is crucial if the exchange is to be anything more than 'white knuckle' adversarial posturing (Marchington 1989, Purcell 1981, Walton and McKersie 1965).

In contrast, other types of voice systems provide individual employees with a direct say through their membership of teams, in quality circles, in the way jobs are designed, in attitude surveys and as shareholders. Figure 8.3 combines direct and indirect forms of employee voice systems with the location of decisions in terms of 'power-centred', 'ownership-centred' and 'task-centred' and shows the wide variety of types of voice mechanisms that can apply. For example, power-centred types of employee arrangements can vary between indirect forms, where there can be high levels of influence seen in worker-director schemes or regular meetings in Joint Partnership Committees between senior executives and union and non-union representatives, to direct, but much weaker, voice systems. These could be no more than regular information flows downward from the board using various channels ('a little' in Figure 8.1) to employee attitude surveys with results reported to board members, who are often surprised to hear that they are not deeply supported! In some cases, for example in a major British bank, the reporting of employee attitude survey results was the first time that HR issues had a distinct place on the board agenda. Following an acquisition, the results proved disturbing for the board which had, until then, believed that integration was going smoothly.

The shift from indirect to direct voice systems

Ramsay (1977, 1983) noted how interest in forms of worker participation (as it was then called) tended to come in waves, often associated with managerial efforts to deal with or buy off labour power. This was most evident in the 1960s and 1970s when union membership and union power seen in strike trends was growing. Marchington

Power-centred

Indirect involvement	• Worker directors • Works councils • Joint partnership committees
Direct involvement	• Attitude surveys • Company communication systems

Ownership-centred

Indirect involvement	• ESOP (Employee share ownership plans) where shares are held by trustees directly elected by employees) • Worker cooperatives
Direct involvement	• Share option (purchase schemes) giving employees 'votes' as shareholders

Task-centred

Indirect involvement	• Shop steward (employee representatives) meeting local/department management
Direct involvement	• Job enrichment (voice in how the job is done) • Seml-autonomous team working • Team briefing • Problem solving group (quality circles/*kaizen* team, continuous improvement group) • Suggestion schemes

Figure 8.3 Types of employee voice mechanism

(1989, 1995) notes how since then, in a period of waning union power, the coverage of voice systems grew in Britain in the last two decades of the 20th century. This was strongly confirmed by trend analysis using the unique UK database on workplace employee relations (WERS) (Millward, Bryson and Forth 2000: 117–37). This shows a strong trend toward a decline in indirect voice arrangements, especially where these were union-focused systems, and a strong rise in the direct forms that they measured, such as regular meetings between management and the workforce. The latter took place in 34 per cent of establishments in 1984 but rose to 48 per cent in 1998. A similar pattern is observed with briefing groups (or team briefing as it is often called), where the proportion of establishments having 25 or more employees using these voice arrangements jumped from just over one third in 1984 to just under two thirds in 1998. Problem-solving groups were found in 35 per cent of workplaces with 25 or more employees in 1990 but by 1998 this had grown to 49 per cent. Similar trends have been observed across Europe (EPOC 1997), North America (Cotton 1993) and Australasia (Davis and Lansbury 1996). The number of workplaces in the UK with no measurable voice arrangements fell from 11 to 9 per cent between 1990 and 1998. Newly-established companies in this period showed a marked preference for non-union voice systems.

It seems clear, then, that there has been both a marked growth in voice arrangements and a substantial change from indirect systems, especially those providing union-only voice through elected union representatives, to direct task-based schemes. This is both important and instructive. The marked decline in indirect representation in the period of the UK WERS surveys coincided with the Conservative Government of Margaret Thatcher and John Major. Thatcherism was very strongly linked with the attack on forms of collective work organisation. While explanations of union decline can be found in structural factors such as growing unemployment in the periods of the 1980s and 1990s, and in the shift towards services from manufacturing, it was especially employees in new workplaces who showed the least likelihood of embracing unions (Millward *et al.* 2000). Beneath these explanations lay a marked change in the basis of legitimacy, with a growing acceptance of individualism, or more precisely 'libertarian individualism' (Purcell 1995) seen in the growth in performance-related pay, individual contracts and direct-voice arrangements. This is a clear indication in the UK of how shifts in beliefs and values impact on structures of HRM, especially in the area of employee voice. In continental Europe, institutions of collective indirect representation are more 'sticky' (Streeck 1990), being enshrined in law and embedded social values. This is the fifth question posed in Figure 8.1. Where voice arrangements are established by law and socially embedded, they last longer since there is 'institutional security' and failure on the part of management to consult, for example over corporate mergers in the Netherlands (Wenlock and Purcell 1992), can lead to the issue being taken to a labour court. Where there is no enforcement mechanism, and where no unions are recognised, voice arrangements can have a short life, as observed by Kessler and Purcell (1996) in their study of joint working parties set up to introduce workplace change with the help of a Government-appointed third party. When the third party left, the joint working parties withered and meetings were no longer held.

The effectiveness of employee voice systems

What is particularly interesting in the UK is the growth in direct-voice arrangements. These are voluntary, and few governments would contemplate trying to legislate in this area due to the problem of definition and enforcement. It is hard to know whether this growth is because of emerging evidence of effectiveness or, as Ramsay (1977) implied, just a fad which will fade in the next recession. There is plenty of evidence (see Marchington 1989, 1995) that voice arrangements can be no more than 'bolt-ons' which become an additional burden on line managers, who fail to provide the necessary support. This is particularly clear in the chequered history of quality circles (Collard and Dale 1989). Here, developing and encouraging employee voice is a fad, or worse, a sop, with little expected or experienced from its introduction.

Not surprisingly, voice systems which are disconnected from organisational life and decision-making, and are irritants to line managers, have a short life. However, when linked to wider changes in work organisation, the growth in employee discretion and changes in managerial values, as we discussed in Chapter 5, these systems very much form part of the capital 'O' in AMO: the opportunity to participate. We know that employee perceptions of the extent to which they are provided with information by their managers, the degree to which she or he provides a chance to comment and respond to suggestions, is associated with higher levels of job satisfaction and organisational commitment, and these variables are linked to performance (Appelbaum *et al.* 2000). Millward *et al.* (2000: 130) show how positive responses in employee attitude surveys on these questions are strongly associated with the existence of direct voice arrangements. Gallie and White (1993) in their large scale survey of employees in the UK conclude that:

> Participation is of fundamental importance for employees' attitude to the organisation for which they work. It is strongly related to the way they respond to changes in work organisation and with their perception of the quality of the overall relationship between management and employees (*ibid*: 44).

Embedded voice systems often lead managers in these firms to assert or affirm that they produce positive outcomes (Marchington, Wilkinson, Ackers and Dundon 2001). It is more difficult to find hard evidence on the performance effects of voice systems. The problems of evaluation are threefold. First, given the very wide range of schemes, as listed in Figure 8.3, it is impossible to take a unified approach boiled down to one question. Second, while one can measure the existence of a structure, mechanism or arrangement, one cannot impute that these lead to certain behaviours. We know that the crucial variable is *how*, and *to what extent*, line managers support and activate employee involvement as a process. Thus, in some companies, these systems are empty of meaning with no more than perfunctory compliance. Yet the voice arrangement does exist. Research which asks if a practice exists, or even what proportion of the workforce are covered by a scheme, is not particularly helpful. Structure does not equate with process. Third, the idea of a bundle of HR practices, discussed in Chapters 1, 3 and 5, is that it is a combination of mutually supportive practices (as expressed in this book as 'AMO') which appear to have performance outcomes where these are appropriate to firm strategy. Thus it becomes hard to sort out individual policies. In the area of voice arrangements, the supporting organisational climate or culture, especially seen in the level of trust, is crucial in providing the seed-bed for effective participation to germinate (Ichniowski, Shaw and Prennush 1995). Indeed, these authors strongly suggest, on the basis of their research in integrated steelworks, which had managed the sort of transformation we explored in detail in Chapter 5, that individual practice changes, such as voice arrangements, have no effect on performance. Bhargava (1994) suggests that, in respect of profit-sharing (which can be a form of voice mechanism if linked to firm ownership), there may be an effect, but it is one-off at the point of implementation and not subsequently.

Despite the difficulties in evaluating a performance effect, we do have some clues if justification is required. Coyle-Shapiro (1999: 45), in a careful time-series study, found that 'the extent of employee involvement is positively related to the assessment of the benefits of TQM'. In particular, and echoing earlier comments on the crucial role of line managers, she found that 'supervisors have a positive role in getting employees involved in TQM' (*ibid*). Kessler and Purcell (1996) in their study of joint working parties found that, according to both the managers and the employee representatives involved, the level of trust between them increased markedly. This was especially the case where employee representatives, and the employees themselves, were actively involved in all stages of the change process overseen by the joint working party. Where this happened well, over half of the managers considered that their organisation had benefited 'a lot' from this form of involvement. Research by Mari Sako (1998), on the impact of employee voice in the European car components industry, is particularly interesting as it shows how it is the combination of direct and indirect forms which have the strongest effect in this sector. She was able to use both 'hard' measures of faulty products and softer attitudinal dimensions in the analysis. Thus, rather than direct and indirect forms of voice systems being alternatives, it is the combination of both which is linked to better performance. The outcome effect of combined types of voice arrangements was clear in the large-scale European survey of participation in the mid 1990s. The greater the number of forms of participation used, the more likely it was that managers reported benefits from increased output through to declining absenteeism (Sisson 2000: 6). This makes a lot of sense, since different forms of involvement play different roles in different organisational settings at the level of the task and amongst decision-makers. It is the climate or style of participation in the organisation as a whole which is crucial. This is considered in the last section of the chapter. Employee financial participation is also often associated with positive performance outcomes (see Hyman (2000) and Pendleton (2002) for reviews of the evidence).

Trade unions and employee voice

The marked decline in union-based, indirect forms of employee voice in the UK, noted above, has been dramatic, and union membership in virtually all advanced industrial countries was in decline in the 1980s and 1990s after a period of sustained growth in the post-Second World War era (Katz and Darbishire 2000). Trade unionism is now a minority activity in most countries outside of Scandinavia and the number of workplaces where unions are recognised to represent employees in collective bargaining and collective consultation has fallen sharply, especially in Britain (Millward *et al.* 2000). Some have argued that in the Anglo-American economies, in particular, we have seen the end of institutional industrial relations in large parts of industry or commerce or the decline in 'organised industrial relations' (Purcell 1995, Tailby and Winchester 2000). Perhaps we should add the caveat, 'the end of institutional industrial relations as we knew it'. That is, while the old landmarks of multi-employer bargaining and adversarial industrial relations have receded, if not quite disappeared, changes are occurring which will fundamentally alter the context in which unions operate. This will be likely to affect the value system of managers as well as employees, the potential union members.

There are three reasons supporting this assertion. First, as we noted at the beginning of Chapter 6, unions have been able in workplace transformations to place emphasis on job security even if their role in gaining above-average wage increases has been emasculated in the face of stronger, and often global, economic forces. That is, all the evidence points to unions making a difference. Sisson (1993) argued on the basis of survey evidence that far from new forms of high-performance work systems, or high-commitment management (HCM), being restricted to the non-union sector, they were more often found where unions were recognised. The presence of unions may encourage workplace transformations even if the unions themselves are not intimately involved in the transformation process: what Storey (1992) calls 'dualism'. Second, as we have already noted, the context of indirect forms of employee voice is changing in Europe at least, as the European Commission pushes ahead with legislation to provide every employee in all but the smallest workplaces with access to representation and a voice. While the legislation focuses on directly-elected employee representatives and gives no explicit role to trade unions, it provides an opportunity for unions to be chosen as the preferred representative body, as they often are in Germany where union-nominated representatives win around three quarters of the elections for works councillors. Within the UK, new legislation introduced by the incoming Labour Government in 1997 provided unions with a statutory mechanism for gaining recognition for collective bargaining from employers. Union membership and recognition agreements grew for the first time for 20 years in the early years of the 21st century.

The third, and most important change, has been to unions themselves in the way they see their role in the global economy. In a review of the role of trade unions at the time of the 1997 general election when the Labour Government came to power, the British Trades Union Congress (TUC), representing all major unions, said 'trade unions must not be seen as part of Britain's problems but as part of the solution to the country's problems' (TUC 1997: 1). The title of this authoritative publication was *Partners for Progress*. Since then, 'partnership' has routinely become accepted in the lexicon of industrial relations, and, to a degree, has been implemented in some workplaces, although it is impossible to say how many. As a rhetoric it is very powerful, implying a markedly new role and new relationship for trade unions both with employers and with union members, potential and actual (Haynes and Allen 2000). In its idealised form, as Tailby and Winchester (2000: 365) put it,

A qualitatively different form of indirect participation or employee representation ... offers each of the parties significant gains: employers are able to secure a greater degree of job flexibility and stronger commitment of employees and union representatives to organisational goals; trade unions are offered a more cooperative form of involvement in enterprise-level employment regulation; and employees are promised greater employment security and the opportunity to participate in new forms of consultation.

This type of partnership, if possible and sustainable, is in marked contrast to the historic role of unions (which is why some sceptical managers doubt 'partnership' since 'the leopard cannot change its spots'). Social values change slowly and 'Thatcher's children' were brought up to be profoundly sceptical of the role of trade unions.

Trade unions inevitably react to the prevailing power and control structures in the world of employment. Adversarial relationships were an inevitable consequence of the command and control management methods of Scientific Management and the exploitative nature of early capitalism. In the UK, craft unions were established to protect the job rights of their members and by restricting entry to the craft and over job allocations, maximised their economic power at the expense of others. General unions sought to mobilise semi-skilled and unskilled workers to act collectively as a means of influencing the power relationship. The same applied to industrial unions in the new industries which emerged in the late 19th century, followed by 'white-collar' unions in banking and insurance, and government services in the inter-war years. The adoption of internal labour markets, explained in Chapter 6, provided regularity and established rules in the employment relationship. Unions sought through collective bargaining to be central to this process of job regulation. In so doing, the outcomes tended to reinforce workplace divisions between categories of workers as well as between management and labour. That is, unions both reflect and reinforce the prevailing employment structures. They could not, and cannot, do so without the agreement and fundamental support of major employers, and the State in providing legislative and legitimatory support. Thus, the spread of collective bargaining in the UK in the 1930s and 1940s, a period of union weakness, can only be explained by Government support behind the growth of employers' associations and union recognition (Clegg 1994). Very similar trajectories were evident in the USA, under the Roosevelt New Deal, and in Northern Europe in the inter-war years in Scandinavia, and the immediate post-war period in (West) Germany. The unique combination of links with political parties, industry structure and wider social beliefs on the role of the unions led to different union structures and agreed institutional arrangements regulating industrial relations. While there may be some convergence of systems, especially in decentralisation and internalisation of the focus of the relationship between capital and labour to the workplace in many countries, the wider structures of industrial relations endure as social institutions (Katz and Darbishire 2000). Multinational companies ignore these at their peril.

The transformation of industrial relations (Kochan, Katz and McKersie 1986), which is especially marked in Anglo-American economies, was strongly influenced by shifts in the underlying beliefs and values of executives in large firms and by the withdrawal of State support legitimising the union role. The latter was most obvious in Britain with Margaret Thatcher's attack on collectivism in all its guises, but was also seen in the USA under President Reagan and in the marketisation of economies and the public services in countries like New Zealand (Boxall and Haynes 1997). The 'root metaphor', as Dunn (1992) put it, changed. Employers' support for unions and collective bargaining was always conditional and a reflection of power structures. This is hardly surprising. The agenda changed with the emergence of new industries in the professional service sector and in the globalisation of markets. Old rules on job grades, demarcation between occupations, and traditional ways of working were questioned. Then, in many places, they were replaced with a new agenda of higher performance, greater flexibility and continuous change.

What, if any, is the union role in these circumstances? Unions can easily be bypassed. Storey (1993: 544) recalls the comment of a senior manager in the Rover Motor Company at the time of its major rescue restructuring in 1991–2: 'Unions were invited to the party but they didn't want to come. So the party went ahead without them.' Subsequently, the unions did accept the invitation and the company concluded that it was foolish to try to exclude them. Unions discovered that fighting to preserve the existing rules and structures is rendered especially hard in circumstances where unemployment is rising fast, as in the recession of both the early 1980s and the 1990s, and now a decade later. If union power is only a function of the propensity to go on strike then fear of long-term unemployment emasculates this. But union influence is more than the imposition of veto power to stop change occurring. Despite the stereotypical imagery of conflict and adversarialism, where union leaders inhibit change, there have always been examples of 'integrative bargaining' and cooperative relationships with employers. This was evident in the era of productivity bargaining in the 1960s and 1970s in the UK (McKersie and Hunter 1973). What is different now, and it is this which helps explain the change to the language of 'partnership' and 'being part of the solution', is that the traditional union roles of job protection through restrictive work rules and gaining above-average pay rises through collective bargaining have been significantly eroded in many, but not all, places. What is left is what Freeman and Medoff (1984) call 'voice-response interaction', that is dialogue and discussion with management about the operation of the firm in general and the management of people in particular. These three roles are shown in Figure 8.4.

The ability of unions to gain 'monopoly' power in wage bargaining (the top line in Figure 8.4) has been much reduced as the coverage of collective bargaining has shrunk from 70 per cent of all employees in 1984 in the UK to 41 per cent in 1998 (Millward *et al.* 2000: 242) and pay systems and contracts of employment individualised (Brown, Deakin, Hudson, Pratten and Ryan 1998). The dilemma too, as the

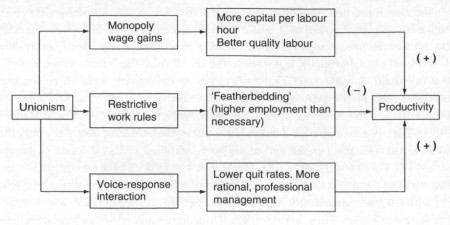

Source: Adapted from Freeman and Medoff (1984)

Figure 8.4 What unions do

model makes clear, is that there is an inevitable trade-off between pay and jobs. Higher wage costs, unless these can be passed on to the customer as in monopolies, make it more attractive to relocate plants overseas and/or invest in labour-saving technologies and work methods which increase productivity. As job security has risen in importance in two decades of high unemployment, the union emphasis has shifted from simple adversarial pay negotiations in the annual ritual of claim, offer and counter-claim. Now job security for existing employees often has priority in negotiations on workplace changes. The middle line in Figure 8.4, restrictive work practices and 'featherbedding', was very common in established manufacturing firms and whole sectors like the newspaper industry (Martin 1981) and the docks (Turnbull, Woolfson and Kelly 1992) where what were called 'Spanish customs' controlled actual hours of work, who did what job, and restricted the adoption of new technology. These restrictive work rules were not always unilaterally imposed by the union and its members but were often reflected in the management organisation of work and the functional structure of the firm – what Mintzberg (1979) called 'machine bureaucracies'. Many of these have been swept away in the last 20 years, either because of the virtual collapse of the industry, as in shipbuilding, or by new entrants to the market being able to utilise the opportunities of greenfield sites. In other cases, change has been imposed on the workforce, as in national newspapers in the UK and the USA. There are relatively few places left where such controls remain. The most obvious remaining examples are, ironically, in the professions such as the law, where barristers in the UK maintain their privileged position to practice in the High Court, despite attempts by Government to break their monopoly.

The type of transformational change required to sweep away restrictive practices has sometimes been achieved by union derecognition, for example by the Murdoch newspapers. More often, it has been the outcome of painful and protracted negotiations with trade unions leading to agreements establishing 'full flexibility' with management. These agreements have achieved or regained the right to design jobs and allocate labour; in other words, a rediscovery of the management prerogative. This process is particularly evident in sectors where competitive pressures have intensified, but it is not universal. In the public sector, for example in teaching and health services, union roles have changed only slowly and adversarial industrial relations remain the norm. Here, where public funding is constrained, adversarialism can remain the only avenue for unions to exert influence on the allocation of resources in terms of jobs and pay (Boxall and Haynes 1997).

The bottom line of Figure 8.4 is more diffuse and ambiguous and is centred on the union role in having a voice, responding to management proposals in consultative forums, and working with management on change agendas. This is where 'partnership' fits in since, if the relationships remain marked by distrust and adversarial posturing by either, and therefore nearly always by both sides, management is unlikely to discuss proposed changes and will not be prepared to listen. Unions in these circumstances will be unwilling to discuss proposed changes without knowing the price beforehand in terms of pay and job security. In effect, with the collapse of unions' traditional roles in many, but not all sectors, they are left with a difficult choice of either being marginalised and continuing to lose members, or of seeking new forms of relationship based on cooperation and joint problem-solving. This presupposes that management is willing to accept a joint philosophy and work to make it meaningful (Haynes and Allen 2000). It is management who are the prime initiators here since they determine the fundamental approach. Unions are inevitably reactive to the style of management. It is extremely difficult for them to be proactive and to create a climate of 'partnership'.

Underlying this new focus on union voice and response is the economic, market-related need for change, leading to an emphasis on productivity and flexibility. The old industrial relations were about control and stability: gaining agreements to keep the production system going and avoiding disruptive conflict. Management needed to make marginal adjustments in terms and conditions of employment and in responding to worker disquiet while preserving their prerogative as far as possible at what was sometimes called the 'frontier of control' (Goodrich 1975). Now the agenda in an increasing number of workplaces is a focus on change. The usual rules of bargaining no longer apply. For one thing, the items placed on the negotiating table become too numerous, too complex and too interwoven for classic trade-off deals. For another, senior management no longer have all the answers. They may know what they want to achieve but remain unclear at a level of detail on how to get there and thus need the cooperation of employees in generating ideas and taking action, as typically found when high-performance work systems are introduced (see Chapter 5). All of the partnership deals analysed by Haynes and Allen (2000) and Tailby and Winchester (2000) have been about the management of change. Where change is not part of the organisation's agenda, or when it is forced, not through market forces (the invisible hand) but by political dictat, the union role can remain one of defending worker interests. This has been seen in recent years in the UK in the prison service, the fire brigade, and the ambulance service (and similarly elsewhere). Thus partnership is not the panacea portrayed by politicians hoping to engender a 'new' social contract but, like much else, is dependent on the mix of circumstances and beliefs.

The fundamental question in unionised work settings is how far the union representatives should be 'invited to the party' (included) or, as critics on the left would say, 'incorporated' in the change process. Or should unions be by-passed, with change imposed by management? This requires unions to decide how far they can go in working with management on a change agenda. In effect, the more they go down a partnership route, broadening the agenda of joint discussion while eschewing industrial conflict as the basis of their power and influence, the more they need to show that dual commitment by employees to both the company and simultaneously to the union is possible and even desirable (Boxall and Haynes 1997). Thus, both parties in change and restructuring have to choose between 'fostering' and 'forcing' strategies or a subtle mixture of both (Walton, Cutcher-Gershenfeld and McKersie 1994). Sometimes the strategy for the employer may be 'escaping' through plant relocation but the threat of this can also be part of a forcing strategy. Fostering and forcing as strategies are not simply about union-management relations but cover the relationship with employees, with different emphasis placed as between 'control' or 'commitment'. Walton *et al.* (1994) call this a 'social contract' and suggest that when management want this contract to be based on commitment and cooperation they will be likely to emphasise fostering in industrial relations, although there may be elements of forcing in order to kick-start the change process. This occurred in Rover when the unions were 'invited' to the party.

Figure 8.5 shows the conditions under which forcing and fostering strategies might be adopted. Walton *et al.* (1994) suggest that an employer will be likely to adopt a forcing strategy, very similar to that employed in national newspapers in the UK, when major, dramatic changes are required and when they believe there is no point in extended dialogue with the unions. They also have to believe they can win, or have the resources to survive a long, drawn-out battle. The battle, at the time, as in newspapers, was not about 'converting' the hearts and minds of existing employees to a new social contract, but about destroying labour resistance, if need be by gaining many new employees to replace others. Fostering strategies focus on the need for a move to new ways of working – the new 'social contract' – that require, or are predicated on, existing employees embracing or at least accepting a high-performance work system as described in Chapter 5. Here the presumed union role is one of helping the management of change, and gaining minimal guarantees of job security. Thus, in forcing the union is seen to be the blocker of change, while in fostering its role is legitimised by management as an agent of change. It is not an easy role to play, as is evident in the recent studies of union-management partnerships in the UK

Question	Conditions that promote	
	Forcing	Fostering
Objectives of initiating party (management)		
Priority for and ambitiousness of substantive change?	High*	Low
Priority for improvement in social contract?	Low*	High
Expected responses (labour)		
Labour expected to be persuaded by business rationale?	Unpersuaded*	Persuaded
Labour believed to be receptive to social contract changes sought by management?	Unreceptive*	Receptive
Power equation		
Management confident it can force substantive change?	Confident*+	—‡

*The more strongly these conditions are fulfilled, the more likely *unrestrained* forcing.
+ When labour and management are both confident of their power, *unrestrained* forcing becomes even more likely.
‡ No hypothesis for this power condition and fostering.

Source: Walton, Cutcher-Gershenfeld and McKersie (1994: 57)

Figure 8.5 Conditions that affect choices to force and foster: Walton *et al.*'s propositions

(Haynes and Allen 2000, Marks, Findlay, Hine, McKinlay and Thompson 1998, Tailby and Winchester 2000).

Conclusions and implications

The choice of strategies in the management of change leads to one final question. What sort of management style does the company want with its employees? Management style can be defined as 'a distinctive set of guiding principles, written or otherwise, which set parameters to, and signposts for, management action regarding the way employees are treated and how particular events are handled' (Purcell and Ahlstrand 1994: 177). In periods of change, managements have to make choices on what sort of relationships they want with employees directly, and with trade unions, and, now that they are required by legislation in Europe, with directly-elected employee representatives in works councils. That is, choices on voice arrangements, while to a greater or lesser extent constrained by legislation and wider beliefs on legitimacy, are taken by management in the sense of wishing to avoid, live with, or embrace forms of partnership with representatives and with employees directly. The way these systems of involvement, participation and negotiation are designed and operated is at the heart of management style. Relationships with unions (and to a lesser extent with works councils and other forms of indirect representation) range along a continuum from low to high forms of cooperation (Boxall and Haynes 1997). Choices here are strongly mediated by the type of 'social contract' or model of human resource management evident in the way individual workers are managed. In crude terms, the choice is between 'control' by authority and command, or 'commitment' as in HCM or HPWSs. Figure 8.6 summarises the main choices. While the figure stylistically describes six distinctive management styles, in practice each of the axes is a continuum and, as we argued in Chapter 3, all styles are the outcome of the complex interplay of tensions and choices between conflicting demands.

Organisations operating with an avoidance strategy, seeking to prevent trade unionism and trivialise legislative voice systems do so either by forceful opposition (Box 1) or by competition in the sense of preferring to provide competitive conditions of employment and extensive use of direct-voice arrangements (Box 2). The former, described by Guest (1995) as 'black hole' firms, have neither high-commitment policies in their relationship with their employees, nor any industrial relations policies of working with trade unions. Most typically, these firms will utilise low-skill employees and minimise investment in people, as seen in low pay, little training and little job discretion. Box 2 firms, like management consultancy organisations or software houses, place emphasis on human capital and knowledge management, seek-

Relationship with employees		Individual-based high-commitment management. Extensive direct-voice systems	Emphasis on individual-based high-commitment management. Hands-off relationship with organised labour. Low trust of external unions	High-commitment management. Partnership with organised labour. Extensive voice systems. High trust
	Commitment/ involvement			
		Box 2	Box 4	Box 6
	Command/ control	Low trust No voice	Low trust Restricted voice Conflict	Emasculated union/representatives No real voice 'Sweetheart unionism'
		Box 1	Box 3	Box 5
		Avoidance	Adversarial	Cooperative

Relationship with trade unions and elected works councils etc

Figure 8.6 Voice systems and management style

ing to get the best out of their core employees and emphasising policies which encourage high performance and retention of the best. They eschew any form of collective representation, focusing on individual, and often competitive, relationships (sometimes seen in the description of career management as 'up or out' (Boxall and Steeneveld 1999).

Boxes 3 and 4 include companies caught in adversarial relationships with trade unions. Traditional patterns of conflict, and Scientific Management control systems, are found in Box 3. These still exist in some manufacturing companies (especially in developing countries) and parts of the public sector like the Royal Mail in the UK and in parts of the service economy like routine, short-transaction call centres. While formal methods of consultation exist at corporate and workplace levels, they are generally seen to be ineffective, being marked by distrust and posturing.

Box 4 organisations are usually in transition. While formal relationships with trade unions or works councils are marked with distrust and a failure by each party to communicate effectively with each other, direct forms of voice are used, often to by-pass and undermine the unions while work organisation places emphasis on HCM/HPWSs. Box 5 is where work organisation is traditional 'command and control' but relationships with unions or works councils are cooperative. This is sometimes called 'sweetheart unionism' and exists where the union is concerned more with its own survival, or its representatives with their own career and wellbeing, than with fighting for the members' interests. Collective voice systems are shallow. While examples are rare, they are most likely to be found where company unions or staff associations exist, in part to keep out external unions.

Box 6 firms exhibit strong voice arrangements, combining both direct and indirect arrangements, and it is likely that a wide variety of schemes operate in tandem and are embedded in a bundle of HR practices which encourage high performance and employee wellbeing. The classic HPWS adopters, described in Chapters 5 and 6, would have these types of voice arrangements, especially those that recognise trade unions and where 'partnership' is accepted as appropriate.

We have explored in earlier chapters dimensions of strategic human resource management in terms of the resource-based view of strategy, changes to work organisation towards HCM/HPWSs, different employment systems, and different types of psychological contracting. All of these concepts are concerned with the extent to which employees are considered to be central to the achievement of firm performance, or are peripheral. Employee voice arrangements in practice will be deeply influenced by choices in these areas. The more central are employees, the more likely voice – meaning involvement and participation in management decisions – will need to be developed and management will wish to do so. That is, the opportunity to participate is strongly linked to the exercise of employee discretionary behaviour for the benefit of the firm and for the employees themselves, provided they have the ability and motivation to do so. This is highly relevant for those firms which see employee initiative and innovation as central to their strategy. Where employees are merely a factor of production to be controlled, with costs minimised, then employer incentives to engage in voice activities with them are minimal.

However, we must be careful not to create the impression that voice arrangements are solely about economic rationality. The beliefs and values of the managers and employees themselves, and the society of which they are part, provide a crucial extra dimension. Few voice systems and positive union-management relations will exist, or exist for long, unless they are valued in their own right as legitimate and morally necessary activities *irrespective* of the performance outcomes. They have to have social legitimacy. Such beliefs and value systems amongst the powerful in society can vary from one generation to another, and from one society to another. The move to market individualism or neo-liberalism in the last two decades of the previous century, especially in Anglo-American societies, challenged this idea of legitimacy, especially in regard to the role of trade unions (Boxall and Haynes 1997). Now in the UK, as a part of Europe, there is a renewed emphasis on the rights of employees, especially a right to have a voice in the affairs of the company. Legislation, to be effective, has to have a catalytic effect on beliefs and values, especially on those who are required to share power and to be accountable to their subordinates, as in most voice systems. The growth in partnership arrangements may be one clue to a change in perspective in some British companies but, in general, it is much too early to say whether underlying changes in values and beliefs will occur in the UK or what form they might take.

The development of voice systems giving employees access to, and involvement in, management decisions is dependent on strategic choice at national and organisational levels. Historically, many employers have opposed legislation yet adapted to it as a political expedient. Taken in isolation, and grudgingly accommodated, voice systems have little impact, or can become a focus for negative adversarial relationships between management and labour. Seen as an important ingredient in advanced forms of human resource management, the way people are managed and their sense of commitment to the organisation is enhanced and made meaningful. This is as much to do with human dignity as it is with performance and flexibility. The search for legitimacy, where employees authorise management in the exercise of its authority, is a necessary feature of strategic human resource management which should not be taken for granted. There are many innovative ways in which the issue can be approached, as we have reviewed in this chapter. Strong evidence points to the use of multiple channels of voice systems at task-, financial- and power-control levels, appropriately integrated together, for positive outcomes for both the organisation and its members to be reaped. The basic requirement is for senior executives to be clear on the fundamental style of management, or the preferred way to manage people, that needs to be, or should be, adopted. This is an ethical choice of practical significance which has implications for every other aspect of HR policy.

part 3

Managing people in dynamic and complex business contexts

9

Human resource strategy and the dynamics of industry-based competition

Chapter 3 of this book made the point that both 'best practice' and 'best fit' have a role to play in the theory and practice of strategic HRM. In Part 3, we move from our discussion of general principles to an analysis of important and complex contexts. In Chapter 10, we examine the twin complexities of HR strategy in multidivisional and multinational firms. In this chapter, we pick up an idea first advanced by Baird and Meshoulam (1988) – that HR strategy should somehow fit with the firm's stage of development.

Our goal in the chapter is to ask: how can HR strategy support business viability and how might it lay a basis for sustained advantage as firms grapple with change in their industries? Readers will recall the argument in Chapter 2 that all firms face strategic problems. The primary problem is how to become and remain a viable player in the chosen industry or sector. Various aspects of management – competitive positioning, technology, operational style, finance, and HRM – have a critical role to play in this. The fundamental priority of HR strategy in a firm is to secure and maintain the kind of human resources that are necessary for the firm's viability. To use mathematical terminology, a reasonably effective HR strategy is a necessary, but not sufficient, condition of firm viability. The 'second order' – or higher level – strategic problem is that of how to develop sources of sustained competitive advantage, a problem which not all firms choose to tackle. In theory, however, there exists opportunity for any firm which remains viable in its industry to build some relatively enduring source of superior performance through outstanding management of human resources. In effect, HR strategy can become a competitive weapon. How it might do so is something that is usefully analysed across cycles of stability and change in industries (Boxall 1998).

Industry dynamics: cycles of stability and change

We begin with the basic observation that firms are located in industries (Carroll and Hannan 1995). Even when we look at firms that have grown by unrelated diversification, we find that their constituent parts – their business units – can be located in particular industries. Individual business units do not compete with every other kind of business: they compete with those who seek to serve the same set of customer needs in much the same kind of way – or in a better way. This doesn't mean that business units compete with every other business in their industry. It is, perhaps, more accurate to identify the 'strategic group' in the industry with which they associate themselves – a cluster of rivals who take significant interest in each other's products, technologies, executives, workforce skills and so on – without overlooking the fact that new competitors can come in 'from left field' (Feigenbaum and Thomas 1993, Peteraf and Shanley 1997). This is why it is useful to speak of *industry-based* rivalry.

It is important to note that the concept of rivalry does not mean that firms are constantly competing. The leaders of firms have a common interest in the health of their industry (Miles, Snow and Sharfman 1993, Nalebuff and Brandenburger 1996). They are certainly engaged in competition for survival and profitability but they also cooperate when it is helpful. Firms are frequently observed in collaborative efforts to develop foreign markets. Australian, South African, New Zealand and Chilean wine exporters all benefit from the joint marketing of 'New World' wines by their national trade organisations in Europe, for example. They also have interests in collaborating in the labour market. The need to build a labour market on which all can draw is often a reason for co-location of firms (Levinthal and Myatt 1994). Good institutions for skill formation and labour supply benefit all firms in the sector. All Australian and New Zealand winemakers, for example, benefit from supporting the excellent educational institutions, such as South Australia's Roseworthy College, that help to ensure a good supply of graduates for the expanding Antipodean industry.

A focus on industry-based rivalry emphasises the point that history matters, a key argument in the resource-based view of strategic management discussed in Chapter 4. Industries emerge at particular points in time and evolve through periods of crisis – in which there are winners and losers – and periods of relatively stable growth (Schumpeter 1950, Miller and Friesen 1980, Tushman, Newman and Romanelli 1986). This understanding of industry evolution is analogous to the well-known biological concept of 'punctuated equilibrium': the idea that the life forms we find around us are not simply the product of incredibly long periods of time, as originally argued by Charles Darwin, but result from alternating periods of intense change and periods of gradual adaptation (Gersick 1991). For convenience, in the argument that follows about the nature of industry evolution, the words 'business' and 'firm' are used interchangeably.

Phases of industry evolution

At the outset of industry formation, pioneering firms introduce technological and/or organisational innovations that create new competitive space. They are typically joined by others who seek to exploit profit opportunities by imitating the pioneers (Carroll and Hannan 1995, Freeman and Boeker 1984). To get established at all, firms must either be successful leaders or successful followers. All industries, in effect, demonstrate a dynamic interplay between innovation and imitation (Schnaars 1994). Over the long haul, resilient firms exhibit an astute blend of the two processes, something that can be difficult for those business leaders who emotionally cannot accept anything 'not invented here' – NIH syndrome.

The microcomputer industry provides an interesting recent example of the dynamics of innovation and imitation. The legendary innovators, Apple Computer, and about a dozen other firms, entered the industry in 1976 (Carroll and Hannan 1995). Apple produced the first personal computer that could display colour graphics and which could operate with floppy disks. IBM, the industry behemoth, entered five years later, in 1981. For quite a while, David thrashed Goliath. Apple enjoyed the fruits of successful leadership through its various innovations (including the ability of Apple 11 to run spreadsheeting software). However, as we all now know, IBM showed an extraordinary ability to execute an astute 'fast-follower' strategy (Carroll and Hannan 1995, Utterback 1994).

The mature context arrives when the industry or sector settles into a period of stable growth based around one or two 'dominant designs' for products or services *and* the organisations that provide them. The development of a dominant design in manufacturing industries enables firms to move quickly up what technology strategists call the S-curve (Foster 1986, Henderson 1995, Utterback 1994), depicted in Figure 9.1. High levels of R and D effort achieve slow progress to begin with but breakthroughs associated with the dominant design create the basis for rapid

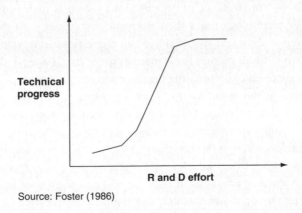

Source: Foster (1986)

Figure 9.1 The S-curve

improvements. Ultimately, the potential of existing technology reaches some kind of performance limit or asymptote.

In the case of personal computers, the IBM PC brought together the defining features that shaped the industry standard: 'a TV monitor, standard disk drive, QWERTY keyboard, the Intel 8088 chip, open architecture, and MS DOS operating system' (Utterback 1994: 25). Dominant designs represent the strategic configurations that have proved more successful than rival models of strategic management in the establishment phase. As Mueller (1997: 827–8) puts it:

> At some point the market begins to select its favourite model designs, producers begin to concentrate upon the best production techniques. Those firms that have selected the 'right' product designs or production processes survive, the others depart. Following this 'shake-out' period, the industry stabilizes and enters a mature phase in which the number of sellers and industry concentration do not change dramatically.

In the mature context, those who remain credible members of the industry enter a period of relative stability in which the emphasis is on continuous improvement within the prevailing business paradigm. They vary, however, in their profitability and in their readiness for change. Stable growth is punctuated by the next crisis which calls for renewal or leads to decline. Renewal crises may be the result of a new round of technological or organisational innovation within the sector – not necessarily by the original pioneers – or may be introduced by a general threat external to all firms – such as a national economic recession, the decline of tariff protection, or a technological revolution in a different field which has dramatic implications across industry boundaries. In the case of technological challenges, particular technologies tend to reach limits (the flat top of the S-curve) and firms must move to new technologies (with their own S-curves) or fail if they cling to an obsolete technology (Foster 1986).

The renewal context challenges the continuities built up over the establishment and mature phases, threatening to turn previous strengths into weaknesses. It is very hard to change the 'core features' of organisations – such as their fundamental mission, their basic technologies and their marketing strategies – so the difficulty of change in the renewal context should never be underestimated (Carroll and Hannan 1995: 26–8). Two kinds of mature firms manage to survive (Baden-Fuller 1995). One is the firm that succeeds in dominating the direction of industry change: the ultimate level of economic achievement for any firm. The other is the firm that manages to adapt to the direction of change. This kind of firm incurs serious costs of adjustment but retains its viability by making the necessary changes without insolvency or loss of investor confidence. It imitates key changes by the new innovators quickly enough to stay afloat. All other firms fail. New entrants may, of course, appear at this point and may hold a winning advantage if they can add new sources of value and behave as nimble entrepreneurial firms which out-manoeuvre the more inertial mature organisations around them.

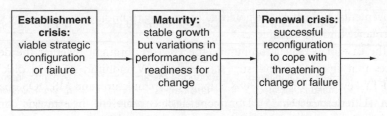

| Establishment crisis: viable strategic configuration or failure | Maturity: stable growth but variations in performance and readiness for change | Renewal crisis: successful reconfiguration to cope with threatening change or failure |

Figure 9.2   Phases of industry evolution

Successful weathering of the renewal crisis ushers in another opportunity for stable growth. In effect, the cycle of stability and crisis continues for as long as the sector remains relevant to a profitable set of customer needs. If it doesn't, the industry enters terminal decline and firms must find something else to do or disappear altogether from the corporate landscape.

The framework shown in Figure 9.2 has been drawn to encompass both goods and service industries. As noted, the S-curve is essentially a concept that relates to manufacturing or to service industries which depend heavily on manufactured technologies for customer service (such as air travel which depends greatly on aircraft technology as well as computerised reservation and passenger management systems). However, all industries – service, manufacturing, public sector and so on – can be thought of as facing alternating periods of change and stability. Change needn't stem from technological breakthroughs: it may stem from ecological, social or political change as well as general economic trends (such as the Asian economic crisis of the late 1990s).

It is also important to note that Figure 9.2 does not imply that all industries change at the same rate across the contexts of establishment, maturity and renewal. Some, like the profession of law, in which precedent and personal service are so engrained, seem to change only in a slow, stately manner. New information technologies are increasingly adopted in law offices but the fundamental nature of legal research and representation has changed very little over the last hundred years or more. Others, such as consumer electronics, seem characterised by what some consultants call 'permanent white water'.

A useful typology of differences in rates of industry change has been developed by Jeffrey Williams (1992). He distinguishes between slow-cycle, standard-cycle and fast-cycle industries (Figure 9.3). One might usefully imagine a dental practice. The dentistry itself (extraction of teeth, filings and so on) is an example of a slow cycle industry. Little has changed in the fundamental nature of dental work for a long period of time. On the other hand, the toothpaste used by the dentist and his/her clients is an example of a standard-cycle industry. The product is mature, controlled by huge oligopolists, and advertising budgets jostle to hold and enlarge market share. Finally, the accounting and client management software on the computer in the dentist's office may be an example of a fast-cycle industry. New upgrades, new versions are almost constantly available.

Aspect	Class 1: slow cycle	Class 2: standard cycle	Class 3: fast cycle
Competitive analogue	Local monopoly	Traditional oligopoly	Schumpeterian
Rivalry	Relaxed: sheltered markets, isolated competition	Extended market share battles, competition on scale	Dynamic: intense rivalry, focus on innovation
Market scope	Narrow: company markets localized	Defined broadly: national or global mass markets and advertising	Varies: overlaps traditional markets, in state of redefinition

Source: Williams (1992)

Figure 9.3 Three types of industry

Despite variations in rates of change, the three phase model of industry evolution – establishment, maturity and renewal/decline – is well supported by research in industrial economics (Mueller 1997) and provides a useful basis for our analysis.

HR strategy and industry dynamics

With this understanding of industry dynamics, we are now in a position to explore the challenges facing HR strategy in each phase or context. Much more research needs to be conducted on the dynamics of HR strategy. Where they are available, key studies are cited but the discussion is necessarily tentative and suggestive of further lines of enquiry. Our concern in each context is with what HR strategy needs to do to help secure the viability of the firm and, secondly, with what it might do to help create some form of sustained advantage.

The establishment context

Any serious search of the HRM literature will confirm that the establishment or founding phase of industry is the least studied of all by HRM researchers. Apart from the work of Hendry, Arthur and Jones (1995) on the role of human resources in the formation of small firms, the typical HRM textbook assumes a ready-made, large scale, bureaucratic corporation with an HR department whose staff are concerned with choosing and improving an appropriate set of human resource policies. Few HR researchers have studied small, entrepreneurial start-ups or even new ventures spawned by large corporations. Yet if we are to take the point seriously that history matters to competitive advantage, we must try to understand the roles human resources play in the establishment phase. Strategic management research indicates that that key decisions taken at founding have profound consequences, establishing a pattern of behaviour that is difficult (though not impossible) to change (Boeker 1989, Eisenhart and Bird Schoonhovern 1990, Freeman and Boeker 1984).

The need for talented entrepreneurs and entrepreneurial teams

What, then, might be said about the likely priorities of HR strategy in this phase? We must begin with the obvious point that all firms depend on appropriate human capital to make any sort of successful beginning. Relevant human resources are a necessary, but not a sufficient, condition of success. This rather obvious point is supported by a major US study of 'entrepreneurial human capital inputs and small business longevity' (Bates 1990). Bates finds that more highly educated entrepreneurs have a better chance of succeeding and of raising capital finance. The likelihood of business failure is lower for high-school graduates and for university graduates than it is for those who did not complete high school. The rate of failure drops markedly if entrepreneurs have four or more years of university education. Better-educated business founders make fewer mistakes, it seems. This result has recently been supported by a study of top management teams in the UK which finds that these teams perform better when the individuals in them are better educated (West, Patterson and Dawson 1999). The greatest benefit comes when at least some team members hold a postgraduate qualification. Not only are these people likely to be more intelligent but their abilities are likely to have been significantly enhanced by the kind of training gained through their postgraduate degrees.

As a general rule, firms are established by entrepreneurs, or 'intrapreneurial' teams in existing corporations, who are either (a) successful pioneers, or (b) successful followers (Freeman 1995, Mueller 1997, Porter 1985, Schnaars 1994, Schumpeter 1950). They are founded by people who create new sources of value or by others who quickly perceive that new value is being created and successfully join the industry. It is possible to fail both at leading and at following. As noted earlier, success depends on being good at one or the other or at demonstrating an astute blend of the two over time.

The need to stabilise a competent and well-coordinated workforce

While entrepreneurial insight is a necessary element, it is not, however, sufficient to ensure successful navigation of the establishment phase. The conventional wisdom is that firms need to be able to secure the kind of 'stable and committed labour force' (Rubery 1994: 47) that will enable them to compete, to deliver on promises to customers. They need to be able to recruit and retain a wider group of employees who work together effectively in expanding the founder's or the founding team's concept of the business. Otherwise, the business will simply not grow. As a study of 122 start-up companies in the USA emphasises, an ability to recruit employees is strategic to business growth, along with an ability to win customers and attract finance (Alpander, Carter and Forsgren 1990). Marketing ability, adequate money, and the people needed to carry out the work come in as the three biggest factors explaining success.

Lack of growth potential is fine in those businesses, such as small professional service firms, that can remain viable as permanently small firms (Storey 1985), but it does not work in other contexts. In many industries, firms need to meet a threshold for 'critical mass'. Viability depends on establishing credible operational capacity in the sector, on recruiting and retaining a pool of people with industry-relevant abilities. Whether firms can do this depends on the degree of labour scarcity in their industry and their ability to make competitive job offers. When labour markets are tight, it is often hard to attract talented people to employment 'in a relatively obscure company' (Alpander, Carter and Forsgren 1990: 14).

A classic example of an attempt to create a viable labour pool in the establishment phase comes from the automobile industry. Henry Ford I began production of the Model T in 1908, the same year in which General Motors was founded (Carroll and Hannan 1995). The Ford Motor Company experienced 370 per cent labour turnover in 1913, a level that was not uncommon in manufacturing at the time (Meyer 1981). In a context of massive product market growth, Henry Ford set out to create a large, competent and stable workforce with a highly innovative 'bundle' of personnel policies. This included a rational system of job grading and promotion based on skill differences, along with the 'Five Dollar Day', an early example of 'efficiency wages' (Lacey 1986, Main 1990, Meyer 1981).[20] Facing a major problem with literacy levels, it also included a schooling system for workforce education. Ford's spectacular and controversial adoption of profit sharing (coupled with a highly demanding pace of work on the moving assembly line) ensured that he attracted and retained much of the best labour then available in the industry. Workers queued to get in. Once recruited, those who couldn't cope with the pace dropped out. Ford built a workforce which was at least equal to that of his rivals, a critical achievement at a time of labour transience in the United States. (His subsequent attempts to fight union organisation are not offered here as a model.)

It is wrong to assume that a good workforce is readily available when the skill requirements of the firm are advanced and specialised. High skill industries can only survive in particular countries if that society generates sufficient numbers of people educated in the relevant science and technology. The great economic historian, David Landes (1998), cites the case of the chemical dye industry which grew phenomenally prior to World War One. Germany trained far more chemists than anyone else, enabling the foundation and growth of the German chemical giants: Hoechst, BASF, Bayer and Agfa, all 'equipped with well-fitted house laboratories and closely tied to the universities' (Landes 1998: 290). When key German chemists teaching in Britain were 'drawn back home by attractive offers, the British organic chemical industry shrivelled' (*ibid*: 290). In an illustration of the role of tacit knowledge (discussed in

---

20 Introduced in 1914. The effect was to roughly double the income of automotive workers employed by Ford. The length of work shifts was reduced at the same time: from 9 to 8 hours. 'Efficiency wages', in this case, means that there can be value in certain circumstances in paying a wage premium (well above the going rate) to improve the recruitment pool and reduce undesirable turnover of highly trained workers (McConnell and Brue 1995: 214).

Chapter 4), the confiscation of German industrial patents during the War did not help American firms to emulate German chemical success. Not to be outdone, they turned to the recruitment of German chemists in the 1920s (Landes 1998: 291).

Our argument, then, is that stabilising a competent workforce of the appropriate size for the sector and the firm's competitive goals is critical to viability in the establishment phase. This should not be thought about simply in terms of individualistic recruitment and retention. As Chapter 2 argued, effective teamwork is also needed. There needs to be reasonably good teamwork among top managers and right throughout the organisation. Research on the establishment of the semiconductor industry in the 1950s helps to illustrate these principles (Holbrook, Chen, Hounshell and Klepper 2000). One of the early leaders, Fairchild Semiconductor, combined a good mix of research and production skills in its core group of executives – the so-called 'traitorous eight' who broke away from the Shockley company (as noted in Chapter 4). Not only did this group work together well as a team but they worked hard to ensure that R and D activities were closely coordinated with the firm's production. When the ability of Fairchild to coordinate R and D and production was undermined in the mid-1960s, a subsequent breakaway team formed Intel (Holbrook *et al.* 2000: 1027).

Sources of human resource advantage?

Large and growing firms that have the ability to pay wage premia, and the capacity to offer superior internal development, are likely to enjoy formidable advantages in the establishment phase. This certainly seems the case with firms such as IBM that enter new markets, and helps to explain why so many small businesses fail to expand successfully or remain small, tenuous organisations with ongoing recruitment and retention stresses (Hendry *et al.* 1995, Storey 1985). The bigger firms operating in the same labour market have better financial resources and more developed 'internal labour markets' (Rubery 1994: 48–51). Large, established firms enjoy superior legitimacy with investors and bankers in the capital markets (Storey 1985). This enables them to offer greater training and career development possibilities to talented employees, something which many people want, as noted in Chapter 7.

What possible routes are available for the very small new venture, founded by an under-capitalised individual rather than a well-known, multidivisional corporation? Arguably, this often means clever use of personal networking (Hendry *et al.* 1995) at a strategic moment in the industry's development. While there is very limited research on this problem, we might consider the example of a young, and very successful, entrepreneurial software engineer (Boxall 1998). This young entrepreneur used their network from engineering school to recruit highly intelligent individuals willing to work outside large organisations (perhaps because they preferred an informal, 'can do' environment) and swiftly offered those who generated outstanding value an ownership stake in the firm to align their interests over the longer term.

Having worked with them at university, the young entrepreneur had special knowledge about the abilities and predispositions of classmates as well as personal ties based on friendship and trust. This created an edge over corporate recruiters forced to rely on formal screening processes and more opaque forms of information (such as university grades) rather than personal knowledge and close connections. In terms of resource-based theory, the young entrepreneur lacked superior financial clout and market reputation but used personal background and social networks to out-manoeuvre recruiters from large, established organisations.

Our knowledge about sources of human resource advantage in the establishment phase is still very limited. It seems likely, however, that *early alignment* of interests among highly talented people plays a decisive role (as was the case at Fairchild Semiconductor). This means that history – being there at the right time – matters enormously in the creation of positions of strength in industries (as argued in the resource-based view). It also implies that clever use of personal knowledge – such as an ability to network among likeminded and similarly gifted people – is needed to overcome the formidable resource barriers associated with firms that are more established in labor and capital markets.

The mature context

We can be somewhat more confident about the priorities of HR strategy in the mature context. This is the familiar terrain of the personnel or HRM textbook. Writers typically assume that a viable business has been handed on from the establishment phase. To be fair, it is only the firms which have grown beyond about 150 to 200 employees that employ HR specialists. This means that the vast majority of HR specialists are working in the mature context or in the renewal context into which it typically leads (see below).

Enduring principles but greater sophistication

Growth beyond the establishment phase into the mature context *does* introduce problems that require a different style of management. It is still vital to create, coordinate and retain a sufficient pool of motivated labour with appropriate industry know-how. This principle is hardly likely to vary with time in the industry. However, the challenges of size, increasing workforce complexity, the need to comply with various employment regulations, and the possibility of unionisation, all mean that HR policies need to become more comprehensive and more formalised (see, for example, Jackson and Schuler 1995). Reliance on the implicit philosophies and informal practices of the small, entrepreneurial firm becomes much less realistic. When recruited into a larger organisation, workers typically expect some formalisation of their role requirements in a written job description. They tend to expect some formal orientation which will introduce them, *inter alia*, to the firm's policies for training, development, pay, promotion and so on. Properly handled, formalisation eases the process of socialisation and psychological contracting by reducing uncertainty and limiting arbitrariness in management practice. Standardisation of policies also makes the management of staff more efficient because it reduces the transaction costs of employing large numbers of people.

On the other hand, the maturing of organisational structure can alienate the very people who have helped to make the firm successful so far. The trend to bureau-cratisation may antagonise those who revelled in the informality and adrenalin-pumping riskiness of the firm's founding years. These individuals may experience a sense of loss, a sense that the company will never again be driven by the same white-hot creativity and sense of fun. Thus, growth can generate a tension around the desirability of bureaucratisation: on the one hand, it is needed to manage complexity and, on the other, it threatens the intimacy and challenge of earlier times.

Supposing this tension does not get out of hand, firms that successfully survive the establishment crisis will have reasonably competent executive leadership and will have built an adequate operating workforce. They will typically have created a sound reputation as a source of respectable employment and have laid the basis of trustworthy employee relations. In terms of the HRM challenges facing the business, they should at least aim to retain 'competitive parity': their employment strategies may not be the best in the sector but they have not so far undermined the firm's growth. Arguably, this situation should persist providing there are no major rever-sals in the quality of recruitment, performance management and employee relations. At the very least, the firm's leaders should avoid turning their competitive parity in HRM into a form of competitive *dis*advantage (Purcell 1999a: 241).

Figure 9.4 summarises the key dimensions of what is required in HRM to help secure a firm's viability. As indicated in our discussion, firms need talented and functioning leadership teams, along with a motivated and capable workforce which can reliably execute its work processes and deliver on promises to customers. These critical human resources are developed through an appropriate mix of HR policies and practices and through supportive non-human resources, including adequate

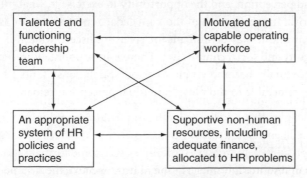

Figure 9.4 HRM and the viability of the firm: key elements

levels of finance. The arrows in the diagram are double-headed because of the inter-action among these elements. For example, good HR practices and adequate fund-ing will help the firm to recruit (or develop internally) good leadership teams. However, it is also true that good leadership teams will, over time, improve the qual-ity of HR practices in the firm and make the kind of financial allocation decisions that enable it to attract and develop other people. Similarly, a motivated and capa-ble workforce will help the firm to generate profits, part of which can be reinvested in recruitment, performance incentives and human resource development.

What, however, might a firm do if it wishes to develop some form of 'human resource advantage' in the mature context? What argument can be built from the resource-based view discussed in Chapter 4? Very little theory is available on this question but one argument is based on the value of improving the quality of man-agement perception in HRM and HR planning systems, and improvements in the consistency of HR practice (Boxall 1998).

The quality of management perception in HRM

Firms vary in the quality of management's *perception* of the firm's strengths and weaknesses in HRM in relation to the strengths and weaknesses of rival employers. Specialised knowledge about *individual* HR practices is widespread (for example, the knowledge developed by recruitment consultants about selection tests or the know-ledge developed by compensation consultants about pay packages) but the ability to discern the *patterns* embedded in the firm's unfolding labour management practices is more likely to be rare. The ability to perceive ways of minimising critical trade-offs in labour management (such as the trade-off between short-run employment flexibility and long-run employee commitment) is also likely to be rare (Boxall 1999).

Research suggests that few managers have a superior understanding of how to 'bundle' or integrate HR practices into high-performance work systems that fit the firm's specific context and its unfolding strategies (Barney and Wright 1998, MacDuffie 1995). If, however, a firm employs individuals with this kind of rare knowledge and perception, and the opportunity to exercise it, what might prevent it being lost to rival firms? If much of the knowledge remains tacit, or associated with executive teamwork, it may be difficult for rivals to discern what it is or who has it (causal ambiguity and social complexity). There is little doubt, however, that this sort of skill will eventually become visible to good search consultants ('head-hunters') and therefore vulnerable to mobility. Individual perception remains, in effect, indi-vidual property.

The quality of HR planning systems

To build human resource advantage in the mature context, the firm needs to develop attributes which are more deeply institutionalised (Mueller 1996). A superior system of human resource *planning*, which identifies and integrates key human variables with other strategic concerns, is one way of institutionalising the perceptual insights of key HR strategists (either specialists or general managers) who may decide to resign from the firm. The kind of human resource planning which encourages firms to manage 'key value generators' proactively and plan to improve key processes (such as learning across intra-firm boundaries) is both valuable and rare (Koch and McGrath 1996). Human resource planning for concerns that transcend the short-term business context helps to avoid the all-too-common situation where financial targets, reinforced in the annual budget cycle, crowd out longer-term strategic issues in management planning (Goold 1991), a theme we take further in Chapters 10 and 11.

Even very large firms have problems developing sophisticated strategic planning systems which incorporate a framework of strategic HR objectives capable of structuring internal debate and decision-making (Boxall 1999, Purcell and Ahlstrand 1994). How might such a discipline be developed and defended? Clearly it depends on the recruitment and retention of leaders who have exceptional HR insight, as discussed above. But this is not sufficient because so much of strategic management depends on good teamwork, as argued in Chapter 2. At some point, a powerful coalition of managers must evolve the conceptual framework and generate the consensus for its ongoing application. At a minimum, a shared understanding between the firm's most influential general managers and its top HR specialists, which persuades other key managers, seems essential. Any firm that achieves this has accomplished an unusual feat in the management process given the political conflicts and paradigmatic disputes that typically afflict the management teams of large organisations. The difficulty of overcoming these internal conflicts is a powerful barrier to imitation. It is not, of course, perfect: the loss of key individuals who act as process champions can compromise the quality of any planning system.

The consistency of HR practice

The possibility of developing HR advantage will be greater to the extent that intelligent HR planning is linked to superior *consistency* of enlightened practice (Benkhoff 1997, Mueller 1996). Inconsistent application of well-designed HR policies often undermines desired impact, as stressed in a study of seven high-profile British organisations (McGovern, Gratton, Hope-Hailey, Stiles and Truss 1997: 12):

> Our evidence, which is drawn from a wider study of HRM in practice, suggests that, while line manager involvement is indeed possible, their practices tend to vary significantly in the consistency of implementation across the organisation (e.g. business units and departments) and in the quality of practice between managers. This finding challenges much of the rhetoric associated with the idea of devolution to the line because it demonstrates that line management practice may itself distort, and possibly even undermine, the contribution which HR policies are supposed to make towards organisational success.

This kind of study should remind us that there is no such thing as *the* single HR practice of the firm. It is more accurate to imagine the HR practices of the firm as norms around which there is variation due to the idiosyncratic behaviour of line managers. In some areas, such as performance appraisal, there is notorious variation, even in the 'best regulated companies'.

As a result, consistency of HR practice is hard to achieve without strong accountability mechanisms for line managers (as noted in the discussion of performance appraisal systems in Chapter 7). A culture of devolution, however, often favours measurement in terms of short-term financial results rather than long-term HR priorities (Goold 1991, McGovern *et al.* 1997, Purcell and Ahlstrand 1994). The prevailing belief in line manager autonomy in the process of HRM is likely to act as a powerful restraint on the ability to develop sources of human resource advantage. While there is value in diversity, too much autonomy can discourage the transfer of excellent models of HRM within a firm across managerial boundaries. In the haste to take out HR department overhead and remove what line managers often regard as the 'policing' of policies, the firm may also lose the power to coordinate objectives for human resource development over the long run. This is not a problem if the firm's main rivals are equally weak at developing plans for long-run human resource development but it is not a recipe for building sustained advantage or undermining a more positively planful competitor.

In summary, the argument here is that the possibility of creating HR advantages for a firm is greater when exceptional perception about HR strategy is embedded in sophisticated planning systems which are connected to consistent practice. The level of insight, and the degree of internal consensus, required to achieve this kind of superiority should not be underestimated. They are likely to be very rare.

The renewal context

The renewal context challenges the continuities built up over the establishment and mature phases. It threatens to turn previous strengths into weaknesses through technological (or other) shocks which call for a reconfiguration of the strategic paradigm in the firm (Barney 1991, Mueller 1997, Schumpeter 1950, Tushman *et al.* 1986). As noted earlier, two kinds of mature firms manage to survive (Baden-Fuller 1995). One is the firm that succeeds in dominating the direction of industry change. The other is the firm that manages to adapt to the direction of change. All other firms fail. New entrants may, of course, appear at this point and may hold a winning advantage if they can behave as clever and nimble entrepreneurial firms. They need not necessarily be small firms: they may, for example, be special business units operating within very powerful multidivisional firms.

What, then, are the implications for human resource strategy? Rather than assuming that firms are privileged by their past, we must now regard history as a double-edged sword.

Conditions for securing viability

There are, arguably, three conditions firms must meet to retain their viability during this kind of industry upheaval (Boxall 1998). Two of these conditions are primarily concerned with HR strategy but the third is not.

The first is *political*. The renewal context threatens the patterns of mutuality – of interest alignment – that have solidified over the establishment and mature phases. The renewing firm needs the kind of mandate from its staff – both managerial and operational – which enables it to bring about major change without enormous resistance. Here the impact of the established hierarchy is important. To begin with, the key players in senior management must be able to form a new 'micro-political' consensus. As noted in Chapter 2, significant, unresolved conflict in the senior management team over the need for change (possibly linked to personal career ambitions and historical power bases) will disrupt renewal efforts at the outset (Hambrick 1987, 1995). Having said this, the ability to open the micro-political gateway at the senior level is necessary but not sufficient for successful renewal in the industry. It is also essential to achieve the necessary change to business capabilities and workplace culture while maintaining an adequate motivational climate throughout the core of the firm's workforce, thus ensuring wider political acceptability for the desired changes. Or, if a large part of the changes are to be formulated from the bottom up, it involves achieving a culture of change acceptability which fosters a willing acceptance of new learning trajectories as a matter of course.

The second condition is *perceptual*. The firm needs leaders who can see what competencies will retain their relevance in the future while perceiving what capabilities have already become liabilities. Where, in effect, should the firm consolidate its learning and what should it 'unlearn' and to what extent (Leonard 1992, 1998, Miller and Friesen 1980, Snell, Youndt and Wright 1996)? And when, and in what order, should it make the desirable changes: how should it shape its 'strategic staircase' (Baden-Fuller and Stopford 1994)? Senior management faces a complex cognitive problem in discerning the kind, extent and timing of the change that is needed to enable the firm to survive. As noted in Chapter 2, this has been called the problem of forming a new 'mental model' (Barr, Stimpert and Huff 1992). It is highly likely, of course, that senior management doesn't have all the answers, in which case the firm's leadership must perceive how to design the sort of participative processes that will generate the necessary learning. The cognitive problem leaders face in renewal is not simply about content: it is also about process. It is altogether more complex than the perceptual problems associated with the mature phase.

The third condition is concerned with *related resources*. The firm must actually have the access to the financial resources it needs to make the necessary changes. As ever, human and non-human resources are interdependent (Mueller 1996). When renewal means radical change, it requires more than human willingness and cleverness. It requires the cash box to make things happen. Lots of firms fail at the renewal phase simply because they are under-capitalised (rather like the establishment phase). Despite great ideas and the best of intentions, no one will lend them any more money.

The three conditions can be illustrated in the case of Ford's dramatic turnaround in the early 1980s. By the early 1980s, the success of Japanese auto manufacturers through superior quality – dependent on good human capital and (what were then) novel processes of 'lean production' – had begun to affect all US firms in the industry. Between 1980 and 1982, Ford lost $3.3 billion. In this context, Ford met the political conditions for renewal. Executives genuinely accepted that the company – an icon of American capitalism – might fail to adapt (Pascale 1991). Furthermore, the realisation that the firm faced a life-threatening crisis permeated all levels of the company, creating the mandate necessary for radical change. Significant lay-offs did occur: the production workforce fell from 191,000 to 105,000 between 1978 and 1986 and white-collar employment fell by 47 per cent between 1980 and 1986 (Schoenberger 1997). Despite this massive reduction, Ford seems to have achieved sufficient mutuality with its remaining workforce through a new profit-sharing agreement and through a genuine shift to a more participative style of management (Collins and Porras 1998, Pascale 1991).

Besides having the political ability to change, Ford was blessed with leadership which met the cognitive condition, which accurately perceived what ought to change. In the early 1980s, Ford drew astute lessons from the Japanese experience while GM and Chrysler struggled to do so (Pascale 1991, Schoenberger 1997). Donald Petersen, Ford's CEO, encouraged the kind of shift to participative management – 'employee involvement' – that was needed to enable Ford's design and production activities to raise their performance much closer to Japanese levels. As Pascale (1991: 117) puts it: 'Petersen did not see himself as having, or needing to have, the answers. He served as the catalyst that enabled Ford's employees to come up with the answers themselves.'

Finally, despite its severe losses, Ford still had the necessary financial resources to invest heavily in product innovation and employee development. Some $3.2 billion was spent on the Taurus vehicle program, an initiative that paid off handsomely (Pascale 1991). The company also had the resources necessary to engage in a major programme of skill formation and process facilitation. In 1986, Ford's profits exceeded those of General Motors for the first time since 1924 (Pascale 1991). In sum, Ford met the political, perceptual and resource conditions necessary for successful renewal.

Opportunities for human resource advantage?

If these are the conditions for retaining viability in the renewal context, where do the opportunities lie for building sustained advantage through human resources? One argument is that it is simply a case of hanging on, of still being there once restructuring and rightsizing strategies – both good and bad – have made their mark on the industry landscape (Boxall 1998). Some rivals will have been fatally weakened in the process – perhaps because they divested the wrong bits – and will go into bankruptcy or suffer the sort of share price collapse that makes them easy takeover targets. The firms with the bigger cash boxes then acquire their weaker rivals, retaining the branches or plants (and people) they really want and divesting or shutting down the rest. The industry concentrates around the strongest survivors. This process may not be pleasant – and is rarely, if ever, discussed in HRM textbooks – but it does suggest that superior human capital will tend to concentrate in the dominant firms despite a prevailing climate of employment insecurity in the industry. On the other hand, the dominant firms cannot afford to be complacent because processes of concentration allow some clever teams to split away from the major firms and occupy specialist market niches (Carroll and Hannan 1995: 215–21).

Human resource strategy and organisational agility

An alternative argument is more proactive, asserting that the surest way to achieve human resource advantage in the renewal context lies in preparing for it more effectively in the mature context (Boxall 1998). Abell (1993) argues that the outstanding firm manages with 'dual strategies': 'mastering the present and pre-empting the future'. Duality implies superior perceptual and planning abilities in all contexts: the firm must not become locked into the inertia of a single strategy at any point in time. Providing the firm's industry does not collapse by becoming techno-logically irrelevant, this scenario is plausible in theory.

Based on exploratory case studies in the USA, Dyer and Shafer (1999) have de-veloped a model of how HR strategy might support organisational agility. In their definition, agile organisations aim 'to develop a built-in capacity to shift, flex, and adjust, either alone or with alliance partners, as circumstances change, and do so as a matter of course' (Dyer and Shafer 1999: 148). In effect, they aim 'to optimise adaptability and efficiency simultaneously' (Figure 9.5). Recalling our discussion of

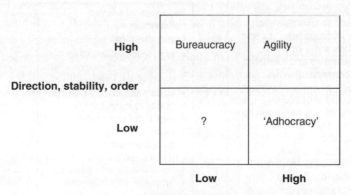

Source: Dyer and Shafer (1999)

Figure 9.5 A definition of organisational agility

HR objectives in Chapter 1, agile organisations can be thought of as firms that aim for high levels of labour productivity (in the current context) and high levels of organisational flexibility. In terms of technology strategy, they are firms that can maximise the gains from their current S-curve while moving when desirable to the next one and reaping its benefits. It might be worthwhile to inject a note of caution here, however. In terms of Jeffrey Williams' framework (Figure 9.3 above), it is firms in fast-cycle industries that most need this capacity. The idea that all industries demand this level of change readiness is exaggerated in popular accounts.

Dyer and Shafer (1999) note that organisational theorists tend to write about organisational agility with little regard for the people elements involved. To help fill this void, their model starts by defining the characteristics of agile organisations and works back through employee behaviours and competencies to desirable HR practices. We have paraphrased and summarised this model in Figure 9.6.

Dyer and Shafer incorporate resource-based thinking in their model: achievement of an agile organisation is very likely to be rare, valuable and hard to imitate. The concept of an agile organisation is fleshed out to mean one that can read markets

Source: Paraphrased and summarised from Dyer and Shafer (1999)

Figure 9.6 Dyer and Shafer's model of HR strategy in agile organisations

well (both current and emerging), can create a culture which welcomes change, and one which readily embeds organisational learning. Like Schuler and Jackson (1987), they then specify certain kinds of desirable employee behaviours and link these to HR practices (see Chapter 3). Much of this thinking is tentative and exploratory but flexible work design is central to Dyer and Shafer's model (fluid job assignments rather than fixed jobs or positions). They then suggest certain kinds of employment practice which should accompany fluid work organisation. The ideas here overlap with typical US models of 'best practice' discussed in Chapter 3, including the emphasis on contingent pay.

As Dyer and Shafer (1999) advise, we need much more research on the nature of 'organisational agility', and the kind of HR strategies that might support it. One critical question must surround the problem of incentives or mutuality. Why would talented workers want to join an agile organisation if very little security is being offered and if, as a relatively flat organisation, little career development is possible? One can imagine that some people will want to buy into the culture for the sheer thrill, the joy of learning, and quite probably, the high pay level if the firm does well. However, as Dyer and Shafer (1999: 169) imply, it is likely that an agile firm will need a stable core of long-term, talented employees if it is to be able to sustain committed learning over time:

> Most agile organisations, contrary to what might be expected, lean toward a so-called closed internal staffing system . . . . They go to great lengths to retain core employees who continue to contribute; most have relatively low voluntary turnover rates and, despite having little reluctance to part company with non-performers, most make every effort to avoid lay-offs because . . . they have rather extensive investments in their core employees.

This brings us back to the need to manage an appropriate core/periphery model of employment, as discussed in Chapter 6. Clearly, the design of agile organisations is a 'frontier area' in strategic HRM and much more work will need to be done, particularly on the management of the strategic tensions involved (Evans and Genadry 1999). The contemporary environment contains major tensions between corporate needs for flexibility, on the one hand, and typical employee needs for certain baseline elements of stability, on the other. Talented, versatile employees have good choices in the international labour market, so the need for compromise and adjustment is not one-way. Further work on how these tensions can be better reconciled is vital.

Conclusions and implications

This chapter has built on resource-based concepts discussed earlier in the book and examined an area that is rarely thought about in HRM texts: the ways in which HR strategy might need to adapt across cycles of change and stability in industries. Not all industries change at the same rate but change pressures are universal.

Drawing on the distinction made in Chapter 2, priorities for HR strategy were considered from two angles: what is needed for viability in the sector and what might contribute to sustained competitive advantage? To achieve viability in the establishment context, firms need talented entrepreneurial leaders and need to be able to stabilise a competent and well-coordinated workforce. Viability depends on establishing credible operational capacity in the sector. Whether firms can do this depends on the degree of labour scarcity in their industry and their ability to make competitive job offers. Firms cannot afford to assume that all the advanced or specialised skills they require will be readily available. Large, well-funded firms are obviously at an advantage when it comes to making offers of good pay and strong internal development to talented individuals. The small, under-capitalised business has great difficulty competing against better funded rivals but astute use of personal networking, and early alignment of interests, may help them to out-manoeuvre more bureaucratic organisations.

In the mature context, it remains important to create, coordinate and retain a sufficient pool of motivated labour with appropriate industry know-how. Firms that survive from the establishment context will have something close to competitive parity in HRM and should aim, at the least, to maintain it. However, they will find that the challenges of growth mean that the style of management will need to change: size, diversity, regulation and the likelihood of employee representation will mean that HR policies need to become more comprehensive and more formalised. Arguably, sources of advantage can be created by firms whose management teams exhibit high levels of perception in HR strategy. Talented HR strategists can be lured away, so it is better if these insights are embedded in excellent HR planning systems and consistent HR practice. This combination of strengths is likely to be very rare. It is not unusual to find ways in which the HR performance of mature firms can be enhanced.

All bets are off in the renewal context. History could now be as much a source of 'core rigidity' as 'core competence' (Leonard 1992, 1998). Simply managing the perceptual, political, and funding problems associated with survival is a major achievement. One of the most interesting questions in strategic HRM theory concerns the characteristics of 'agile organisations', firms that anticipate the need for renewal and are well prepared to take advantage of it (Dyer and Shafer 1999). Arguably, this is more important in fast-cycle industries. Existing work is exploratory and research in this area needs to consider ways in which tensions between company and employee goals can be managed more effectively. There is no doubt that agile organisations need greater flexibility but they are unlikely to reach high performance levels without stabilising at least a critical core of highly talented individuals and teams who can help them find the future. In working out the tension between stable harvesting of the current environment and preparation for radical change, firms are likely to find that at least some commitments need to be made to fair, interesting and reliable employment relationships if they are to attract and hold talented staff.

10

Corporate human resource strategy in the global economy

Most models of business strategy, and strategic human resource management, start with the premiss that the firm is both independent, with a direct relationship between it and the shareholders, and engaged in a single business activity. With these two assumptions in place, it is possible to model the behaviour of the firm in response to specific, or changing, product market conditions and competitor challenges within the sector (as we did in Chapter 9). This has allowed us to show the linkages between competitive strategies and configurations of policies and practices associated with productivity, flexibility and legitimacy in human resource management. All models need to reduce the infinite complexity of organisational life, as revealed over time, through a process of variable reduction, enabling us to make some sense of what is going on and extrapolate trends. Sensible though this is, it can reduce complexity too far. We need in this chapter to take account of the effect on HR strategy of being a multi-business, and often multinational, firm.

In fact, most workplaces are part of larger organisations where top management is geographically remote. For example, in the UK, only just over a quarter of establishments with 25 employees or more were 'stand-alones' in 1998 (Cully *et al.* 1999: 16). Of those that were part of a wider organisation, 38 per cent belonged to firms with 10,000 or more employees. Around one fifth of workplaces were wholly or partially foreign-owned, and this foreign ownership became more visible, or more dominant, the larger the size of the workplace. Thus, 28 per cent of establishments with 500 or more workers belonged to, and were controlled by, companies with headquarters outside the UK. Foreign ownership in the UK more than doubled between 1980 and 1998 (Millward, Bryson and Forth 2000: 32). This foreign direct investment (FDI) is, of course, not restricted to Britain. 'The UK, Germany, Holland and France hosted 40 per cent of worldwide FDI in the early 1990s. There were 3500 cross-border mergers in the run-up to the creation of the Single European Market (European firms buying other European firms) . . . (at the same time) UK firms were investing \$27 billion in the US: the largest single country-to-country movement in its history' (Sparrow 2002). Predictions for the first five years of the 21st century are for FDI worldwide to grow from $6500 billion to $10,000 billion (*ibid*). A representative study of large companies in the UK in the early 1990s, each employing over 1000 people, found that 60 per cent were multinational corporations (MNCs) (Marginson, Armstrong, Edwards and Purcell 1993). Of the 24 per cent of these big firms which were foreign-owned, half were North American, 38 per cent had their headquarters elsewhere in Europe, with the remainder coming from other parts of the world.

To get to grips with the critical issues that impact on human resource strategies, and the extent to which HRM is a strategic issue in the management of large firms, we need to look at trends in the structure and control of large multi-business firms, both nationally and internationally. This takes us into an understanding of the dynamics of the multidivisional company (M-form) and the way the M-form company has spread to a dominant position worldwide. At the same time, we are seeing the emergence of a new type of M-form based around networks: the N-Form (Hedlund 1994). The development of an N-form company has profound implications for HRM, especially in the way the critical resources of these companies, including managers and professional workers, are developed (the pursuit of 'human capital advantage') and interact across boundaries, whether political-geographic or organisational (the pursuit of 'organisational process advantage').

At the same time, we need to look at the impact of ownership and control on workplace employment systems. Here the current mantra for MNCs is to 'think global, act local'. This implies a separation of corporate strategy dealing with the whole of the corporation (think global), from the delivery of productivity and flexibility at the local level in different ways and in different forms to take account of institutional and cultural differences (act local). Thus, our concern is with dilemmas in structural configuration and with forms of control exercised from headquarters, the corporate office. Do firms centralise or decentralise, or achieve both, and with what implications? And should corporations seek to integrate the different businesses they own, or treat them as separate entities but try to manage them better than if they were wholly independent? The crucial question is how does the centre add value, how does it develop what has been called 'parenting advantage' (Goold, Campbell and Alexander 1994)? We need to ask, what contribution, if any, does HRM make to parenting advantage?

Most large companies have grown by buying other companies, and simultaneously selling parts of their portfolio businesses. We need to consider the special challenges that mergers and acquisitions (M&A) pose for HRM. This is a particularly acute question since around half of all M&As are deemed failures (KPMG 1999) with implementation problems relating to people, employment and cultural issues the main reasons for failure (Hubbard and Purcell 2001: 17–18). We consider this problem in the third part of the chapter.

Traditionally in a book of this sort there would be a separate chapter on MNCs. Here we would chart the growth of these firms (many with revenues which exceed the GNP of some nation states), note the changing form of organisations within them (Bartlett and Ghoshal 1998), and consider the special HR issues. In practice, nearly all HRM research in this area has been on staffing, with a particular focus on expatriates (see Scullion and Brewster (2001) for a summary and analysis). Formidable though some of these HR issues are, often requiring the attention of internationalist, specialist HR managers, they do not address the strategic issues of integration or separation, centralisation or decentralisation, and the HR strategies embedded within them. In practice, virtually all MNCs adopt an M-form structure. The merging of the M-form with MNCs is, in part, an outcome of shifts in global markets. When there were predominantly national markets in, say, cars or soap powders, or hotels and banks, MNCs were distinct in that the question was, how did the corporation manage its assets (including its people) in distinct national markets? Increasingly markets are global, or at least regional, in many areas. Soap packets now come in 14 languages on the back. The 'world car' is premissed on global design and global sourcing of components. Insurance companies are too small to survive in one country alone, and hotel chains straddle most parts of the world with a global branding strategy. Increasingly, the organisational form of MNCs is not one of separate companies in each country with their own national strategies but divisions based on products or services facing end markets across boundaries. One consequence is that labour markets for managerial and professional workers become themselves global. Increasingly, recruitment agencies are taking on global roles for sourcing specialist skills as well as local labour, but with global supply contracts with major employers. Manpower Inc. is now the largest firm worldwide in terms of the number of people on its books (2.7 million in 2000).

Thus, it is not sensible to separate a consideration of the dominant form of large firm organisation – the M-form company – from MNCs. The key strategic factors are common to both. The international and global issues that confront large corporations in HR terms, such as variances in cultures, forms of regulation and institutional frameworks and their effect, are woven into the chapter.

Strategy, structure and the divisionalised company

Most firms start as single businesses. As they grow and mature and as the market they serve changes (as explored in Chapter 9), a number of critical choices are faced. Is the competitive position in the current markets sustainable given new entrants, is there sufficient capital available from revenue to fund future investment needs, is the market maturing such that growth potential and margins are likely to be eroded in the medium term? Another type of question faced is whether there are opportunities to use distinctive technologies or knowledge to enter other markets. What is certain is that doing nothing is rarely viable, and for many business leaders rather boring too. One route to growth is to branch away from the traditional market, in other words to diversify. This could be to do the same thing in a new market, as UK retailers Marks and Spencers tried unsuccessfully to do by buying their way into the USA. Another route is by vertical integration, seeking both to protect the supply chain and to enter new markets where there is growth potential, or to make life more difficult for competitors in cornering a market position. It may also be that another firm possesses knowledge of a technology or market that the single business firm lacks, or indeed they may feel the lack of general management expertise. Whatever the reason, the critical choice that follows is how best to manage a diversified business, nationally and internationally, and how far should diversification go?

The traditional firm usually adopts a functional or unified form where functional specialists in marketing, operations, finance and HRM each coordinate their own areas, having representation on the board of directors under the command of the chief executive (CEO) and sometimes a separate chairman. The board may also contain non-executive directors drawn from the great and the good in the corporate world to provide oversight, advice and access to networks. As firms diversify, this structure is placed under strain. Executive directors are responsible for operational decisions but find that the scope of their responsibility in multiple sites and two or more markets is difficult to handle. They tend to suffer from 'bounded rationality' as we discussed in Chapter 2.

An alternative organisational form for the multi-business company is the holding company, where the corporate office holds the assets of each of the companies in the portfolio but allows each to manage its own affairs and to retain most of the profits that it generates. In effect, the holding company is a type of institutional shareholder or friendly banker. The problem is that the holding company does little to add value since it is not actively managing its assets, and indeed may destroy value by protecting the inefficient or preventing the good from gaining access to the capital market to fund further expansion.

The American solution to this problem of how best to manage diverse businesses was the adoption of the M-form structure. In a famous book in the early 1960s, Chandler (1962) extrapolated from the experience of General Motors under Alfred Sloan to assert that 'structure follows strategy'. This meant that decisions on the long-term direction of the firm and the scope of its activities (its corporate strategy) should be the dominant factor in decisions on the structure of the corporation. These 'second-order decisions' on internal operating procedures, and, especially for our purposes, the relationship between parts of the organisation, thus flowed from first-order corporate strategy. This had a profound influence on the location of decision-making in HRM, both directly and indirectly (seen in how corporate control was exercised over operating decisions and activities). HR strategies in operating units are then best seen as a 'third-order' activity or downstream process which is deeply influenced by first and second-order strategy (Figure 10.1).

The distinctive feature of the M-form organisation is a clear separation of 'operational management' from 'strategy-makers' in the corporate office. All profits are

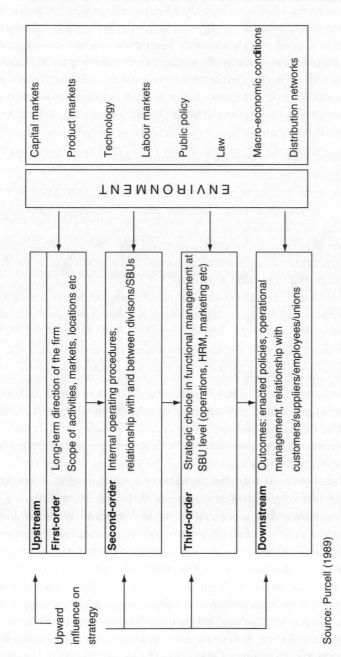

Figure 10.1 Three levels of strategic decision-making in Anglo-American multidivisional firms

Source: Purcell (1989)

returned to the corporate office and regular weekly or monthly reports are required on aspects of performance, especially on rate of return on sales (ROS) or rate of return on investment (ROI). In effect, the M-form company is composed of a number of U-form organised profit centres, or, to use the preferred term, strategic business units (SBUs). These SBUs are often limited-liability companies in their own legal status. Between SBUs, which often face distinct, narrowly defined markets, and the corporate office, divisional structures often exist to coordinate whole sectors or geographic areas. M-form companies in the rational minds of industrial economists have five advantages over other forms of corporate control. Williamson (1970: 120–1) argues that these are:

- the responsibility for operating decisions is assigned to (essentially self-contained) operating divisions;
- the elite staff attached to the general office perform both advisory and auditing functions. Both activities have the effect of securing greater control over operating division behaviour;
- the general office is principally concerned with strategic decisions involving planning, appraisal and control, including the allocation of resources among the (competing) operating divisions;
- the separation of the general staff from operations provides general office executives with the psychological commitment concerned with overall performance rather than becoming absorbed in the affairs of the functional parts;
- the resulting structure displays both rationality and synergy: the whole is greater (more effective, more efficient) than the sum of the parts.

Whittington and Mayer (2000: 67), following the work of Jelinek (1979), note the similarity with the Scientific Management of F.W. Taylor (discussed in Chapter 5): 'The separation of strategy and operations . . . was the analogue of Taylor's own separation of conception from execution on the shopfloor. Divisionalisation was the scientific management of the corporation.'

Seen in this way, the M-form becomes less of a structure than a process of managing: a universal theory of asset management that could be applied anywhere. The marketisation of the public service sector in the 1980s and 1990s was built on the principle of the separation of strategy from operations, adopted with new performance reporting requirements and the single-minded pursuit of efficiency or, to use the language of the private sector, 'shareholder value'.

The ultimate logic of the M-form structure or process of control was that an increasing number of firms would move from being single businesses through a process of gradual diversification and divisionalisation into a collection of related businesses, and from there to become unrelated conglomerates. At this final stage, no one business would dominate the portfolio by having 70 per cent or more of corporate turnover and there would be little or no market or technological relationship between businesses. Evidence collected in Britain by Channon (1982) between 1950 and 1980 showed a clear growth in the number of conglomerates. Firms like BTR and Hanson became known for the ruthless way in which they managed acquired businesses. Hanson typically stripped out 25 per cent of the labour costs in each of a succession of hostile acquisitions. In recent years, the attractiveness of conglomerates has waned and many have divested some of their businesses in order to refocus the corporation around a few related businesses. In a sense, the high point of the M-form was reached in the last quarter of the last century, but it still remains the dominant logic for organising and control of many multi-business firms.

The M-form company developed in the USA and spread to the UK and other parts of the Anglo-American world. The superiority of it, seen in terms of profitability and shareholder value (Hill and Pickering 1986; Rumelt 1982) has often been observed. It was assumed, however, that the very different institutional environment in continental Europe would limit its impact and growth in these other societies. For example, 'in France and Germany the systems of ownership have been consistently less market-based than in the UK, control has been more personal and the technical backgrounds (of senior executives) more important' (Whittington and Mayer 2000: 121). Added to this, the regulatory and institutional frameworks in these countries are more extensive than in the Anglo-American world, especially in regard to employment matters. Despite these national and institutional differences, there is clear evidence of a growth in diversification and a move to M-form structures in these countries, as shown in Figure 10.2.

It is clear that the dominant pattern is the emergence of the 'related diversified' company. This is where no one business contributes more than 70 per cent of the turnover to the corporate whole but where there is a market or technological relationship between different businesses in the portfolio. As we shall see, how large firms manage these relationships is crucial. Figure 10.2 also clearly indicates that the

Aspect	France		Germany		UK	
	1970	1993	1970	1993	1970	1993
(a) *Diversification*						
Single	20	19.4	27	12.7	6	4.5
Dominant	27	15.2	15	7.9	32	10.4
Related diversified	43	51.5	38	47.6	57	61.2
Unrelated diversified	9	17.6	19	31.7	6	23.9
(b) *Organisational structure*						
Functional	18	1.5	27	3.2	8	1.5
Functional-holding	24	9.1	21	14.3	1	0
Holding	16	13.6	14	12.7	18	9
Divisional	42	75.8	40	69.8	74	89.5

Source: Adapted from Whittington and Mayer (2000)

Figure 10.2 Trends in diversification and M-form structures in France, Germany and the UK, 1970–1993, among top 100 industrial firms (%)

M-form or divisional structure is now by far the most important organisational form adopted for large businesses.

The HR implications of divisionalisation

What are the implications of divisionalisation for HRM? We can assess this in three ways. First, there is a need to look at the form of control exercised from the centre. Second, we can try to assess what role there is for HRM in the corporate office in determining corporate strategy and involvement in the budgetary control process. And third, we can ask specifically, what role do HR specialists play in the development of the management cadre?

Forms of control

Hill and Hoskisson (1987) examined the different approaches that divisional firms use to extract value by gaining certain economies:

Financial economies are found where the superior allocative properties of the internal capital market are maximised. That is to say that financial criteria dominate the goals set by the corporate office, compared with long-term growth or market development, for example. These enterprises are likely to have diversified into unrelated activities and to structure the firm in such a way as to minimise or ignore interdependencies between business units and between divisions.

Synergistic economies exist where common techniques, skills, or market knowledge are utilised across a range of products or services. These companies are capable of organising around key values and are usually concerned that acquisitions match and enhance their business mission. 'Second-order' integration strategies are likely here.

Vertical integration happens where a closely coordinated and integrated chain of activities from raw material sourcing to final distribution allows vertical economies to be realised. Here there is likely to be a strong central planning influence and an emphasis on administrative coordination.

Relatively few firms are still organised around the principle of vertical integration, in part because of the growth in outsourcing and the focus on core markets. The choice is between those firms emphasising the achievement of synergies and those focusing on financial economies and financial control. It is this latter type of company which, in HR strategy terms, is a cause for concern (we will return to synergistic companies in the next section). As Hill and Hoskisson (1987) show, these firms place heavy emphasis on a clear separation of the centre from the operational units or SBUs, and are unlikely to have divisional offices. This decentralisation of businesses places emphasis on profit responsibility and short-term financial targets.

Budgets are negotiated or imposed annually, planning horizons are short, and performance measured against targets is reported frequently:

> These companies are willing to act speedily to exit from the businesses that are not performing or do not fit . . . and are quicker to replace managers, fiercer in applying pressure through the monitoring process and more effective in recognising and acclaiming good performance (Goold and Campbell 1987: 126, 132).

This decentralisation of operating decisions but with strong control over budgets has important implications. First, operating units are given much greater autonomy on many aspects of HRM such as how many people to employ, the payment system to use, and decisions on recruitment, training and development (Marginson *et al.* 1993). There are exceptions: for example, few organisations give *carte blanche* to SBUs on questions of trade union recognition. The corporation will often have firm views on such matters. The logic of the financial control, M-form company is a focus on the performance control system and a minimisation of administrative controls or guidance where head office instructs on what is to be done in a particular area. As Goold and Campbell (1987) note, this can be liberating for SBU managers and the use of high value, performance-related pay, where bonuses constitute one third or one half of salary, can be a real incentive for the SBU manager. The structure of the SBU facing a distinctive, defined market can also allow for unique product and market knowledge to be applied.

The problem with relatively high degrees of freedom for SBU managers is that they need the financial freedom to invest in HRM processes and this is much less likely. Investment decisions are made by the corporate office and the operating budget, as approved, often has no reserved area for HR issues such as training and development, for example. Short-run targets render long-run HR goals difficult to achieve, if not impossible. Since human resourcing is an indirect cost (as opposed to being directly relevant to production or service), there is always strong pressure for HR overheads to be reduced. Returning HRM to the line is as much about budgetary constraint as it is about progressive policies to encourage line managers to be responsible for the management of their own people. Surveys of long-term trends in the UK by the authoritative WERS (Workplace Employee Relations Survey) show that:

> the job of workplace employee relations managers working in a multi-plant organisation appears to have become more difficult over time. First, . . . the decision making capacity . . . has been curtailed . . . second, the facilities devoted to employee relations management have been streamlined as evidenced by the reduction in the number of non-clerical staff assisting employee relations managers (Millward *et al.* 2000: 82).

The way these pressures are imposed will depend on the business's place in the corporation's portfolio. If a business is seen as a 'star' that is growing in a buoyant market, it may get heavy investment and be allowed to place emphasis on critical resources such as HR recruitment and development. A good business in a static or mature market is likely to be 'milked' (as a 'cash cow'), required to strip out costs, and have its profits reinvested elsewhere in the portfolio. An unsuccessful firm in an unattractive market is squeezed before being spat out (often termed a 'dog'). Each of these types of companies in the portfolio has very different HRM consequences (Purcell 1989). Managing the portfolio means a centralisation of budgetary control. The WERS trend survey noted that 'the proportion of workplaces able to decide upon the use of any financial surplus fell from one third in 1990 to 14 per cent in 1998. In over half of the cases this decision was made elsewhere without reference to the workplace concerned' (Millward *et al.* 2000: 79). Sharing in economic success – what might be called 'gainsharing' – depends exclusively on the generosity of the corporate office, but as we noted earlier, the classic model of rationality in the M-form fosters in executives the psychological commitment concerned with overall performance rather than a psychology of absorption into the affairs of the SBUs. Thus, even if local management wished to engage in 'gainsharing', they may be prohibited from doing so.

HRM in the corporate office

The classic structure of the corporate board of the M-form is to have only one functional specialist – the finance director – as a member together with the CEO and the chairman. Other members, apart from non-executives, will tend to be the managing directors of the main operating divisions. The role of HR specialists is ambiguous. Much depends on the personal preferences of the CEO and the historical role of personnel managers in the centre. All the evidence points to a marked decline in board membership for HR directors in the UK. The WERS trend data shows that the proportion of head offices employing specialists in HRM (or 'ERM' as they call it) fell from nearly half in 1990 to just over a third in 1998 (Millward *et al.* 2000: 76). The 1992 Company Level Industrial Relations Survey found that only 30 per cent of companies with a thousand employees or more had an HR director on the executive board, and as few as 14 per cent had the combination of a director, a specialist manager, and a dedicated specialist board sub-committee dealing with HR matters (Marginson *et al.* 1993: 31). As the researchers noted at the time, 'if one of the defining characteristics of human resource management is the explicit link with corporate strategies, then this survey has failed to find it for the majority of companies' (*ibid*: 71).

It is not that there is a shortage of issues where HR or 'people-related' considerations are likely to loom large. The sort of big change decisions where HR considerations always emerge like acquisitions, divestments, the development of greenfield site operations, plant closure and so on had taken place in over half of these big companies in the five years before the survey. Having an HR director does make a difference since there is much more likely to be an HR voice in the corporate corridors of power.

The management of ongoing operations is important too. This is especially the case in the budget review process. Budget formulation and control constitute one of the most important regular activities that corporate offices undertake. They establish key performance indicators (KPIs) for the SBU and for managers themselves. These KPIs emphasise financial performance, with HQ managers often 'managing by numbers'. Intangible, more human assets and behaviours tend therefore to be ignored since they cannot be 'counted' (a matter we shall pursue in Chapter 11). Once agreed, the budget sets the agenda for at least a year ahead, and more if rolling forecasts are used. By using a battery of measures, most of which include labour costs and performance data (Armstrong 1995), the process determines the boundaries for HR initiatives. Thus, budget meetings at both corporate and SBU levels are of fundamental importance, yet HR people attend these relatively rarely. At the corporate level, this was true in the 1992 survey in less than one third of the cases but rose to half where there was an HR director. An HR director on the main board made it much more likely that HR managers locally were involved in budget-setting, indicating the symbolic importance of an HR director (Purcell 1995: 79).

Management development

The most obviously important area in a corporate office for an HR role is in the management of careers for managers who populate divisions and SBUs (as noted in Chapter 2). These individuals are a critical resource for the corporation. The extent to which careers are planned varies considerably. In conglomerates and financial control companies, there is clear evidence that this activity is under-developed (Marginson *et al.* 1993: 38). This fits the pattern noted earlier where excessive decentralisation and separation of businesses to expose profit responsibility renders it difficult to emphasise or build on relationships between business units. Each is treated as an atomised unit. It is often the case that managers beyond head office will have contracts of employment with the operating company, not with the corporation. They are not considered as a corporate resource. In one case known to us the only managers who moved between the SBUs to and from the corporate office were financial controllers, emphasising the dominant role of this function. Career expectations for others within the parent group were discouraged since what was required was 'focus' on local profit generation, and they competed fiercely with each other for survival and reward. Cooperation between business unit leaders was seen as a weakness. The culture favoured 'male' attributes, fighting for the survival of the fittest.

Unilever, the long established, Anglo-Dutch, food, detergent, personal products and speciality chemicals MNC, takes a fundamentally different approach. Although it is heavily decentralised, there is a strong culture of coordination and linkages between businesses. This is achieved by building elaborate networks and lateral relationships between managers in different businesses and retaining tight control over career management and promotion decisions. All managers worldwide are considered a corporate resource. The process starts with recruitment. 'The greatest challenge of recruiting is to find the best and the brightest who will fit into the company . . . For international careers in our current operating company we look for people who can work in teams and understand the value of cooperation and consensus' (Floris Maljers, a joint chairman of Unilever, quoted in Goold *et al.* 1994: 154). Around a thousand graduate management trainees are recruited each year. Thereafter, career movement for the best takes on a triple spiral: between functions, between divisions, and between countries. An elaborate, knowledge-based information system for careers is widely used to aid this process. Looking at Unilever's parenting advantage in the way the centre adds value, strategy analysts concluded that:

> Unilever's system for managing its human resources creates a direct linkage benefit by providing the businesses with a larger pool of suitable management talent to draw on. It is also a mechanism that promotes other linkages. By fostering a common culture, promoting networks, and exposing managers to a broad range of experiences, the Unilever system speeds up the circulation of product knowledge and best practice (Goold *et al.* 1994: 155).

This is an excellent example of a combination of strengths in human capital and organisational process helping to create sustained competitive advantage.

From structure to synergy

A different word can be used to capture the Unilever experience: synergy. The modal pattern for divisionalised companies in terms of the scope of their activities, as shown in Figure 10.2, is to organise around related businesses where market or technological relationships exist between divisions. Corporations can choose to ignore these in the search for financial performance through a process of decentralisation and separation. Alternatively, the corporation can organise around these linkages in order to maximise the synergies that exist between them. These may be by vertical integration along the supply chain, requiring integrated scheduling and development to spread, build or exploit innovations. Increasingly, however, vertical integration is giving way to outsourcing, sub-contracting and strategic alliances. Alternatively, relationships may be designed to achieve 'scope' economies through shared distribution channels, for example, or the exploitation of a common root technology. One example here is the Japanese company, Canon, where 'most of the product groups share overlapping technologies that come together in the research rather than development phase, and central technologists are able to stimulate new combinations and generate new ideas' (Goold *et al.* 1994:169). Here, organisational practices which focus on flexibility, knowledge creation, and collaboration are crucial (Volberda 1998).

A third type of synergy is achieved spatially where the same tasks are carried out in each division. This is especially the case in MNCs where product integration across boundaries is emphasised. This allows for 'economies of replication to be secured' (Marginson 1993: 6). In particular, direct comparisons between operating units in different countries can be made, enabling the centre to reward or punish in future investment decisions, and to encourage the spread of best practice (Mueller and

Purcell 1992). The Ford Production System (FPS), for example, is applied in great detail across the globe and new acquisitions, like the luxury car makers Jaguar and Volvo, are required to adopt FPS with the centre using a battery of performance measures like 'Six Sigma' to encourage, cajole and sanction. This is not a remote form of surveillance but active management aided by the movement of executives between divisions and countries, and now by an extensive, knowledge-based IS system. The plan is to provide all employees worldwide with a home PC with access to the Ford intranet and within it to a range of learning packages. Managing knowledge world-wide allows for a process innovation in, say, Brazil to be tapped into by others. This can be work team to work team, not merely restricted knowledge exchange among senior managers. Management consultancies operating globally, like McKinsey, oper-ate in the same way through the replication of knowledge.

This does not mean doing the same thing in the same way everywhere since dif-ferences in institutional frameworks and national cultures, and in the particular his-tories and traditions of the operating unit, SBU or division, establish different contexts for policy implementation and innovation. The successful divisionalised firms, especially global ones, require strong performance but recognise the need for local diversity. Thus, there can be simultaneous divergence and convergence in multi-national companies: 'think global, act local' (a phrase coined by Asea Brown Boveri).

The crucial point of this search for synergies between divisions, and internation-ally, is that corporate management cannot simultaneously seek to achieve the finan-cial economies of separation and decentralisation and the achievement of vertical, horizontal or spatial synergies. Choices have to be made. It is here that the trade in management knowledge and ideas between generations is important. If the true div-isional company is the bedfellow of Scientific Management (the separation of strat-egy from operations in the former, and between planning and execution in the latter), then both were shaken to the core by the success of Japanese corporations worldwide in the 1980s:

> The most disturbing aspect, it seemed, was that the Japanese challenge could not be attrib-uted to the successful imitation of American management techniques but to the adoption of a completely different model . . . Being more specialised, Japanese corporations seem to have less need for the multidivisional structure . . . as a consequence while the American corporation makes a virtue of separating strategy from operations, the Japanese corpor-ation keeps them closely interrelated (Whittington and Mayer 2000: 80).

Leading strategy analysts turned on the M-form company in the 1990s. To Bettis (1991), it was an 'organisational fossil'. Prahalad and Hamel (1990), in a famous paper in *Harvard Business Review,* referred to the 'tyranny of the SBU' and argued for an emphasis on linked core competencies crossing the corporation's businesses (as we explained in Chapter 4). This is where the management of synergies and espe-cially the management of critical resources in the managerial cadre become vital. After the logic of separation in the M-form has come the N-form organised around networks (Hedlund 1994). 'The N-form works best with the Eastern appreciation of the tacit, the embedded and the ambiguous, rather than the explicit, tightly specified knowledge systems of the West' (Whittington and Mayer 2000: 81). If the Scientific Management of Fordism gave way to post-Fordism (as discussed in Chapter 5), then the modernist organisation of the M-form gave way to a new era of the postmodern organisation in the N-form. A different and instructive metaphor is between the masculinity of the M-form and the femininity of the N-form. Of course, trends in management thinking are often far in advance of practice. Just as there are plenty of examples of Scientific Management in the 21st century, so there are many tradition-al divisionalised firms still exercising strong financial control over their subsidiaries worldwide. Evolution and adaptation are slow but the rise of firms like ABB (Goold *et al.* 1994: 164–7, Whittington and Mayer 2000: 81–2), the continuing success of Unilever and Canon, and the resurgence of Ford over the last 20 years (discussed in Chapter 9), point the way to new strategies in corporate control. A summary of these trends is shown in Figure 10.3.

The human resource function, it will be noted, is argued to be the key function in the N-form company. A good example of what this might mean comes from the transformation of General Electric (GE) under the leadership of Jack Welch (who retired in 2001):

> By 1990, Jack Welch had formulated his notions of coordination and integration within his view of the 'boundaryless company'. A key element of this concept was a blurring of internal divisions so that people could work together across functions and business bound-aries. Welch aimed at 'integrated diversity' – the ability to transfer the best ideas, most developed knowledge, and most valuable people freely and easily between businesses (Grant 1998: 415).

The N-form company, and more generally those that emphasise synergistic inte-gration, place much greater emphasis on human resource management:

> The new strategies and structures require new ways of managing and new kinds of man-agers . . . The human resource function has become central to making the new forms of organisation work. These new HR practices have two broad dimensions in the emerging model of organisation: those concerned with supporting horizontal networking, and those

Aspect	Investor	Managerial	Network
Origins	1920s–	1960s–	1980s–
Key resource	Capital	Scale and scope	Knowledge
Key technique	Accounting ratios	Planning	Exchange
Key function	Finance and accounting	Corporate planning	Human resources
Structure shape	Pyramid	Pear	Pancake
Example	DuPont	General Electric	ABB

Source: Whittington and Mayer (2000)

Figure 10.3 Evolving types of multidivisional company

with maintaining organisational integration' (Whittington, Pettigrew, Peck, Fenton and Conyon 1999: 587).

National business systems, especially types of capital structures and traditions of management development and careers, make a difference here. Whittington *et al.* (1999), in their extensive study of European firms between 1992 and 1996, show how German companies seemed better able to manage the complementarities associated with changing structures, changing processes and changing boundaries. German companies more often used project type structures or matrix organisational forms and this was associated with HR innovations. The authors link this to the 'patient' capital market in Germany. The contrast is with British firms, operating in a short-term capital market, which emphasise decentralisation and 'downscoping', but which are not innovative in HR terms (*ibid*: 591). That is, they often change structures and boundaries but are less adept at process change. Yet 'high performing firms were characterised by denser and more inclusive webs of relationships between design variables than low performing firms' (*ibid*: 597). Whether this results from the capital market in Germany being more patient or from the career structures and preferred technical background of senior managers is hard to say. What seems clear is that the combination of the short-term capital market in the UK (and, by extension, the Anglo-American world), and the preference for general managers with background in no one sector, makes it especially hard to manage integrated, organic, matrix-type organisations when human resources become a key function.

On an international scale, Bartlett and Ghoshal (1998) term the emergent organisation a 'transnational corporation'. Here, each national or regional unit operates independently but is a source of ideas and capabilities for the whole corporation. National units seek to achieve global scale through specialisation on behalf of the whole corporation. Crucially, the corporate centre manages this global network by first establishing the role of each business unit, then sustaining the system through relationships and culture to make the network of business units operate effectively. 'They must foster the process of innovation and knowledge creation. They are responsible for the development of a strong management centre in the organisation' (Johnson and Scholes 2002: 460). These types of firms are the most innovative in developing human resources strategies and more able to spread best practice from unit to unit.

Generally, there is strong evidence that foreign-owned firms are more innovative than UK firms in HR policies. They are more likely to have HR directors in their national subsidiaries, more often use specialist HR sub-committees and have more specialist HR professionals (Marginson *et al.* 1993, Walsh 2001). Variations in institutional arrangements, whether regulatory or cultural, make many foreign companies more sensitive to context and, with the pressure on performance between units in different countries, they become more innovative. That is, they learn to enhance productivity and flexibility within constraints. And, for some, the need to be seen as global citizens aware of their ethical responsibilities leads them to seek evidence of legitimacy in the way they manage employees locally. The ethnocentric international companies of the 1960s, where one best way (usually the American way) was forced on reluctant overseas subsidiaries, are giving way to more polycentric, adaptable behaviour. This in turn places pressure on national systems of regulation and institutional frameworks to adapt to global competitive pressures (Katz and Darbishire 2000). This does not necessarily mean the need to deregulate and free up the labour market to become more like the Anglo-American model. National requirements for involvement and participation, and for training and development, provide the basis for 'AMO' in the firm. Boselie, Paauwe and Jansen (2001) argue that these national institutions have contributed to the ability of the Dutch economy, for example, to outperform its neighbours in the 1990s.

The HR implications of mergers and acquisitions

The volume of mergers and acquisitions (M&As) has risen considerably in the last two decades (Hubbard 1999) in response to a variety of environmental changes such as the privatisation of State assets, pressures on cost reduction, especially in banking and insurance, the development of global markets, the spread of information technologies, growing costs in product development, and the availability of capital in search of higher shareholder value. Cross-border acquisitions are particularly noticeable. What is curious is that around half of acquisitions are deemed failures in the sense of either having an inability to provide shareholder value greater than the sum of the previous two companies, or an inability to maintain market dominance, achieve promised cost reductions, or manage synergies between the new firms effectively. Difficulties in achieving organisational fit, especially the meshing of cultures or management styles, are often identified (Buono, Bowditch and Lewis 1985; Datta and Grant 1990). Marks and Mirvis (1982) showed that people and employee issues accounted for a third to a half of all merger failures and there is no indication that things have improved in the last two decades. Most often, the failure of M&As occurs not at the negotiation or purchase stages, although this can be important if a firm pays excessively for a purchase, but at the implementation stage when two firms come together. Hunt, Lees, Grümber and Vivian (1987) found a positive correlation between success of implementation and the overall perceived success of the acquisition in 83 per cent of cases, making it the 'most decisive variable in success and failure'. KPMG (1999) distinguishes between 'hard keys' to successful mergers which need to happen at the start of the process, such as synergy evaluation, integration project planning and due diligence, from 'soft keys'. These soft keys cover the classical HR issues such as the selection of the management team, resolving cultural issues, and communication inside the two companies (which needs to be compatible with communication externally to shareholders and the business press). According to

KPMG, these soft or behavioural issues of implementation should be considered at the beginning of the acquisition process. According to their research, where they were, there was a strong association with success measured in terms of shareholder value. Thus 'human factors' loom large in M&As from the beginning, but become especially acute during the post-acquisition implementation phase, and beyond in what is sometimes called the stabilisation period (Hunt *et al.* 1987, Cartwright and Cooper 1992, Hubbard and Purcell 2001).

Employee expectations and breaches of the psychological contract

A crucial element is the uncertainty generated by the acquisition process and the response of employees to it. It is hardly surprising to find that employees suffer from uncertainty in acquisitions (Buono and Bowditch 1989) and this is linked to per-ceived breaches of an individual's psychological contract with the employer, espe-cially the new employer (recall Chapter 7). Such breaches typically lead to a withdrawal of support for the organisation and a reduction in discretionary behav-iour and motivation (Robinson 1996). In an acquisition, this psychological breach can occur on a large scale, covering groups of employees leading to distinctive, and for the acquirer, damaging consequences of a withdrawal of trust and commitment. In practice, the political and politicised environment of an acquisition severely reduces the opportunities to participate. People often feel powerless and suffer from anomie. They may ask their manager what is happening but it is rare for her or him to know any more than they do. Trade unions may be informed one or two days before the public announcement but are generally unable, at that time, to raise issues of concern on the details of the acquisition consequences, unless provided with legal rights to do so, as in the Netherlands (Wenlock and Purcell 1990).

Beyond this, there can be a profound sense of loss – a form of bereavement (Cartwright and Coooper 1992) – when a long established company is swallowed up and effectively dies. Symbolically, decisions such as where to locate a new head office become touchstones of the new corporation. When Lloyds Bank 'merged' with TSB in the UK in the mid 1990s, once the decision was taken to locate the HQ in the Lloyds building the game was up, whatever the protestations of senior management. It was an acquisition, not a merger, and the 'dominant coalition' was to be found in Lloyds. Much the same happened when the 'marriage' of CGU with Norwich Union, two giants of the UK insurance industry, took place in 1999. The head office was to be in Norwich, and Norwich Union imposed its own management style on CGU, which had prided itself on inclusion and consensus. The outcome in cases of these sorts can be substantial voluntary labour turnover, reductions in effort and forms of cooperation, and resistance to integration moves, which thus take longer and cost more in terms of performance dips than anticipated.

Senior managers can often take the view that the only HR issue of immediate con-cern in an acquisition announcement is to deal with job security and job loss. This is the question that is always asked by the press. In Hubbard's (1999) acquisition research, there was quite commonly an early announcement that it was to be 'business as usual' and that both companies would be stronger by coming together. This was rarely the case, and at times announcements to employees of 'business as usual' were at odds with statements to the business press on the need to reduce costs and increase margins. Of course, employees read these and note the incompatibility of the internal with the external statement.

The employee response to an acquisition announcement, especially those in the 'target' firm to be acquired, is much more multi-faceted than a single concern with job security. Hubbard (1999) calls this 'dual expectations theory'. This covers both the individual's perception of their immediate future (what will happen to me, do I have a job?) and their concern with their team and the wider social networks (what will happen to us?). Beyond that, this bifurcation between the individual and the group continues into concerns about assimilation into the new organisation and what sort of firm it is. Thus, for the individual, the issue is 'what sort of job will I have, what type of future, how do I know what is expected of me in terms of performance and will I fit into the new organisational culture?' These concerns of individuals coalesce into wider group or collective worries about the culture and style of the new management. This 'cultural behaviour' means learning about and internalising as a group 'the shared patterns of beliefs, assumptions and expectations held by organisational members, and the group characteristic way of perceiving the organisation's environment and its norms, roles and values as they exist outside the individual' (Schwartz and Davis 1981: 33).

These expectations may come to the fore at different times in the acquisition process. Senior managers involved, directly or indirectly, in the negotiations have particular concerns at the first planning phase. Due diligence may well (and certainly should) involve an appraisal of top management capabilities with decisions taken on who is vital in terms of client or customer knowledge, or technical or product knowledge, while others are deemed less important. The issue, too, is who is to get the senior positions. If satisfied at this stage, the next stages of announcement and implementation may be of less concern to these top managers, although cultural concerns, such as the form of communication used in the new firm, often emerge later in the final, but ongoing, stabilisation phase. Middle managers, unaware of the negotiations, often find the announcement and implementation stages especially difficult. Hubbard's (1999) research showed that this group have considerable worries about organisational culture and the way they fit into the new organisation and whether they both have, and wish to have, a future in it. Quit rates for this group can be especially high in the year after an acquisition. Non-managerial employees are most concerned about job security at the point of transfer but are particularly concerned with group issues in the way redundancies are handled. The existence of legal guarantees at the point of transfer helps, but by no means overcomes, these concerns.

These types of concerns and their consequences for individuals and for the organisation seem to be common but, as the KPMG (1999) research implies, some firms are adept at handling acquisitions and learn from experience, while others are inept, especially if there is no prior experience and little understanding of behavioural issues. The finance director in one of Hubbard's cases referred to the 'abattoir effect'. 'He expressed the belief that employees actually preferred the quick, unsuspected process of redundancies . . . The brutality of the day shocked and appalled those employees being made redundant, and those remaining' (Hubbard and Purcell 2001: 24). Within four months, 15 per cent of the middle managers who had stayed after 'Black Monday', as it was called, had left. The company completely failed the 'legitimacy test'. By contrast, one of the most successful acquirers, with over 40 acquisitions in the period 1993–1999, is Cisco Systems based in Silicon Valley. In that period the number of employees grew from less than 4000 to 26,000. Cisco chooses small, compatible, entrepreneurial companies and pays particular attention to cultural integration but within the dominance of the Cisco Way. This is seen in the parties having a shared vision and cultural compatibility at the start of the acquisition process:

> When we acquire a company, we do not tell them 'we'll leave you alone'. We say, 'we'll change everything'. We try to establish an environment where we are attractive to small innovative companies. We have learned that to make it [the acquisition] successful you have to tell employees up front what you are going to do, because trust is everything in this business. You've got to tell them early so you do not betray their trust later (quoted in O'Reilly III and Pfeffer 2000: 61).

The strategic nature of acquisitions and their consequences for HRM

Strategically for Cisco, the crucial aspect of all their acquisitions is the retention of the people. Cisco is a software knowledge business. The intellectual capital of the firm is about the only 'asset' that they have. Thus for them, capability transfer and retention are crucial (Haspeslagh and Jemison 1991). Not all acquisitions, of course, are driven by the same strategic need for talent and growth. The strategic purpose of an acquisition will deeply influence the process and the type of HR issues to be faced. In particular, the crucial issue is the degree of organisational integration required for the combined firms and the underlying reasons for it. The greater the degree of organisational integration, the greater the HR issues that come to the fore since sites are likely to close, rationalisation occurs in department amalgamations (a single sales team, a single finance office and so on), and there will be 'winners' and 'losers' in the organisational musical chairs that follow (Hubbard and Purcell 2001: 21).

A whole range of issues needs to be faced in organisational integration. It is likely that most if not all of the HR policies and practices associated with 'AMO' will need to be integrated. Since the nature of these policies is a reflection of wider, yet ill-defined, beliefs about organisational culture, the change process can be fraught, especially if the acquired employees refuse to legitimate the new economic and social order. 'If the corporate culture makes no sense of the organisational realities experienced by the employees other than senior management, it will not be internalised outside that small group' (Legge 1995: 187). Culture change programmes are hard at the best of times within existing companies but in acquisitions they are especially fraught. The outcome can often be no more than 'resigned behavioural compliance' (Ogbonna and Wilkinson 1990).

Stand-alone acquisitions may be easier until the new owner seeks to exercise control with the appointment of new managers or the imposition of new reporting procedures or a performance management system. These are the artefacts of cultural control. This is particularly an acute problem in cross-border acquisition, for example when a French company acquires a British utility company. The utility company is left alone in an operational sense for a while but very different forms of corporate control and expectations come from the new owners. French management is, naturally, somewhat different from British management (Barsoux and Lawrence 1990, Lawrence and Edwards 2000). More generally, 'if we accept that HRM approaches are cultural artefacts reflecting the basic assumptions and values of the national culture in which organisations are embedded, international HRM becomes one of the most challenging corporate tasks in multinational organisation' (Laurent 1986, quoted in Schneider and Barsoux 1997: 128). This is even more challenging in cross-border acquisitions. Becoming an integrated multinational, let alone a transnational corporation, developing networks and powerful international systems of knowledge building, exchange and intellectual capital, as Unilever has done, often via acquisition, is a daunting task. Or in the language of the RBV (Chapter 4), it is a rare organisational attribute that combines people and processes and can become a powerful source of sustained competitive advantage that others find extremely hard to copy.

The most frequent way acquisitions are intended to create value, for the shareholder at least, but not for the employee, is by 'resource sharing' (Haspeslagh and Jemison 1991). Primarily, although often dressed up in terms of synergistic value creation, this means a focus on cost reduction while at times increasing the scope of business activities. Analysis of bank mergers in the 1990s concluded that value came more from cost reduction than from enhanced revenue generation (Houston, James and Ryngaert 2001). 'Resource sharing' is seen in branch closures where there is overlap in a town, operational rationalisation in the home country or overseas, and call and contact-centre amalgamations. Significant savings, too, can occur within management from specialist departments coming together and from property sales and other direct savings. The problem is how this can be done quickly, leaving behind a committed, integrated, innovative workforce able to maximise customer service. Just taking one issue alone, that of IS integration, the J-curve problem, where performance dips in a change programme at the start, is painfully clear. The J-curve (Figure 10.4) draws attention to the requirements for 'competency destruction' or 'unlearning' before new learning can occur (Pil and MacDuffie 1996). It is clear even for a

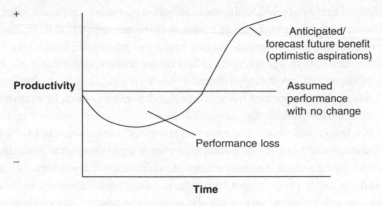

Figure 10.4 The J curve of productivity loss in the management of change

firm like Cisco, with all of their experience, that 'when you combine (even good) companies, for a period of time, no matter how smoothly they operate, you lose business momentum' (John Chambers CEO of Cisco, quoted in O'Reilly III and Pfeffer 2000: 56). Cisco, of course, are trying to retain talent and go for growth with all of the opportunities that can mean. Where, however, competency destruction means job loss, often in large numbers, and, for those that remain, a requirement to learn new cultures, new operating procedures and to deal with new bosses, the slope of the J-curve coming out of the transitional period is tantalising but unachievable. The loss of productivity or profitability, while anticipated, is both deeper and lasts longer than hoped for, and greatly exceeds that told to the shareholders in the prospectus. It is easy to see how shareholder value is lost, let alone employee value. Cultural integration is especially hard but even system integration is difficult and requires planning, project teams and high levels of involvement at operational level between employees from the two companies, learning to work together.

One of the key, defining moments in the acquisition process, where integration is required in order to achieve cost reduction, is the way announcements are made and especially how redundancies are handled. Companies may sometimes make generous cash offers to those being made redundant and think they have done enough but this nearly always misses the crucial issue of how decision-making is perceived and legitimated. Why is it that people often refer to 'survival guilt' or 'survivor syndrome' in these circumstances? This refers to those who survive the job-cutting rationalisation programmes feeling emotional, disturbed and guilty that they have been spared. Far from being grateful to management, they tend to be highly critical of it.

In recent years, increasing attention has been given to the idea of organisational justice (Folger and Cropanzano 1998). This concept focuses on the way people evaluate the fairness of a decision. This does not mean the extent to which the decision is accepted as appropriate in the circumstances (although employees are often realistic about the inevitability and even the necessity of a redundancy programme) but the fairness of the way in which the decision was taken. There are three elements of justice in an organisational context: distributive, procedural and interactional. Distributive justice (the fairness of the outcome) and procedural justice (the fairness with which the decision was taken, including the extent to which there is an employee voice (Chapter 8)) are strongly related. 'Procedural justice both mediates perceptions of distributive justice and has important independent effects from distributive justice' (Cox 2001: 16). As Folger (1998: 32) puts it, 'The more someone considers a process fair, the more tolerant the person is about the consequences of the process'. In redundancy (and closure) decisions, this means that open communication and discussion of the need for, and procedures of, selection, and the design of compensation and assistance programmes (procedural justice) are important in their own right but also affect perceptions of the outcome of the programme in terms of who is selected (distributive justice). People sometimes use the term 'equality of misery' here to signify that the pain of downsizing is shared across the organisation with no group especially favoured or protected. Interactional justice focuses on how decisions are communicated to those affected by them. This covers the sincerity with which procedures are followed, the politeness and courtesy with which the individual is treated, which affect the maintenance of their sense of dignity and self-worth, and the way in which apologies, explanations and justifications are communicated (Cox 2001: 17–18). This is particularly important when the outcome is adverse for the individual, as in most cases of redundancy.

Referring back to the finance director who valued 'the abattoir effect' in dealing with post-acquisition redundancies, it is abundantly clear that he failed all three elements of organisational justice. The outcome, as one of the employees put it, was to destroy trust in management: 'I do not know if they [the employees] will trust again, it will take a long time if they do. People can forget things and go on but it never goes away completely. Once it has been done, you never forget it totally' (Hubbard and Purcell 2001: 26).

Conclusions and implications

The fundamental problem for large multi-business firms, and especially those organised internationally, is to find an effective way to manage the relationship between parts of the business. This is both vertical, in the relationship from the centre to the outposts, and horizontal, in the way in which parts of the business collaborate or compete with each other, and the extent to which networks develop and synergies are emphasised or denied. One of the key influences on this complex problem is the extent to which the firm operates in related markets and related businesses, or has a wide range of unrelated activities. The record of many businesses, especially conglomerates, is poor, certainly in recent times as the business environment globally became less stable and predictable. We have seen how the logic, in economic and rational terms, of the multidivisional firm has tended to favour decentralisation and the separation of the firm into discrete accounting units, allowing the centre to 'manage by numbers'. There is evidence that this form of management is supported by the particular features of the Anglo-American share market, with the requirement for quarterly reporting using ROI and PE (price/earnings) ratios. The more 'patient' continental European capital markets seem to allow for longer-term development and types of management control associated with project teams, networks and HR innovations.

Quite how far how organisations are moving from the M-form model towards the networked or N-form or, in multinationals, towards the 'transnational' model is hard to say. There are some powerful and persuasive examples but they are relatively few in number. What we can say is that when networks are developed, the way people, especially managers and professional workers, are managed plays a crucial, if not the crucial role. Once knowledge is defined as the key resource and exchange as the key technique, HR practices that support and facilitate horizontal networking and organisational integration between markets, countries and technologies become vital.

Growing by acquisition makes this harder to achieve since different cultures and different operating processes and procedures need to be understood. Some may be eradicated but others are a source of value where to impose a standardised, internally consistent solution may destroy more value than it creates. Too much can be made of the differences in national cultures and the different forms and strength of institutions in the labour market and the way these impinge on international management operations. There is clear evidence that MNCs are innovators in HR practices at the local level, in developed as well as developing countries (Budhwar and Debrah 2001). Not all of these innovations, especially those linked to cost reduction, are necessarily welcome but 'think global, act local' means adapting to local circumstances and traditions while pushing for performance and market leadership. It is possible for powerful firms (and large firms have resources and access to capital denied smaller organisations) to push for productivity and flexibility in nearly all countries whatever the institutional rigidities, and if they fail, most have the capacity to relocate at relatively low cost, but often with a high cost to the host country.

The search for legitimacy is different. It is here that issues of organisational justice – distributive, procedural and interactional aspects of decision-making – come into play, as we saw with redundancy programmes in acquisitions. This is where local requirements for, and expectations of, voice systems and for redress become important, not just because local laws need to be followed but because the way decisions are made and communicated (and their internal logic) establishes the baseline of legitimacy necessary for their implementation.

11

Conclusion: implications for the strategic management process

If we now have a greater appreciation of the strategic significance of human resource management, what can we practically do about it? How can strategic management processes in firms be improved to deal more effectively with the critical HR problems they face and, if possible, to take advantage of the competitive opportunities that HRM presents? The final chapter is dedicated to these questions. It begins with a review of the debate over the value of strategic planning and examines the question of how to design HR planning systems. This leads to a discussion of the more integrative approaches to strategic management that have become associated with the notion of the 'balanced scorecard' (Kaplan and Norton 1996, 2001). Such approaches to strategic management are concerned with relating critical non-financial factors to financial outcomes, with assisting firms to map the key cause-effect linkages in their desired strategies. They challenge the short-termism of traditional budgeting processes. They imply a central role for HRM in the strategic management of the firm and suggest practical ways of bringing it about.

Can strategic planning be a valuable resource in the firm?

The resource-based view (RBV) of the firm has occupied an important role in this book. We should ask whether it is supportive or otherwise of the discipline of strategic planning. Does it suggest that better planning, with all the effort it entails, is a valuable use of executive time and the firm's money? Doesn't the RBV say that 'causal ambiguity' helps to protect a firm's key resources? In which case, doesn't this imply, paradoxically, that we cannot plan for improved performance in HRM? Furthermore, don't Henry Mintzberg's (1990, 1994) stinging criticisms of strategic planning caution us against bureaucratic planning routines? Doesn't long-range planning suit static rather than dynamic environments? Doesn't it undermine the very flexibility that firms need today?

Like Ansoff (1991) and Wilson (1994), we reject this anti-planning perspective. Chapter 4 considered three barriers to imitation: unique timing and learning, social complexity, and causal ambiguity. It argued that the notion of causal ambiguity is the least significant of the three. Ambiguity around key causes of a firm's success (and especially the way these interact) must be present to some extent in any firm. As Chapter 2 explained, strategic management is cognitively or intellectually challenging. If there were no ambiguities, senior management teams would never make blunders. However, we all know they do, and often with disastrous consequences.

Having said this, we argued that unique timing and learning ('path dependency') and social complexity (the system of collaboration and teamwork in the firm) are more important barriers to imitation than causal ambiguity. In other words, first-mover or fast-follower strategies, when well executed, build positions of competitive strength which other firms find very difficult to emulate. There are therefore advantages to be gained from planning to build the firm's human capital and create faster learning in the firm.

Research supports this interpretation, as we noted in Chapter 9 in our discussion of the value of planning skills in the mature and renewal contexts of the firm's life-cycle. Koch and McGrath's (1996) study of human resource planning practices and business outcomes is instructive. The sample studied consists of 319 business units drawn from the Standard and Poors' database of companies in the USA. Measures of business performance include labour productivity (defined as sales per employee). Their main finding is that:

> Labor productivity . . . tend(s) to be better in firms that both formally plan how many and what kinds of people they will need, as well as where employers systematically evaluate their recruitment and selection policies . . . *proactive* firms that *plan* for their future labor needs, as opposed to reacting to changes, as well as those firms making investments in getting the right people for the job *at the outset*, tend to be the ones with better labor productivity (Koch and McGrath 1996: 350).

Koch and McGrath (1996: 352) go on to argue that superior HR planning skills, which enhance the quality of the firm's investment in human capital, can provide a form of resource-based advantage.

This is only one study and we should be cautious about concluding anything from a single study. What other evidence is there? The largest study so far is associated with a 'convenience sample' of 656 firms[21], located mainly in the USA or in South Africa (Brews and Hunt 1999). This study was set up to examine the debate between Ansoff's

---

21 The sample was constructed from executives attending certain business education programmes in the USA but is large and covers a diverse set of industry circumstances.

'planning school' and Mintzberg's 'learning school'. While based on executive assessments of planning practice and business performance, the study argues that unstable environments require *more* rather than less planning, thus challenging the idea that planning systems make firms inflexible. It also argues that firms gain greater advantages from planning when they persist with it: benefits are greater after four or more years of working at a planning system (Brews and Hunt 1999: 905). This finding is consistent with the analysis of the US railway companies – the Chicago & North Western (C&NW) and the Chicago, Rock Island and Pacific (Rock Island) – discussed in Chapter 2 (Barr *et al.* 1992). Both firms faced an unstable environment in the 1950s (as railroads faced serious threats from alternative forms of transport) but the directors of C&NW began to change their mental model and take responsibility much more quickly than those at Rock Island (which subsequently went bankrupt).

These studies suggest that 'learning to plan' counts for something. They imply that successful firms find ways of incorporating lessons from learning-by-doing into their planning routines and of making their planning systems more flexible. Formal planning processes, when they involve the key line managers who manage the majority of staff, offer a way of surfacing informal learning about what does and doesn't work in the management of people. When designed competently, planning sessions provide a means for periodic review: they can be used both to make emergent learning explicit and to consider new external threats and opportunities. Rather than upholding the Mintzbergian criticisms of formal planning, these studies imply that planning systems can be reformed in ways that make them more valuable in changing times. As Brews and Hunt (1999: 906) put it: 'When the going gets tough, the tough go planning: formally, specifically, yet with flexibility and persistence. And once they have learned to plan, they plan to learn.'

The value to be gained does not lie solely in the capacity to improve the analytical abilities of the firm but also has a political dimension, something which Chapter 2 argued is always present in strategic management. As Lam and Schaubroeck (1998) explain, formal planning processes can be used to bring together key constituencies in the firm, thus hammering out new compromises and building commitment for desirable change. We conclude that strategic planning systems should not be abandoned but their design should be reviewed on a regular basis and enhanced. Part of this enhancement should involve improving the way they tackle the HR challenges facing the firm.

The design of HR planning processes

The argument that HR planning should be linked to strategic planning did not suddenly emerge with the advent of practitioner and business school interest in HRM in the 1980s. Planning the human aspects of business strategy has a long tradition. For example, the role of planning in personnel management, including planning for recruitment and succession, was emphasised in the publication of the UK Institute of Personnel Management's booklet on *Functions and Organisation of a Personnel Department* in 1964 (Crichton 1968: 42–3). And it should surely be obvious that military and industrial planning techniques were absolutely central to labour force planning, training and production management in both World Wars and, indeed, much earlier than this (Smith and Bartholomew 1988). The idea that we are finally discovering the value of good integration between organisational goals and labour requirements is an insult to former generations of managers. We are, however, in a position to identify some key lessons about how HR planning should be conducted.

Improving the quality of HR planning: process principles

Drawing on research and historical learning about HR planning, what principles can be used by executive teams to improve the quality of HR planning in their firm?

The stakeholder principle

As explained in Chapter 1, it is vital to recognise that HRM does not belong to HR specialists. HR planning should aim to meet the needs of the key stakeholder groups involved in people management in the firm. In the broadest sense, stakeholder groups include shareholders, creditors, managers, employees, customers, suppliers, competitors, the local community and environmental interests. In HR planning, however, we need to focus on those stakeholder groups who are most affected by the quality of labour management in the firm. This means the process ought to be designed to consider the interests of:

Operations and other line managers: these are the managers who manage the vast majority of people in any firm. Their views can be canvassed in various ways. For example, all line managers might be surveyed on HR issues in the firm. Alternatively, or in addition, a representative group of line managers might be involved in the planning team. As part of their perspective, line managers, including senior executives, should bring into the process an assessment of how other stakeholder groups, such as shareholders, customers and competitors, are affected by the firm's HR strategies.

Employees themselves: it should be obvious that employees and potential recruits are 'clients' of HRM in the firm. Any HR planning process will be better if it allows for employee involvement, particularly the involvement of those core workers whose ongoing commitment is needed by the firm (for example, through staff surveying and the use of focus groups to look more qualitatively at key issues). Data on how employees have reacted to HR policies in the past typically helps to improve the quality of HR planning in firms.

The State: over time, governments play a key role in providing 'social capital'. In the sense used here, this means the quantity and quality of the country's labour pool and its educational and social infrastructure. In exchange for access to these resources, governments require certain levels of compliance with labour statutes and regulations. The requirements of labour law ought always to influence the design of HR policy in firms.

The last point helps to remind us that legitimacy, as argued in Chapters 1, 3 and 8, is one of the key goals of human resource management. Some reviews of the role of HR planning assume that HR planning systems are only relevant to the 'bottom line' (see, for example, Murphy and Zandvakili 2000) but the HR goals of any firm ought to be broader than this. How to improve productivity and flexibility ought to be major concerns in HR planning but firms are also embedded in societies. Their performance should never be regarded as solely financial.

The involvement principle

The stakeholder principle implies that only through dialogue among those centrally involved in managing people in the firm can the quality of HR planning be improved. The research of Hart and Banbury (1994), discussed in Chapter 2, suggests that firms that master a range of styles of strategic management, including the more participative ones, are likely to be superior performers. As a general rule, the senior management team should drive HR planning (with the chief executive and top team leading but involving the key managers throughout the firm who manage the majority of people). HR specialists should *facilitate* the process, contributing their specialist expertise (for example, in research reports on the state of internal and external labour markets and on the HR strategies of rival firms (Craft 1988)), but not creating the situation where strategic HR planning is seen purely as their hobbyhorse.

The rivalry principle

HR planning is of little use if it is just navel-gazing. Labour markets are competitive, and intelligent rivals will attempt to recruit the best workers and build the best management processes. As a result, the firm's executive team should aim to understand the HR strengths and weaknesses of key competitors (Craft 1988). Does the company have good data on the employment strengths and weaknesses of rivals? While this is a competitive question, it should not simply be seen in a competitive light (Nalebuff and Brandenburger 1996). Rival firms may be competing in the labour market but also have common interests in improving labour supply to the network or cluster of firms, a key reason for co-location of facilities in many industries. This is one of the secrets of 'Silicon Valley' in California and of many other examples of co-located firms.

The dynamic principle

As argued in Chapter 1, it is vital to accept that change is inevitable and that some preparation for the future is therefore crucial. We have not so far discussed the issue of the planning horizon but, as in all planning, this is important. Most HRM textbooks cover the techniques of short-run HR planning well and companies typically find they need at least some of them. Some short-run planning is necessary just to stay afloat. Any type of recruitment, for example, involves some kind of thinking in advance about the firm's skill deficits and desirable types of candidate (even if this thinking becomes much sharper as the selection process unfolds). Where firms tend to be much weaker, however, is in the quality of their long-run HR planning (Gratton, Hope-Hailey, Stiles and Truss 1999a, 1999b). As argued in this chapter, planning for the next three to five years is a good thing providing it does not make the organisation unduly inflexible (which it can do if done badly).

The most obvious approach in this context is scenario planning which can be used to create readiness for a range of competitive futures. One thing that must be accepted about the future is that it is uncertain. As Anthony Giddens repeatedly emphasised in the 1998 BBC Reith Lectures on globalisation, we should 'expect the unexpected' and learn to manage risk. The example shown in Figure 11.1 involves defining three competitive scenarios and exploring their HR implications. One scenario is based on the most desirable business case. Such scenarios tend to assume that intelligent rivals do not exist and that the environment is generally benign, so it pays to define a second, more likely scenario. Finally, one can define a least desirable case, a scenario in which there are major downturns or reversals in business fortunes. The bombing of the World Trade Centre and the Pentagon in September 2001 should remind us that there are factors well beyond business control that can disrupt business performance. Certainly in the case of airlines, and those in their supply chains, contingency planning for downsizing helps firms to adjust to such unexpected circumstances.

In this context, Shell's multiple planning system is a celebrated case (De Geus 1988, Grant 1998). In the aftermath of the 1970s oil shocks, most oil companies in the 1980s planned for a scenario of permanently rising oil prices. Shell did this but also planned for significant price decreases, a scenario that was played out in early 1986 as oil prices fell from US$27 a barrel to $17 in February and $10 in April. As a result of the lateral thinking encouraged by its scenario planning, Shell was better prepared than other companies in the industry.

The model shown in Figure 11.1 deliberately uses three scenarios. As argued by Eisenhardt, Kahwajy and Bourgeois (1997), whose work on strategic decision-making was noted in Chapter 2, it helps if more than two options are generated in thinking about the future. Two decision options can degenerate into a political slugfest between two executives or two sides of the team. Three or four options help to reduce this kind of political in-fighting and to keep us open to the possibility that we might combine ideas from different options in the eventual decisions we take.

Step 1: Identifying long-run business scenarios

- Identify the key rivals in your industry-based 'strategic group'
- Identify three scenarios that might be played out in the group over the next five years (eg most desirable case, most likely case, and least desirable case)

Step 2: Assessing the firm's HR readiness
For each scenario ask:

- What are the HR challenges posed by this scenario (eg challenges posed by inadequate social capital, by labour market rivals, or by the attitudes to the firm of current or potential employees)?
- What are our HR strengths to meet these challenges (eg existing depth of know-how in a key business area, strength of reputation as an employer)?
- What are our HR weaknesses in relation to these challenges (eg recruitment not yet focused on capabilities needed in the future, lack of training for future competitive needs, excessive turnover of core staff)?

Step 3: Identifying key stakeholder trends relating to HRM
Over the next five years, what are the likely trends in the following and what should the company do to prepare?

- HR strategies of key rivals – what are the threats they will most likely pose (eg 'poaching' of star employees)? What opportunities do they present (eg joint training initiatives)?
- Needs and aspirations of key workers – how might they differ from current needs and aspirations? What should the company do to prepare for these possible changes?
- Quality of social capital and changes in labour market regulation – how might the quality of the labour pool change? How might labour law change?

Step 4: Planning HR strategies to meet long-run business needs and cope with stakeholder trends

- Focusing on the most desirable business scenario, list the key *long-run* HR research, review, policy or programme initiatives that must be taken for this scenario to become a reality and develop milestones for them over the next five years (eg a staged leadership development programme with an increasing annual budget, development of an annual employee attitude survey linked to customer surveying and jointly linked to annual business planning)
- Focusing on the most likely business scenario, list key HR policies and programmes that should be put in place to improve readiness to cope with it
- Focusing on the least desirable business scenario, list key HR policies and programmes that should be put in place to improve readiness to cope with it
- Identify HR initiatives that are (a) common across all scenarios, and (b) those that are unique and will require some development of flexible skills and processes in HR management

Figure 11.1 An example of scenario-based HR planning

The integration principle

The last principle is one that has been continually emphasised in the literature for many years, as noted above. Processes for HR planning ought to be integrated with processes used for:

- long-run strategic planning and business development;
- short-run planning and budgeting.

It is not a question of choosing between short-run and long-run planning systems. Both forms of planning are important and HR planning needs to play an appropriate role in both.

In reality, no-one seriously challenges this principle. The key question is always: 'Yes, of course, we should integrate – but how?' In the next section, we turn to a closer examination of this issue by considering a key set of ideas about integrating financial and non-financial planning which have become very influential in contemporary strategic management.

Seeking integration: HR planning and the new management accounting

Chapter 3 in this book notes that Michael Porter's *Competitive Strategy* (1980) and *Competitive Advantage* (1985) were landmark contributions to the literature on strategy in the 1980s. These books offered useful analytical frameworks, particularly the notion of 'industry analysis' which helped firms to analyse the economic and political dimensions of industries. Porter's ideas were very much concerned with forging a competitive vision: with strategy as something 'out there'.

From the mid 1990s, another perspective grew up alongside the positioning model, as Chapter 4 explained. In popular reading lists, Hamel and Prahalad's (1994) *Competing for the Future* became a counterpoint alongside Porter's frameworks, encouraging firms to apply some of the internally-oriented notions associated with the resource-based view of the firm. Hamel and Prahalad's work, however, has been more difficult to apply in concrete ways. If we want to locate the most practically influential ideas of the 1990s on how to reshape strategic management they are to be found in the 'new management accounting' associated with two books by Robert Kaplan and David Norton: *The Balanced Scorecard* (1996) and, most recently, *The Strategy-Focused Organization* (2001). Traditional approaches to management accounting have been roundly criticised for focusing managers on short-term performance and for failing to encourage intelligent management of the links between financial and non-financial variables in the firm (Johnson and Kaplan 1991). As a discipline that heavily influences the strategic management process, traditional management accounting has to be treated with great care if it is not to produce dysfunctional outcomes.

Not unreasonably, Kaplan and Norton start from the premiss that it is *executed* strategy that counts in a firm's performance. This, of course, was Mintzberg's (1978) fundamental point in his classic work on emergent strategy. Formulation of strategy may seem incredibly important but what customers and business rivals take most seriously (and what researchers are most interested in) is the strategy that is actually implemented. Business failure is seen to stem mostly from failing to implement and not from failing to have wonderful visions (Kaplan and Norton 2001: 1). In their view, good implementation of well-formulated strategy is rare, an argument consistent with the resource-based view of the firm. This stems from lack of consensus about what the firm's strategy actually is. All too often, they argue, senior managers overestimate what people understand about the firm's espoused strategy.

Balancing performance measures in the firm

There are two key sets of ideas that are important in Kaplan and Norton's (1996, 2001) work. The first is concerned with balancing the measures that focus management attention. The balanced scorecard involves a process of developing goals, measures, targets and initiatives in four perspectives on business performance (Figure 11.2).

An edited example of a balanced scorecard, based on a US retail chain store ('Store 24'), is shown in Figure 11.3 (Kaplan and Norton 2001: 82). This edited version is depicted in vertical format rather than as a wheel. It does not show all the links involved and only includes some measures that the company uses (in the top and bottom perspectives). Kaplan and Norton recognise that financial outcomes are important to shareholders (the perspective at the top of the scorecard) but that they are 'lagging' and short-term indicators. To improve a business, management needs to look at desirable long-term outcomes and improve the 'leading indicators' or 'performance drivers' that generate them.

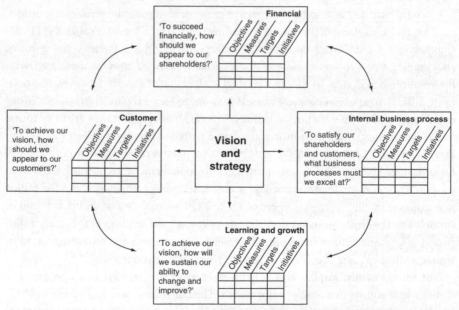

Figure 11.2 The four perspectives in the balanced scorecard

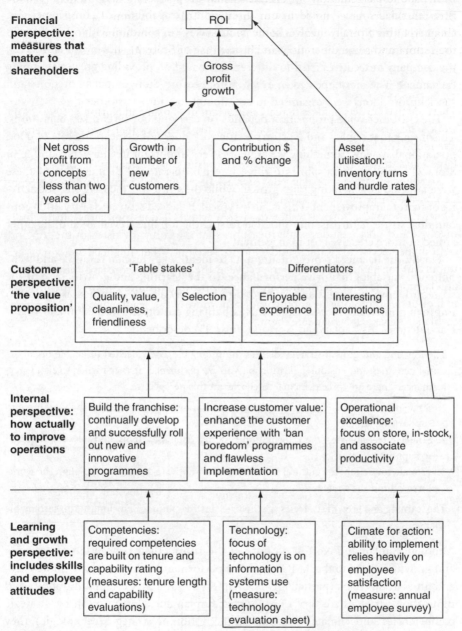

Financial perspective: measures that matter to shareholders

ROI

Gross profit growth

| Net gross profit from concepts less than two years old | Growth in number of new customers | Contribution $ and % change | Asset utilisation: inventory turns and hurdle rates |

Customer perspective: 'the value proposition'

'Table stakes'

Quality, value, cleanliness, friendliness

Selection

Differentiators

Enjoyable experience

Interesting promotions

Internal perspective: how actually to improve operations

Build the franchise: continually develop and successfully roll out new and innovative programmes

Increase customer value: enhance the customer experience with 'ban boredom' programmes and flawless implementation

Operational excellence: focus on store, in-stock, and associate productivity

Learning and growth perspective: includes skills and employee attitudes

Competencies: required competencies are built on tenure and capability rating (measures: tenure length and capability evaluations)

Technology: focus of technology is on information systems use (measure: technology evaluation sheet)

Climate for action: ability to implement relies heavily on employee satisfaction (measure: annual employee survey)

Figure 11.3 Example of a strategy map and some balanced scorecard measures

Performance drivers are located in the three perspectives that underpin the financial one. Customers must perceive a 'value proposition' if they are to reward the firm financially. As we noted in our discussion of capabilities or competencies in Chapter 4, this typically involves some 'table stakes' (in common with other firms in the sector) and some differentiators. In the case of Store 24 shown in Figure 11.3, the company's executives tried to differentiate based on providing greater shopping excitement. The motto, posted in every store, became 'Store 24 bans boredom' and special promotions were organised in an attempt to amuse customers.

The customer value proposition depends on carrying out certain key operations. This means that Kaplan and Norton's framework does not demean the role of good operational systems, something we argued is very important in Chapters 2 and 5. In Store 24's case, this was split into three internal operational themes. Two of these were targeted at generating sales growth while the third was focused on productivity or margin improvement. This is fairly typical. Balanced scorecards very often contain dual strategic thrusts: one aimed at raising the top line (revenue) and the other aimed at more effective cost management.

Finally, the balanced scorecard attempts to identify key human resource and technological variables that drive performance. In the 'learning and growth' base of the scorecard, employee skills and satisfaction are nearly always identified as critical to improving internal processes, and thus enhancing customer satisfaction and financial outcomes. As Kaplan and Norton (2001: 93) describe it:

> The learning and growth strategy defines the intangible assets needed to enable organizational activities and customer relationships to be performed at ever-higher levels of performance. There are three principal categories in this perspective:
>
> 1. Strategic competencies: the strategic skills and knowledge required by the workforce to support the strategy
> 2. Strategic technologies: the information systems, databases, tools, and network required to support the strategy
> 3. Climate for action: the cultural shifts needed to motivate, empower, and align the workforce behind the strategy.
>
> The learning and growth strategies are the true starting point for any long-term, sustainable change.

Although Kaplan and Norton do not use the rubric, their conception of 'learning and growth' is close to the 'AMO' model of performance which we have quoted several times in this book (particularly in Chapters 1, 5 and 7). Certainly, the ability and motivation variables are very close to what Kaplan and Norton mean by 'strategic competencies' and 'climate for action'. In the notion of 'strategic technologies', they also identify part of what it means to provide workers with the opportunity to perform because good systems and tools are needed if people are to work effectively. However, their thinking here does not go as far as we would like. It helps to see the structure of work – the forms of work organisation used in the firm – as facilitating or constraining employee opportunity to make a difference. Online and offline opportunities for participation in problem-solving and decision-making are typically very important in creating 'high-performance work systems', as we argued in Chapter 5.

Through this kind of framework, then, Kaplan and Norton encourage business unit managers to define desirable long-run strategic goals and make short-run plans based on 'milestones' toward long-run goals. This provides a simple, practical way of integrating strategic planning and annual budgeting. Budgeting is a very strong corporate ritual which tends to over-emphasise short-run profitability and undermine long-run efforts to build the business. The balanced scorecard can be used to re-work budgets around steps towards the desired long-run strategy. Some short-run targets are always needed (because survival into the long-run depends on surviving today) but such targets should not create perverse long-run consequences. Given business unit goals, the scorecard can then be used to create departmental and personal scorecards for individual managers.

It can also be used in multidivisional firms to open up a better dialogue between corporate and business unit management about the role of both (Kaplan and Norton 2001: 161–5). Rather than simply considering figures on return on investment, balanced scorecards can open up debate around the performance drivers of financial outcomes, including HR variables. Such an approach challenges some of the modes of corporate control discussed in Chapter 10. Corporate scorecards in multidivisional firms, argue Kaplan and Norton, should identify synergies across the group (why else have a group?). This includes ways in which central service units (such as corporate finance, IT and HR departments) can add value to particular business units. In those companies moving from M-form to N-form structure (see Figure 10.3 in Chapter 10), the balanced scorecard could be a valuable tool for identifying synergies across business units and between business units and corporate service centres.

The Kaplan and Norton scorecard is thus better balanced than typical financial reports that only report history and which do not identify underpinning sources of success. Our discussion indicates that it is also better balanced in the sense that it recognises outcomes that matter to other *stake*holders (particularly customers and employees) besides *stock*holders. This emphasis is consistent with a range of contemporary efforts to encourage broader reporting, such as the notion of the 'triple bottom line' (financial, environmental and social) (Elkington 1997).

Building a theory of the business or 'strategy map'

The second key idea in the balanced scorecard is that senior managers should build a 'theory of the business' or what Kaplan and Norton (2001) are increasingly calling a 'strategy map'. This is a map of causes and effects, of performance drivers and their key outcomes. In the edited version of a scorecard depicted in Figure 11.3, key elements of a strategy map become apparent, including the role of skill-building and employee motivation in producing good encounters with customers and, thus, better financial returns.

Another example of a strategy map is shown in Figure 11.4. This map depicts the 'service-profit' or 'employee-customer-profit chain' at Sears (Heskett, Jones, Loveman and Schlesinger 1994, Rucci, Kirn and Quinn 1998). Sears uses the idea that the company will become a 'compelling place to invest' if it is a 'compelling place to shop' and a 'compelling place to work'. The map argues that differences in employee satisfaction and capabilities have direct impacts on customer satisfaction in service firms and important indirect impacts on profitability. As Becker, Huselid and Ulrich (2001) note, the links between HR strategy, employee behaviour and what happens to customers are very clear in this kind of service business. The vast majority of employees are working directly with customers and their attitudes to the work and the company become very apparent to customers, something to which we can all attest.

Another strategy map, this time in a five-star hotel is shown in Figure 11.5 (Haynes and Fryer 2000). The hotel, having over 400 rooms and located in a large New Zealand city, aims to outperform industry rivals through the quality of its people management. Like all luxury hotels, physical amenities and the refurbishment of properties drive one aspect of the strategy but tend to fall into the category of 'table stakes'. With enough money, hotel owners can create the kind of opulent surroundings that position them in the luxury hotel segment. However, the bricks and mortar (or, in this case, the marble and polished wood) do not confer any form of sustained advantage in the segment. The key to superior returns really lies in the way staff deal with customers in the context of these surroundings. This includes the way in which guest preferences are discovered and catered for in successive visits. It means that there is a role for investments in the more intangible variables: in broader, more empowering job design, in development interviews and more comprehensive training, and in staff committees and surveys through which management learns about employee motivators. As Figure 11.5 illustrates, HR strategy becomes the primary driver of competitive differentiation in this context. The case helps to illustrate the way in which there are opportunities to make better use of staff discretion in many types of services, not simply in those, such as professional services, where skill levels are traditionally perceived as high.

The key point about strategy maps is that they open up debate about what really makes the business successful or could make it more successful, particularly when staff at all levels of the business are included in the process (Kaplan and Norton 2001). 'Making strategy everyone's everyday job' is one of the key principles (as opposed to making it the exclusive knowledge of a top-management 'secret society'). Over time, management should postulate and measure various hypotheses about cause and effect in the business and thus improve their 'theory of the business', something that is also emphasised by HR scholars such as David Guest

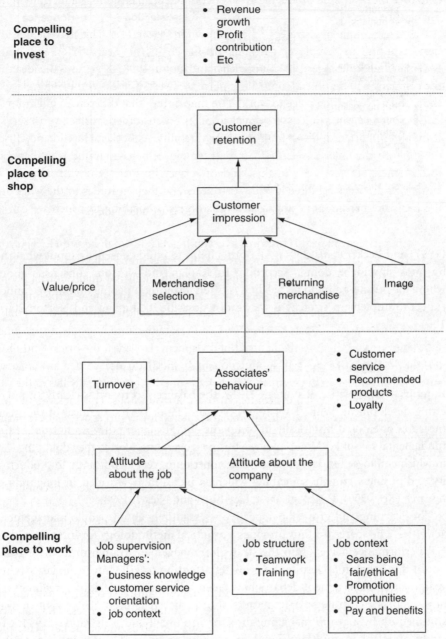

Compelling place to invest

- Revenue growth
- Profit contribution
- Etc

Compelling place to shop

Customer retention

Customer impression

Value/price

Merchandise selection

Returning merchandise

Image

Compelling place to work

Turnover

Associates' behaviour

- Customer service
- Recommended products
- Loyalty

Attitude about the job

Attitude about the company

Job supervision Managers':
- business knowledge
- customer service orientation
- job context

Job structure
- Teamwork
- Training

Job context
- Sears being fair/ethical
- Promotion opportunities
- Pay and benefits

Figure 11.4 The employee-customer-profit chain at Sears

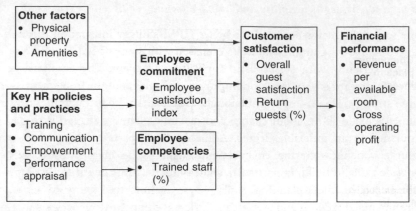

Source: Haynes and Fryer (2000)

Figure 11.5　A strategy map in the luxury hotel industry

(1997) and Becker *et al.* (2001). All of this helps to build consensus about what the business should be doing. According to Kaplan and Norton, consensus about where the business should be heading is often lower than people think. 'We cannot expect to implement strategy if we cannot describe it' (Kaplan and Norton 2001: 100).

Strategic HRM and the balanced scorecard: an evaluation

In terms of the practice of strategic HRM, the balanced scorecard is clearly an interesting development. While Kaplan and Norton (1996: 144) are critical of the weak measures often used historically in companies on HR issues, they do not doubt the fundamental role of HRM in building a business over time. Nor do they doubt the way in which employee satisfaction, over time, contributes very significantly to productivity and business growth, something which is increasingly affirmed in longitudinal research (Koys 2001, Patterson, West, Lawthorn and Nickell 1998).

The 'learning and growth' perspective is essentially about people management activities. The scorecard thus provides a practical methodology for integrating key HR performance drivers into the strategic management framework. There is no doubt this is helpful. Despite the growing attention to HRM over the last twenty years, senior management debates have been hamstrung by lack of agreement on how reports on strategic HR matters should be structured. The problem was summed up by a group managing director in Purcell and Ahlstrand's (1994: 61) study of HRM in multidivisional firms. This individual commented that the board in his company: ' . . . had decided on thirty priorities in the last few years, with the people ones being the most woolly, the hardest to measure, and the easiest to forget'.

The need for strategic flexibility and 'meta-planning' skills

While seeing the major potential for better HRM-strategy integration through the balanced scorecard, caution should be exercised with some of Kaplan and Norton's ideas, or certainly with a simplistic application of them. The emphasis of the balanced scorecard is very much on improving the quality of the implementation of a *given* strategy. This is important enough, as Kaplan and Norton argue. However, arguments made above about change and dynamic planning suggest it should not be pursued to an inflexible degree. Arguably, those parts of the process which encourage openness to the environment ought to be highlighted more fully. Alongside skills in building particular strategy maps, firms ought to develop what might be called 'meta-planning' skills. These include the ability to sense new environmental directions and to switch to different competitive scenarios, something that was shown to be valuable in our earlier discussion of the US railway cases.

This criticism is increasingly recognised by Kaplan and Norton. In the *Strategy Focused Organisation* (2001: Chapter 12), they accept the role and importance of environmental and competitor analysis prior to formulating strategy. They also discuss examples of 'dynamic simulation' and note the value of calibrating scorecard measures against industry rivals (thus benchmarking the firm in terms of industry change). They further argue that the firm's leaders should aim to identify and support the Mintzbergian 'emergent learning' that occurs in their organisation. They note, for example, that Store 24 (Figure 11.3) has now modified its strategy because the 'ban boredom' approach did not impress customers (Kaplan and Norton 2001: 318–19). It turns out the customers valued fast service and good selection rather than in-store entertainment. The slogan has changed to "Cause you just can't wait' and the scorecard has been revised accordingly. All these points help to underline the value of strategic flexibility and meta-planning skills.

However, more is needed. Building the capacity for strategic management depends heavily on the quality of the *management* of managers, something we emphasised in Chapters 2, 7 and 10 and which does not figure in typical scorecards. Recruitment, development and team-building activities at the top levels of management (and at the middle levels which supply them) need to be planned for in astute ways. Some recognition of the importance of senior management team-building is contained in Kaplan and Norton's latest work (2001: 345–8) but much greater emphasis could be placed on this area. The balanced scorecard does contain an emphasis on the management of the non-management workforce and is obviously a way of structuring executive performance measurement. This is absolutely critical but it needs to be complemented with a more comprehensive conception of HR strategy for managing managers.

The need to recognise multiple 'bottom lines' in HRM

A second caution is closely related to the first. The importance of productive pursuit of the current strategy is the key theme in Kaplan and Norton's framework. This is, of course, vital in any business. However, this should not make us blind to the fact that some HR policies are not connected directly to productivity or indeed to organisational flexibility. Compliance and employment citizenship goals have a role to play in HRM irrespective of competitive goals. All reputable firms should comply with labour laws in their countries of domicile, as we noted in Chapters 3 and 8. This means that the firm's scorecard for HRM should never be totally dominated by a single 'bottom line'.

How can firms practically deal with this and the preceding criticism? It helps if three 'bottom lines' are identified, based around the three goals we have argued in this book are important in HRM: labour productivity, organisational flexibility, and social legitimacy (Chapter 1). Each of these goals gives rise to a cause-effect chain or strategy map, as we depict in Figure 11.6. The first chain is the one most readily associated with Kaplan and Norton's scorecards: it runs from HR practices through operating processes and customer reactions to productivity and profit. The key concern in this chain is with adopting the cost-effective set of HR practices needed to underpin profitable operations in the firm. This would normally include a suitable mix of practices concerned with hiring and developing employee skills, with motivating appropriate performance and with work structure and voice systems. The second cause-effect chain is concerned with creating organisational flexibility, with the need to think above and beyond the current business context. The HR practices here are concerned with long-run capability development, both for managers and for the workforce generally. This could include, for example, forms of training that build skills in creative thinking and environmental sensing. The third cause-effect chain is

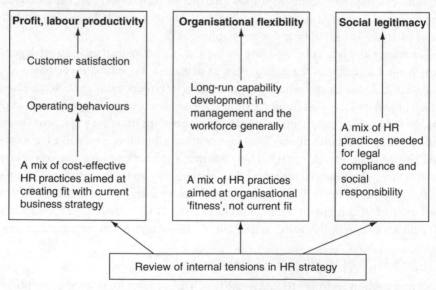

Figure 11.6 Three 'bottom lines' or cause-effect chains in HR strategy

concerned with social legitimacy. There is no necessary connection here to the traditional bottom line of profit (although there may be). This chain identifies the HR practices needed to underpin legal and socially responsible employment relationships in the firm. Included here are minimum employment standards and occupational health and safety systems, among others.

All of this, of course, begs the question of how to reconcile these three sets of HR practices. As the bottom box in the diagram recognises, a process is needed to review 'internal fit' in HR strategy, a concept discussed in Chapter 3. As argued there, there will be tensions in any HR strategy: 'fit' in the sense of a single, uncomplicated theme is not possible. Multiple themes are needed in an effective HR strategy. The key thing is to identify and face up to the main tensions. For example, it is important to learn how to balance HR practices that reinforce the execution of a given strategy with practices that help the firm to conceive of a completely different one.

The need for caution with specific HR practices

A final criticism of the balanced scorecard concerns Kaplan and Norton's assumptions about desirable kinds of HR practice. Like many US 'best practice' writers, they tend to place too much faith in incentive remuneration (the 'balanced paycheque') (see also Becker *et al.* 2001). The principle of aligning employer and employee interests is, of course, absolutely fundamental but this doesn't mean that bonus systems are always desirable, a point we covered in our discussion of agency theory in Chapter 7. There are many situations in which the better focus a scorecard can bring will work well alongside high wage levels but without mechanistic bonuses. If, however, the scorecard process encourages firms to find out more about employee motivations (through, for example, encouraging greater use of employee surveying), it should improve the design of work and reward systems over time. The stakeholder and involvement principles we noted earlier in relation to HR planning systems imply this kind of consultative process. What is needed is a way of identifying that mix or bundle of HR practices that will be relevant in a particular context. While some practices have almost universal relevance, others are heavily shaped by industry and societal contexts, among other factors. The need to recognise and manage the tension between 'best practice' and 'best fit' is a key theme in this book.

Conclusions and implications

While recognising that strategic management is broader than strategic planning, many of the ideas about how to improve strategic management come back to ideas about how to improve the planning debate in the firm. In most situations, there is competitive value in finding ways to improve the quality of strategic planning, including finding ways in which human resource problems and opportunities can be better understood and tackled. Far from being outdated or inappropriate in changing times, the discipline of strategic planning is something that can yield greater value, particularly when firms show persistence and develop 'meta-planning' skills in environmental analysis and flexible thinking. Scenario planning is important in this regard, particularly those models that involve planning for the HR challenges presented by different scenarios.

At the base of all strategies, there are things that firms need to do with people, as Kaplan and Norton's (1996, 2001) 'balanced scorecards' and 'strategy maps' indicate. Human resources may not be sufficient for competitive success but they are a necessary part of the system of resources that is. There is no doubt that in many firms, the creation and testing of a strategy map would constitute a major breakthrough by helping to identify the key linkages between HR practices and a desired competitive position. As the new management accountancy recognises, there is then less likelihood that critical resources, including human ones, will be subject to counter-productive forms of cost-cutting in the firm. Such frameworks represent an important, integrating step forward, one in which management can move beyond mere assertion about the value of human capital to a planning regime in which measurement and modelling confirm these important assertions by making them specific and transparent.

As Kaplan and Norton argue, human resource variables, such as employee skills and satisfaction levels, are 'performance drivers' in all firms. However, this perspective cannot encompass all that is important about HR strategy. The strategic goals of HRM should be understood in a broader sense. They include productive exploitation of current strategy (labour productivity) but also the building of certain types of organisational flexibility and social legitimacy. They involve strategic tensions that are never easy to handle even where measurement is improved. The 'bottom line' for organisations, including private sector ones, is more complex than it first appears. A good performance is multidimensional. As we have argued in this chapter, three 'bottom lines' are useful for planning in HR strategy: one for productivity, another for flexibility and yet another for legitimacy. New frameworks in strategic planning have lessons for HRM and are more embracing of HRM. The traffic, however, is not all one way. Human resource management also has some enduring lessons for the new planning frameworks.

References

Abell, D. F. (1993) *Managing with Dual Strategies: Mastering the Present, Preempting the Future*. New York: Free Press.

Adams, J. S. (1965) 'Inequality in social exchange'. In Berkovitz, L. (ed.) *Advances in Experimental Social Psychology*, Vol. 2. New York: Academic Press.

Adler, P. S., Goldoftas, B. and Levine, D. I. (1999) 'Flexibility versus efficiency? A case study of model changeovers with Toyota production system'. *Organization Science* 10(1): 43–68.

Albert, S. and Bradley, K. (1998) 'Professional temporary agencies, women and professional discretion: implications for organizations and management'. *British Journal of Management* 9: 261–72.

Alpander, G., Carter, K. and Forsgren, R. (1990) 'Managerial issues and problem-solving in the formative years'. *Journal of Small Business Management* 28(2): 9–19.

Amit, R. and Shoemaker, P. (1993) 'Strategic assets and organizational rent'. *Strategic Management Journal* 14: 33–46.

Ansoff, I. (1991) 'Critique of Henry Mintzberg's "The design school: reconsidering the basic premises of strategic management" '. *Strategic Management Journal* 12(6): 449–61.

Appelbaum, E. and Batt, R. (1994) *The New American Workplace*. Ithaca, NY: ILR Press.

Appelbaum, E., Bailey, T., Berg, P. and Kalleberg, A. (2000) *Manufacturing Advantage: Why High-Performance Systems Pay Off*. Ithaca, NY: ILR Press.

Armstrong, P. (1995) 'Accountancy and HRM'. In Storey, J. (ed.) *Human Resource Management: A Critical Text*. London: Routledge.

Atkinson, J. (1984) 'Manpower strategies for flexible organisations'. *Personnel Management* August: 28–31.

Audit Commission (2001) *Brief Encounters: Getting the Best from Temporary Nursing Staff*. London: Audit Commission.

Baden-Fuller, C. (1995) 'Strategic innovation, corporate entrepreneurship and matching outside-in to inside-out approaches to strategy research'. *British Journal of Management* 6(Special issue): 3–16.

Baden-Fuller, C. and Stopford, J. (1994) *Rejuvenating the Mature Business*. London: Routledge.

Bailey, T. (1993) 'Organizational innovation in the apparel industry'. *Industrial Relations* 32: 30–48.

Baird, L. and Meshoulam, I. (1988) 'Managing two fits of strategic human resource management'. *Academy of Management Review* 13(1): 116–28.

Bamberger, P. and Meshoulam, I. (2000) *Human Resource Strategy: Formulation, Implementation and Impact*. Thousand Oaks, CA: Sage.

Barker, J. (1993) 'Tightening the iron cage'. *Administrative Science Quarterly* 38(3): 408–37.

Barnard, C. (1938) *The Functions of the Executive*. Boston, MA: Harvard University Press.

Barney, J. (1991) 'Firm resources and sustained competitive advantage', *Journal of Management* 17(1): 99–120.

Barney, J. and Wright, P. (1998) 'On becoming a strategic partner: the role of human resources in gaining competitive advantage'. *Human Resource Management* 37(1): 31–46.

Baron, J. and Kreps, D. (1999) 'Consistent human resource practices'. *California Management Review* 41(3): 29–53.

Barr, P., Stimpert, J. and Huff, A. (1992) 'Cognitive change, strategic action, and organizational renewal'. *Strategic Management Journal* 13: 15–36.

Barsoux, J. and Lawrence, P. (1990) *Management in France*. London: Cassell.

Bartel, A. (2000) *Human Resource Management and Performance in the Service Sector: the Case of Bank Branches*. NBER Working Paper Series. Cambridge, MA: National Bureau of Economic Research.

Bartlett, C. and Ghoshal, S. (1998) *Managing Across Boundaries: The Transnational Corporation*. New York: Random House Business Books.

Bartol, K. and Durham, C. (2000) 'Incentives: theory and practice'. In Cooper, C. and Locke, E. (eds) *Industrial and Organizational Psychology*. Oxford: Blackwell.

Bates, T. (1990) 'Entrepreneur human capital inputs and small business longevity'. *Review of Economics and Statistics* 72(4): 551–9.

Batt, R. (2000) 'Strategic segmentation in front-line services: matching customers, employees and human resource systems'. *International Journal of Human Resource Management* 11(3): 540–61.

Batt, R. (2001) 'The economies of teams among technicians'. *British Journal of Industrial Relations* 39(1): 1–24.

Baumeister, A. and Bacharach, V. (2000) 'Early generic educational intervention has no enduring effect on intelligence and does not prevent mental retardation: the infant health and development program'. *Intelligence* 28(3): 161–92.

Becker, B. and Gerhart, B. (1996) 'The impact of human resource management on organizational performance: progress and practice'. *Academy of Management Journal* 39(4): 779–801.

Becker, B., Huselid, M. and Ulrich, D. (2001) *The HR Scorecard: Linking People, Strategy, and Performance*. Boston, MA: Harvard Business School Press.

Becker, G. (1964) *Human Capital*. New York: Columbia University Press.

Beer, M., Spector, B., Lawrence, P., Quinn Mills, D. and Walton, R. (1984) *Managing Human Assets*. New York: Free Press.

Belbin, M. (1981) *Management Teams: Why They Succeed or Fail*. Oxford: Butterworth-Heinemann.

Bendix, R. (1956) *Work and Authority in Industry*. Berkeley, CA: UCLA Press.

Benkhoff, B. (1997) 'A test of the HRM model: good for employers *and* employees.' *Human Resource Management Journal* 7(4): 44–60.

Berg, P. (1999) 'The effects of high performance work practices on job satisfaction in the United States steel industry.' *Relations Industrielles* 54(1): 111–134.

Berggren, C. (1992) *The Volvo Experience: Alternatives to Lean Production in the Swedish Auto Industry*. London: Macmillan (now Palgrave Macmillan).

Bettis, R. (1991) 'Strategic management and the straight-jacket: an editorial essay'. *Organization Science* 2(3): 315–19.

Bhargava, S. (1994) 'Profit sharing and the financial performance of companies: evidence from UK Panel data'. *The Economic Journal* 104: 1044–56.

Bird, A. and Beechler, S. (1995) 'Links between business strategy and human resource management strategy in US-based Japanese subsidiaries: an empirical investigation'. *Journal of International Business Studies* 26(1): 23–46.

Blyton, P. and Turnbull, P. (1998) *The Dynamics of Employee Relations*. London: Macmillan (now Palgrave Macmillan).

Boeker, W. (1989) 'Strategic change: the effects of founding and history'. *Academy of Management Journal* 32(3): 489–515.

Boselie, P., Paauwe, J. and Jansen, P. (2001) 'Human resource management and performance: lessons from the Netherlands'. *International Journal of Human Resource Management* 12(7): 1107–25.

Boxall, P. (1992) 'Strategic human resource management: beginnings of a new theoretical sophistication?' *Human Resource Management Journal* 2(3): 60–79.

Boxall, P. (1994) 'Placing HR strategy at the heart of business success', *Personnel Management* 26(7): 32–5.

Boxall, P. (1995) 'Building the theory of comparative HRM', *Human Resource Management Journal* 5(5): 5–17.

Boxall, P. (1996) 'The strategic HRM debate and the resource-based view of the firm'. *Human Resource Management Journal* 6(3): 59–75.

Boxall, P. (1998) 'Achieving competitive advantage through human resource strategy: towards a theory of industry dynamics'. *Human Resource Management Review* 8(3): 265–88.

Boxall, P. (1999), 'Human resource strategy and industry-based competition: a conceptual framework and agenda for theoretical development'. In Wright, P., Dyer, L., Boudreau, J. and Milkovich, G. (eds) *Research in Personnel and Human Resource*

Management (Supplement 4: Strategic Human Resources Management in the Twenty-First Century). Stamford, CT and London: JAI Press.

Boxall, P. and Haynes, P. (1997), 'Strategy and trade union effectiveness in a neo-liberal environment', *British Journal of Industrial Relations* 35(4): 567–91.

Boxall, P. and Purcell, J. (2000) 'Strategic human resource management: where have we come from and where should we be going?' *International Journal of Management Reviews* 2(2): 183–203.

Boxall, P. and Steeneveld, M. (1999) 'Human resource strategy and competitive advantage: a longitudinal study of engineering consultancies'. *Journal of Management Studies* 36(4): 443–63.

Bracker, J. (1980) 'The historical development of the strategic management concept'. *Academy of Management Review* 5(2): 219–24.

Bradley, K. and Gelb, A. (1983) *Worker Capitalism: The New Industrial Relations* London: Heinemann Educational.

Bradley, L. and Ashkanasy, N. (2001) 'Formal performance appraisal interviews: can they really be objective and are they useful anyway?' *Asia Pacific Journal of Human Resources* 39(2): 83–97.

Braverman, H. (1974) *Labor and Monopoly Capital*. New York and London: Monthly Review Press.

Brews, P. and Hunt, M. (1999) 'Learning to plan and planning to learn: resolving the planning school/learning school debate'. *Strategic Management Journal* 20: 889–913.

Brewster, C. (1999) 'Different paradigms in strategic HRM: questions raised by comparative research'. In Wright, P., Dyer, L., Boudreau, J. and Milkovich, G. (eds) *Research in Personnel and Human Resource Management (Supplement 4: Strategic Human Resources Management in the Twenty-First Century)*, Stamford, CT and London: JAI Press.

Brown, C. and Reich, M. (1997) 'Micro-macro linkages in high-performance work systems'. *Organization Studies* 18(5): 765–81.

Brown, W., Deakin, S., Hudson, M., Pratten, C. and Ryan, P. (1998) *The Individualisation of the Employment Contract in Britain*. Employment Relations Research Series No. 4. London: Department of Trade and Industry.

Bruce, A. and Buck, T. (1997) 'Executive reward corporate governance'. In Keasey, K., Thompson, S. and Wright, M. (eds) *Corporate Governance: Economic and Financial Issues*. Oxford: Oxford University Press.

Bruegal, I. and Perrons, D. (1998) 'Deregulation and women's employment: the diverse experiences of women in Britain'. *Feminist Economics* 4(1): 103–25.

Budhwar, P. and Debrah, U. (2001) *Human Resource Management in Developing Countries*. London: Routledge.

Buono, A. F. and Bowditch, J. L. (1989) *The Human Side of Mergers and Acquisitions*. San Francisco: Jossey-Bass.

Buono, A. F., Bowditch, J. L. and Lewis III, J. (1985) 'When cultures collide: the anatomy of a merger'. *Human Relations* 53(5): 477–500.

Burgess, S. and Rees, H. (1998) 'A disaggregate analysis of the evolution of job tenure in Britain, 1975–1993'. *British Journal of Industrial Relations* 36(4): 629–55.

Buxton, J. (1998) *Ending the Mother War.* London: Macmillan (now Palgrave Macmillan).

Cam, S., Purcell, J. and Tailby, S. (2002) 'Contingent employment in the UK'. In Bergstrom, O. and Storrie, D. (eds) *Contingent Employment in Europe and the US.* Cheltenham: Edward Elgar.

Cameron, K. (1986) 'Effectiveness as paradox: consensus and conflict in conceptions of organizational effectiveness'. *Management Science* 32(5): 539–53.

Campbell, J. P., McCloy, R., Oppler, S. and Sager, C. (1993) 'A theory of performance'. In Schmitt, N. and Borman, W. (eds) *Personnel Selection in Organizations.* San Francisco: Jossey-Bass.

Cappelli, P. (1995) *Airline Labor Relations in the Global Era.* Ithaca, NY: Cornell University Press.

Carroll, G. R. and Hannan, M. T. (eds) (1995) *Organizations in Industry: Strategy, Structure and Selection,* New York and Oxford: Oxford University Press.

Cartier, K. (1994) 'The transaction costs and benefits of the incomplete contract of employment'. *Cambridge Journal of Economics* 18: 181–96.

Cartwright, S. and Cooper, C. (1992) *Mergers and Acquisitions: the Human Factor.* Oxford: Butterworth-Heinemann.

Castells, M. (1996) *The Information Age. Volume 1: The Rise of the Network Society.* Malden, MA and Oxford: Blackwell.

Chandler, A. (1962) *Strategy and Structure: Chapters in the History of Industrial Enterprise.* Cambridge, MA: MIT Press.

Channon, D. (1982) 'Industrial structure'. *Long Range Planning* 15(5): 78–93.

Child, J. (1972) 'Organizational structure, environment and performance: the role of strategic choice'. *Sociology* 6(3): 1–22.

Child, J. (1997) 'Strategic choice in the analysis of action, structure, organizations and environment: retrospect and prospect'. *Organization Studies* 18(1): 43–76.

Child, J. and Smith, C. (1987) 'The context and process of organizational transformation: Cadbury Limited in its sector'. *Journal of Management Studies* 24(6): 564–93.

Clegg, H. (1975) 'Pluralism in industrial relations'. *British Journal of Industrial Relations* 13(3): 309–16.

Clegg, H. (1994) *The History of British Trade Unions Since 1889, Vol. III.* Oxford: Oxford University Press.

Coase, R. (1937) 'The nature of the firm'. *Economica* 4: 386–405.

Coff. R. (1997) 'Human assets and management dilemmas: coping with hazards on the road to resource-based theory'. *Academy of Management Review* 22(2): 374–402.

Coff, R. (1999) 'When competitive advantage doesn't lead to performance: the resource-based view and stakeholder bargaining power'. *Organization Science* 10(2): 119–33.

Collard, R. and Dale, B. (1989) 'Quality circles'. In Sisson, K. (ed.) *Personnel Management in Britain*. Oxford: Blackwell, 356–77.

Collins, J. and Porras, J. (1998) *Built to Last: Successful Habits of Visionary Companies*. London: Century.

Conner, K. (1991) 'A historical comparison of resource-based theory and five schools of thought within industrial organization economics: do we have a new theory of the firm?' *Journal of Management* 17(1): 121–54.

Conyon, M. (1997) 'Institutional arrangements for setting directors' compensation in UK companies'. In Keasey, K., Thompson, S. and Wright, M. (eds) *Corporate Governance: Economic and Financial Issues*. Oxford: Oxford University Press.

Cotton, J. (1993) *Employee Involvement*. Newbury Park, CA: Sage.

Cox, A. (2001) *Managing Variable Pay Systems: A Question of Form Over Substance?* Unpublished PhD thesis, University of Bath.

Coyle-Shapiro, J. (1999) 'Employee participation and assessment of an organizational change intervention'. *The Journal of Applied Behavioural Science* 35(4): 439–56.

Coyle-Shapiro, J. and Kessler, I. (2000) 'Consequences of the psychological contract for the employment relationship: a large scale survey'. *Journal of Management Studies* 37(7): 903–30.

Craft, J. (1988) 'Human resource planning and strategy'. In Dyer, L. (ed.) *Human Resource Management: Evolving Roles and Responsibilities*. Washington: Bureau of National Affairs.

Crichton, A. (1968) *Personnel Management in Context*. London: Batsford.

Cronshaw, M., Davis, E. and Kay, J. (1994) 'On being stuck in the middle or good food costs less at Sainsbury's'. *British Journal of Management* 5(1): 19–32.

Crouch, C. (1979) *The Politics of Industrial Relations*. London: Fontana.

Crouch, C. and Pizzarno, A. (1978) *The Resurgence of Class Conflict in Western Europe Since 1968*. Basingstoke: Macmillan (now Palgrave Macmillan).

Cully, M., Woodland, S., O'Reilly, A. and Dix, G. (1999) *Britain at Work: As Depicted by the 1998 Workplace Employee Relations Survey*. London: Routledge.

Dany, F. and Torchy, V. (1994) 'Recruitment and selection in Europe: policies, practices and methods'. In Brewster, C. and Hegewisch, A. (eds) *Policy and Practice in European Human Resource Management*. London: Routledge.

Dattta, D. and Grant, J. (1990) 'Relationships between types of acquisition, the autonomy given to the acquired firm, and acquisition success: an empirical study.' *Journal of Management* 16: 29–44

Davis, E. and Lansbury, R. (eds) (1996) *Managing Together: Consultation and Participation in the Workplace*. Melbourne: Longman.

De Cieri, H. and Dowling, P. (1999) 'Strategic human resource management in multi-national enterprises: theoretical and empirical developments'. In Wright, P., Dyer, L., Boudreau, J. and Milkovich, G. (eds) *Research in Personnel and Human Resource Management (Supplement 4: Strategic Human Resources Management in the Twenty-First Century)*, Stamford, CT and London: JAI Press.

De Geus, A. (1988) 'Planning as learning'. *Harvard Business Review* March/April: 70–4.

Deane, P. (1969) *The First Industrial Revolution.* Cambridge: Cambridge University Press.

Deephouse, D. (1999) 'To be different, or to be the same? It's a question (and theory) of strategic balance'. *Strategic Management Journal* 20: 147–66.

Delbridge, R., Lowe, J. and Oliver, N. (2000) 'Worker autonomy in lean teams: evidence from the world automotive components industry'. In Procter, S. and Mueller, F. (eds) *Teamworking.* Basingstoke: Macmillan Business (now Palgrave Macmillan), 125–42.

Delery, J. (1998) 'Issues of fit in strategic human resource management: implications for research'. *Human Resource Management Review* 8(3): 289–309.

Delery, J. and Doty, D. (1996) 'Modes of theorizing in strategic human resource management: tests of universalistic, contingency, and configurational performance predictions'. *Academy of Management Journal* 39(4): 802–35.

Deming, W. E. (1982) *Out of the Crisis.* Boston, MA: MIT Press.

Dierickx, I. and Cool, K. (1989) 'Asset stock accumulation and sustainability of competitive advantage'. *Management Science* 35(12): 1504–14.

DiMaggio, P. and Powell, W. (1983) 'The iron cage revisited: institutional isomorphism and collective rationality in organizational fields'. *American Sociological Review* 48(2): 147–60.

Doeringer, P. and Piore, M. (1971) *Internal Labor Markets and Manpower Analysis.* Lexington, MA: Heath.

Donaldson. T. and Preston, L. (1995) 'The stakeholder theory of the corporation: concepts, evidence, and implications'. *Academy of Management Review* 20(1): 65–91.

Doogan, K. (2001) 'Insecurity and long-term employment'. *Work, Employment and Society* 15(3): 419–41.

Dowling, P., Schuler, R. and Welch, D. (1994) *International Dimensions of Human Resource Management.* Belmont: Wadsworth.

Dreher, G. and Dougherty, T. (2002) *Human Resource Strategy: a Behavioral Perspective for the General Manager.* Boston, MA: McGraw-Hill Irwin.

Drucker, P. (1968) *The Practice of Management.* London: Pan.

Dubin, R. (1954) 'Constructive aspects of industrial conflict'. In Kornhauser, A., Dubin R. and Ross, M. (eds) *Industrial Conflict.* New York: McGraw-Hill.

Dunlop, J. (1958) *Industrial Relations Systems.* New York: Henry Holt.

Dunlop, J. and Weil, D. (1996) 'Diffusion and performance of modular production in the US apparel industry'. *Industrial Relations* 35(4): 334–55.

Dunn, S. (1992) 'Root metaphor in the old and the new industrial relations'. *British Journal of Industrial Relations* 28(1): 1–31.

Dyer, L. (1984) 'Studying human resource strategy'. *Industrial Relations* 23(2): 156–69.

Dyer, L. (1988) 'A strategic perspective of HRM'. In Dyer, L. (ed.) *Human Resource Management: Evolving Roles and Responsibilities*. Washington: Bureau of National Affairs.

Dyer, L. and Holder, G. (1988) 'A strategic perspective of human resource management'. In Dyer, L. (ed.) *Human Resource Management: Evolving Roles and Responsibilities*. Washington: Bureau of National Affairs.

Dyer, L. and Reeves, T. (1995) 'Human resource strategies and firm performance: what do we know and where do we need to go?'. *International Journal of Human Resource Management* 6(3): 656–70.

Dyer, L. and Shafer, R. (1999) 'Creating organizational agility: implications for strategic human resource management'. In Wright, P., Dyer, L., Boudreau, J and Milkovich, G. (eds) *Research in Personnel and Human Resource Management (Supplement 4: Strategic Human Resources Management in the Twenty-First Century)*. Stamford, CT and London: JAI Press.

Edvinsson, L. and Malone, M. (1997) *Intellectual Capital*. London: Piatkus.

Edwards, R. (1979) *Contested Terrain: the Transformation of the Workplace in the Twentieth Century*. London: Heinemann.

Edwards, P. K. and Whitson, C. (1991) 'Workers are working harder: effort and shop-floor relations in the 1980s'. *British Journal of Industrial Relations* 29(4): 593–601.

Edwards, P., Collinson, M. and Rees, C. (1998) 'The determinants of employee responses to total quality management: six case studies'. *Organization Studies* 19(3): 449–75.

Eilbert, H. (1959) 'The development of personnel management in the United States'. *Business History Review* 33: 345–64.

Eisenhardt, K. M. and Bird Schoonhovern, C. (1990) 'Organizational growth: linking founding team, strategy, environment, and growth among US semiconductor ventures, 1978–1988.' *Administrative Science Quarterly* 35(3): 504–29.

Eisenhardt, K. M. and Zbaracki, M. J. (1992) 'Strategic decision making'. *Strategic Management Journal* 13: 17–37.

Eisenhardt, K. M., Kahwajy, J. L. and Bourgeois, L. J. (1997) 'How management teams can have a good fight'. *Harvard Business Review* July/Aug.: 77–85.

Elger, T. and Smith, C. (1998) 'Exit, voice and "mandate": management strategies and labour practices of Japanese firms in Britain'. *British Journal of Industrial Relations* 36(2): 185–207.

Elkington, J. (1997) *Cannibals With Forks: The Triple Bottom Line of 21st Century Business*. Oxford: Capstone.

EPOC Research Group (1997) *New Forms of Work Organisation: Results of a Survey of Direct Employee Participation in Europe*. Dublin: European Foundation for the Improvement of Living and Working Conditions.

Evans, P. (1986) 'The strategic outcomes of human resource management'. *Human Resource Management* 25(1): 149–67.

Evans, P. and Genadry, N. (1999) 'A duality-based perspective for strategic human resource management'. In Wright, P., Dyer, L., Boudreau, J. and Milkovich, G. (eds) *Research in Personnel and Human Resources Management (Supplement 4: Strategic Human Resources Management in the Twenty-First Century)*, Stamford, CT and London: JAI Press.

Feigenbaum, A. and Thomas, H. (1993) 'Industry and strategic group dynamics: competitive strategy in the insurance industry'. *Journal of Management Studies* 30: 69–105.

Ferguson, N. (1998) *The Pity of War*. London: Penguin.

Ferlie, E., Ashburner, C., Fitzgerald, L. and Pettigrew, A. (1996) *The New Public Management in Action*. Oxford: Oxford University Press.

Folger, R. (1998) 'Fairness as a moral virtue'. In Schminke, M. (ed.) *Managerial Ethics: Morally Managing People and Processes*. Mahwah, NJ: Lawrence Erlbaum Associates, 13–34.

Folger, R. and Cropanzano, R. (1998) *Organizational Justice and Human Resource Management*. Thousand Oaks, CA: Sage.

Foster, R. (1986) *Innovation: the Attacker's Advantage*. New York: Summit Books.

Foulkes, F. K. (1980) *Personnel Policies in Large Non-Union Companies*. Englewood Cliffs, NJ: Prentice-Hall.

Fox, A. (1974) *Beyond Contract: Work, Power and Trust Relations*. London: Faber.

Freeman, J. (1995) 'Business strategy from the population level', in Montgomery, C. (ed.), *Resource-Based and Evolutionary Theories of the Firm: Towards a Synthesis*, Boston, MA: Kluwer, 219–50.

Freeman, J. and Boeker, W. (1984) 'The ecological analysis of business strategy'. *California Management Review* 26(3): 73–86.

Freeman, R. and Medoff, J. (1984) *What Do Unions Do?* New York: Basic Books.

Freeman, R. and Rogers, J. (1995) 'Worker representation and participation survey: first report of findings'. In Voos, P. (ed.) *Proceedings of the 47th Annual Meeting*. Madison, WISC: Industrial Relations Research Association.

Frenkel, S. (1994) 'Patterns of workplace relations in the global corporation: toward convergence?'. In Belanger, J., Edwards, P. K. and Haiven, L. (eds) *Workplace Industrial Relations and the Global Challenge*. Ithaca, NY: ILR Press.

Gallie, D. and White, M. (1993) *Employee Commitment and the Skills Revolution*. London: Policy Studies Institute.

Gallie, D., White, M., Cheng, Y. and Tomlinson, M. (1998) *Restructuring the Employment Relationship*. Oxford: Clarendon Press.

Gant, J., Ichniowski, C. and Shaw, K. (1999) 'Getting the job done: inside the production functions of high-involvement and traditional organizations'. In *Industrial Relations Research Association 51st Proceedings*, 43–52.

Geare, A. J. (1977) 'The field of study of industrial relations'. *Journal of Industrial Relations* 19(3): 274–85.

Gersick, C. (1991) 'Revolutionary change theories: a multilevel exploration of the punctuated equilibrium paradigm'. *Academy of Management Review* 16(1): 10–36.

Ghemawat, P. and Costa, J. E. (1993) 'The organizational tension between static and dynamic efficiency'. *Strategic Management Journal* 14: 59–73.

Gilligan, C. (1982) *In a Different Voice: Psychological Theory and Women's Development*. Cambridge, MA: Harvard University Press.

Gittleman, M., Horrigan, M. and Joyce, M. (1998) ' "Flexible" workplace practices: evidence from a nationally representative survey'. *Industrial and Labor Relations Review* 52(1): 99–115.

Glover, I. (1998) 'Ford, Henry (1863–1947)'. In *The Handbook of Human Resource Management*. London: Thompson Business Press, 871–9.

Godard, J. (2001a) 'Beyond the high-performance paradigm? An analysis of variation in Canadian managerial perceptions of reform programme effectiveness'. *British Journal of Industrial Relations* 39(1): 25–52.

Godard, J. (2001b) 'High performance and the transformation of work? The implications of alternative work practices for the experience and outcomes of work'. *Industrial and Labor Relations Review* 54(4): 776–805.

Godard, J. and Delaney, J. (2000) 'Reflections on the "high performance" paradigm's implications for industrial relations as a field'. *Industrial and Labor Relations Review* 53(3): 482–502.

Goodrich, C. (1975) *The Frontier of Control*. London: Pluto Press.

Goold, M. (1991) 'Strategic control in the decentralised firm'. *Sloan Management Review* 32(2): 69–81.

Goold, M. and Campbell, A. (1987) *Strategies and Styles: the Role of the Centre in Managing Diversified Corporations*. Oxford: Blackwell.

Goold, M., Campbell, A. and Alexander, M. (1994) *Corporate-Level Strategy: Creating Value in the Multibusiness Company*. New York: Wiley.

Gospel, H. (1973) 'An approach to a theory of the firm in industrial relations'. *British Journal of Industrial Relations* 11(2): 211–28.

Gospel, H. (1992) *Markets, Firms, and the Management of Labour in Modern Britain*. Cambridge: Cambridge University Press.

Granovetter, M. (1985) 'Economic action and social structure: the problem of embeddedness'. *American Journal of Sociology* 91(3): 481–510.

Grant, D. (1999) 'HRM, rhetoric and the psychological contract: a case of "easier said than done" '. *International Journal of Human Resource Management* 10(2): 327–50.

Grant, R. (1991a) *Contemporary Strategy Analysis*. Cambridge, MA: Blackwell.

Grant, R. (1991b) 'The resource-based theory of competitive advantage: implications for strategy formulation'. *California Management Review* 33(2): 114–35.

Grant, R. M. (1998) *Contemporary Strategy Analysis*, Malden, MA and Oxford: Blackwell.

Gratton, L., Hope-Hailey, V., Stiles, P. and Truss, C. (1999a) 'Linking individual performance to business strategy: the people process model'. *Human Resource Management* 38(1): 17–31.

Gratton, L., Hope-Hailey, V., Stiles, P. and Truss, C. (1999b) *Strategic Human Resource Management: Corporate Rhetoric and Human Reality*. Oxford: Oxford University Press.

Green, F. (2001) 'It's been a hard day's night: the concentration and intensification of work in late Twentieth-Century Britain'. *British Journal of Industrial Relations* 39(1): 53–80.

Grimshaw, D., Ward, K., Rubery, J. and Beynon, H. (2001) 'Organisations and the transformation of the internal labour market'. *Work, Employment and Society* 15(1): 25–54.

Guest, D. (1987) 'Human resource management and industrial relations'. *Journal of Management Studies* 24(5): 503–21.

Guest, D. (1990) 'Human resource management and the American dream'. *Journal of Management Studies* 27(4): 377–97.

Guest, D. (1995) 'Human resource management, trade unions and industrial relations', in Storey, J. (ed.) *Human Resource Management: A Critical Text*. London: Routledge.

Guest, D. (1997) 'Human resource management and performance: a review and research agenda'. *International Journal of Human Resource Management* 8(3): 263–76.

Guest, D. (1998) 'Is the psychological contract worth taking seriously?' *Journal of Organizational Behavior* 19: 649–64.

Guest, D. and Conway, N. (1997) *Employee Motivation and the Psychological Contract*. Issues in People Management No. 21. London: CIPD.

Guthrie, J. (2001) 'High-involvement work practices, turnover, and productivity: evidence from New Zealand'. *Academy of Management Journal* 44(1): 180–90.

Guthrie, J., Spell, C. and Nyamori, R. (2002) 'Correlates and consequences of high-involvement work practices: the role of competitive strategy'. *International Journal of Human Resource Management* 13(1): 183–97.

Hall, R. (1993) 'A framework linking intangible resources and capabilities to sustainable competitive advantage'. *Strategic Management Journal* 14: 607–18.

Hambrick, D. (1987) 'The top management team: key to strategic success'. *California Management Review* 30(1): 88–108.

Hambrick, D. (1995) 'Fragmentation and the other problems CEOs have with their top management teams'. *California Management Review* 37(3): 110–27.

Hamel, G. and Prahalad, C. (1993) 'Strategy as stretch and leverage'. *Harvard Business Review* 71(2): 75–84.

Hamel, G. and Prahalad, C. (1994) *Competing for the Future*. Boston, MA: Harvard Business School Press.

Hart, S. L. (1992) 'An integrative framework for strategy-making processes'. *Academy of Management Review* 17(2): 327–51.

Hart, S. L. and Banbury, C. (1994) 'How strategy-making processes can make a difference'. *Strategic Management Journal* 15: 251–69.

Haspeslagh, P. and Jemison, D. (1991) *Managing Acquisitions: Creating Value Through Corporate Renewal*. New York: The Free Press.

Haynes, P. and Allen, M. (2000) 'Partnership as union strategy: a preliminary evaluation'. *Employee Relations* 23(2): 164–87.

Haynes, P. and Fryer, G. (2000) 'Human resources, service quality and performance: a case study'. *International Journal of Contemporary Hospitality Management* 12(4): 240–8.

Hedlund, G. (1994) 'A model of knowledge management and the N-form corporation'. *Strategic Management Journal* 15: 73–90.

Heery, E. and Salmon, J. (eds) (1999) *The Insecure Workforce*. London: Routledge.

Henderson, R. (1995) 'Of life cycles real and imaginary: the unexpectedly long old age of optical lithography'. *Research Policy* 24: 631–43.

Hendry, C., Arthur, M. and Jones, A. (1995) *Strategy Through People*. London and New York: Routledge.

Heneman, H. G. (1969) 'Toward a general system of industrial relations: how do we get there?'. In Somers, G. G. (ed.) *Essays in Industrial Relations Theory*. Ames, IO: Iowa State University Press, 3–24.

Heskett, J., Jones, T., Loveman, G. and Schlesinger, A. (1994) 'Putting the service-profit chain to work'. *Harvard Business Review* March/April: 164–74.

Hill, C. W. L. and Hoskisson, R. (1987) 'Strategy and structure in the multi-product firm'. *Academy of Management Review* 12(2): 331–41.

Hill, C. W. L. and Jones, T. M. (1992) 'Stakeholder-agency theory'. *Journal of Management Studies* 29(2): 131–54.

Hill, C. W. L. and Pickering, J. F. (1986) 'Divisionalization, decentralization and performance of large United Kingdom companies'. *Journal of Management Studies* 23(1): 26–50.

Hochschild, A. (1986) *The Managed Heart: Commercialization of Human Feeling*. Berkeley, CA: University of California Press.

Holbrook, D., Chen, W., Hounshell, D. and Klepper, S. (2000) 'The nature, sources, and consequences of firm differences in the early history of the semiconductor industry'. *Strategic Management Journal* 21: 1017–41.

Hoskisson, R., Hitt, M., Wan, W. and Yiu, D. (1999) 'Theory and research in strategic management: swings of a pendulum'. *Journal of Management* 25(3): 417–56.

Houston, J., James, C., and Ryngaert, M. (2001) 'Where do merger gains come from? Bank mergers from the perspective of insiders and outsiders'. *Journal of Financial Economics* 60(2–3): 285–331.

Hubbard, N. (1999) *Acquisition Strategy and Implementation*. Basingstoke: Macmillan (now Palgrave Macmillan).

Hubbard, N. and Purcell, J. (2001) 'Managing employee expectations during acquisitions'. *Human Resource Management Journal* 11(2): 17–33.

Huber, V. and Fuller, S. (1998) 'Performance appraisal'. In Poole, M. and Warner, M. (eds) *The IEBM Handbook of Human Resource Management*. London: Thomson Business Press.

Hunt, J. and Boxall, P. (1998) 'Are top human resource specialists "strategic partners"? Self-perceptions of a corporate elite'. *International Journal of Human Resource Management* 9(5): 767–81.

Hunt, J. W., Lees, S., Grümber, J. and Vivian, P. (1987) *Acquisitions: The Human Factor*. London: London Business School and Egon Zehnder International.

Hunt, S. (1995) 'The resource-advantage theory of competition'. *Journal of Management Inquiry* 4(4): 317–22.

Hunter, J. E. and Hunter, R. F. (1984) 'Validity and utility of alternate predictors of job performance'. *Psychological Bulletin* 96: 72–98.

Hunter, J. E., Schmidt, F. L. and Judiesch, M. K. (1990) 'Individual differences in output variability as a function of job complexity'. *Journal of Applied Psychology* 75(1): 28–42.

Hunter, J. E., Schmidt, F. L., Rauschenberger, J. and Jayne, M. (2000) 'Intelligence, motivation, and job performance'. In Cooper, C. and Locke, E. (eds) *Industrial and Organizational Psychology*. Oxford: Blackwell.

Hutchinson, S., Kinnie, N., Purcell, J., Collinson, M., Scarborough, H. and Terry, M. (1998) *Getting Fit, Staying Fit: Developing Lean and Responsive Organisations*. London: Institute of Personnel and Development.

Hutchinson, S., Kinnie, N., Purcell, J., Rees, C. L., Scarbrough, H. and Terry, M. (1996) *The People Management Implications of Leaner Ways of Working*. Issues in People Management No. 15. London: Institute of Personnel and Development.

Hyman, J. (2000) 'Financial participation schemes'. In White, G. and Drucker, J. (eds) *Reward Management: A Critical Text*. London: Routledge.

Hyman, R. (1975) *Industrial Relations: a Marxist Introduction*. London: Macmillan (now Palgrave Macmillan).

Hyman, R. (1978) 'Pluralism, procedural consensus and collective bargaining'. *British Journal of Industrial Relations* 16(1): 16–40.

Hyman, R. (1987) 'Strategy or structure? Capital, labour and control'. *Work, Employment and Society* 1(1): 25–55.

Ichniowski, C., Shaw, K. and Prennush, G. (1995) *The Impact of Human Resource Management Practices on Productivity*. International Bureau of Economic Research Working Paper 5333. Cambridge, MA: IBER.

Ichniowski, C., Kochan, T., Levine, D., Olson, C. and Strauss, G. (1996) 'What works at work: overview and assessment'. *Industrial Relations* 35(3): 299–333.

Isenberg, D. J. (1984) 'How senior managers think'. *Harvard Business Review* Nov./Dec.: 81–90.

Jackson, S. and Schuler, R. (1995) 'Understanding human resource management in the context of organizations and their environments.' *Annual Review of Psychology* 46: 237–64.

Jacoby, S. (1984) 'The development of internal labor markets in American manufacturing firms'. In Osterman, P. (ed.) *Internal Labor Markets*. Cambridge, MA: MIT Press, 23–70.

Janis, I. (1972) *Victims of Groupthink*. Boston: Houghton Mifflin.

Jelinek, M. (1978) *Institutionalizing Innovation: A Study of Organizational Learning*. New York: Praeger.

Jensen, M. and Meckling, W. (1976) 'Theory of the firm: managerial behavior, agency costs and ownership structure'. *Journal of Financial Economics* 3: 305–60.

Johnson, G. (1987) *Strategic Change and the Management Process*. Oxford: Blackwell.

Johnson, G. and Scholes, K. (1997) *Exploring Corporate Strategy*. London: Prentice-Hall.

Johnson, G. and Scholes, K. (2002) *Exploring Corporate Strategy: Text and Cases*. Harlow: Pearson Education.

Johnson, H. and Kaplan, R. (1991) *Relevance Lost: the Rise and Fall of Management Accounting*. Boston, MA: Harvard Business School Press.

Jones, S. R. H. (1994) 'The origins of the factory system in Great Britain: technology, transaction costs or exploitation?'. In Kirby, M. W. and Rose, M. B. (eds) *Business Enterprise in Modern Britain*. London: Routledge.

Judge, T., Higgins, C., Thoresen, C. and Barrick, M. (1999) 'The big five personality traits, general mental ability, and career success across the life span'. *Personnel Psychology* 52: 621–52.

Kamoche, K. (1996) 'Strategic human resource management within a resource-capability view of the firm'. *Journal of Management Studies* 33(2): 213–33.

Kamoche, K. and Mueller, F. (1998) 'Human resource management and the appropriation-learning perspective'. *Human Relations* 51(8): 1033–60.

Kaplan, R. and Norton, D. (1996) *The Balanced Scorecard: Translating Strategy into Action*. Boston, MA: Harvard Business School Press.

Kaplan, R. and Norton, D. (2001) *The Strategy-Focused Organization*. Boston, MA: Harvard Business School Press.

Katz, J. and Darbishire, O. (2000) *Converging Divergences: Worldwide Changes in Employment Systems*. Ithaca, NY: Cornell University Press.

Kay, J. (1993) *Foundations of Corporate Success*. Oxford: Oxford University Press.

Keenoy, T. (1992) 'Constructing control'. In Hartley, J. and Stephenson, G. (eds) *Employment Relations: the Psychology of Influence and Control at Work*. Oxford: Blackwell.

Keenoy, T. and Anthony, P. (1992) 'HRM: metaphor, meaning and morality'. In Blyton, P. and Turnbull, P. (eds) (1992) *Reassessing Human Resource Management*. London: Sage.

Keltner, B., Finegold, D., Mason, G. and Wagner, K. (1999) 'Market segmentation strategies and service sector productivity'. *California Management Review* 41(4): 84–102.

Kessler, I. (1998) 'Payment systems'. In Poole, M. and Warner, M. (eds) *The IEBM Handbook of Human Resource Management*. London: Thomson Business Press.

Kessler, I. and Purcell, J. (1992) 'Performance-related pay: objectives and application'. *Human Resource Management Journal* 2(3): 16–33.

Kessler, I. and Purcell, J. (1996) 'The value of joint working parties'. *Work, Employment and Society* 10(4): 663–82.

Kessler, I., Coyle-Shapiro, K. and Purcell, J. (1999) 'Outsourcing and the employee perspective'. *Human Resource Management Journal* 9(2): 5–19.

Kets de Vries, M. and Miller, D. (1984) *The Neurotic Organization*. San Francisco: Jossey-Bass.

King, A. and Zeithaml, C. (2001) 'Competencies and firm performance: examining the causal ambiguity paradox'. *Strategic Management Journal* 22: 75–99.

Koch, M. and McGrath, R. (1996), 'Improving labor productivity: human resource management policies do matter'. *Strategic Management Journal* 17: 335–54.

Kochan, T., Katz, H. and McKersie, R. (1986) *The Transformation of American Industrial Relations*. New York: Basic Books.

Koerne, B., Pot, F. and Paauwe, J. (2001) 'Establishment and acceptance of an emerging industry: what factors determine the development and growth of the temporary work industry in Europe?'. Paper presented to the 17th EGOS Colloquium, Lyon, July 2001.

Koys, D. (2001) 'The effects of employee satisfaction, organizational citizenship behavior, and turnover on organisational effectiveness: a unit-level, longitudinal study'. *Personnel Psychology* 54: 101–14.

KPMG (1999) 'Unlocking shareholder value: the key to success'. In *Mergers and Acquisitions: A Global Research Report*. London: KPMG.

Kristof, A. (1996) 'Person-organization fit: an integrative review of its conceptualisations, measurement, and implications'. *Personnel Psychology* 49: 1–49.

Kruger, J. (1999) 'Lake Wobegon be gone! The "below-average effect" and the egocentric nature of comparative ability judgments'. *Journal of Personality and Social Psychology* 77(2): 221–32.

Lacey, R. (1986) *Ford: the Men and the Machine*. London: Heinemann.

Lam, S. and Schaubroeck, J. (1998) 'Integrating HR planning and organisational strategy'. *Human Resource Management Journal* 8(3): 5–19.

Landes, D. (1998) *The Wealth and Poverty of Nations*. London: Abacus.

Lane, C. (1990) 'Vocational training and new production concepts in Germany: some lessons for Britain'. *Industrial Relations Journal* 21(4): 247–59.

Latham, G. and Latham, S. (2000) 'Overlooking theory and research in performance appraisal at one's peril: much done, more to do', in Cooper, C. and Locke, E. (eds) *Industrial and Organizational Psychology*. Oxford: Blackwell.

Laurent, A. (1986) 'The cross-cultural puzzle of international human resource management'. *Human Resource Management* 25(1): 91–102.

Lawler, E. (1987) *High-Involvement Management*. San Francisco: Jossey-Bass.

Lawrence, P. and Edwards, V. (2000) *Management in Western Europe*. Basingstoke: Macmillan (now Palgrave Macmillan).

Lazear, E. (1999) 'Personnel economics: past lessons and future directions'. *Journal of Labor Economics* 17(2): 199–236.

Lees, S. (1997) 'HRM and the legitimacy market'. *International Journal of Human Resource Management* 8(3): 226–43.

Legge, K. (1978) *Power, Innovation, and Problem-Solving in Personnel Management*. London: McGraw-Hill.

Legge, K. (1995) *Human Resource Management: Rhetorics and Realities*. Basingstoke: Macmillan (now Palgrave Macmillan).

Leonard, D. (1992) 'Core capabilities and core rigidities: a paradox in managing new product development'. *Strategic Management Journal* 13: 111–25.

Leonard, D. (1998) *Wellsprings of Knowledge: Building and Sustaining the Sources of Innovation*. Boston, MA: Harvard Business School Press.

Lepak, D. and Snell, S. (1999) 'The strategic management of human capital: determinants and implications of different relationships'. *Academy of Management Review* 24(1): 1–18.

Levinson, D. (1978) *The Seasons of a Man's Life*. New York: Knopf.

Levinson, D. and Levinson, J. (1996) *The Seasons of a Woman's Life*. New York: Knopf.

Levinthal, D. and Myatt, J. (1994) 'Co-evolution of capabilities and industry: the evolution of mutual fund processing'. *Strategic Management Journal* 15: 45–62.

Lovas, B. and Ghoshal, S. (2000) 'Strategy as guided evolution'. *Strategic Management Journal* 21: 875–96.

Lowe, J., Delbridge, R. and Oliver, N. (1997) 'High-performance manufacturing: evidence from the automotive components industry'. *Organization Studies* 18(5): 783–98.

MacDuffie, J. P. (1995) 'Human resource bundles and manufacturing performance: organizational logic and flexible production systems in the world auto industry.' *Industrial and Labor Relations Review* 48(2): 197–221.

MacDuffie, J. P. and Pil, F. T. (1996) 'Changes in auto industry employment practices: an international overview'. In Kochan, T. A., Lansbury, R. D. and MacDuffie, J. P. (eds) *After Lean Production: Evolving Employment Practices in the World Auto Industry*. Ithaca, NY: Cornell University Press, 9–42.

Macky, K. and Johnson, G. (2000) *The Strategic Management of Human Resources*. Auckland: McGraw-Hill.

MacNeil, I. (1985) 'Relational contract: what we do and do not know'. *Wisconsin Law Review* : 483–525.

Mahoney, J. and Pandian, J. (1992) 'The resource-based view within the conversation of strategic management'. *Strategic Management Journal* 13(5): 363–80.

Main, B. (1990) 'The new economics of personnel.' *Journal of General Management* 16(2): 91–103.

Marchington, M. (1989) 'Joint consultation in practice'. In Sisson, K. (ed.) *Personnel Management in Britain.* Oxford: Blackwell.

Marchington, M. (1995) 'Involvement and participation'. In Storey, J. (ed.) *Human Resource Management: A Critical Text.* London: Routledge.

Marchington, M. and Grugulis, I. (2000) ' "Best practice" human resource management: perfect opportunity or dangerous illusion?' *International Journal of Human Resource Management* 11(6): 1104–24.

Marchington, M. and Wilkinson, A. (2000) 'Direct participation'. In Bach, S. and Sisson, K. (eds) *Personnel Management: A Comprehensive Guide to Theory and Practice.* Oxford: Blackwell.

Marchington, M., Wilkinson, A., Ackers, P. and Dundon, T. (2001) *Management Choice and Employee Voice.* Research report. London: CIPD.

Marginson, P. (1993) *The Multi-Divisional Structure and Corporate Control: Explaining the Degree of Corporate Coordination Over Decisions in Labour Relations'.* Papers in Organization, No. 12, Institute of Organization and Industrial Sociology, Copenhagen Business School.

Marginson, P., Edwards, P., Martin, R., Purcell, J. and Sisson, K. (1988) *Beyond the Workplace: Managing Industrial Relations in the Multi-Establishment Enterprise.* Oxford: Blackwell.

Marginson, P., Armstrong, P., Edwards, P. and Purcell, J. with Hubbard, N. (1993) 'The control of industrial relations in large companies: an initial analysis of the second Company Level Industrial Relations Survey'. *Warwick Papers in Industrial Relations,* No.45. Coventry: University of Warwick.

Marks, M. and Mirvis, P. (1982) 'Merging human resources: a review of current research' *Merger and Acquisitions* 17(2): 38–44.

Marks, A., Findlay, P., Hine, J., McKinlay, A. and Thompson, P. (1998) 'The politics of partnership? Innovation in employment relations in the Scottish spirits industry'. *British Journal of Industrial Relations* 36(2): 209–26.

Marsden, D. (1999) *A Theory of Employment Systems: Micro-Foundations of Societal Diversity.* Oxford: Oxford University Press.

Marshall, D. (2001) *The Outsourcing Process: From Decision to Relationship Management.* Unpublished PhD thesis, University of Bath.

Marshall, V. and Wood, R. (2000) 'The dynamics of effective performance appraisal: an integrated model'. *Asia Pacific Journal of Human Resources* 38(3): 62–90.

Marsick, V. and Watkins, K. (1990) *Informal and Incidental Learning in the Workplace.* London and New York: Routledge.

Martell, K. and Carroll, S. (1995) 'Which executive human resource management practices for the top management team are associated with higher firm performance?' *Human Resource Management* 34(4): 497–512.

Martin, R. (1981) *New Technology and Industrial Relations in Fleet Street*. Oxford: Clarendon Press.

Matusik, S. F. and Hill, C. W. (1998) 'The utilization of contingent work, knowledge creation and competitive advantage'. *Academy of Management Review* 23(4): 680–97.

McConnell, C. and Brue, S. (1995) *Contemporary Labor Economics*. New York: McGraw-Hill.

McGovern, P., Gratton, L., Hope-Hailey, V., Stiles, P. and Truss, C. (1997) 'Human resource management on the line?' *Human Resource Management Journal* 7(4): 12–29.

McKersie, R. and Hunter, L. (1973) *Pay, Productivity and Collective Bargaining*. London: Macmillan (now Palgrave Macmillan).

McLean Parks, J. and Kidder, D. (1994) ' "Till death us do part . . . " changing work relationships in the 1990s'. In Cooper, C. and Rousseau, D. (eds) *Trends in Organizational Behaviour, Vol. 1*. New York: Wiley.

McLoughlin, I. and Gourlay, S. (1992) 'Enterprise without unions: the management of employee relations in non-union firms'. *Journal of Management Studies* 29(5): 669–91.

McMillan, J. (1992) *Games, Strategies and Managers*. New York: Oxford University Press.

McWilliams, A. and Smart, D. (1995) 'The resource-based view of the firm: does it go far enough in shedding the assumptions of the S-C-P paradigm?' *Journal of Management Inquiry* 4(4): 309–16.

Meyer, A. D., Tsui, A. S. and Hinings, C. R. (1993) 'Configurational approaches to organizational analysis'. *Academy of Management Journal* 36(6): 1175–95.

Meyer, S. (1981) *The Five Dollar Day: Labor Management and Social Control in the Ford Motor Company 1908–1921*. Albany, NY: State University of New York Press.

Miles, R and Snow, C. (1984) 'Designing strategic human resources systems'. *Organizational Dynamics* Summer: 36–52.

Miles, G., Snow, C. C. and Sharfman, M. P. (1993) 'Industry variety and performance'. *Strategic Management Journal* 14: 163–77.

Milkovich, G. and Boudreau, J. (1997) *Human Resource Management*. Chicago: Irwin.

Miller, D. (1981) 'Toward a new contingency approach: the search for organizational gestalts'. *Journal of Management Studies* 18(1): 1–26.

Miller, D. (1992) 'Generic strategies; classification, combination and context'. *Advances in Strategic Management* 8: 391–408.

Miller, D. and Friesen, P. (1980) 'Momentum and revolution in organizational adaptation'. *Academy of Management Journal* 23(4): 591–614.

Miller, D. and Shamsie, J. (1996) 'The resource-based view of the firm in two environments: the Hollywood film studios from 1936 to 1965'. *Academy of Management Journal* 39(3): 519–43.

Millward, N., Bryson, A. and Forth, J. (2000) *All Change at Work: British Employment Relations 1980–1998 as portrayed by the Workplace Industrial Relations Survey Series*. London: Routledge.

Mintzberg, H. (1978) 'Patterns in strategy formation'. *Management Science* 24(9): 934–48.

Mintzberg, H. (1990) 'The design school: reconsidering the basic premisses of strategic management'. *Strategic Management Journal* 11(3): 171–95.

Mintzberg, H. (1994) 'Rethinking strategic planning part 1: pitfalls and fallacies'. *Long Range Planning* 27(3): 12–21.

Mintzberg, J. (1979) *The Structuring of Organizations*. Englewood Cliffs, NJ: Prentice-Hall.

Morgan, G. (1997) *Images of Organization*. Thousand Oaks, CA: Sage.

Mueller, D. (1997) 'First-mover advantages and path dependence'. *International Journal of Industrial Organization* 15(6): 827–50.

Mueller, F. (1994) 'Teams between hierarchy and commitment: change strategies and the international environment'. *Journal of Management Studies* 31(3): 383–404.

Mueller, F. (1996) 'Human resources as strategic assets; an evolutionary resource-based theory'. *Journal of Management Studies* 33(6): 757–85.

Mueller, F. and Purcell, J. (1992) 'The Europeanization of manufacturing and the decentralisation of bargaining: multinational management strategies in the European automobile industry'. *International Journal of Human Resource Management* 3(2): 15–35.

Murphy, K. and Cleveland, J. (1991) *Performance Appraisal: an Organizational Perspective*. Boston, MA: Allyn & Bacon.

Murphy, T. and Zandvakili, S. (2000) 'Data- and metrics-driven approach to human resource practices: using customers, employees, and financial metrics'. *Human Resource Management* 39(1): 93–105.

Murray, A. (1988), 'A contingency view of Porter's "generic strategies"'. *Academy of Management Review* 13(3): 390–400.

Nahapiet, J. and Ghoshal, S. (1998) 'Social capital, intellectual capital and the organizational advantage'. *Academy of Management Review* 23(2): 242–66.

Nalebuff, B. and Brandenburger, A. (1996) *Co-opetition*. London: Harper Collins Business.

Nelson, R. (1991) 'Why do firms differ, and how does it matter?'. *Strategic Management Journal* 12: 61–74.

Nelson, R. and Winter, S. (1982) *An Evolutionary Theory of Economic Change*. Cambridge, MA: Belknap Press.

Noe, R., Hollenbeck, J., Gerhart, B. and Wright, P. (2000) *Human Resource Management: Gaining a Competitive Advantage*. Boston: Irwin McGraw-Hill.

Nonaka, I. and Takeuchi, H. (1995) *The Knowledge-Creating Company*. New York: Oxford University Press.

Nord, S. (1999) 'Sectoral productivity and the distribution of wages'. *Industrial Relations* 38(2): 215–30.

O'Reilly III, C. and Pfeffer, J. (eds) (2000) *Hidden Value: How Great Companies Achieve Extraordinary Results with Ordinary People*. Boston, MA: Harvard Business School Press.

O'Reilly III, C. and Pfeffer, J. (2000) 'South West Airlines: if success is so simple, why is it hard to imitate?'. In their (eds) *Hidden Value: How Great Companies Achieve Extraordinary Results with Ordinary People*. Boston, MA: Harvard Business School Press, 21–48.

Oakeshott, R. (2000) *Jobs and Fairness: The Logic and Experience of Employee Ownership*? Norwich: Michael Russell.

Odiorne, G. (1985) *Strategic Management of Human Resources*. San Francisco: Jossey-Bass.

Ogbonna, E. and Wilkinson, B. (1990) 'Corporate strategy and corporate culture: the view from the checkout'. *Personnel Review* 19(4): 9–15.

Oliver, C. (1997) 'Sustainable competitive advantage: combining institutional and resource-based views'. *Strategic Management Journal* 18(9): 697–713.

Oliver, N. and Wilkinson, B. (1992) *The Japanization of British Industry*. Oxford: Blackwell.

Organ, D. (1988) *Organizational Citizenship Behavior: the Good Soldier Syndrome*. Lexington, MA: Lexington Books.

Osterman, P. (1982) 'Employment structures in firms'. *British Journal of Industrial Relations* 20(3): 349–61.

Osterman, P. (1987) 'Choice of employment systems in internal labor markets'. *Industrial Relations* 26(1): 46–67.

Osterman, P. (1994) 'How common is workplace transformation and who adopts it?' *Industrial and Labor Relations Review* 47(2): 173–88.

Osterman, P. (2000) 'Work reorganization in an era of restructuring: trends in diffusion and effects on employee welfare'. *Industrial and Labor Relations Review* 53(2): 179–96.

Pascale, R. (1985) 'The paradox of "corporate culture": reconciling ourselves to socialization'. *California Management Review* 27(2): 26–41.

Pascale, R. (1991) *Managing On the Edge*. London: Penguin.

Patterson, M., West, M., Lawthorn, R. and Nickell, S. (1998) 'Impact of people management practices on business performance'. *Issues in People Management* No. 22. London: Institute of Personnel and Development.

Peck, S. (1994) 'Exploring the link between organizational strategy and the employment relationship: the role of human resource policies'. *Journal of Management Studies* 31(5): 715–36.

Peel, S. and Boxall, P. (2001) 'Contracting versus employing: bringing together organisation and worker perspectives'. Paper presented at 17th EGOS Colloquium, Lyons, July 2001.

Pendleton, A. (2000) 'Profit sharing and employee share ownership'. In Thorpe, R. and Homan, G. (eds) *Strategic Reward Systems*. Harlow: Pearson Educational.

Penn, R., Rose, M. and Rubery, J. (eds) (1994) *Skill and Occupational Change*. Oxford: Oxford University Press.

Penrose, E. (1959) *The Theory of the Growth of the Firm*. Oxford: Blackwell.

Peteraf, M. (1993) 'The cornerstones of competitive advantage: a resource-based view'. *Strategic Management Journal* 14: 179–91.

Peteraf, M. and Shanley, M. (1997) 'Getting to know you: a theory of strategic group identity'. *Strategic Management Journal* 18(S): 165–86.

Peters, T. and Waterman, R. H. (1982) *In Search of Excellence: Lessons from America's Best-Run Companies*. New York: Harper & Row.

Pfeffer, J. (1994) *Competitive Advantage Through People*. Boston, MA: Harvard Business School Press.

Pfeffer, J. (1998) *The Human Equation: Building Profits by Putting People First*. Boston, MA: Harvard Business School Press.

Pfeffer, J. and Salancik, G. R. (1978) *The External Control of Organizations: a Resource Dependence Perspective*. New York: Harper & Row.

Pil, F. K. and MacDuffie, J. P. (1996) 'The adoption of high involvement work practices'. *Industrial Relations* 35(3): 423–55.

Pinfield, L. and Berner, M. (1994) 'Employment systems: toward a coherent conceptualisation of internal labour markets'. In Ferris, G. (ed.) *Research in Personnel and Human Resources Management, Vol. 12*. Stamford, CT and London: JAI Press, 41–78.

Piore, M. and Sabel, C. (1984) *The Second Industrial Divide: Prospects for Prosperity*. New York: Basic Books.

Polanyi, M. (1962) *Personal Knowledge*. New York: Harper.

Porter, M. (1980) *Competitive Strategy*. New York: Free Press.

Porter, M. (1985) *Competitive Advantage: Creating and Sustaining Superior Performance*. New York: Free Press.

Porter, M. (1990) *The Competitive Advantage of Nations*. London: Macmillan (now Palgrave Macmillan).

Porter, M. (1991) 'Towards a dynamic theory of strategy'. *Strategic Management Journal* 12(S): 95–117.

Porter, M. (1996) 'What is strategy?' *Harvard Business Review* Nov./Dec.: 61–78.

Prahalad, C. and Hamel, G. (1990) 'The core competence of the corporation'. *Harvard Business Review* May/June: 79–91.

Priem, R. and Butler, J. (2001) 'Is the resource-based "view" a useful perspective for strategic management research?' *Academy of Management Review* 26(1): 22–40.

Procter, S. and Mueller, F. (eds) (2000) *Teamworking*. Basingstoke: Macmillan (now Palgrave Macmillan).

Purcell, J. (1981) *Good Industrial Relations: Theory and Practice*. Basingstoke: Macmillan (now Palgrave Macmillan).

Purcell, J. (1987) 'Mapping management styles in employee relations'. *Journal of Management Studies* 24(5): 533–48.

Purcell, J. (1989) 'The impact of corporate strategy on human resource management'. In Storey, J. (ed.) *New Perspectives on Human Resource Management*. London: Routledge.

Purcell, J. (1995) 'Ideology and the end of institutional industrial relations: evidence from the UK'. In Crouch, C. and Traxler, F. (eds) *Organized Industrial Relations in Europe: What Future?* Aldershot: Avebury.

Purcell, J. (1996) 'Contingent workers and human resource strategy: rediscovering the core/periphery dimension'. *Journal of Professional HRM* 5: 16–23.

Purcell, J. (1999a) 'High-commitment management and the link with contingent workers: implications for strategic human resource management'. In Wright, P., Dyer, L., Boudreau, J. and Milkovich, G. (eds) *Research in Personnel and Human Resources Management (Supplement 4: Strategic Human Resources Management in the Twenty-First Century)*, Stamford, CT and London: JAI Press.

Purcell, J. (1999b) 'The search for "best practice" and "best fit": chimera or cul-de-sac?'. *Human Resource Management Journal* 9(3): 26–41.

Purcell, J. and Ahlstrand, B. (1994) *Human Resource Management in the Multidivisional Company*. Oxford: Oxford University Press.

Quinn, J. B. (1980) *Strategies for Change: Logical Incrementalism*. Homewood, Ill: Irwin.

Ramsay, H. (1977) 'Cycles of control: worker participation in sociological and historical perspective'. *Sociology* 11: 481–506.

Ramsay, H. (1983) 'Evolution or cycle? Worker participation in the 1970s and 1980s'. In Crouch, C. and Heller, F. (eds), *Organisational Democracy and Political Processes*. London: Wiley, 203–25.

Ramsay, H., Scholarios, D. and Harley, B. (2000) 'Employees and high-performance work systems: testing inside the black box'. *British Journal of Industrial Relations* 38(4): 501–31.

Reed, R. and DeFillippi, R. (1990) 'Causal ambiguity, barriers to imitation, and sustainable competitive advantage'. *Academy of Management Review* 15(1): 88–102.

Riordan, M. and Hoddeson, L. (1997) *Crystal Fire: the Birth of the Information Age*. New York: Norton.

Robinson, S. (1996) 'Trust and the breach of the psychological contract'. *Administrative Science Quarterly* 41(4): 574–99.

Robinson, S. and Rousseau, D. (1994) 'Violating the psychological contract: not the exception but the norm'. *Journal of Organizational Behavior* 15: 245–59.

Rose, M. (1994) 'Job satisfaction, job skills, and personal skills'. In Penn, R., Rose, M. and Rubery, J. (eds) *Skill and Occupational Change*. Oxford: Oxford University Press.

Rose, M. (2000) 'Work attitudes in the expanding occupations'. In Purcell, K. (ed.) *Changing Boundaries in Employment*. Bristol: Bristol Academic Press.

Rousseau, D. (1995) *Psychological Contracts in Organizations*. Thousand Oaks, CA: Sage.

Rowlinson, M. (1997) *Organisations and Institutions: Perspectives in Economics and Sociology*. London: Macmillan (now Palgrave Macmillan).

Rubery, J. (1994) 'Internal and external labour markets: towards an integrated analysis'. In Rubery, J. and Wilkinson, F. (eds) *Employer Strategy and the Labour Market*. Oxford: Oxford University Press.

Rucci, A. Kirn, S. and Quinn, R. (1998) 'The employee-customer-profit chain at Sears'. *Harvard Business Review* 76(1): 82–97.

Rumelt, R. (1982) 'Diversification strategy and profitability' *Strategic Management Journal* 3: 359–69.

Rumelt, R. (1987) 'Theory, strategy and entrepreneurship'. In Teece, D. (ed.) *The Competitive Challenge*. New York: Harper & Row.

Rynes, S., Barber, A. and Varma, G. (2000) 'Research on the employment interview: usefulness for practice and recommendations for future research'. In Cooper, C. and Locke, E. (eds) *Industrial and Organizational Psychology*. Oxford: Blackwell.

Sako, M. (1998) 'The nature and impact of employee 'voice' in the European car components industry'. *Human Resource Management Journal* 8(2): 6–13.

Sanz-Valle, R., Sabater-Sanchez, R. and Aragon-Sanchez, A. (1999) 'Human resource management and business strategy links: an empirical study'. *International Journal of Human Resource Management* 10(4): 655–71.

Schein, E. (1977) 'Increasing organizational effectiveness through better human resource planning and development'. *Sloan Management Review* 19(1): 1–20.

Schein, E. (1978) *Career Dynamics: Matching Individual and Organizational Needs*. Reading, MA: Addison-Wesley.

Schnaars, S. (1994) *Managing Imitation Strategies*. New York: Macmillan.

Schneider, S. and Barsoux, J-L. (1997) *Managing Across Cultures*. London: Prentice-Hall.

Schoenberger, E. (1997) *The Cultural Crisis of the Firm*. Oxford: Blackwell.

Schoenberger, R. (1982) *Japanese Manufacturing Techniques*. New York: Free Press.

Schuler, R. (1989) 'Strategic human resource management and industrial relations'. *Human Relations* 42(2): 157–84.

Schuler, R. (1996) 'Market-focused management: human resource management implications'. *Journal of Market-Focused Management* 1: 13–29.

Schuler, R. and Jackson, S. (1987) 'Linking competitive strategies and human resource management practices'. *Academy of Management Executive* 1(3): 207–19.

Schumpeter, J. (1950) *Capitalism, Socialism and Democracy*. New York: Harper & Row.

Schwartz, H. and Davis, S. M. (1981) 'Matching corporate culture and business strategy'. *Organizational Dynamics* 10(1): 30–48.

Scullion, H. and Brewster, C. (2001) 'The management of expatriates: messages from Europe?' *Journal of World Business* 36(4): 346–65.

Senge, P. (1992) *The Fifth Discipline: the Art and Practice of the Learning Organization*. London: Random House.

Sewell, G. (1998) 'The discipline of teams: the control of team-based industrial work through electronic and peer surveillance'. *Administrative Science Quarterly* 43: 397–428.

Sheehy, G. (1977) *Passages: Predictable Crises of Adult Life*. New York: Bantam.

Simon, H. A. (1947) *Administrative Behavior*. New York: Free Press.

Simon, H. A. (1985) 'Human nature in politics: the dialogue of psychology with political science'. *American Political Science Review* 79(2): 293–304.

Sisson, K. (1989) 'Personnel management in perspective', in Sisson, K. (ed.) *Personnel Management in Britain*. Oxford: Blackwell.

Sisson, K. (1993) 'In search of HRM'. *British Journal of Industrial Relations* 31(2): 201–10.

Sisson, K. (2000) *Direct Participation and the Modernisation of Work Organisation*. Dublin: European Foundation for the Improvement of Living and Working Conditions.

Smith, A. (2001) 'Perceptions of stress at work'. *Human Resource Management Journal* 11(4): 74–86.

Smith, A. R., and Bartholomew, D. J. (1988) 'Manpower planning in the United Kingdom: an historical review'. *Journal of the Operational Research Society* 39(3): 235–48.

Snell, S. and Dean, J. (1992) 'Integrated manufacturing and human resources management: a human capital perspective'. *Academy of Management Journal* 35(3): 467–504.

Snell, S., Lepak, D. and Youndt, M. (1999) 'Managing the architecture of intellectual capital: implications for human resource management', In Wright, P. Dyer, L. Boudreau, J. and Milkovich, G. (eds) *Research in Personnel and Human Resources Management: Strategic Human Resource Management in the Twenty-First Century*. Stamford, CT and London: JAI Press.

Snell, S., Youndt, M. and Wright, P. (1996) 'Establishing a framework for research in strategic human resource management: merging resource theory and organizational learning'. *Research in Personnel and Human Resources Management* 14: 61–90.

Sparrow, P. (2002) 'Globalization as an uncoupling force: internationalisation of the HR process?'. In Gunnigle, P. (ed.) *The John Lovett Lectures: A Decade of*

Development of Human Resource Management in Ireland. Dublin: Gill & Macmillan.

Steedman, H. and Wagner, K. (1989) 'Productivity, machinery and skills: clothing manufacture in Britain and Germany', *National Institute Economic Review*, May: 40–57.

Stewart, T. A. (1998) *Intellectual Capital.* London: Nicholas Brealey.

Storey, D. J. (1985) 'The problems facing new firms'. *Journal of Management Studies* 22(3): 327–45.

Storey, J. (1992) *Developments in the Management of Human Resources* Oxford: Blackwell.

Storey, J. (1993) 'The take-up of human resource management by mainstream companies: key lessons from research'. *International Journal of Human Resource Management* 4(3): 529–53.

Storey, J. (1995) *Human Resource Management: a Critical Text.* London: Routledge.

Storey, J. and Sisson, K. (1993) *Managing Human Resources and Industrial Relations.* Buckingham: Open University Press.

Strauss, G. (2001) 'HRM in the USA: correcting some British impressions'. *International Journal of Human Resource Management* 12(6): 873–97.

Streeck, W. (1987) 'The uncertainties of management in the management of uncertainty: employers, labour relations and industrial adjustment in the 1980s'. *Work, Employment & Society* 1(3): 281–308.

Streeck, W. (1992) *Social Institutions and Economic Performance: Studies of Industrial Relations in Advanced Capitalist Economies.* London: Sage.

Swart, J. and Kinnie, N. (2001) 'Human resource advantage within a distributed knowledge system: a study of growing knowledge intensive firms'. Paper presented at ESRC Seminar 'The Changing Nature of Skills and Knowledge'. Manchester School of Management, September 2001.

Tailby, S. and Winchester, D. (2000) 'Management and trade unions: towards social partnership?'. In Bach, S. and Sisson, K. (eds) *Personnel Management: A Comprehensive Guide to Theory and Practice.* Oxford: Blackwell.

Taira, K. (1993) 'Japan', In Rothman, M., Briscoe, D and Nacamulli, R (eds) *Industrial Relations Around the World.* Berlin: de Gruyter, 218–33.

Taylor, M. S., and Collins, C. (2000) 'Organizational recruitment: enhancing the intersection of research and practice'. In Cooper, C. and Locke, E. (eds) *Industrial and Organizational Psychology.* Oxford: Blackwell.

Thompson, M. (1998) 'Jet setters'. *People Management* 4(8): 38–41.

Thompson, M. (2000) *The Competitiveness Challenge: Final Report: the Bottom Line Benefits of Strategic Human Resource Management.* The UK Aerospace People Management Audit. London: Society of British Aerospace Companies.

Tomer, J. (2001) 'Understanding high-performance work systems: the joint contribution of economics and human resource management'. *Journal of Socio-Economics* 30: 63–73.

Towers, B. (1997) *The Representation Gap: Change and Reform in the British and American Workplace*. Oxford: Oxford University Press.

TUC (1997) *Partners for Progress*. London: Trades Union Congress.

Tuchman, B. (1996) *The March of Folly: From Troy to Vietnam*. London: Papermac.

Turnbull, P., Woolfson, C. and Kelly, J. (1992) *Dock Strike: Conflict and Restructuring in British Ports*. Aldershot: Avebury.

Tushman, M., Newman, W. and Romanelli, E. (1986) 'Convergence and upheaval: managing the unsteady pace of organizational evolution.' *California Management Review* 29(1): 29–44.

US Department of Labor (2000) *International Comparisons of Hourly Compensation Costs for Production Workers in Manufacturing, 1999*. Washington, DC: Bureau of Labor Statistics.

Utterback, J. (1994) *Mastering the Dynamics of Innovation*. Boston, MA: Harvard Business School Press.

Veliyath, R. and Srinavasan, T. (1995) 'Gestalt approaches to assessing strategic coalignment: a conceptual integration'. *British Journal of Management* 6(3): 205–19.

Volberda, J. (1998) *Building the Flexible Firm: How to Remain Competitive*. New York: Oxford University Press.

Wajcman, J. (2000) 'Feminism freeing industrial relations in Britain'. *British Journal of Industrial Relations* 38(2): 183–202.

Wallace, T. (1998) 'Fordism'. In Poole, M. and Warner, M. (eds) *The IEBM Handbook of Human Resource Management*. London: Thomson Business Press.

Walsh, J. (2001) 'Human resource management in foreign-owned workplaces: evidence from Australia'. *International Journal of Human Resource Management* 12(3): 425–44.

Walton, R. and McKersie, R. (1965) *A Behavioural Theory of Labor Negotiations*. New York: McGraw-Hill.

Walton, R. E., Cutcher-Gershenfeld, J. E. and McKersie, R.B. (1994) *Strategic Negotiations: A Theory of Change in Labor-Management Relations*. Boston, MA: Harvard Business School Press.

Ward, K., Grimshaw, D., Rubery, J. and Beynon, H. (2001) 'Temporary workers and the management of agency staff'. *Human Resource Management Journal* 11(4): 3–21.

Warner, M. (1994) 'Japanese culture, Western management: Taylorism and human resources in Japan'. *Organization Studies* 15(4): 509–33.

Warner, M. (1998) 'Taylor, Frederick Winslow (1856–1915)'. In Poole, M. and Warner, M. (eds), *The IEBM Handbook of Human Resource Management*. London: Thompson Business Press, 931–5.

Watson, T. (1986) *Management, Organization and Employment Strategy: New Directions in Theory and Practice*. London: Routledge.

Webb, S. and Webb, B. (1902) *Industrial Democracy*. London: Longman.

Weinstein, M. and Kochan, T. (1995) 'The limits of diffusion: recent developments in industrial relations and human resource practices in the United States'. In Locke, R., Kochan, T. and Piore, M. (eds) *Employment Relations In a Changing World Economy*. Cambridge, MA: MIT Press.

Wenlock, J. and Purcell, J. (1990) 'The management of transfer of undertakings: a comparison of employee participation practices in the United Kingdom and the Netherlands'. *Human Resource Management Journal* 1(2): 45–59.

Wernerfelt, B. (1984) 'A resource-based view of the firm'. *Strategic Management Journal* 5(2): 171–80.

West, G. and DeCastro, J. (2001) 'The Achilles heel of firm strategy: resource weaknesses and distinctive inadequacies'. *Journal of Management Studies* 38(3): 417–42.

West, M., Patterson, M. and Dawson, J. (1999) 'A path to profit? Teamwork at the top'. *CentrePiece* 4(3): Winter.

Wever, K. (1995) *Negotiating Competitiveness: Employment Relations and Organizational Innovation in Germany and the United States*. Boston, MA: Harvard Business School Press.

Whitfield, K. and Poole, M. (1997) 'Organizing employment for high performance: theories, evidence and policy'. *Organization Studies* 18(5): 745–64.

Whittington, R. (1993) *What Is Strategy – And Does it Matter?* London: Routledge.

Whittington, R. and Mayer, M. (2000) *The European Corporation: Strategy, Structure and Social Science*. Oxford: Oxford University Press.

Whittington, R., Pettigrew, A., Peck, S., Fenton, E. and Conyon, M. (1999) 'Change and complementarities in the new competitive landscape: a European panel study, 1992–1996'. *Organization Science* 10(5): 583–600.

Whyte, W. F. (1956) *The Organization Man*. New York: Simon and Schuster.

Whyte, W. F. and Whyte, K. K. (1989) *Making Mondragon: The Growth and Dynamics of the Worker Cooperative Complex*. Ithaca, NY: ILR Press.

Wilkinson, A. and Willmott, H. (1995) *Making Quality Critical: New Perspectives on Organisational Change*. London: Routledge.

Wilkinson, B., Gamble, J., Humphrey, J. and Morris, J. (2001) 'The new international division of labour in Asian electronics: work organisation and human resources in Japan and Malaysia'. *Journal of Management Studies* 38(5): 675–98.

Williams, J. (1992) 'How sustainable is your competitive advantage?' *California Management Review* 34(3): 29–51.

Williamson, O. E. (1970) *Corporate Control and Business Behavior*. Englewoood Cliffs, NJ: Prentice-Hall.

Williamson, O. E. (1975) *Markets and Hierarchies: Analysis and Antitrust Implications*. New York: Free Press.

Williamson, O. E. (1985) *The Economic Institutions of Capitalism*. New York: Free Press.

Williamson, O. E., Wachter, M. L. and Harris, J. E. (1975) 'Understanding the employment relation: the analysis of idiosyncratic exchange'. *Bell Journal Economics* 6(1): 250–78.

Wilson, I. (1994) 'Strategic planning isn't dead – it changed'. *Long Range Planning* 27(4): 12–24.

Windolf, P. (1986) 'Recruitment, selection, and internal labour markets in Britain and Germany'. *Organization Studies* 7(3): 235–54.

Wolfe Morrison, E. and Robinson, S. (1997) 'When employees feel betrayed: a model of how psychological contract violation develops'. *Academy of Management Review* 22(1): 226–56.

Womack, J., Jones, D. and Roos, D. (1990) *The Machine that Changed the World: The Triumph of Lean Production.* New York: Rawson Macmillan.

Wood, S. (1989) 'The transformation of work'. In Wood, S. (ed.) *The Transformation of Work.* London: Allen and Unwin, 1–43.

Wood, S. (1996) 'High-commitment management and payment systems'. *Journal of Management Studies* 33(1): 53–77.

Wood, S. and Albanese, P. (1995) 'Can we speak of high-commitment management on the shop floor?' *Journal of Management Studies* 32(2): 215–47.

Wright, P., McMahan, G. and McWilliams, A. (1994) 'Human resources and sustained competitive advantage: a resource-based perspective'. *International Journal of Human Resource Management* 5(2): 301–26.

Wright, P. and Snell, S. (1998) 'Toward a unifying framework for exploring fit and flexibility in strategic human resource management'. *Academy of Management Review* 23(4): 756–72.

Youndt, M., Snell, S., Dean, J. and Lepak, D. (1996) 'Human resource management, manufacturing strategy, and firm performance'. *Academy of Management Journal* 39(4): 836–66.

Author index

Bourgeois, L.   43, 233
Boxall, P.   7, 9, 11, 13, 30, 32, 35, 41, 48,
      49, 50, 54, 55, 56, 57, 58, 73, 82, 85, 86,
      87, 123–4, 131–2, 134, 146, 147, 175,
      177, 178, 179, 181, 182, 185, 193, 196,
      197, 199, 200, 201
Bowditch, J.   220, 221
Bracker, J.   28
Bradley, K.   133, 162
Bradley, L.   144
Brandenburger, A.   186, 232
Braverman, H.   16
Brews, P.   229–30
Brewster, C.   50, 207
Brown, C.   16
Brown, W.   175
Brue, S.   146, 192
Bruce, A.   148
Bruegal, I.   119
Bryson, A.   169, 205
Buck, T.   148
Budhwar, P.   227
Buono, A.   220, 221
Burgess, S.   159
Butler, J.   78
Buxton, J.   159

Cam, S.   132
Cameron, K.   8, 14
Campbell, A.   206, 213
Campbell, J.   137–8
Cappelli, P.   102
Carroll, G.   33, 81, 148–9, 150, 161, 186,
      187, 188, 192, 201
Carter, K.   191–2
Cartier, K.   15
Cartwright, S.   221
Castells, M.   19
Chandler, A.   208
Channon, D.   210
Chen, W.   193
Cheng, Y.   106, 144
Child, J.   34, 35, 36, 39
Clegg, H.   16, 174
Cleveland, J.   145
Coase, R.   124
Coff, R.   14, 54, 75, 86
Collard, R.   170
Collins, C.   141

Collins, J.   34, 200
Collinson, M.   110
Conner, K.   72
Conway, N.   168
Conyon, M.   148, 218–19
Cool, K.   72
Cooper, C.   221
Costa, J.   36
Cox, A.   226
Coyle-Shapiro, J.   132, 151, 153, 172
Craft, J.   232
Crichton, A.   61, 143, 231
Cronshaw, M.   55
Cropanzano, R.   225
Crouch, C.   96, 99
Cully, M.   66, 130, 134, 205
Cutcher-Gershenfeld, J.   58, 178

Dale, B.   170
Dany, F.   143
Darbishire, O.   172, 174, 220
Datta, D.   220
Davis, E.   55, 169
Davis, S.   222
Dawson, J.   191
Deakin, S.   175
Debrah, U.   227
DeCastro, J.   80
DeCieri, H.   50
DeFillippi, R.   33, 76, 77
DeGeus, A.   233
Dean, J.   55, 58
Deane, P.   93
Deephouse, D.   33, 81
Delaney, J.   9
Delbridge, R.   18, 111
Delery, J.   55, 56, 57, 61
Deming, W. E.   138
Dierickx, I.   72
DiMaggio, P.   33
Dix, G.   66, 134
Doeringer, P.   116
Donaldson, T.   35, 39
Doogan, K.   103, 120
Doty, D.   55, 61
Dougherty, T.   137
Dowling, P.   50, 145
Dreher, G.   137
Drucker, P.   2, 4, 7

Subject index